PRIESTLY EXISTENCE

PRIESTLY
EXISTENCE

Rev. Michael Pfliegler

translated from the German by
FRANCIS P. DINNEEN, S.J.

THE NEWMAN PRESS · WESTMINSTER
MARYLAND · 1958

First published, 1957
Second printing, 1958

Originally published as *Priesterliche Existenz* by Verlagsanstalt Tyrolia, Innsbruck, Austria. All rights reserved.

FOREWORD

Most of what I have written has first been given as lectures; the same is true of this attempt to outline priestly existence: I had been asked to give a lecture, and that lecture left me no peace, when once the problem had been posed and expressed. In fact, the story of how this book came about is practically the key to its understanding.

The Vienna Pastoral Institute, founded just after World War I, has been wisely and surely guided through the vicissitudes of the past thirty years by Dr. Karl Rudolf. It has also set the pattern for similar institutes in almost all the dioceses of Central Europe. In all its meetings, it has been concerned with the problems of a timely pastoral program, but its leaders soon realized that the answer to the problem lay first and last with the priests themselves. Why did some cooperate and others not? What was behind the faithful attendance of some and the qualified adherence of others to the program? What was behind the reluctance and criticism? Why was it necessary again and again to appeal to ecclesiastical authority to implement even obvious suggestions? Could it be that there was a multiplicity of priestly types behind the many forms of their reactions? What was the reason for it?

The question of the priest as a pastor was proposed. At first an attempt was made to explain—and this was quite pertinent—the difference in attitude toward pastoral duties on the basis of the different degree of theological education and the different measure of ascetical and religious training. But that was only part of the explanation.

Could we get any information from characterology? We heard of a man who had devoted half of his life (Prof. Dr. Liener) to the study of the types of priests—this was in the early 'forties—according to the book *Rasse und Seele* (Munich, 1940). It was a refreshing and in part striking gallery of priests, of whom some were from Nordic races, and therefore men of action, while others were phlegmatic and therefore not to be aroused from their deeply rooted conservatism. Then, besides scattered examples of the Mediterranean opportunists whom we cannot take very seriously, there were numerous examples of Eastern shirkers who delight in avoiding all duties that come up, especially new ones. The insights were stimulating, but the application to the examples at hand did not fit, and therefore the whole explanation was unreliable. Among the faithful adherents to the reforms which originated with the Institute were certainly portly pastors who were of the Eastern races; but among those who shirked their work there were long-legged Nordics, with a whole shock of blond hair. The typology was correct, but the parallels founded on race were not. Or, at least, not always.

Another attempt was made in Edward Spranger's *Lebensformen* (Halle, 1930). Spranger divided men according to the values which were their ultimate guides. However, isn't the only value which is decisive for the priest a religious one? But wait a minute! That makes sense in the realm of norms and theories, but the question still remains whether in a concrete case the decisive value is the true motive power. In answering this, the following priest-types appeared:

1. the man interested in theory: that is, one concerned only with theological problems and not with their application;

2. the man of economic interests, even though he would not admit it. That is, his concern is for the "better" parishes, for stole-fees and questions of stipends and their canonical solutions;

3. the esthetic type who makes much of nice vestments, beautiful services, cultured society, and a purple rabat;

4. the socially-minded man for whom the words of Our Lord (Mark 8:2) "I have compassion on the multitude" is the origin and meaning of his priestly vocation;

5. the power-type of cleric who can't endure anyone having more influence than he; or who cannot live if *he* is not the one who organizes and runs everything, or if he hasn't power over a few typewriters and the typists that go with them. And if he doesn't succeed in all that, he intrigues against those who do have the power he wants.

And the sixth type—we hope the most common—the priest whose life is spent in pure love of God and immortal souls.

Did all this cast light on the attitudes of all priests?

It cannot be denied that with these norms we now had a means of making a good deal intelligible. But even with this typology, the norms were too general and not really valid when applied to priests: we still had a good deal to explain.

Such inadequacy is even more true of C. G. Jung's *Psychologishe Typen* (Zürich, 1925). Obviously, there are priests who are introverts—quiet, reflective, shy, and retiring, likely never to get beyond reflecting and analyzing. Instead of working, they sink into mistrust and intransigence. Obviously, too, there are extrovert priests who meet all men and challenges freely and openly, who quickly adopt and apply good ideas, only to give up too soon, uncritically waiting for more and more new stimulation. But these norms explained even less.

G. Phalheer's *System der Typenlehre* (Leipzig, 1929) was too little known in our circles. His division according to the four fundamental functions of the life of the soul (awareness, perseverance, emotional susceptibility, and vital energy) is subdivided into twelve character types. But these are too clearly set up with schools and students in view to serve as a basis for a characterological grouping for priests.

It was clear that these typologies did make it possible to distinguish different levels within the priesthood and therefore could be cause for an examination of conscience. Each priest would have to ask himself, "In my inmost being, to which of these types do I belong? What are the strong points and dangers of that type?" This can be said especially of Edward Spranger's *Lebensformen,* despite the predisposition to relegate priests and monks, individually and collectively, to the religious type.

Therefore, when I was approached and asked to give a lecture at a congress of priests in Vienna on April 28, 1943, with "The Psychology of the Priesthood" as my topic, I introduced Spranger's *Lebensformen,* along with the other attempts described above, because I knew that it was essentially a matter of characterology in which the delegates were interested. But it was clear from the beginning that we would have to arrive at a key-typology which would be proper to the priestly state alone. It had to be a key-typology that did not divide priests *a priori* according to race or soul or value theory, but which arose from the very existence of the priesthood and which was based on fundamental priestly experience.

I became even more certain of this, when, at the invitation of the bishop, I had to speak on the same theme before
the deans' meeting at Innsbruck on September 7, 1943.
But the problems that were raised by the lecture were not
solved and, therefore, still plagued me. The Pastoral Institute during the war invited all the priest-soldiers stationed
in Vienna to come to a meeting held every Thursday evening, and each time there were from fifty to a hundred
priests present. They came from all parts of Germany; besides the secular priests, nearly all the large Orders were
represented. On November 27, 1943, I conducted a long
meditation for them on vocation and perseverance. Then, as
custom demanded, there followed a frank exchange of opinion. They had their experiences with their fellow-soldiers.
They had all formed their own opinions about the reasons
for perseverance and non-perseverance. It struck me particularly that most of them thought that preparatory seminaries were a bit of a problem; indeed, they rejected them,
and I had my hands full, trying to make them appreciate
the advantages as well as the weaknesses and dangers of
the institution. It first became clear to me when I was preparing the lectures for the Theological Convention in Vienna
(July 24-26, 1950) that my theme was no longer "The Psychology of the Development of the Priestly Vocation," nor
could it be called a "Typology of the Priesthood." Rather,
it was "Priestly Existence." That is why I declined to have
my lectures printed in the reports, since my talks no longer
answered the questions that had occurred to me during the
lecture series. (There did appear, in a special printing, the
"Correspondence of the Priests' Prayer Union of the *Asso-
ciatio perseverantiae sacerdotalis*.")

What, then, is the purpose of this book?

This book does not intend to provide a typology on the
grounds of any characterological predisposition, nor one

based on a predetermination dating from the time before a man has chosen the priesthood. We want to try to explain the modes of priestly existence from the data of the priestly experience itself, from the experience of the tension, the necessary and unavoidable tension between the vocation to be a priest and the fact that such a vocation is given to a man who lives in this world.

We do not merely want to oppose the final types to each other by a cross-section, showing only their variety, at least not at first, but we will attempt to come to an understanding of how they come about through a longitudinal section, by analyzing and tracing their development from the foundations of priestly existence and its tensions. I hope—or, in the interest of the purity of the analysis I should almost say, "I'm afraid"—that the original purpose of these lectures breaks through at least in places. I refer to the interpretation of various priestly attitudes as a basis for a serious examination of conscience. As far as the demands of scientific clarity are concerned, that will be the weakness of this work. As one whose life-long task it has been to educate those called to the priesthood, I am not unhappy that this is so.

Philosophical Existentialism, aside from its being dynamic and time-conditioned, is a reaction against two philosophical tendencies which give a false understanding of man. It is a reaction against Idealism, in which man pales to a mere idea, to nothing more than a temporary state of absolute spirit in its course of evolution, at the term of which there is only the concept of all-spirit. And, secondly, it is a reaction against Positivism which misunderstands man as a part of nature and therefore denies to man anything in the realm of motivation and causality which lifts him above nature.

Similar to this misunderstanding in the literature dealing

with the priesthood are those idealized representations, un-
realistically devoid of any tension, which have St. John
Chrysostom's treatise "On the Priesthood" as their model.
This was the first of the ideal descriptions of the priestly
vocation, but the later ones are unmindful of the existential
necessity in which the saint wrote his description. To this
type belong novels about priests, often very entertaining,
which depict the priest's life, or part of it, in all its bril-
liance. The tensions never even appear, or if they do, they
are treated with affection and humor, according to the situation, as the little necessary shadows which make the light
just that much brighter.

In opposition to this kind of literature there is another, a
reaction, if you will, against idealization, by those who take
the concrete individual fate of the priest as their theme. But
they regard it from the viewpoint of a naturalistic predetermination which is unintelligible when compared to Christian
or priestly existence. Thus many things are left unexplained:
celibacy (e.g., in *Allerseelen,* by Rudolf Greinz, 1910),
or the struggle between the enlightened priestly philanthro-
pist and the ecclesiastical zealot, or the tension between the
"progressive," likewise enlightened, young idealist and his
dour, politicking ecclesiastical "boss," or any other opposition of cultural attainments. Emile Marriot, himself a believer, has published a typical example in his novel *Der
Geistliche Tod* (Berlin, 1924)). The "classical" themes of
novels about priests are represented here: a noble young
man becomes a priest for his mother's sake; he finds celibacy a burden, and although a kindly man, is inwardly unhappy. Finally he falls in love. His dean, a correct man, but
utterly lacking in fraternal charity, effects his transfer to
the most unhealthy parish of the diocese as a punishment.
This is a spot high in the mountains, called "Spiritual
Death." Here the tubercular George Harteck dies amid

much suffering. Stylistically, the novel belongs in the company of those by Marlitt, Werner, and Eschstruth. Ludwig Anzengruber developed similar "tensions" in his book *Pfarrer von Kirchfeld* (1870) and in his play *Die Kreuzelschreiber* (1872). They are also treated, in a repulsive way, in his *Dorfgängen.* They appear in a more exalted vein in two novels by Peter Rosegger, *Ewigen Licht* (1897) and *Die beiden Hänse* (1897). Here, too, an idealistic young priest dies in banishment to the mountains. This is the problem of the priest as seen from the outside.

One book that preserves a moderate stand between these two extremes, as well as between the demands of history and the pressures of the present, is Joseph Sellmair's *The Priest in the World* (1955). I was much impressed when it first appeared, but have not consulted it when putting this present book together, so that the train of thought I am following would not be diverted. Sellmair was aware of and expressed a number of the problems which determined me to write this book.

Priestly existence is neither a general picture, colorless or rosy, nor some priestly ideal, although one can make out a case for either of these extreme descriptions. Nor is it just the individual case, radiant with the beauty we so often read about in monographs and even in novels. Neither is it an illustration of collapse in pursuit of an ideal, or its deterioration. What we are trying to present here is an outline of the condition in which the priest lives and of his attempts to master it. Let it not be supposed that there is no head-on meeting with life in this book because it refers so repeatedly to literary sources. This is done only to make the references available to all, and such books are the only possible ones which are so available. But one who knows these novels realizes how deeply grounded in real life their problems and characters are. And in using them, we intend to show, as a secondary aim, a kind of fiction that is not just a pastime, but impels one to a sincere self-examination and knowledge. And they do so with more warmth than many meditations we know of, whose correctness no one ever doubted, but whose effusions never moved anyone. But we must emphasize the fact that we do not consider the following investigation to be in any sense a literary one. As for examples from real life, the reader will find them all about him, if he but chooses to look. Obviously, so can the author. But they would be documentary proof only if names and addresses were given, and that is precisely a detail which is unimportant.

The final types are not predetermined by any characterology previously established. As much as modern characterology can contribute to clarifying them, our types are empirical categories. Of course, we have tried as much as we could to make them complete, but such completeness is impossible. It is left consciously to the reader to fill in the details that are yet wanting.

When the present investigation was almost completed, I came across a typology which originated with a professor of the Passau *Hochschule,* Dr. Alois Winklhofer. It appeared in the *Oberrheinishen Pastoralblatt* of August and September, 1951 (Vol. 52, pp. 209-16, 232-44). It does not give a typology of priestly existence as such, but is, as its title suggests ("Priest-characters in Modern Literature"), a synthesis of priestly types in present-day literature. He finds six types: 1. the Vianney type, 2. the St. Francis de Sales type, 3. the sinner type, 4. the man-of-the-world type, 5. the apostate, and 6. the Sebastian-vom-Wedding type.

The typology which is presented by Bert Herzog in *Orientierung* (Zürich, February 29, 1952) under the title "Priest-characters in the Modern Novel" is similar. He distinguished 1. the *Padre* type of the Southern, Latin area, "internally and externally neglected, unjustifiably concerned about his future, grinding out his Mass at a terrific speed"; 2. the French type (in Bernanos, Mauriac, Queffelec): ". . . dry realism . . . penchant for intellectual adventure, Celtic phantasy, a feeling for sanctity, ecstasies, sensing the presence of demons . . ." In contrast to that, the "robust Curé who squares accounts in the confessional." 3. The German type: on the one hand, the Sebastian-vom-Wedding type, ". . . impatient for martyrdom" and on the other, ". . . they tend neither to the right nor to the left, but are never found in the middle." But the predominant type is the German "Big Shot" Priest (a clerical Babbitt), ". . . the typical bureaucrat, who has canon law at his finger-tips, correct from top to toe and a talented organizer, a sworn enemy of all slovenliness . . . the sophisticated older man, who must impart his pastoral experiences to the zealous young curate . . . always in a hurry, involved in a hundred projects and businesses . . . the harassed big-city pastor of the hurly-burly present . . . much like that type of priest which is now appearing in American fiction." 4. There is the priest of American fiction: ". . . neither exotic nor a theorist, neither a fanatic nor a mystic, neither rustic nor conservative, but a priest of the masses. For him, preaching is a 'psycho-technical arithmetic problem': tricks, systems and advertising. Fresh and untroubled he tumbles into situations, boxes, swims, plays tennis, and talks with everybody." Then there is, finally, the priest of the novel of the future: "the underground priest in the totalitarian state": no rectory, "no well-stocked theological library," no income, no faculties, "supporting himself as a tractor driver."

"This whole literature encompasses an unhealthy atmosphere and portrays the priest of today in a dangerous period of transition, in a storm of forced adaptation, in an uncertain situation."

The inventory which we attempt in the following pages will come to similar conclusions. It will embrace only what is revealed in the present. But yesterday is contained in today, and tomorrow can only be derived from the complete today. Be derived? No: at best, it can only be surmised. Over all this determinism and its offspring, pessimism, stands the grace of God and His mercy—and our prayers.

CONTENTS

BOOK ONE

Foundations and Development of Priestly Existence

I. PRIESTLY EXISTENCE

1. EXISTENCE

Before we try to explain what is meant by *priestly existence,* it is necessary to clarify what is meant here by *existence* in general.

In the following pages we do not conceive of *existence* in the sense of the ancient philosophies, i.e., what is actually at hand as opposed to what is merely thought of or attempted. We consider rather under this concept of existence that mode of being proper to a *human being.* It is in this mode of being that man experiences all the baffling and menacing aspects of his life as something proper to him and to him alone. At the same time, he becomes aware of the summons within him to take this life upon him, despite its dangers and obscurity and in spite of the temptation to escape from it. This man must save his humanity, that is, realize it in its individuality. That his life is endangered is something that every man can experience for himself. The forms that such threats take are indescribably various and numerous, ranging from bodily hunger (and all the needs of "existence" in the every-day sense) to the hopeless impotence of his thought, which, face to face with ultimate questions, demands certainty and does not get it. The experience of the pain of living is not only universal; it is more piercing and therefore more convincing than all talk, all philosophizing about it.

Great is the danger of trying to avoid the burdens of this existence which has been assigned to us; and in our cowardice and weakness, we side-step and fall daily. "One" lets oneself go and therefore is lost. If a man wants to prove himself, to secure his individuality and dignity, then he must take this life decisively upon him and dare its fulfillment; he must keep himself constantly taut and alert, lest he betray himself. This decisiveness, for the existentialist, has no other motive than that of saving dignity and individuality, despite the fact that we cannot know where life comes from or whither it is tending. It is a matter of individual and universal experience only that it is lost in death. Existentialism does not transcend life. The decisiveness of Heidegger and Sartre merely serves to rescue man from the anonymity of "one" and so wards off despair.

The Man of Faith, whose experience of the fragility of this life is even more urgent, and who is beset by the same existential seriousness to master it, tears it loose from its senseless and abandoned surroundings and casts it before the One Absolute. He places it inseparably before the word and judgment of his God. The Christian does this in the faithful conviction that, with the Incarnation of the Second Person of the Blessed Trinity, each person is faced inexorably with a choice between resurrection and fall. But because this choice itself, just as existence under the judgment of this choice, is necessarily determined by the tension between sin and grace, life for the Faithful is much more than the world-immersed existentialist suspects. The believer is pulled and torn between fear and confidence, between his own questionability and an unquestionability even more obscure to him, between his own helplessness and the faith that he can do all things through the power of Him who gives him strength (Phil. 4: 13). Above all, the decision to prove himself is made infinitely more profound through his Faith, which tells him that it is not just a matter of preserving himself from oblivion for this "life unto death." Rather, with the grace of God, and under the continual judgment of His infinite knowledge, he is to save every moment of this life for eternal life.

Whoever supposes that life loses something of its earnestness and awareness if it is lived in and through Faith, has but to try it himself. Doubtless the obscurity of our life is illuminated by Faith and its senselessness is removed, but the mystery remains, buried in infinite depths. A life of Faith demands more awareness and decision of a man than the "conscience" of Heidegger and Sartre can provide. Nor need it be overlooked or denied that, just as in the world of secular existence the number of those who sink into an impersonal "one" is doubtless in the majority, so, too, of those to whom the Faith has been given, there are some who mistake it as the impersonal "one" of a secure life for this and the other world, and who therefore would like to live up to it by mere pious industry. The impersonal "one" is always that broad mass which, wherever and whenever it exists, accustoms itself to every challenge and levels existence down to a path that "one" can travel.

2. CHRISTIAN EXISTENCE

In the existential *experience* we become frighteningly aware of the obscurity of our life, seek to fathom it, and then learn that anxiety itself is what constitutes life, that life is anxiety.

The experience of *Christian existence* is based on the practical knowledge of our sinfulness and the dangers to our life attendant upon it. "Fear of the Lord" is its beginning (Ps. 110: 10), "fear and trembling" is its path (Phil. 2: 12;

1 Pet. 1: 7), trust in the mercy of God is its salvation. The Christian is far more conscious than the existentialist that his life tends to being and non-being. But being for him means being grounded in Absolute Being, and non-being for him is not a name for a shapeless terror, but a state of being rejected by God. It is a matter for him of beatitude or rejection, and not only for this life. Both are for all eternity; both are an inescapable either-or; both are provided as an object of choice, yet are not determined by freedom alone. Much more consciously and concretely than anyone else, the Christian suffers his way through that universal human condition of tension between a longing for salvation and all that menaces it. This tension cannot be ignored. The fear of the judgment is unbearable. The obscure word of prophecy, that mercy and truth have met each other, justice and peace have kissed (Ps. 84: 11) would have been, in man's experience, something wholly improbable, had not the union of ultimate justice and ultimate love become existential in the Incarnation of the Son of God and His abandonment upon the cross.

Since then, life glows with faith, trust, and love; its power comes from grace and sacrament, but it remains a life of peril. It is not uncertainty in the face of something unknown that determines Christian existence, but the possibility of rejection that follows us as long as we live, the uncertainty of our personal redemption. There are historical examples of rejection for incredulity. But does faith in a certain salvation save you? "Thou standest by thy faith. Be not highminded, but fear!" (Rom. 11: 20). And besides all uncertainty, there is the fear of one single, clearly recognized enemy: "Be sober, be watchful! For your adversary the devil, as a roaring lion, goes about seeking someone to devour. Resist him, steadfast in faith" (1 Pet. 5: 8). He goes about! He ranges even farther, despite the fact that the Sun of Grace has risen over the kingdom of the redeemed and over the soul of each individual. He goes about as "prince of this world," as our Lord Himself called him (John 12: 31; 14: 30), and he even dares to let his sun, the "sun of Satan," shine, despite the fact that he is already judged (John 16: 11). Further, the life of the Christian must be lived, decisively, in "uncertainty and hazard" and all darkness, which are ever with the man in grace, even in the loftiest heights of mystical communion with God. Darkness and light? How easy the decision would be if that were the case. But we are faced instead, and more often, by the question: "sun of God"? or "sun of Satan"?

This general world of Christian life is the background for priestly existence. It is not the task of this volume to describe the former. But it is essential for what is to follow that we stress the fact that a disservice is done to Christian existence if one were to make it seem harmless and ordinary, or would try to obscure the tensions in it. What we have to deal with is a pregnant reality which even our Lord and Master could illustrate only in terms of paradox.

Let us hear what our Lord Himself had to say: The Prince of Peace, foretold by the prophets, confesses of His mission: "Do not think that I have come to send peace upon the earth; I have come to bring a sword, not peace" (Mt. 10: 43; Luke 12: 51). "He who finds his life will lose it, and he who loses his life for my sake, will find it" (Mt. 10: 39; Mt. 16: 25; Mark 9: 35; Luke 9: 24; 17: 33).

In this world there is a necessary conflict between the wisdom of this world and the folly of the cross. (1 Cor. 1: 20, 27; 4: 10.) Wisdom is the first of the cardinal virtues and according to the words of Our Lord, we are to be "wise as serpents" (Mt. 10: 16). Nevertheless, in praising the Father, Jesus gave thanks ". . . that thou didst hide these things from the wise and prudent and hast revealed them to the little ones" (Luke 10: 21). "Blessed art thou, Simon Bar-Jona, for flesh and blood has not revealed this to thee, but my Father who is in heaven" (Mt. 16: 17). He accepts the reproach of the man who had buried his talent: "Thou reapest where thou hast not sowed and gatherest where thou hast not winnowed" (Mt. 25: 24). Then there are surprising laws of value and reward: "For to everyone who has, shall be given, and he shall have in abundance, but from him who does not have, even that which he seems to have shall be taken away" (Mt. 25: 29). For the lost son, the fatted calf is killed; and for the good son, who had remained at home, working, none. (Luke 15: 1 ff.) For "I say to you, that even so, there will be more joy in heaven over one sinner who repents, more than over ninety-nine just who have no need of repentance" (Luke 15: 7).

Although Christ certainly founded His Church upon earth with all the visibility it needs and obligated it to ranks and orders, His warnings to those who exercise power in His Kingdom surely sound anarchistic. "The kings of the Gentiles lord it over them and they who exercise authority over them are called Benefactors. But not so with you. On the contrary, let him who is the greatest among you become as the youngest, and him who is the chief as the servant" (Luke 22: 25 ff). A child is the greatest in this kingdom. (Luke 18: 17; Mt. 18: 1 ff.) Thus: "Whoever exalts himself shall be humbled, and whoever humbles himself shall be exalted!" (Mt. 23: 12; Luke 14: 11). "Whoever wishes to be great among you shall be your servant; and whoever wishes to be first among you shall be the slave of all" (Mark 10: 44), since "what is exalted in the sight of man is an abomination before God" (Luke 16: 15).

When it is a question of God, all earthly bonds, even those most sacred to men, count for nothing. This is true even in the case of the love of one's parents and children, and between husband and wife. That is why our Lord uses the word *hate* for all this. The constitution of this Kingdom begins with: "Blessed are the poor . . . blessed are the meek . . . blessed are they who mourn . . . blessed are the peacemakers . . . those who suffer persecution . . ." (Mt. 5: 3-12). Then "many who are first now shall be last, and many who are last now shall be first" (Mt. 19: 30; Mark 10: 31). Then there are demands that can only be expressed in paradox: "It is easier for a camel to pass through the eye of a needle than for a rich man to enter the kingdom of God" (Mark 10: 25).

The only explanation of this the terrified disciples heard (Luke 18: 25) was that "things that are impossible with men are possible with God" (Luke 18: 27). Who belongs to this kingdom? "He who is not against us is for us" (Mark 9: 40). And then again: "He who is not with me is against me, and he who does not gather with me scatters" (Luke 11: 23). And yet again: "The kingdom of God is within you" (Luke 17: 21).

And repeatedly we find mention of that mysterious *necessity,* linked none the less with *responsibility*: "For it must needs be that scandals come, but woe to the man through whom scandal does come!" (Mt. 18: 7; Luke 17: 1). "Did not the Christ have to suffer these things before entering into his glory?" (Luke 24: 27). He was seized *"in order that* the scripture might be fulfilled" (Mt. 26: 56).

In the face of all these obscurities, does not the word which our Lord spoke apply as well to the priest as it did immediately to His head-shaking disciples: "To you it is given to know the mystery of the kingdom of God, but to the rest in parables" (Luke 8: 10)?

The explanation of these passages can be found in any commentary; and although we accept it, we know at the same time that the paradox in what our Lord said remains for the Christian conscience a persistent appeal, and no exegesis can silence it.

The tension which is presented to us in these paradoxes provides us with an understanding of Christian existence. That existence has neither the right to ignore nor the possibility of ignoring the tension which has been assigned to it. It cannot disregard the challenging aspects of its position by eliminating one or another of its potencies. We dare not rest. We must remain in suspense and prove ourselves in it. At every moment! It is at the very breaking point of both dynamisms that we do prove ourselves. It is at this point that great saints and great heretics are made. The former derive their growth from the necessity and grace of this point of stress, and the latter decide for one or another path and become either apostates or heretics. But every individual Christian must stand between these two dynamisms and, by resisting their attraction, prove himself.

Therefore it is only one side of Christian existence and false when "poor Reinhold" lays aside his office of abbot with the words: "Jesus is not a man of order—by no means!" (Rudolf Krämer-Badoni, *Der arme Reinhold*, Hamburg, 1951, p. 240). Later, as a poor lumberman, he answers the Communist who tries to win him over, "What I have against the present order is that it *is* an order" (p. 268); "I snap my fingers at the right order, just as I do at the wrong one." And when the Communist mocks him, "But now your mistake is in claiming that all would be in the best possible order if all men lived a Christian life," he answers: "I don't say that. On the contrary, if all men lived as Christians, the world would be in the most perfect disorder" (p. 270). Everyone would have to become poor. That would be the solution.

And there is one more terrible saying: "Be you perfect as your heavenly Father is perfect" (Mt. 5: 48). Where is God and His perfection, and where are we? "For the imagination and thought of man's heart are prone to evil from his youth" (Gen. 8: 21). Who are we, that this model is set before us as though it were a matter of course? We stand in a field of tension between two eternities, faced both with the impossibility of fulfillment and its actuality, and with the necessity of the appeal which forces us to recognize our lot and assume it with full consciousness.

3. PRIESTLY EXISTENCE

The origins of priestly existence lie deep-rooted in the common experience of Christian existence: the experience of the hazard of life and its destitution, out of which it cannot lift itself unaided; in the vision of Faith with regard to sin and death as the end of sin; in the terror which our fallen condition of being-in-the-world entails; in the disgust caused by such a life.

But the fixed purpose of the priest today is not directed—and this is the ultimate drive of *his* existence—merely toward saving and proving himself. This could lead to monasticism in its ancient form, and radical negation. The experience of a vocation to be a priest, a *secular priest*—it is only of this that we speak—has its roots in a concept of living which means sharing life with mankind endangered, in the experience of being united with them and of being responsible for them. It is an experience which is so intense that it amounts to risking a life for one's fellow men, to see oneself and one's brothers in the light of what is necessary to bring them safely out of their abandonment and sins to God the merciful Savior and Sanctifier.

But this fixed purpose is not, at least usually, a matter of reflection and subsequent free decision. It is built upon the experience of a vocation. He knows that he is chosen and called by God, and therefore is obliged to answer. Therefore, there is a certain inevitability about it. Every attempt to evade it is answered by an uneasy conscience. Time and eternity are no longer decided for him only in the preservation of his Christian existence, but in the closest friendship with God, by which he keeps faith with Him who has called him to this lot. Let us try to sketch the existence of the priest from its roots and beginnings by a sort of anticipation of what will be unfolded in the following pages.

Different callings determine existence with varied intensity. There are some which completely fill it up, or almost do so. There are others which stand on the side-lines of life, so to speak, and can be dispatched with one hand. The ticket collector, the factory worker, for example, do their jobs for a certain number of hours. Only after that do they really begin to live as human beings. The man flies from his office to his family or into the open air, or to his friends, or to a favorite hobby, and only then does he begin to "come to life." But there are other vocations which cannot be set aside after the clock has ticked off eight hours. They take hold of a person and determine his existence. Such is the vocation of a mother. The priestly vocation is so much the vocation of the man who is a priest that the person involved is only a tool. The human being is a victim of his vocation. This can even be literally true in the sense of a bloody imitation of his Master. It is a possibility the priest must reckon with. But the usual case is that the one who has been ordained lives a life of total surrender of his talents and person for perpetual service.

Priestly existence does not merely begin with a vocation. Vocation is the continued existential fact in the life of a priest. The fact that remains is that he has been selected from among all Christians, not merely from the world. The priest is *segregatus a populo*—separated from the people— not in the sense that at one time he is summoned from the ranks to assume a position opposed to them and later returns as one of the rank and file. This is sharply accentuated in the Western Church through the assumption of celibacy, remaining ever unmarried, in order to belong to God alone. The vocation is a vocation of heroes. Celibacy is the deciding test and touchstone of that heroism. With ordination, he becomes a *sacerdos in aeternum,* a priest forever, with a *character indelibilis,* signed with the seal of the priesthood which will be his mark forever, and which, God forbid, if he be lost, cannot even be burnt away in the flames of hell. The determination and ordination of a twenty-four-year-old create a condition which is settled for time and eternity. The canonical prescriptions describe only his external condition.

The inexorability and inescapability which go with his freely accepted ordination are part and parcel of the existence of the priest. The decision for the priesthood is an irrevocable one. That is what makes it so serious. Besides, there is the fact that no one who decides for the priesthood makes that decision for himself alone. It affects countless others. The priest can never be saved alone and can never be lost by himself. Indeed, in many respects, he no longer has any other possibility of saving his own life than through saving his fellow men.

For the sacrament of Holy Orders which he receives is not given to him for his own salvation. He receives it *tam pro vivis quam pro defunctis,* both for the living and the dead: as a power which works even beyond this our time for the salvation of his fellow men. By his ordination, not only is a sacrifice made, but he becomes a priest-victim in union with his Lord and Master, a mediator between men and their heavenly Father. He becomes a preacher of the Word, like his Lord and Master: of the Word first of all as the form of the sacraments, as the Word which wells up from the springs of grace. But above all, he is a preacher of the word which the Lord received from His Father and hands on to His disciples (John 14: 10; 17: 8; Mt. 28: 19). He becomes a preacher of *the* Word, that is to say, the Word of God. This is a terrifying task for a man: he is burdened with the fear that he may preach his own word as the Word of God.

For the Word which he is to preach is the final word of God to man. Christ is not only the fulfillment of all the longing for redemption which awaited the fullness of time perfected in His Incarnation; Christ is the only and final Redeemer. There will be no other after Him. His Word is the last that the merciful God directs to mankind. The Holy Spirit will only receive of His Word and proclaim it. (John 16: 14.)

Since this is the case, all comparisons of the priest of Christ with the other historical forms of priesthood in other religions fall short; there is no possibility of making his existence relative to any other. For he represents the last stage of the history of salvation, the final hour of human history, one which will never strike again. That is an essential part of the consciousness of his existence. He has, therefore, the duty of representing every man, for every man that he meets can be given to him. He is, as was Christ his Master, set for the rise and fall of many. "The prince of this world" knows that. This fact explains the unmotivated hatred for a priest whom a particular individual meets for the first time. It is probably a sign that the person is rejecting one grace, perhaps his deciding grace. Hate is always the expression of the helplessness which follows wasted freedom. This eschatological seriousness is also essential to priestly existence. The priest experiences it as subjectively as a child. He is simply a priest. He cannot understand hatred, because he is a child and a lover.

But in the final analysis, this is determined by the tension which exists between the tremendous thing that is required of him and his poor humanity. God has laid His hand upon a human being. The mystery of such a choice, always obscure and inconceivable, now becomes a palpable terror. One can only answer yes to such a call when one is convinced that there is always a disproportion between the vocation and its fulfillment. Indeed, it is the holiest of priests who have grasped that best of all and have most often expressed it. Just as Christ has given Himself in His earthly life to all men, saints and sinners alike, desiring only to do the will of Him who sent Him, even unto His death on the cross (John 4: 34; 19: 30), so, too, He has surrendered His mystical life to be continued by men who are led now by nothing other than the call of their Lord; men who set themselves the task of fulfilling the call given to all the world, in all simplicity; men who must carry it out, even if it means becoming like their crucified Master. Sensibly, i.e., if all this were subject to the common sense of *men,* only saints could accept such a vocation. But the paradox becomes more apparent when we hear that it was precisely the saintly men who wanted most of all to escape—the burden? No, rather the dignity! In his rule, St. Pachomius forbade his monks to accept the priesthood because of its dignity. Of course, this was because of the reverence paid to the priest himself, consequent upon the dignity of his office—a consequence obvious at first glance, but still tragic.

So the priest assumes the burden and honor of his existence in faith, and he is convinced that the disproportion between priest and man, between his task and how he fulfills

it, will never fully disappear, that the complete fulfillment
of priestly existence is impossible, or, better, that even the
holiest fall short of the ideal because they can do no more.
Nonsense? No, it is merely the obscurity that exists between the *omnipotence* of grace and—hard as it is to believe
—the *necessity* of our cooperation. Heresies would not admit the paradox. But there it is, and it remains a factor
determining the existence of the priest. He is required by his
Master to endure it and he may not hesitate. What is it that
the Lord says in Luke 17: 10? "When you have done everything that was commanded you, say, 'We are unprofitable
servants.' "

That is equally true of the saint and the sinner: the commandment as well as the confession.

Georges Bernanos has his saintly pastor of Lumbres, who
dies of a heart-attack sitting upright in the confessional, say
this prayer: ". . . You have cast us like a leaven into the
lump. The universe, of which sin has stripped us, we shall
recover, inch by inch, we shall hand it back to you just as
we received it, in its order and in its holiness, on the first
morning of the days. Reckon not the time for us, Lord! Our
heedfulness falters, our mind so quickly turns aside. Constantly the eyes espy, both right and left, no possible way
out; constantly one of your workmen casts aside his tool and
goes away. But your pity, no, your pity grows not weary and
everywhere you hold out to us the tip of the blade; the run-
away will resume his task, or he will perish in the wilderness . . ." (*Under the Sun of Satan*, 1949).

II. THE FOUNDATIONS OF
PRIESTLY EXISTENCE

1. VOCATION

The priestly vocation is a vocation in the truest sense of the word. It is not chosen, in the sense of deliberation about a vocation in which there is left to the young man the choice of many possible states of life, all offering good prospects. It is essentially rooted in a calling. And this comes from God. It is God who calls. A man hears that call. That is the rock-bottom of priestly existence.

What our Lord said in parting from His Apostles is true of every priest: "You have not chosen me, but I have chosen you and have appointed you . . ." (John 15: 16). No one who is not called can take this vocation upon himself. The vocation is an act of God alone, reserved to Himself. It is in this that the dignity of the vocation lies. "And no man takes the honor to himself; he takes it who is called by God, as Aaron was. So also Christ did not glorify Himself with the high priesthood, but He who spoke to Him, 'Thou art my Son . . .'" (Heb. 5: 4 ff). The priesthood, even before it becomes existent, has a strict parallel with the priesthood of Christ.

Whether one receives this call of God with rejoicing or terror changes nothing in the fact of the call. That is part and parcel of priestly existence, right from the beginning. God has laid His hand upon the young man. It would not be the first time that one should seek to tear himself loose, as the prophet Jonas tried to do. The attitude of the prophet Jeremias stands as a timeless symbol: (Jer. 1: 4-10) "And the word of the Lord came unto me, saying: 'Before I formed thee in the bowels of thy Mother I knew thee, and made thee a prophet unto the nations.' And I said: 'Ah, ah, ah, Lord God! Behold, I cannot speak, for I am a child.' And the Lord said to me: 'Say not, I am a child: for thou shalt go to all that *I* send thee: and whatsoever I shall command thee, thou shalt speak. Be not afraid of their presence: for I am with thee to deliver thee . . .' " Since the time of Jeremias, vocation and consolation have remained the same thing.

This does not take anything away from the gravity of the moment when the young man makes his assent to his vocation—for God desires free acquiescence to His call—or if the choice which is thrust upon him comes in the form of a question, as it did to St. Francis of Assisi. It is infinitely significant for the uneasy certainty of this summons as well as for the shadowy possibility of explaining away this moment that St. Francis heard a voice when he was *half asleep*. While riding to a knightly contest at Apulia, he heard a voice: "Francis, who can do better for you, the Lord or the servant?" "The Lord," said Francis. "Then why do you abandon the poor for the sake of the rich, and the Lord for the sake of the servant?" For this assent is not just taking a position on a theoretical question. In this moment, life itself is at stake, life for time and eternity, and that for a young man in the spring of his awakening life, in a world full of enticements and attractions. Do you, who would skim over this, realize what a burden this vocation is, whose aim is so high—in fact, the highest? It is precisely the highest of goals that is not easily taken. It must be bought dearly, most dearly. And do you realize that the world and the "prince of this world" show their splendor most dazzlingly to one who would bear testimony against them? Even here, the servant is not greater than the Master (John 13: 16; Mt. 4: 9). Who can take it ill of the young life that does not wish to surrender itself immediately? Franz Michael Willam (*The Life of Jesus Christ*, St. Louis, 1936) sees in the God-Man Himself, when He is faced on Olivet with the last and most terrifying assent to His vocation, a secret longing for the life of the ordinary man.

Besides, this call to decision is one to the concrete form of the *Catholic* priesthood. Although celibacy does not belong to the essence of the priesthood, it has solid foundation in Holy Scripture (Mt. 19: 12; I Cor. 7: 32); it is inseparably bound up with the priesthood in the West by legislation and a tradition which goes back to early Christianity. The quiet feeling of attraction to the priesthood is felt even in children,[1] but the conscious choice faces the young man at the end of his adolescence. The divine love which beats in his heart is ready for all sacrifices. He still has five or six years of self-testing ahead of him. For countless youths who are all called by God, the choice they regard as most painful, if not the deciding one, is that between earthly and heavenly love. Even for St. Augustine, a woman was the last thing that hindered him from surrendering to God. (Conf. VIII, 2, 5) The celibacy of the Bishop of Milan whom he so revered seemed a burden to Augustine (Conf. VI, 3). The Church could then, and can even today, use only heroes. This sacrifice is, in her eyes, the touchstone of their genuine desire to be heroes.

Ultimately, the "undivided service" of the Kingdom is the

---

[1] Two Catholic newspapers for children in Germany (10 to 14 years of age) asked this question of their readers: "What do you want most of all?" Of thousands of replies, 4.97% of the boys answered that they wanted to become priests.

reason. This led the greatest Protestant of the nineteenth
century, Sören Kierkegaard, to break off his engagement (W.
Ruttenbock, *Sören Kierkegaard,* Berlin, 1929, p. 23). The
sacrifice is great; it should not be glossed over. If R. Kass-
ner, in speaking of Rilke, can dare to say: "From fervor
to greatness there is only one path: sacrifice!"—then what
is the vocation of a poet compared to that of the priest?

There are clear hours of vocation, especially when one
is conscious of it in the early years of youth. Mostly there
is a long period of unrest preceding it. "It is just impossible
for me to go on living like this," thought the young Baron
von Ketteler, during nights of unrest. "But then, it's equally
impossible to give in. What shall I do then, just to get moving? Always the same vicious circle . . . help me, Oh God,
almighty God. Oh, I beseech Thee, help me on the way. I
am lost unto death in the mist, and cry to thee for help!"
(Franz Herwig, *Der grosse Bischof,* Munich, 1932, p. 122).
And God answers! He calls. And Ketteler replies with decision and greatness, waiting for the grace which alone gives
him the strength to endure. After he is almost driven mad
by the way that a priest, whom he met by chance, made
light of his confession, he gives his final assent (p. 171).
"Terror, coming from afar, coursed over him . . . was this
last hour a reality . . . have I really made the decision to
be a priest? . . . Had he really, for now and always, laid his
life at the feet of God? . . . Yes, really and truly, I can no
longer retreat!" (p. 150) Then more difficulties: am I worthy
then? The question tortures him for some time (p. 166).
Only when he is fully determined does a holy joy come over
him, such as he had never known. "Yes, I am coming—
thank You! Thank You! How wonderful, all is decided!
It really had been decided long ago while he was still in
doubt. He had not been deceived in the emotion he experienced in the Frauenkirche at Munich when he felt that

the bishop was a messenger from God, summoning him" (p. 186). "Never, I felt, could life seem sweeter to a man of another calling. The *Rorate Coeli*, it seemed, had been fulfilled in me" (Joseph Bernhart, *Der Kaplan*, 1919, p. 65).

Subsequently Bernhart asks the question (*Der Kaplan*, p. 9): "Was I free? I entered this course of my own free will, but who knows who guides the decisions which seem to us to be free and of our own making?" Life, every human life, is *essentially* a *hazard;* and the more important a decision is, so much the more necessary the risk.

There have been vocations that were so palpable—literally!—that we can only shake our heads and say that they are understandable only in the light of mass psychology. But as was shown in time, they were genuine, and, even today, there are inspiring priestly figures who were chosen by God in this way. Let us not deceive ourselves! The symbolism can be the same among us, only more hidden. The cry, "Let Ambrose be made bishop!" struck the governor of Emilia and Liguria with fear; he was not even baptized. He demurred, but recognized in the voice of the child who had started the cry of the community at Milan the voice of God. He received baptism and a week later, December 7, 374, was consecrated bishop. And when Augustine came into the cathedral of Hippo, unsuspectingly making a tour of the churches, he was recognized. Of a sudden, a couple of men took hold of him and dragged him before the throne of their bishop, Valerius. Then the cry, "Let Augustine be ordained a priest!" echoed through the house of God. Augustine, too, heard the *vox Dei* in the *vox populi* and acquiesced (Louis Bertrand, *St Augustine*, Paderborn, 1930, pp. 213 ff.).

And that is the key to an understanding of how a son becomes conscious of God's will in the vow of a pious or despairing mother. This was the theme of the tragedies in the cheap novels about priests in the second half of the nineteenth century (e.g. Emile Marriot, *Der geistliche Tod;* Ludwig Anzengruber, *Sündkind;* Maria Ebner-Eschenbach, *Glaubenslos?*). With difficulty, the Beneficiary of Ried, Marcus Rusch, strives to convince a mother that her son is not bound by her vow (Arthur Schubart, *Pfarrergeschichten,* Munich, 1932). Here the times have sorely changed. The opposite case—a refreshing sign—is more frequent today; now the young man, often an only child, conscious of his vocation, must work it out in the face of parental opposition. But it must not be overlooked that even Anthusa, the mother of St. John Chrysostom, at first begged him not to become a priest, lest she be widowed a second time. (*On the Priesthood,* I, 5). And when the handsome young Stephen Fermoyle, the future Cardinal, returns to his family as a newly ordained priest, following his studies at the American College in Rome, his sister cries out rather mischievously, "Oh Stevie . . . You're so handsome. The girls of St. Margaret's will be mad for you" (p. 42). And when they are alone, his mother asks him a question that has caused her much anxiety: "Tell me truly—did my wanting you to be a priest make you decide to be one?" And she is put at rest when he answers: "No . . . I'm a priest because there's nothing else on earth that I want to be" (Henry Morton Robinson, *The Cardinal,* New York, 1950, p. 46).

The world asks why and looks for reasons. What is it that determined a young man to follow such a vocation, despite all obstacles? "In no other religion was there ever given a man a more merciful task or a more exalted mission. Exalted above all mankind by his ordination, armed with the power of God by his priestly office, and even as the immediate representative of God, the servant of the Lord can walk to the brink of the abyss, when the earth

rocks and groans, and come to the aid of the poor abandoned wretch whom the Church once baptized, but who
later forgot her or perhaps even persecuted her unto death."
This is what J. K. Huysmans has his Durtal say when he
witnesses an ordination (*Unterwegs*, Hildesheim, 1926,
p. 35). But do these arguments explain everything?

Does a vocation always start with an indescribable,
shrouded meeting of the young man and God? Is there only
the mystery of vocation, impenetrable by reason? Are there
no traits which anyone could recognize, so that the one who
is called, or even one who *wants* to be a priest, can know
that he dare try this vocation? And there is another need
—one of the most awful responsibility. Those who educate
and train candidates for the priesthood must have *certain*
norms to enable them to sift, evaluate, and decide among
their applicants.

At the turn of the century, and even earlier, France was
the scene of bitter ecclesiastical controversies. The law of
December 11, 1905 (during the regime of Combes), which
completed the separation of Church and State, plunged the
Church of that land into unavoidable external difficulties.
These were contributing factors in the decreasing number
of candidates for the priesthood. Also, there was apparently
a continually decreasing number of vocations. There then
arose a heated discussion of the question "How can a man
know that he is called to the priesthood?"

There were two opposed answers. One opinion (represented especially by Louis Branchereau's *De la vocation sacerdotale*, Paris, 1896) taught this: the most important
thing is the summons, the vocation by God. From this comes
the inclination to the priesthood and the feeling of attraction
on the part of the one called by God.

The other opinion contradicted this: (Joseph Lahitton, *La Vocation sacerdotale*, Paris, 1909). Neither the vocation, in the sense of an extraordinary invitation from God, nor a sensible attraction for the priesthood need be present. He may decide that he has a priestly vocation, i.e., feel himself "called," who has the intellectual and moral qualities necessary, and possesses a good intention (*bona fides*).

The quarrel went back and forth for years. Pope Pius X assigned a Commission to decide it and they found in general for Lahitton (June 26, 1912, A.A.S., IV, 485):

1. An "inspiration of the subject" is not necessary for the priestly vocation.
2. A sensible attraction for the priesthood and consolations of divine grace are not preconditions.
3. These suffice: the right intention (*intentio bona*), the ability, spiritual and intellectual, and freedom from impediments such as irregularities (e.g. illegitimacy, serious bodily deformity, epilepsy, insanity, etc.).
4. The bishop alone (or the superior of a Religious Order) decides whether a candidate is to be admitted to the priesthood. There is no prior right to a vocation, nor any other opposing that of the bishop. That means that even the refusal of a vocation on the part of the one truly called would not be a sin against justice (although it might be against some other virtue). One who feels himself called, but whose vocation cannot be recognized by the bishop after the years of seminary training has no right of complaint against the bishop.
5. Anyone who is fit for the priesthood in this sense is not under any obligation of sin to become a priest. (Obviously. Such "sinners" would be running around by the hundreds, all unsuspecting.)

This decision is canonically clear. In virtue of it, we have the answer to the question, "Who *may* become a priest?" but not to the question, "Who *should* become a priest, with the inner call from God?" (The bishop, of course, decides whether he will or can become a priest, externally.)

The words of St. John Climacus apply to everyone whom the Lord calls. "Let us take care that, if the King of Kings, the Lord of Lords, the God above all gods, should call us to this heavenly state, we may not refuse out of scruple or vanity, and so be found unworthy before the judgment" (Migne, PG, 88, 640).

Life, every life, is a hazard. The decisions which most determine our life, and especially these, cannot be so nicely calculated that we can know within a decimal point that we are right. And yet a man must make up his mind. Freedom and risk are essential parts of life. And obscurity, too. All is uncertainty and hazard.

These two existential realities, the earmarks of our life, are so much a part of it that they remain in even the highest degrees of mystical experience (so with St. Teresa). The deepest meaning of our wandering on earth is not explainable. It is only bearable. Any rebellion on our part is childish. God has an absolute right to us. He lays His hand upon a human life. What sense is there to any further question? What "happens" after that is hidden from the world, as are all the greatest "happenings." "In the cubicles or cells of our seminary, there hung only a poor, small crucifix. The cross was of wood and the Crucified of porcelain or something like that, such as one would find in the poorest of homes. Now between that crucifix and the young candidate for the priesthood there passed the confidences that are so soul-shaking since they precede so serious a choice of vocation. Then it struck me for the first time how silently the Crucified hung on His cross. No longer are there seven words to be heard. There are only five wounds that bleed" (Joseph Wittig, *Roman mit Gott,* Stuttgart, 1950, p. 190).

A young man makes his decision and says yes. There are people who ask, shocked, "How can an inexperienced and weak man take upon himself such a *difficult* vocation?" And there are others who are shocked, but their question is, "How can a man choose such a *holy* vocation himself?"

What has happened? Something very simple and understandable. Once I had to preach on the occasion of a friend's silver jubilee of ordination. It was the fourth Sunday after Pentecost. I gave a homily on the Gospel of the day, about the miraculous draught of fish and the calling of Peter (Luke 5: 1-11). What happened here? And what has happened a million times since then? *Christ entered into the little ship of Peter's life.* And he calls out, "Depart from me, for I am a sinful man!" But the Lord remained. Peter could have fled. He could have put the Lord out of his ship. But without fault? At any rate, Peter did not do the choosing; he was chosen. And he heard, too, the comforting words, "Do not be afraid; henceforth thou shalt catch men." "And when they had brought their boats to land, they left all and followed Him." They showed no hesitation. That was grace. "Whatever lack of fitness we may feel in ourselves, we are no less able to do all that God wishes from us with Jesus Christ. 'I can do all things in Him who strengthens me.' And we can never be so unfit that Jesus Christ cannot do in us and with us all that our vocation demands" (Charles de Condren, *Geistliche Briefe,* Freiburg i.B., 1939, p. 38).

Vocation is "knowledge" of the summons to a total dedication of one's life to God. This knowledge may not be much more than an intimation, but the test of its reality is a certain unrest that besets the one who will not listen to it. The "yes" given to this call is an act of love and a "yes" of distress. For in it lies the hazard of an entire life. There are times when the joy of being called makes you happy and times when the possibility of refusing strikes terror. But most of the time, joy and sorrow strike a balance. Accepting the vocation is above all a single-minded act of confidence in the grace of Him who calls us.

It is the call of God Himself which creates a situation of inevitability. The acceptance fixes it. The one who has made the decision knows of the inexorability of his existence. It is that which indelibly marks the ordained priest through all eternity. The law of the Church and her administration, as well as the concurring judgment of the faithful, clearly say the same thing. And not least of all, so does the conscience of the one who has given his acceptance to God.

On the feast of St. Philip Neri we read in the second Nocturn *"Sacerdos ex obedientia factus"* (he became a priest out of obedience); on the day of St. Paulinus (May 22), that he had to be forced to become a priest. And we read the same thing often of the priest-saints. Why did they resist? It was their fear of the dignity and, in those days, also of the external honor. It was humility. We say this only to point out *one* defense.

No one is forced. Each must freely decide. Everyone can retract his decision, according to canon law, as long as he has not received major orders. Before the first of the major orders, there is set aside a week for earnest consideration.

The need of priests cannot be so great that the Church would ever force anyone. The contrary is true. All during the years of his preparation, he is faced, day by day, with his decision. In one of his writings, St. Bernard says that the number of priests is often in inverse proportion to their fitness. That was true not only in the twelfth century.

And nevertheless, or perhaps precisely because of that, there is great joy in those who are called. It manifests, humanly speaking, their fidelity. It is an unintelligible riddle to those outside. Anyone who sees in our universities those happy, black-cassocked young theologians striding through the throngs of their fellow students in other faculties, has an inkling of the living paradox they represent for all who seldom consider the choice of a vocation from any viewpoint but that of a profitable future.

Let no one suppose that these young idealists suspect nothing of the dangers, that they have no knowledge of the ones who turned their backs on their vocation. They have often met them. They were often held up to them as examples. Perhaps it was these very scandals which made them want to try to do better. Let no one reproach their sense of mission! It is rarely personal pride; and if it is, then this conceit leads quickly to leaving the seminary. It is a holy fixity of purpose that animates them. It cannot be the prospect of a secure life, nowadays. Persecution and martyrdom, by no means just something they read about in old stories of the saints, do not frighten them.

But at the same time, their ideal can be colored, or even soiled, by their own ideas and desires. The ideal is so great and those who follow it are so young that this is possible —and often enough the source of later tragedy. *The* ideal, at different times, has always had different aspects, conditioned by these times. And it is also very different in different countries. There may be different "states in life" more in accord with one's talents behind these plans for the future. It is imaginable that its economic value could make this state attractive for someone—though the poor fellow's in for a shock! It is obvious that for the poor farmer boy of yesteryear the parish with a solid income had a powerful attraction. The idealist dreams of a life in a parish as beautiful as only the Flemish authors could make it: e.g. Ernst Claes, *Der Pfarrer von Kempenland* (Munich,

1939); Felix Timmermans, *Der Pfarrer vom blühenden Weinberg* (1927). And to be a pastor is still an attractive calling. A man given to theorizing may dream of a priestly life in which he can devote long hours to his books, or of a doctorate in theology, for which he is trying, or he may think of himself as a future professor. The esthete sees himself in gleaming vestments or as a celebrated preacher, a famed organizer, or—just imagine!—as a monsignor in glowing red. The words of our Lord, "I have pity on the multitude" (Mark 8: 2), can more immediately determine the socially-minded man than religious distress and salvation. The man who craves for power dreams of being a pastor against whose will not a cock can crow in the village. He thinks of mighty movements and organizations, with himself at their head, demanding respect of friend and foe alike—but he finally winds up at a desk from which he can "dictate" to his own secretary-typist. (A caricature of his own dictatorial plans, but he's gotten bald in the meantime and is satisfied anyway.)

It is the task of the five or six years of philosophical, theological, and, above all, ascetical training, to see to it that these distortions of the ideal do not become a danger to it.

2. THE SEMINARY

A Test of the Genuineness of Vocation

The first task of a seminary is *to try* the vocation for its genuineness and endurance. This is equally true of the seminarian and of those in charge. The latter have, in the decision of June 26, 1912, a certain norm for their responsible decisions. But they are not so much troubled with the question of whether this or that particular man has a vocation. Rather, their problem is: "Who is fitted for the life?" Who is so far well enough established that perseverance is to be expected? The authorities have the responsibility for those whom they propose to the bishop for ordination.

It is different with the seminarians. If they were faced only with the sober task of testing themselves to find out whether they really had the qualifications mentioned in the clarification from Rome, and therefore *might* choose a priestly vocation, their decision would be fairly painless. For the final result would be that those who did find themselves equipped with all of the required prerequisites for a priestly vocation's acceptance could still refuse it without any sin.

But what makes it so serious? These young men *know* they have a vocation. This call from God, which decided them in both peace and trouble of soul, in inclination and distress, in longing and fear, is being tested, tested to see whether it is *real*, or whether their enthusiasm for a priestly career did not stem from the romanticism of youth, released by some internal or external experience. That punctilious counting up of the conditions under which a candidate may apply for the priesthood still remains sufficient foundation for acceptance of a doubtful case. There are incomparably more young men today who could become priests according to the norms of 1912 than was the case in 1912. None the less, there are fewer today who decide on that vocation. We live in a time of World Congresses of the Lay Apostolate, but not of parish priests—these, of course, are not really necessary. The army of truly devoted lay helpers grows, but the numbers of priests, by comparison at least, decreases.

If one asks around, the reason is by no means to be found in the fear of a life of service in the Church nor in any lack of love of God. The reason is mostly that the young man does not trust himself in a life of celibacy. There is a remote and unconscious infection in their thinking, derived from the psychoanalysts, which, despite the protestations of psychologists and pedagogs, teaches that unmarried life is not only harmful to body and mind, but even impossible. Then there is the vitalism and naturalism of the last century. And even the literature for young Catholics praises a pure youth almost exclusively as the preparation for happy marriage and, of course, the personal love for a pure girl. These are the reasons known to all why countless young men who might have applied for the priesthood without further ado, according to the clarification of 1912, did not report for entry into the seminary.

And yet the decision for a pure and unmarried life is still the test for the genuineness of vocation in general.

It would be wide of the mark to center the will to persevere in the priestly state—to center this will in the desire for celibacy. It must be the other way around. There are countless laymen, scientists, artists, and politicians who considered that their vocations would only be hindered by marriage. Hence, they often broke engagements upon which they had already entered, e.g., Beethoven, Kierkegaard; they did not want the responsibility of burdening another life with their own. So, too, the seminarian offers himself as a holocaust to God, for the service of the Church and of souls. He knows that all the energy and days of his life will not suffice to fulfill his chosen vocation. "Undivided service" [1] in the kingdom of God is its steadfast will. All else, hard as it may seem at the moment, is only a consequence of that will.

[1] cf. Johann Adam Möhler, *Der ungeteilte Dienst. Von der Grösse und Fährnis jungfräulichen Priestertums,* New Edition, Salzburg, 1933.

Religious Foundation

The second task of the seminarian is to lay the foundation of a healthy, true religious life which takes into account the fact that crises will not be lacking and that they must be endured. The challenge, "Be ye perfect as your heavenly Father is perfect," was directed to all. To whom does it apply more intimately than to those who are to be the salt of the earth (Mt. 5: 13), the city on a mountain, the light on the bushel (Mt. 5: 14)? But the infinite goal of this finite journey, a goal unattainable for those travelers who tire, who want to rest, who become discouraged or even despair, must be grasped in its essence. For only in this way will they continue to see themselves as fellow-pilgrims with all the poor, the weak, and the wandering. It is in this way that they will be able to approach them. Then they will understand our Lord's words, "Judge not that you may not be judged" (Mt. 7: 1). To be a Christian means to be on the way. Or, better, one can never *be* a Christian; one can only try to *become* one and to become one more and more. That removes all Pharisaism from the world of the kingdom of God. For our Lord warns His disciples more clearly against this than against many things which are apparently worse. For even the Pharisees *did have* their justice. The Lord was acquainted with that. He merely states the difference between that justice and the justice of those who belong to the kingdom: "Unless your justice exceeds that of the Pharisees, you shall not enter the kingdom of Heaven" (Mt. 5: 20). "Beware of the leaven of the Pharisees . . ." (Mt. 16: 6). The fervent, untiring journeying toward the infinite goal of perfection, which takes into account weariness, weakness, and crises, both in oneself and others, but which continues undiscouraged on the way, is healthy piety.

The religion of the New Testament does not consist in just performing acts, so that we can then say that we have done our part. The Sermon on the Mount is a singular challenge, and only when one is beyond the bare fulfillment of the law does the new life of grace and freedom begin. The Lord does not want to dissolve the natural moral order nor the revealed law of the Old Testament; He wishes to perfect both of them (Luke 16: 16 ff). The law of Christ is that of spirit and of grace (Rom. 8: 2). "For the law was given through Moses; grace and truth came through Jesus Christ" (John 1: 16). We have become the children of God, and God allows us to call Him Father. He gives us the power to become the "children of God." We are no longer servants, but friends (John 15: 15). Therefore, love, not fear, is the basic drive of Christians. The servant fulfills the job assigned to him. The child asks: "Can I do more?" because it loves.

Therefore, love is the external sign of His disciples, and woe to those in whom it is no longer visible! "A new commandment I give you, that you love one another: that as I have loved you, you may love one another. By this shall all men know that you are my disciples, if you have love for one another" (John 13: 34 ff). Therefore, the Christian does not live as one chained by the necessity of performing many tasks, but rather he serves, yes, *serves* out of the freedom of being a child of God. "But now we have been set free from the law, having died to that by which we were held down: so that we may serve in a new spirit and not according to the outworn letter" (Rom. 7: 6).

It is fundamental to Christian existence that we be conscious of the dignity of a child of God and of the conduct that follows from it. That is something far more fearful for such as we than for non-Christians. But for the same reason, the return of the prodigal son to his father is much more understandable and consoling. And it is a joyous event that the good son cannot understand at all.

Therefore, there has been no single life since Christ that is not under the call of grace at every hour. The "Here I am!" that the seminarian says upon entering must be repeated every day as his prayer. To dedicate himself to God daily is for him and all Christians something that determines their existence. Fulfillment is not a single act, in the sense of the Old Testament, short of which there is sin and beyond which duty ceases. Fulfillment of duty, with respect to the next instant, is only the first step. Not that there is anything wrong with fulfilling one's duty! But to educate a seminarian to that alone is to lay the foundations of a type of priest with whom we will have an unpleasant meeting in the typology that follows later. One can "get through" the Breviary, and canonically, at least, everything will be in order. But the Breviary must be prayed. We are living in the New Testament. For the priest, the Breviary is either a daily admission to the sources and greatest treasures of self-sanctification or the school in which he gradually, but completely, loses all knowledge of how to pray. Where else will the priest derive the strength needed to endure, or to pick himself up after a fall, if not from the daily fountain of youth of his sanctification—Holy Mass and the Breviary? "While your lips repeat the divine words which have been handed down through the inspiration of the Spirit of God, let nothing of this great treasure be lost to you, so that your spirit may answer the voice of God faithfully" (Pius XII).

To understand this is the second task of the seminary period.

Freedom from the World

Further, the cleric must develop, in these years, a clear and full view of the world and its importance in the eyes of God. The dubious nature of all that is temporal, of all earthly assurances, must become part of his flesh and blood. He devotes his life entirely to God, without fear: for God keeps His word. That means freedom in the face of the world's society and environment, indifference to the needs, satisfactions, comforts which seem to be necessities to those in the world about us. He chooses a state of life which is the last one remaining of a society once divided according to a person's state. It has duties, customs, and rights proper to it and its own particular dignity. It is a state of the most ancient nobility, far beyond the nobility of this world. And yet it is grand and pure. God is his liege lord, the greatest there is. He it is Who loves freedom from the goods of this world. He it is Who came into this world in a dress the world despised, that of poverty. But it is this alone which beseems the priest, for his freedom and independence are rooted in it. So too is his power over men.

The splendid pastor of Torcy puts these words into the mouth of the Savior, rebuking His disciples when they complained about Mary, who anointed Him "for His burial"; "Poverty weighs heavily in the scale of my heavenly Father and all your treasure of idle mist cannot level it" (Georges Bernanos, *Diary of a Country Priest*, New York, 1937). A holy, no, a healthy indifference toward all possessions is necessary for the priestly candidate. The talk against the bourgeois priest is gradually becoming pointless, for, as a class, he is gradually disappearing. "The comfortable, bourgeois happiness which is forced upon us is so little adapted to our needs. It isn't difficult for the most extreme poverty to retain its dignity. Then to what purpose are such appearances preserved? Why are necessities forced upon us?" (*Ibid.*).

We are living in a time when the "*Mission de France*" of the Catholic priesthood is living an experiment of priestly existence in poverty before the eyes of the world. And all this in a country of the strongest bourgeois tradition, even among the clergy. No one can say whether this form of life will not become common. It is one of the most wonderful things to see that those who have been called to the priesthood in the most troubled decades of this century, here, there, and everywhere, have not been mistaken in their ideal, despite any revolution in or deprivation of—as this foolish world thought—the "reason for its being." But what does this world know of *priestly existence*?

It is not necessary that all seminarians devote their free time to charitable occupations, wherever this is possible, during the years of their formation, as do the seminarians of Lisieux. There are seminaries which send their students into factories or farms to work during their vacations. At any rate, it is the task of the seminary to instill, as a part of the cleric's fundamental notion of priestly existence, the conviction that a priest's life is essentially a co-existence with men and a state of concern about them. That is more than an understanding of the "social question." It is even more important that they become united among themselves by a bond of love and remain so united. The brotherly union that exists among priests is so much a part of their existence that nothing can replace it. Living side by side in a restricted area always results in a smoothing out of the rough edges and weaknesses of the individuals, and that in all charity. But it should be done only with charity and good humor. It is only right that the individual get rid of the idiosynrasies which disturb or even strike the community as odd. But no member of the community should be a defenseless *ens foppabile*" (object of constant ridicule).

There is food for thought in the fact that Emile Baumann, in his book *Exkommunizierte* (Vienna, 1947, p. 72) traces the downfall and embitterment of the apostate priest back to the uncharitable jokes made at his expense during his seminary days. Of course, Radec himself was an unsociable boor. But the well-meaning mockery of his companions could not have made him more sociable. There remained a "trauma" which served to lay the foundation for the later revolutionary.

Priests volunteer for the *Mission de Paris*. They do not constitute an order and take no vows. Each can leave at any time he wants. Anyone with good will is accepted, but there are those who are not welcome; these exclusions are not arbitrary, as they may seem, but the result of bitter experience; unwanted are all who are furtive, sly, devious, hypocritical and querulous. The unctuous and artificial are undesirable. Here a finger is laid on a dangerous wound. This type which is refused is one incapable of existential (therefore, true) work for souls. It is the type that rebels, that compromises the Church of Christ by his very appearance and slanders the love of Christ, which he is bound to preach.

It is one of the most weighty duties of self-examination on the part of those who conduct the seminaries to ask themselves whether certain methods of training, discipline, and surveillance, which they employ, do not really destroy the childlike, Christian, and indeed, interiorly honest man (Mt. 18: 3; 19: 14; Luke 10: 21). In a case like this there is a later lack of foundation, and no devotion, however intense it be, can make up for the damage already done. Even his piety is overpowered by the gathering shadows, and ends in a feigned gesture of shocked innocence. We are acquainted with the efforts of the enemies of Christian teaching to represent the morality of Christianity as inferior. Such attempts must fail, of course, but the type mentioned above gives a certain credibility to their objections.

Personality Training

A very serious source of failure in later life is the suppression or even the neglect of *personality*. Only strong, rounded, healthy, and energetic men will be able to master the huge task that awaits them, humanly speaking. They alone make an impression; they alone will remain firm rocks of support in times of stress. Only they can comfort the faithful. The priestly vocation, the holiest, greatest, and most difficult of all vocations, requires in the person who bears it a strong natural foundation. The great saints, especially those who made history, were all outstanding personalities.

The simple priest cannot claim for himself either their greatness of nature or grace, but they are symbols and models, according to the measure in which the individual is gifted.

It is not belittling to recall that it is not unspoiled nature but *natura cruciata*, which will carry the supernatural power which constitutes the priest. Therein lies a confusion between *natura cruciata* and *natura denaturata*. Whoever has promised himself to the kingdom of God and its lot of persecution has likewise promised himself to the cross: the unbloody cross, usually, but if it must be, the bloody cross. "Finally, it is necessary that all of us, united in Christ, suffer the mystical death of the cross so that we can apply the words of St. Paul to ourselves: 'I am crucified with Christ'" (Pius XII, *Menti Nostrae*, 33). But the sacrifice, if such ve want to call it, is only great when the whole, strong man teps under the cross. It is a fateful ascetical mistake to suppose that a man is only rightly prepared for the cross vhen his backbone has first been broken. He must be able o *carry* the cross.

It is a tremendous mistake when candidates of a strong, self-willed character are regarded with suspicion or even rejected. It would be different if the training aimed at a herd of sheep which would be as free as possible of all distractions. But in this way, how the kingdom of God is deprived of forces it needs so desperately!

"I am an old priest," says the Canon de la Motte-Beuvron in Bernanos' *Diary of a Country Priest*, "and I know how the seminaries mould boys down to the same ordinary level, till often, unfortunately, there's nothing left to choose between them." Anyone, anywhere, who keeps his eyes open can see that. Then, years later, you have submissive, frightened, unenergetic priests, incapable of initiative or of the right idea at the right time. There was something that happened to Friedrich Perthes which apparently had never happened to him before: he met Saint Clement Mary Hofbauer (1816) and—"his eye, without the usual look of the Catholic priest, was full of fire, looking at you directly and sharply; the features were quite mobile and yet his whole face was suffused with a peace which one must call heavenly" (J. Hofer, *Saint Clement Maria Hofbauer*, Freiburg, 1923). The man had to wait until he was forty-four years old to meet a priest who was still a real man. Maybe that was just bad luck.

Therefore, it is the task of the seminary to try each one with regard to his vocation and not to exclude the troublesome candidates. Regents of seminaries must themselves be free, open, and healthy confidants of their charges. They must see to it that they keep healthy in body and soul. The times can only make use of priests capable of hard work They must build up precisely those human capacities which the priest needs as a healthy foundation for grace: upright ness, sincerity, nobility, bravery, magnanimity, courage, self lessness, the ability to listen to others' opinions, respect fo every honest conviction: for these alone will later admit him into the company of those he wants to win over. The Holy Father warns that ". . . pupils be educated to integrity and honesty, esteeming the purity of their lives and that o others and every power of their souls over all else, avoiding all deception and deceit" (*Menti Nostrae*).

Attention must be given to the formation of a genuine moral personality based on the moral qualities already pos sessed and upon conscience. The old objection that a "Chris tian is lacking in fundamentals," that is, in fundamental natural morality, need not be true. It should not be voiced again when speaking of a priest. The future priest, like every other Christian, owes his moral and social develop ment to his environment, and it is out of this that he grows and matures. It is a caricature of the Christian, and even more so of the priest, if he is a two-legged ghost who fright ens people, who fulfills his individual moral obligations imperfectly and only after a casuistic *pro* and *con*, without *himself* growing in moral maturity.

The religious goal, the greatest possible perfection under grace, is most exalted by reason of its infinity, more exalted than we shall ever be able to attain. But the higher the build ing, the stronger the foundation must be. In this case, to plan and to try for the highest possible goal is not merely understandable, but simply necessary.

Humility comes from the knowledge of one's own poverty. It is an insight into reality. It is knowledge of our limita tions and faith in the fact that grace can do all things. It is a realization that even the best that we can put at the disposal of grace is really nothing. But it is not humility to put nothing at the disposal of grace.

It is an old composition theme that the God-willed and God-given singularity of every human existence is a lofty good; we would be depriving God of an honor that no one else could supply, were we to forget that. Why is this idea not taken more seriously? Why is it not the starting point and motive power of everyone's personal education? The thing that is peculiar to a person is also the thing that he alone can do. For a priest, it is the way in which he alone can serve God.

Priests are sometimes called "Reverend Father." No one can ever come up to the honor which is intended by that greeting. But if the person to whom this honor is given should be a weak and feeble man, the effect is so comic as to make one laugh out loud. Once a malicious fellow asked, "What would be left if the priests were stripped of their cassocks?" It is a provoking deformity and self-mockery— not that that is so bad! But it is a cause of a mockery of the things of God if the world sees in a poor specimen an overweening consciousness of his own dignity of manhood.

It is also part of the seminary training to see to it that each student keep a sense of proportion. The vocation is always great, the fulfillment is always holy, always beyond the means of this world; there is never a proportion between the man and his priesthood. Every priest must know that. But there are cases in which this knowledge becomes especially pressing, because it is fully wanting. Since the tension that exists between the man and the priest is there of necessity, it cannot be the cause of criticism, but rather a warning to those who educate men for the priesthood. The priest is necessarily in danger of "living above his environment intellectually," as Ludwig Hänsel once put it (Rudolf, *Das Christentum in der Neuheit der Tage,* Vienna, 1940, p. 47);

and that means both poses and expressions which arouse distrust. That distrust hinders men's approach to the priest.

All insincerity stems from one's personality. What is the source of that affected pathos in some sermons? the repulsive unctuousness in conversation? There is something missing, down deep in a man, even in the natural order. And the man who approaches a priest in a time of real need, only to sense in him an attitude which destroys his hope, just gives up.

The roots lie deeper. Prudence indeed is the first of the cardinal virtues. But it has nothing to do with slyness, or with speculation about another's weak points, or the compliments that have the purpose of—winning the other fellow over? No, they are just soft soap. We need open, straight, upright priests, guileless as children. The consecration of the priest is in no way disturbed by the true personality of the man so consecrated. The power to win people, even that of religion, is given only to what is healthily natural.

Priestly Piety

The foundations of priestly existence are laid in the seminary. The seminary bears the responsibility, therefore, for both the priest's power for good and his possible failure. The foundations of priestly piety are there.

As in every Christian, it is the love of God that must be the source of power which sustains, vivifies, and enlightens all the virtues. The priest is daring to live amid the confusion of the world, bound, and necessarily so, to the people of his congregation; and yet in the final analysis his life must be one of loneliness with God.

All his works must take their origin from this union with God, and all must be referred to it. It is in this love that his love of souls is rooted. This love, rooted in God, cannot be lost on men in the long run. It is the magnet which attracts the sinner to penance; indeed, it is precisely what is needed in order that the sinner be known for what he is and helped because of it. It overcomes the enemy with the might of Christ, though all else be dubious or remain unexpressed. It is sufficient, as the legend of the Apostle John tells us. It is not only the bond and heart of every perfection of the priest, but it is the mark of the faithful for the world at large. *"Magna res est amor"* (*Imit. Christi*, III, 5, 8). It is not faith which distinguishes the redeemed from the unredeemed, but love. Even "the devil believes, but does not love" (St. Augustine). Newman says somewhere that it is the greatest mystery of our Faith, that the Son of God loves us as the Father loves Him. Then it is the greatest mystery of our priestly lives that we hand on this love of Christ to our fellow men in the same degree as we have received it. "According to the teaching of our Divine Master, the perfection of Christian life consists in the love of God and our neighbor, a love which must be fervent as well as zealously active" (*Menti Nostrae*, 23).

The second point is that the priest must be convinced that he has chosen a calling which has meaning only in loving co-existence with his congregation, a calling that can be perfected daily only in that union.

We must be convinced that we have chosen a calling which must stand fast in the tension between the love of God and the fear of God's daily nearness . . . For the whole of our lives—a whole lifetime—without ever experiencing a lessening of the power of fascination (*fascinosum*), as Rudolf Otto puts it, nor of the power of the terrifying, fearful nearness of God (*tremendum*). For a whole lifetime!

This life, this tension between loving God and fearing Him—yes, even fleeing from Him, can only be endured because the Church has given us a grand, holy form of association with God, without which we would perish in defenselessness. It is the liturgy. She places us in the midst of the splendor of God's presence and, at the same time, protects our eyes from its consuming fire. It is not only a work of grandeur beyond dimension, since ultimately it is the work of the Holy Spirit; it is also the discovery of His love. Thus we can live in the presence of God.

It is an essential task of seminary training to show that by this loving act of God, the liturgy holds that tension in check. But it must not be so explained that the tension is no longer felt, nor can the *opus operantis* be forgotten when it is explained how the *opus operatum* is veiled from us.

In the novels *Über die Brücke* by Joseph Weingartner (Innsbruck, 1929) and *The Chosen* by Rev. E. J. Edwards (New York, 1949) the problems of seminary training are most extensively treated. In both, there are striking parallels. A group of high-minded young men enter the seminary as close friends. In one book, the five young men go from New York to the remotely situated seminary of St. John in Ohio. In the other book, three young men cross over the bridge which leads to the boarding school in Brixen. In both stories it is a young man named Martin who seems most unlikely to persevere; yet he is the only one who does. Marty is the only one of the five to be ordained. At the same time, Alice, who had tried to win him away from his vocation for herself, kneels at a statue of the Sorrowful Mother and resigns herself to God's will. Berta Kamployer in Brixen takes Martin Schöpf's decision a little less dramatically and adapts herself to it with understandable Catholic hardihood.

But what a humane atmosphere there is in Brixen! The professors are friendly and close to their students. In this atmosphere, everyone can express himself. In St. John's College, the impersonal House Order is the single cold test of perseverance, from which one automatically expects the miracle of spiritualization. The five leave the confusion of New York for the isolation of St. John's. They have torn themselves away from a world of business and noise: Rube junks his car; Steve, star fullback, says goodbye to his coach; Joe escapes from his well-to-do middle-class family with great difficulty and resistance; Ruby is quite upset by Dick's parting; Marty consoles his mother who will now be left alone; and they all leave. The inseparables arrive at the silent Ohio seminary, to be met with some distrust, since they come not from the minor seminary, but from the "World."

They meet an entirely new world behind the gates: isolation, silence, and a most strict daily order. The first retreat hits them like a cold shower. But they get through it well enough. The high goal is worth it. It is just their training to be future "soldiers of Christ." "Renouncing the world, they would have to go out to a very worldly world, and their renunciation as priests would have to be the answer to the many questions which would be asked". Their studies are mostly in the foreground. It is striking that there is never any discussion of things spiritual. The educational skill of the prefects, all blameless priests, is limited to surveillance and checking to see what paragraph of the house rules might have been broken. The one exception is Father White. It is the scandal of this novel that, although the seminary "was renowned throughout the country, not only because of the erudition of its faculty and the capability of its graduates, but also because of its excellent discipline," yet it was unable to bring these idealistic young men, with the best of good will, to the priestly life, with the exception of Marty. Only Dick leaves of his own accord, after changing his dangerous attitude of "both—and" to one of "either—or."

The title of the book refers to the students. But after a look at Stoner, Carroll, McClellan, and others, even including the Rector, who only appears once in the book, the title could easily be changed to "Many are chosen but few are called." At the end, of course, they know themselves that they are through with Latin. Father White sums it up this way: "This whole formation that we submit them to, seems so useless. And of those that last it out, there are still a few who are unsuitable for the demands of the priesthood." Of course, even the best seminary cannot give a guarantee like that with its diploma. It is very important, but it isn't the only thing which marks the future priest.

3. FORMATION IN THEOLOGY

Its Secondary Importance

In the preparation for the priesthood, the thing that most engrosses the seminarian, even from the point of time, is the study of theology. But this is of secondary importance, in comparison with the religious and ascetical-humanistic foundation, not to mention the sacramental. This was clear in the time of the Fathers of the Church, as can be seen when one considers their varied callings. Later centuries have effected a reversal in the order of importance and, at first glance, we find this quite as it should be. Even in the most recent times, however, God has faced us with some challenging figures, seeming to smile indulgently at His theology professors.

The saintly Curé D'Ars is a case in point. When thirteen years of age, he keeps hearing the words, "Follow Me!" as he lies on his pallet in a horse stall. At seventeen, he is convinced of his vocation. Then, after a long struggle, he begins his humanities at the age of twenty (1806). The splendid Curé Balley d'Ecully, to whom we must be grateful, humanly speaking, for the saint, considers the case hopeless. Latin just could not enter that peasant head; apparently he had never heard of Greek. So Vianney becomes a joke to his fellow students. And after three years, at most, of the humanities, taken privately with Père Balley, he wants to start his theological studies, which consisted at that time only of one year of philosophy, two years of theology. It was hopeless. At home only with common-sense reasoning, he can make nothing of logic. And Latin! He was accepted at the major seminary as "an extremely weak student," but was soon dismissed as totally unfit. A new attempt by Balley comes to nothing. He has to teach theology privately to Vianney. Even though this was done in French, it was only partially successful. Nor was it easy to find a bishop willing to assume the responsibility for his ordination. Finally, the Bishop of Grenoble took a chance on him. By reason of the *litterae testimoniales* of the Bishop of Lyon, Vianney's native diocese, he was ordained on July 13, 1815, but—and here the smile of the Heavenly Father must have been broadest, meant even for His troubled bishops—only on the condition that he receive jurisdiction for hearing confessions a year after his ordination. He, the greatest confessor of the century, to whom a few years later, hundreds of thousands of sinners and troubled minds from all the countries of Europe and abroad would flock! They came in such numbers that Vianney spent 16 to 18 hours in the confessional, day in and day out, for years! The influence of this poor priest who could not qualify theologically, pastor of a hitherto unknown hamlet of three hundred souls, was greater than that of hundreds of learned doctors of theology put together. And it will be felt for a long, long time.

But that is the most recent and perhaps most provocative example. Another is that of St. Clement Maria Hofbauer. He made his theology in Vienna, at a time when the faculty there was strongly tainted with Josephinism, protesting silently, and even aloud at times. The second nocturn of his feast tells us, of course, that he made a pilgrimage to Rome *ex puriore fonte sacras disciplinas hausurus* (to learn his theology from a purer source). But if we trace his life year by year, it appears that there was insufficient time for that.

Or what should one say, as a theologian, of the case of St. Joseph Cupertino? Dear Lord, he could pray, that former lay brother! Praying, he forgot the whole world and detected saints and sinners among men as though by smell. He had not volunteered to be a candidate for the priesthood. He *knew* no theology. And now he was sitting among the examinees, equipped only with his merry Franciscan trust in God. One after another they answered the bishop's questions brilliantly: the bishop was quite delighted. And just before it was Joseph's turn, he stopped. The splendid attainments of the other candidates caused him to suppose that it would be a waste of time to bother the others with an examination. That is how Joseph Cupertino became a priest —and what a priest!

Then there is the sacristan Thomas Gouvernec, who naively wanted to replace the priests who had abandoned his island. The simple, pious fellow is summoned by the bishop, who wanted to make him pastor of the tiny abandoned reef. But he can't get the abstractions of theology into his poor head, and he is sent home. But the longing of the people of the island becomes a cry of pious despair. Then the bishop calls him again and ordains him. That is how it was in the early days of the Faith. The fishermen of Lake Genesareth and the fisherman of the Breton coast, the beginning and the end, salute one another (Henri Queffelec, *Island Priest*).

Even aside from the early years of the Church, these examples could be multiplied. They support the remark we made at the beginning of the section, but they do have one weakness: all the examples that can be cited are those of saints. But we speak here of the ordinary case. So, naturally, there are rules of procedure and canonical prescriptions. Their dignity and the differentiating between what is absolute and what is more or less important is really of no practical moment.

But let us adduce, for the sake of example, a parallel in Protestantism as it is found in the United States. Here theology is not only of secondary importance, but is banished to such a place in their consciousness that it almost becomes superfluous or harmful. When we say Protestants, we do not mean the Lutherans (3,300,000) nor the congregations of Calvinistic origin (Presbyterians, 2,600,000; Congregationalists, 1,100,000; Reformed, 900,000), nor even the descendants of the former Anglican Church (Protestant Episcopal, 1,300,000). But rather we mean the largest Christian groups outside of the 30,000,000 Catholics in the United States, the Baptists (10,000,000) and the Methodists (over 8,000,000). To a greater degree, this is true of the small sects (Brethren, Adventists, Quakers). "In individual churches, that is, in those of Methodist or Baptist stamp, in the South of the United States, only a relatively small number seek their education as preachers in a theological school. Many content themselves with attending Bible schools" (Adolf Keller, *Amerikanisches Christentum heute*, Zollikon-Zürich, 1943, p. 154). "A naive biblicism takes the place of doctrine. Belief in the Bible takes the place of all theological formulae" (p. 155). Scarcely a third of the ministers of the nineteen

Protestant denominations have a theological education (p. 189). Therefore it is not unusual that "ministers go over to another denomination without any internal conflict at all" (p. 292).

Significance

The significance of theology for the foundation of priestly existence is granted; it is ineffably important. It gives the future priest a knowledge of the content of his priestly work and is intended to give him clarity and certainty. He is the dispenser of the mysteries of Christ. He must know what these are and what they mean. He is the preacher of the Word. He must know what the content of his message is. Religion, revelation, and theology are not the same thing. One cannot suppose, however, that there is any contradiction between them (not so Rudolf Otto, *Das Heilige*, Munich, pp. 117 ff.). Here there is only the difficulty of a concrete case. Theology is not meant to be, nor can it be, an immediate source of preaching. Attempts to make it so have failed. But all study of theology, according to the rule of St. Dominic, should be directed toward the care of souls. Theology is intended to give the future apostle a clear framework of the spiritual and religious world in which everything can be reviewed in a systematic synthesis of order and relations. An immediate application to the concrete is seldom possible. In the years of his formation, the young theologian must make a path in his mind from the sources of revelation through the theological disciplines to an understandable synthesis of Catholic doctrine. With this equipment, he must then go back through pastoral theology to the sources, to their objective pure meaning and refined application. Theology makes it possible for him to preach the

one Word of God in the unity of the Faith of all the priests
of the entire Christian world. That is not merely something
tremendous. It is absolutely necessary for his work. The
power of the priests and, therefore, that of the Church, both
in conquering and defending, lies in their thorough theological training. The unity of action of priests over the whole
world is an unmistakable and irresistible bulwark in this
lost world.

A lack of theological background brings the priest into
tension between what is demanded of him and what he is
able to do. It is a reason why many simply rely on the ready
answer that covers any situation. Or he restricts himself to
the administration of the sacraments, and little more. He
never has a right to do that. The command "Go forth and
teach . . . " is a duty that binds him for all time. The New
Testament does not recognize the difference between priest
and Scripture scholar. The priest of the New Testament
must be both because he is necessarily the bearer of the
Word which transforms men. He is a servant of the Word,
the written word of God.

It is true that theological learning is not the same as spiritual power. But it is just as certain that without an up-
to-date theological background, today's priest cannot be
effective. It isn't the knowledge that does it; he must have
a love for holy theology. There is an *Eros theologikos*. The
second nocturn of his feast says of Saint Anselm that he
studied theology with tears in his eyes; of others we read
that they studied it on their knees. This love of the holy
science will impel the seminarian to go beyond the basic
matter given him in the lectures to plumb its depths for
himself. It has been said that no one can be considered truly
educated unless he has his favorite poet. The same thing
can be said of a theologian. He should have his favorite
author and favorite work, one that he consults constantly,

if he is to be truly a theologian. A poor man's knowledge of examination theology will be quickly lost in the apostolate. He will find out later how he is to extend his theological learning from the jobs he is given by his bishop, the assignments he receives, the people he meets. Above all, he himself must never try to evade a question. He must master his uncertainty, especially his doubts, right down to the last subtle distinction. The necessary tension that exists between knowledge and mystery should not be covered up by a premature act of Faith. The borders of one must be seen clearly and the profundity of the other must be endured in the existence of the man of Faith.

Theology Today

Needless to say, this places tremendous responsibilities upon theology itself.

Theology has no easy time of it. It is her task to delimit the mysteries and the infinity of revealed truth and present them in an intelligible synthesis. By clean-cut definitions, theology must bring within the limits of human understanding the *Deus incomprehensibilis*, the incomprehensible Divinity, the *Deus ineffabilis*, the ineffable God, the limitless infinitude. It is an audacious thing to attempt, and often enough pious folk have considered it blasphemy. The *tremendum* of God's presence is subjected to a microscope, and His infinity is inspected with a telescope, as we try to reduce them to our systems. Is this profaning them? Surely not that! See how modestly St. Thomas approaches the mysteries of God in the first part of his *Summa*!

In the eighteenth century, an attempt was made to impart theology to the thousands of monks who lived in their own city on Mount Athos. But they destroyed the Athos Academy erected there by Efjenios Vulgaris as an outpost of the devil and let it fall into ruins, still to be seen today. (Franz Dölger, *Mönchsland Athos,* Munich, 1943, p. 262). There has been no similar mad defense against this danger in the West. The most extreme profanation of things sacred *and* theological was Hegel's *Religion als Wissen von Gott.* This it was that aroused Sören Kierkegaard to the defense of what was sacred, declaring that theology was necessarily an existential science. He was certainly not the first to do that. Pious complaints about theology for its own sake have often been voiced. *"Quid prodest tibi alta de Trinitate disputare, si careas humilitate, unde displiceas Trinitati?"* What good does it do you to hold learned disputations on the Trinity, if you are lacking in humility and so displease the Trinity? (*Imit. Christi,* I. 1, 3). *"Opto magis sentire compunctionem quam scire ejus definitionem."* I would rather feel compunction than know how to define it (*Ibid.*). *"Noli autem discutere opera Altissimi, sed tuas iniquitates perscrutare, in quantis deliquisti et quam multa bona neglexisti."* Don't presume to examine the works of the Most High, but rather your own sins; how much evil you have done and how much good omitted (*Ibid.* III, 4, 19).

These words, and the same is true for so much written in Kempis' *Imitation of Christ,* are valuable for all time, not merely in the light of the period in which they were written—and that was when the theological hair-splitters were in full swing. They express the secondary place of theology in the whole plan of Christian living. Or better, they bear witness to the fact that theology has meaning and being only in existential union with a Christian life. The necessity of a theological education as a preparation for the priesthood is beyond cavil.

What is more, theology must regain the leading place in intellectual life. Let no one be surprised at this demand:

not the theologian, surely, because what it says is something obvious; for either theology is the queen of sciences, or it simply does not exist. And not the opponent of theology, because neither the hierarchy nor primacy in the world of science can be usurped. The only thing that enables one science such preeminence in this world is real accomplishment.

That is why we theologians are faced with the necessity of producing something in the totality of the intellectual world that both makes the primacy of theology effective and is worthy of it. A theology will never attain that primacy by living a ghetto existence, nor by producing mere ghetto evidence. It cannot be a theology taught by men who are glad that the rest of the world—naturally evil, of course—cares nothing about them. Nor can the problems of theology be treated like dried out, well-assorted flowers in a herbarium. In a herbarium, there are merely plants that once were alive. But the medicinal and poisonous plants of the day blossom and ripen in the green meadows of every era. It cannot have as its Bible an old, carefully preserved tome that is completely out of touch with theology, containing an exclusive canon of problems and errors beginning with the Docetism of the first centuries, with a pat presentation and refutation that will hold for all time to come. It must be a theology which will familiarize the future priest with the theological, philosophic, spiritual, and social problems and tasks of this his day and enable him to master them. It must on its own merits attract auditors from among the students of other faculties, because they know that it is here and only here that they will get a picture of the world which transcends their special fields; here a valid answer to their ultimate questions is to be found. The timidity of theologians must be overcome. Long ago Father Faber asked, "Why is it that we are so enchanted with the material and philosophic studies and find theology alone insipid?" (*Creator and Creature,* New York, 1923). His answer is that such a theology is a sign of lifeless Faith. Actually, it is worse, for it is a slander of the things of God by one whose duty it is to protect them. It is the duty of theology —again and again we must insist upon this—in an age when the world is withdrawing from it, to cease being the secret knowledge of priests and monks. Only such a theology is capable of contributing to the building up of priestly existence; only such a theology has rights over that existence.

For the task of the future priest will be to preach to the men of his own day—he must be able to do that. If he is not equipped to do so, then his theological preparation has failed him and must share the guilt of those who fall on the broad front of every-day life. There is an existential theology, not only in the sense of a theology that is alive, but one which feels the needs and challenge of the moment. It is that theology which comes alive as a result of the meeting of eternal truths with the current problems and anxieties of the day. Without making the claim itself, such a theology would be a theology of preaching even for those who must go out into the whole world and teach it.

It is one of the most terrible mysteries of our time and indeed of every time that its questions and tasks are the things that fully occupy it. It will only find its way to eternal truth when it can find a temporal answer to its temporal problems. Have we fully understood the demands and validity of this law? What is even more frightening is the fact that if the questions of the hour, and therefore the demands of God, are not dealt with in the name of God, they will be taken up in the name of atheism, and their solutions will be fraught with danger. It is needless to mention the examples we could all name from our own time. Who will answer for it? Above all: what theologian, leaving behind him the needs of our time, believes that he would be justified in excusing himself before God by saying that he had taught solid, timelessly valid theology? As though there were any other kind! And yet it must give every age its answer. It must know, experience, and master the concrete needs of men.

Nikolai Berdyaev claims that the atheism of Bolshevism is explained by the hatred of suffering man for the universal and abstract, which lectures far from the actual misery of man and yet still lays claim to rulership over his life. (*Sinn und Schicksal des russischen Kommunismus,* Lucerne, 1937, pp. 56, 69, 46 ff.). Impeachment of the attempts of atheistic forces which are objectively justified can now only be made with veiled heads, for now it is the act of the servant who buried his talent so that he could hand it back unchanged to his demanding Lord: unchanged, and therefore timelessly valid. It is the annoying alibi of the man who wasn't there when the crisis broke, and now he wants to blame the poor fellow he neglected to help. It is likewise the reason for the co-responsibility for the misery that of necessity must come when man seeks his happiness contrary to the Name of God. What will the Lord say to the apologete of the timelessly valid, who is eternally behind the times? "Out of thy own mouth I judge thee, thou wicked servant!" (Luke 19: 22).

We must refute the errors of our day, but we can only do it with a bad conscience, not because error has stolen a march on truth, but because the truth we do preach is powerless to banish error of itself. Why is it powerless? That is a question which should weigh heavily on every conscience.

It is clear that a theology is existential, in the sense of a living, effective theology, because of its impact on the world of today, because of its daily new, living response to the daily new, living problems and needs of the world about us. Effectiveness comes from real accomplishment. Real accomplishments alone have real power. Experience shows that this power is conditioned by the degree of understanding of being at every instant of the time in which alone it can work. And this depends on the timely conviction and existential seriousness of the theologians who are aware of the fact that there are not only eternal orders and truths, but also that life now and always presents a new and unfulfilled challenge. The fulfillment of that challenge is an obvious duty to which God constantly summons His own. And there is always danger of failure because of the fault of His own. They know that at every moment there is a concrete duty that cannot be repeated or brought back in this challenge of fulfillment. The only thing that is objective and absolute is the revelation of the eternal plan and the superabundance of Redemption. But since this objective reality does not yet mean subjective redemption, each age of the world can meet the reality and power of eternity clearly and with conviction only when it has mastered its own needs. Do we take into account how fearful this state of affairs is? For the modes of living and knowing are as numerous as the seconds in the time-span of this world. And the modes of awareness and understanding—therefore the paths to grace and faith—are equally numerous.

This is where we find the concerns of theology which are determined by time. They are just as necessary as its timeless task, because the present and constant anxiety of the priest lies with whatever congregation is his.

Besides, who will reproach the lonely priest at his post amid chimneys, flats, or dying farms? Did he receive the equipment that gave him confidence and daily renews it, when he was sent to the front, a confidence that enables him to endure with courage and trust in God?

Does not theological training often share the responsibility for the priest who goes wrong?

Again: the task of today's Christians, and especially the priests, is to reclaim the lost provinces of the Church. It is the task of theology to equip the layman and priest intellectually for this task. How easy it is to say something like that! In this world, so much a prey to confusion, in which even the thinking man finds an erratic mixture of good and bad, true and false, even the provinces of truth and falsehood are divided by no known border, so that they seem well on the way to a world-spanning State.

Whose State? The absolute is sought in the name of man. But it is the will of God alone that is the absolute and it can only be realized in the Name of God. For the same world is "equally ready for every form of cruelty as for every form of fanaticism and superstition" (Bernanos).

Every age stands under the judgment of God, each in its own way. Every time has its own symbolism, proper to it. It is universal and contains its physical, as well as its spiritual, reality. The atom bomb, whose workings every fool is acquainted with, is only a symbol of how this time, as no other heretofore and probably no other afterwards, is faced with being and non-being. This is true also in its spiritual existence. Also? No, rather precisely because of it!

The feeling about today is so universal that every theologian and every priest, be he in the most remote mountain parish, works with it ever before his eyes. It is a simple fact that all men share the same fate because of the technical means of travel and communication. Economic relationship and mutual interdependence are only the most keenly felt aspects of the unity of the world. And the political unity of the world which is now being demanded, is already decided upon. There is only a difference of opinion as to the form and spirit of the world-kingdom. Even the Church had and still has the idea of a religious and hierarchically arranged world-union in the words of our Lord, "Go forth and teach all nations" (Mt. 28: 19). The heart of this union can only be spirit and life: life from the Spirit of the Son. His kingdom is not of this world. But His Spirit must be the spirit of this world. It must be the spirit of the future world-kingdom. To work for that we have need of existential theological weapons.

III. THE DEVELOPMENT OF THE
FORMS OF PRIESTLY EXISTENCE

1. THE NEWLY ORDAINED

The first Holy Sacrifice of the newly ordained priest has always been not only an occasion of the greatest solemnity, but also one full of mystery, even for the theologian. Granted the offering of the first fruits always had special significance (Deut. 8: 8; 18: 4; Numb. 28: 26; 1 Cor. 16: 15; Apoc. 14: 4), what occurs there is nothing different from what happens at the Consecration of every other Mass. The first blessing has scarcely any more effect than every other priestly blessing.

How is it, then, that on this day the people flock from all over? Why is it that the newly ordained is received with the outward signs of solemnity that his congregation usually reserves for a bishop's visit? Certainly, the excitement and emotion of the people is much greater and deeper than when the bishop comes.

Why?

Is it only the joy of having a new priest? It is something more: one has to look into the eyes of the parishioners, especially those of his relatives, and most especially, his mother's, to know for the first time what pure, true joy is. To be the mother of a priest is the most glorious crown of Christian motherhood. By that fact, the mother becomes like the

Mother of God Herself. When the mother of a priest dies, it often happens that more priests accompany her coffin than attend the funeral of another priest.

But this joy is not without a tacit unconfessed tension, a sense of the difficulty and risk now confronting the newly ordained priest. Isn't the solemnity just a little bit too solemn? In the tears of joy, a still anxiety is also found. There was an elderly pious woman who once told me that she could never attend a First Mass because she couldn't keep from crying. I asked her why. Her answer was that she didn't *know*. Women never know, but their intuition is seldom wrong. Perhaps that is what is behind the folk-custom of the First Mass bride. She is usually the sister of the newly ordained, or a child, wearing a garland of myrtle, like any other bride, carrying the garland of the new priest before him on a white silk cushion. Is it a symbol of the congregation he will soon have? Of the Church? Or of a sad rejoicing over the sacrifice? At any rate, there is an analogy with the wedding ceremony. It is the marriage of renunciation. That such a marriage is celebrated on purpose is wonderful, but deeply moving as well.

The newly ordained priest himself now lives days and weeks of the greatest joy. The real crisis has long since passed, months ago, when he was ordained to the subdiaconate. God answers his "great decision" with the gift of heart-felt joy. The last hesitations were burned away in the glow of the final retreat; ordination exalted him above the rest of the Christian people; the celebration of his First Mass confirmed that and, humanly speaking, strengthened his self-confidence. He is still such a young man. The people press around him: Bless us! Bless us! And he does not weary of spreading his hands over their bowed heads. The grace of ordination flows out of him in a new vital power. His hands still smell of the holy oils. The faithful have an almost magic confidence in these consecrated hands—all try to cling to them. In a trance, blessed Catherine Emmerich lay stiff, cut off from her surroundings. But whenever a priest was near, she felt for the consecrated fingers and held them fast. There are powers of which no one is conscious and which none can understand. But they do exist. Nothing seems too impossible, too difficult, for the powers conferred in ordination. And that fact is in complete accord with reality; the opposite is untrue.

With child-like trust, he said *"Ecce adsum"*—"I am here." And as far as he knows, that is completely foreign to any *"Ecce Homo!"* Here I am, a man! It is the farthest thing from his thoughts.

The faithful have a single-minded faith in the power of the young priesthood. The proverb still goes about, even though one no longer hears it in so many words: to get a first blessing, you ought to walk right through new shoes or ride your horse to death. And his fellow-priests share in this conviction.

The sermons preached at a First Mass express all this well. It is rare that they make much of anything but the grandeur of the priesthood, but it does happen. The pastor of St. Peter's in Ahrntal (East Tirol) speaks soberly and bravely when preaching at a First Mass. Even the word *tension* occurs here in speaking of the priestly life. "Even you, Brother in Christ, who have offered up the sacrifice of the New Testament, full to overflowing with heart-felt joy, even you will not be spared hours of bitter struggle, sour disappointment, and deepest discouragement. You, too, will feel often enough to your sorrow that in you the Lord has chosen a poor specimen of manhood as His servant. But even if I do not pass over these facts in silence, do not let it discourage you" (Joseph Weingartner, *Über die Brücke*, Innsbruck, 1929, p. 122). The *Pfaffenspiegel* uses one of the panegyric types of First Mass sermons to give its readers a laugh at popish pretensions: it was delivered by the parish priest Anton Häring in 1868, at the parish church of Elbersberg. "With the power of absolution, Jesus has given the priest a power which is fearful to hell itself, which even Lucifer cannot resist. It is a power which reaches even unto the measureless stretches of eternity, where every other earthly power finds its limit and dies. It is a power, I tell you, capable of smashing chains forged from all eternity, forged by the commission of the most grievous sins. Yea, in very truth, the power to forgive sins makes the priest a second God, for in the nature of things, God alone can forgive sins. And yet that is not the highest pinnacle of priestly power. His authority reaches even higher. For he can make God Himself serve him. How is this? When the priest strides to the altar to offer up the Mass, then at the same moment, Jesus Christ, who sits at the right hand of the Father, arises from His throne to be ready for the signal of his priest on earth . . .

"Therefore, all nobility and royalty of this world disappear before the power of the priest; all saints and angels together step back from him; yea, even the Mother of God, who once said her '*fiat mihi*' and cannot repeat it, at least not every day and in a '*Hoc est enim* . . .' which makes the Son of Man present . . ."

Exception can be taken to some of the expressions used in this sermon, but what the priest *wanted* to say then in Elbersberg is true and, we hope, better expressed in untold other First Mass sermons. The ultimate source of these superlatives is the monograph of St. John Chrysostom in which he justifies his fleeing the priesthood by telling of its dignity.

But these sermons are only expressions of that feeling of joy that surrounds the newly ordained priest and the Christian people on the day of his First Mass. Weeks of purest priestly joy follow it. He waits for his first apostolate with longing. Perhaps there is even a bit of trepidation in the back of his mind, wondering whether he will hit it off well or not. Both are understandable, but both show how many human elements are involved. There are stations in every diocese'that are eagerly desired, and others that are feared. In this twilight of fear and longing, both as yet unreal and inexperienced, anxiety regarding possible dissension makes itself felt. But the young priest is looking for it so far in the wrong direction.

With a start, he awakes a few weeks later from the heaven of his First Mass in a little room in a country rectory.

Maybe even earlier than that! There is a psychological law which says that no exalted state of soul can last for long; and a second, that it can easily change into its opposite at the very moment when it is at its height. This can be a state of weariness or even of oppression. Hours of convincing certainty can dissolve into times when all the doubts come back as strong as ever. That this up and down is one of the ordinary phases of man's existence, even on that level of rational assurances on which we exist, is brought out convincingly in Peter Wust's book *Ungewissheit und Wagnis* (Graz, 1946). Four hundred years ago St. Teresa enunciated this law for Christian existence in her *Seelenburg*: she tells us that it applies even in the loftiest heights of mystical companionship with God.

Therefore, no one, not even the young priest, should be frightened at the ups and downs of this life, at the trough of disenchantment which may follow upon the crest of mystic exaltation. The pastors who receive new priests into the Lord's vineyard should pay especial attention to this. The disenchantment must come. We are responsible to God for everything over and above what we contribute to it.

At any rate, priestly life is no eternal First Mass. The triumphal arches are cleared away and the festive decorations of the altar are packed up. The First Mass panegyric suddenly seems unreal, even untrue. The myrtle of the First Mass crown begins to wither, and its green becomes more and more gray. It is the gray of the priest's everyday life.

This everyday life must be mastered by the love of the young priest. He will still be praying his daily "I will go unto the Altar of God, to God who giveth joy to my youth" when his hair is snow-white. The altar of God and God Himself must be what preserve in him the devotion of his First Mass for his whole lifetime. It need not be true what someone—I've forgotten quite who—either said or wrote: "Most priests have only one high point in their lives: their First Mass." That need not be true. The First Mass, with its festivities and power, need not be the high point, but the starting point of his priesthood, and the preservation of the grandeur of that priesthood is his everyday life.

That grandeur may be preserved, even if life brings on cruel disenchantment. Life is no joke. Moods cannot prevail in it: in no life, and, above all, not in a priest's life! It shows what is real in a man if he can unhesitatingly turn away from the feast and look the difficulties and dangers of this life in the eye. It shouldn't follow so closely as it did in that terrible chapter of Joseph Bernhart's novel, *Der Kaplan* (pp. 167 ff.), where, during the festivities of a First Mass, a degraded priest who had long been in prison for a moral crime returns home to the same village, where, years ago, he had celebrated his First Mass.

The holocaust of a life, which makes the First Mass so grand and moving in the eyes of the people, is not the sacrifice of a festal hour of joy. A holocaust is the sacrifice of a whole life. In the fulfillment of that and in that alone, without the festive congregation or panegyric, and even in the

grayest days of his humdrum life, a priest's life is still one
long First Mass celebration. That is surely the idea behind
the verse by the priest-poet Ernst Thrasolt which is often
read to candidates for the priesthood (*Witterungen der
Seele,* 1911, p. 60):

> A life you want, that like a weight
> Of woeful curse your soul depresses?
> Then be a priest—and be but half a priest.
> But if you want your fill of joys,
> A friend in God, who loves you solely,
> Then be a priest—and be one wholly!

> *Willst du ein Leben, das schwer wie ein Alp*
> *Auf Dir liegt und wie ein Fluch,—*
> *Werde ein Priester und werde es halb.*
> *Willst Du Freude übergenug*
> *Und die Seele voll Frieden und Gottesglanz—*
> *Werde ein Priester und werde es ganz.*

While I was working on this book, I had occasion to give
an extension course to some two hundred priests during
Easter Week of 1951. I stayed at the Linz Seminary, living
in the room of one of the students. I was told that his was a
delayed vocation, and that after he had worked as a farm-
hand, he started his secondary education only at the age of
twenty. There hung on his bedstead, written out in an artistic hand, the following lines. It is an old prayer for new
priests:

THE PRIEST

MUST BE, OH, SO GREAT, YET HARD TO SEE, NOBLER
OF MIND THAN A KINGLY BAND, SIMPLE AND PLAIN
AS A FARMER'S HAND, A HERO WHO KNOWS NOT
DISASTER, ✠ BUT BOWS TO GOD AS HIS MASTER ✠
A SOURCE OF THE LIFE THAT IS GRACE ✠ WHO

FROM SINS HAS AVERTED HIS FACE ✠ A SLAVE
OF THE FEARFUL AND WEAK ✠ UNWILLING HIGH
FAVORS TO SEEK ✠ RECEIVING FROM GOD ALL HIS
LORE ✠ A LEADER IN SPIRITÜAL WAR ✠ A BEGGAR
WHOSE HANDS STILL BESEECH ✠ YET ANOINTED,
GLAD TIDINGS TO TEACH ✠ A GOD WHEN THE BAT-
TLE SMOKES THICKEN ✠ A MOTHER WHOSE POOR
CHILDREN SICKEN ✠ A SAGE IN VIEW ✠ A CHILD
IN TRUST ✠ WHOSE AIMS ARE HIGH ✠ WHOSE
FRIENDS ARE DUST ✠ A SON OF JOY ✠ WHO LIVES
WITH PAIN ✠ WHOSE THOUGHTS ARE TRUE ✠
WHOSE SPEECH IS PLAIN ✠ A FRIEND OF PEACE ✠
THE SLUGGARD'S FOE ✠ WHO STANDS ALONE ✠
WOULD I WERE SO!

PRAY FOR ME ✠

2. THE FIRST YEARS AS A PRIEST

There sits the priest a few weeks after the triumphant days
of his First Mass, in that little room in a country parish.
There are still a few embers of the glow that was these past
few weeks, for he is still giving the children of the parish
his first blessing. Then suddenly he's just another one of
the curates, one of many, and since he is the youngest, he's
the least of all. He is on the bottom rung of the "hierarchy,"
so to speak. But it would be more fitting to speak of his
rank as part of the deaconry.

He is certainly not depressed. Nor is he particularly
worried about his first appearance in the school or on the
pulpit. He is stirred with joy: he has reached his goal and
is allowed to work in the vineyard of God. The love of the

ewly ordained priest is a fire within him. He is full of
ious, semi-pious, inexperienced, and unrefined zeal.

My first station was Kirchberg am Wechsel, and I went
here for the first time on September 4, 1915. It was a
aturday. My pastor asked: "You'll want to start preach-
ng tomorrow, won't you?" Did I want to! I was already
repared. It was the fifteenth Sunday after Pentecost, and
he Gospel told of the widow of Naim and her dead son
Luke 7: 1-16). I gave it to them straight from the shoulder:
he weeping mother as Mother Church, the dead son a sym-
ol of the sinner over whom Mother Church weeps. Sin
s death, eternal death. Is there no salvation? Christ and
Ie alone can say to a Christian who has lost his salvation
hrough sin: "Young man, I say to thee, arise! Today we're
ttending a funeral. Are we among the living or are we on
he bier? If we are, do we want to cause Mother Church
urther tears? Shall Christ pass us by and allow us to be
arried to the grave without His 'Arise'?"

I was uncommonly pleased with my sermon. And the
empter whispered in my ear (and the devil is always quot-
ng Scripture, even as he did in Mt. 4): "The people will
e whispering or thinking to themselves what it says in the
ast verse of today's Gospel (Luke 7: 17): 'A great Prophet
as risen amongst us and God has visited His people . . .
And this report concerning him went forth throughout the
vhole of Judea and all the country roundabout.'"

Ecce Homo! But it is not at all the One who was covered
vith blood under His fool's cloak, whom Pilate had shown
o the people.

In the meantime, I felt pretty good: my pastor, who was
istening behind the pulpit to hear what his new helper was
vorth, said dryly as I came back to the sacristy: *"Prima
ectio brevis!* (The first lesson is always short.) Next time
ou'll have to speak longer." That was all.

The Importance of the First Pastor

The kind of pastor the newly ordained priest gets is of the utmost moment to him. Experience shows that neither the seminary nor his theological training is as important for him as the priest who introduces him to his apostolic life—or who doesn't introduce him to it. "We call to the attention of all priests that the future success of young priests lies to a great extent in their hands" (Pius XII, *Menti Nostrae* 100). The pastors to whom the newly ordained are entrusted should be the best in the diocese, both as men and as priests. Any measures taken against those who fail in this delicate task are perfectly justified, considering the importance of their duties. Anyone who searches to find out why a priest has turned out the way he is, will find, practically without exception, that it all began in his first assignment as a curate. These pastors must be truly priestly and understanding men of experience, kindly yet firm. They don't have to be models in every respect. Who is, anyway? But they must have so much brotherly love that it nurtures the young priesthood of their charges and helps them to grow in it. They are helping to lay the foundations of the entire later apostolate of the young priest. They must have a deep knowledge of human nature, and be attentive to their role in laying these foundations; they must be able to judge how deep and well-grounded these foundations are. They must be selfless, without envy. Joseph Bernhart tells of a pastor who would not allow his curate to do anything for fear he would excel him in it.

Even the reception of the new curate has a decisive influence. The "new curate," in the book of the same name by Canon Sheehan, is received by his pastor with great dis-

ust. But why? The pastor had said, rather rashly, "What
an a bishop do to a pastor?" "Good friends" reported these
words, spoken in anger, to the bishop. His answer was:
What can I *do*? I can send him a curate who will break
is heart in six weeks." There are some like that, and after
ll, the bishop does have one over a barrel. But he didn't
o through with his threat. The good-natured old curate was
alled away, and on the very night of his departure, the
new curate" was knocking on the door. "A real gentleman," the cook announces. Father Dan greeted his new
cooperator heartily, "as much as he could, under the circum-
tances," but soon learned that he had an ideal type of
young priest before him. "Then my heart rose up to this
right, cheery, handsome fellow, who had no more pride in
him than a barelegged gossoon; and who was prepared to
nd his pleasure amongst such untoward circumstances. But
didn't like to let myself out as yet. I had to keep up some
how of dignity" (p. 8). He had little need for his authority;
he had a good priestly heart and Father Letheby yielded
more to that than to his pretended dignity.

Peter Schwabentan is met at the station by his "boss,"
ity pastor Scharf, and in no time is up to his neck in work.
One can hardly expect a pastor, who gets a new curate every
two or three years, to be choked with emotion each time
a new one comes into the rectory. (Hermann Herz, *Peter
Schwabentans Schaffen und Träumen*, Regensburg, pp. 19
f). But that can happen, too. Joseph Bernhart (*Der Kaplan*,
Munich, 1924) tells of meeting his first pastor: "How kindly
he received me! just like a favorite guest; how he treated
me at table and each time we met, almost to my embarrassment, as his younger friend and companion. And how en-
couragingly he showed me what I had to do! It lit up the
start of my path like the sun of a noble manliness" (p. 10).
His second "boss" received him gruffly, but this was only

to test his new arrival's humility and self-possession, to "take the starch out of him" right in the beginning. He was really a good-hearted man. Later he was sent to a pastor who dealt with his curates officiously and only in writing. He kept his distance, passing out the "job" in sullen silence (pp. 183 ff).

When Father Francis Chisholm arrived at the station of his first assignment, late at night, in the coal mining town of Shalesly, it was raining and there was no one to meet him. Father Kezer and he met at supper. His first words were: "Sit down and stop looking like the lost chord. I hope you play cribbage. I like a game of an evening" (A.J. Cronin, *The Keys of the Kingdom*, p. 100). How international—I almost wrote how universally "catholic" these virtues and failings are! It was just like the first question that Ignatius Seipel's pastor in Staatz asked of him: "I hope you play Taroc—or do you?"

Father Kezer passed Francis a bowl of kippers and poached eggs. "He himself ate rapidly, his strong crunching jaws and capable hands, felted with black hairs, never at rest. He was burly, with a round cropped head, and a tight mouth. His nose was flat, with wide nostrils out of which sprouted two dark snuff-stained tufts. He conveyed the impression of strength, of authority. Every movement was a masterpiece of unconscious self-assertion. As he cut an egg in two and slipped one half into his mouth his little eyes watched, formed an opinion of Francis, as a butcher might weigh the merits of a steer.

"You don't look too hardy. Under eleven stone, eh? I don't know what you curates are coming to. My last was a weak-kneed effort! Should have called himself flea—not Lee—he hadn't the guts of one. It's this Continental la-de-da that ruins you. In my time—well, the fellows who came out of Maynooth with me were men" (101).

Father Kezer was a grim preacher. His natural ire was a poor substitute for tact. Planted solidly on his feet, head thrust aggressively forward, he lashed in his sermons the sparse congregation for its neglect. "How do you expect me to pay the rent, and the taxes, and the insurance? And keep the church roof over your heads . . . ?" (102). These repeated complaints won him the enmity of his parishioners. They were poor miners and felt that he demanded too much of them. They listened to him in stony silence, or just didn't come to him any more. Father Chisholm wanted to win back their confidence, but Father Kezer, "astute and watchful, seemed to sense, with a kind of grim humour, the difficulties his curate was experiencing and to anticipate slyly a readjustment of the other's idealism to his own common sense" (104). Chisholm learned only at the end of the first month that Lee had gone off with a nervous breakdown. The pastor forbade his prayers at night: "I won't have it. I never heard such nonsense in my life. I'm running a parish, not a religious order" (105). Kezer is suspicious of his curate's attempt to win people over, even though the first step was only a club. Chisholm had to keep his superior's good qualities in mind all the time, so as not to lose courage. And when he finally meets with great success, and the employer of the men of the parish speaks about it, contrary to Chisholm's will, the people applaud him thunderously. Kezer wants to see no more: "In the last ten years he had knocked out more curates than Henry VIII had wives. And now a curate had knocked him out" (116). He asks the bishop to change his curate. Things like that have happened often enough, and not only in Scotland.

The Code of Canon Law lists the duties of the pastor: "*qui eum paterne instruat ac dirigat in cura animarum, ei invigilat*" (Can. 476, 7). He is supposed to give his curate fatherly instruction, introduce him to his spiritual labors, and keep watch over him. He should not rob the young idealist of any of his fire, but protect him by relentlessly showing him what the realities involved are, so that his ideals will become more manly and mature. He should not expose him to danger. Heinrich Federer describes in his book *Miss Therese* how a young priest is left to himself, as happens in the country. He gives up his fantastic plans for the apostolate one after another merely because of the silent criticism of his portly housekeeper. He had to learn everything by his own experience. "Therefore you must be sure," says Pius XII, "that the good hopes one has for newly ordained priests can be disappointed if they are not introduced to their labors gradually, or if no one watches over their work with wisdom and fatherly care" (*Menti Nostrae*, 97).

Youth sees things in contradictions. It is either black or white: theirs is an attitude of either-or. The young priest must learn that between the last and final "either-or" of the Last Day and the "either . . ." of his world and the " . . . or" of this world, there is quite a lot of room, and that is his true field of labor. That is where the real problems of the priest are waiting, and they are much more complex than his gruff "either-or" suspects. Still less should the dynamic "either-or" of his youth transform him into unalterable rigidity and resignation. "My dear sir," said Father Johannes to the young curate, with resignation, "always remember this: people are as good and as bad as you can possibly imagine. So the best thing that you can do is to get the strength from the one to help you put up with the other. You can't hope for more than that" (Joseph Bernhart, *Der Kaplan*, p. 99). There is a great deal of experience behind that. But it is still bad advice. The young priest cannot begin by being resigned. He must live through the give and take himself and grow in it.

Yet, he has to lead an economic existence in this world

and still remain a priest. That doesn't hurt. It was only when he heard about things of such a nature that the young pastor of Ambricourt, attending the pastoral conference, came awake: "During the discussion of the economic reports I felt like a child that had stumbled upon a conversation of its elders . . . I was amazed to see how easily my companions plunged into such discussions, though they are nearly all poor and resigned to it" (Georges Bernanos, *The Diary of a Country Priest*). It is often amazing how easily curates pile up debts. "That is because we become accustomed right from the seminary on, to receiving our daily bread and plate of beans from the hands of Superiors; we remain pupils and children right to the hour of our death." (*Ibid.*) There is a light side to it, but there are also shadows.

The young priest should not be deprived of his zeal, but the pastor must be even more careful that he is not confused and disillusioned, that he does not lose hope or even give up entirely. Father Dan (the pastor) is reading to his young helper from the letter of Saint Francis de Sales to the Abbess of Port Royal; consequently, it is not exactly the situation of the young curate. But the analogy is plain: "Accustom yourself to speak softly and slowly, and to go—I mean walk —quite composedly; to do all that you do gently and quietly and you will see that in three or four years you will have quite regulated this hasty impetuosity. But carefully remember to act thus gently and speak softly on occasions when the impetuosity is not urging you . . ." This calmness is still missing in his new curate, all right. He is hasty, impatient; he judges too quickly; he thinks that he can do everything at once and that he must do so. He's troubled when he can't remake the entire parish of Kilronan into one of saints. He is an anachronism, a being set down from another world in sleepy Kilronan. For the first few weeks, the dogs used to bark as he hurried along the streets, and all the neighbors asked wildly: "Who's dead? what happened? where's the fire?" And then there was universal wrath when it became known that it was Father Letheby who had frightened them all out of their peace without a reason in the world. "Why the mischief doesn't he go aisy? Sure, you'd think he was walking for a wager" (Sheehan, *My New Curate*, p. III).

It is the task of the pastor to see all this, to rejoice over the zeal displayed, but to try to bring his curate into some more sensible and considered form of consistency in his care of souls. It is not an easy job at all. And it would be wrong to say that it is the pastor's fault whenever there is a conflict. But it would be a way of constantly renewing and guaranteeing real service to the faithful if both pastor and curate would learn from one another. For even as in the rest of life, it is the function of youth to see to it that life doesn't grow old and stagnant. The eagerness to try to do everything should be regarded in this light, and not as a case of personal presumption.

The term cooperator (συνεργός) is Biblical and in this sense it was first used of Epaphroditus by Saint Paul, for he was the Apostle's first fellow-worker. What he has to say of him would be the ideal description of the relationship between pastor and curate: He should be a "brother," a "fellow-worker," a "fellow-soldier," and a "minister to the need" of his pastor; for the pastor does need him, if only for the physical labor of the parish.

Tensions between Pastor and Curate

Tensions between pastor and curate are necessary, unavoidable, and completely understandable. So there's no reason to get excited about them, but there is reason for trying to control them. The reasons for them are:

a. In the light of psychological development, they are opposites in many ways: youth–age; start–decline; inexperience–insight; developing–developed; audacity–resignation; idealism–realism (and often optimism–pessimism); the will to do something–the need for rest; *"ecce nova facio omnia"*– *"quieta non movere!"*

We do not only need to find a way of smoothing over the tacit and frequently vocal reproach that arises out of these tensions. Youth and age both have their duties to each other, and both can be enriched because of them.

b. Then there are often instances of character conflict. Two opposed temperaments have a connatural antipathy to one another. On the other hand, if both are of a choleric temperament, they split more easily over divergencies of opinion. Everyone can see that those curates who complained most about overbearing pastors later make the most unbearable superiors themselves. That gives one food for thought.

c. Another cause can be differing intellectual backgrounds. The tempo of development in a mechanized age is faster even in the Church of God, which is oriented toward eternity. One generation already looks upon the other as a stranger. But these tensions existed as such a long time ago. The "reform priests" of the sixteenth century approached their elders with suggestions about more frequent Communion, with demands for a more solemn Divine Service, with remarks about the necessity of more work among the young; the older priests immediately called it—the method is always the same!—a "revolution in the apostolate" (Alois Schrott, *Seelsorge im Wandel der Zeiten,* Graz, 1949, pp. 60 ff.). Look how difficult it was for the Catholic Cooperative Movements to take hold in the second half of the nineteenth century. Consider the resistance that is met with today when attempts are made to break them up, and substitute the "principle of the parish" as the only one that is valid! Look at the resistance the Liturgical Movement met with when it started fifty years ago. The opposition amounted to persecution, and today—its results are the Church's official program. We young curates of thirty years ago had to go through a great deal with many pastors to put into effect the decree of Pius X regarding more frequent Communion! My old pastor, Joseph Wüsinger, an irreproachable priest and apostle, an ecclesiastic through and through, a dean and honorary canon, was an opponent of daily Communion, and we had to tear permission from him for each new daily communicant.

d. Besides these, there are differences in method. Differences between men can easily become contradictions and opposites. One is more disposed to fight; the other, to win over. The one relies almost exclusively on one class in a parish which is composed of many different groups. For example, one relies on the farmers, while the other sees in this a danger to the whole congregation. One is a pastor of the old politician type (Hermann Herz, in the novel *Peter Schwabentan*, pp. 24 ff., paints a portrait of the clerical politician at the height of his powers), while another sees that the salvation of the priest lies in a religious freedom from the politics of the day. The "Lord" pastor and dean of "St. Jakob" in East Tirol is not supported in his campaign for the Legislature by some of his parishioners, and therefore has a falling-out with them. His curate Father Harteck wants to associate with all of the parishioners in spite of this enmity, and therefore has a tiff with his superior (Emile Marriot, *Der geistliche Tod*, Berlin, 1924, pp. 17, 35). One man is a liturgical "innovator," while another can see only a cause of confusion among the faithful if they are required to participate in the liturgy. One wants to incorporate the laymen into the parish work in the sense of Catholic Action, while another sees the layman only as an object of the apostolate.

e. Then there are human weaknesses and differences, none of which are worth talking about, since people put up with them everywhere men live together because they have to. But some of them can make common life miserable, because the atmosphere is already charged. The young unpolished idealist comes and meets a pastor who does not suit his taste. The pastor, on the other hand, loves a comfortable home; he's a business man and has his bowling club. He spends less time with the Book of Kings than he does with his bookmaker. The curate finds a kind of priest who has developed over decades and through difficult experiences, who represents a type we will study and come to know better later on—but the newly arrived priest doesn't understand that. Or he finds that it isn't the pastor who gives orders in the rectory, but the housekeeper.

f. Of all the things that make for tension, the one that is most provoking for the curate is his canonical insecurity as opposed to the security of the pastor. The curate can be replaced at any moment; the pastor is immovable or quasi-immovable. There is no *a pari* relationship between them. In real chivalry, the pastor should see to it that his curate is not conscious of this fact when there is a difference of opinion between them.

Idealism in Danger and Distress

All of these elements play a part in the formation of the maturing priest, especially in the first few years. They have less and less influence as the years go on, as long as the bright flame of his love of God and souls is not extinguished. When the fire flickers so low that he can no longer see his way, that can happen early in some cases. But all of them will be considerably disenchanted by the first five years. In some cases it happens too quickly. A year after his First Mass, Dick Ouwendijk visits his brother Auke in his parish: "What a difference between the humble figure of the new priest in his white alb and the bowed figure of this priest with his head held despairingly in his hands" (Dick Ouwendijk, *Das geschändete Antlitz*, Warendorf, Westfalen, 1950, p. 26). And Auke confesses: "If you only knew what was left of my ideals . . . naturally after a while you learn to put up with the fact that your ideals have paled and gone up in smoke . . . but to think that even our priesthood, dear God, one's own consecration, vocation, all the duties for which one thought he could shed his blood—for all that to go the way of every ideal—to disappear, go up in smoke!" (*Ibid.* pp. 38 ff.)

And what is the reason? We are taking examples from novelists, sober Catholics who apparently write what they have seen happen in life. Almost always it starts with a different approach to the apostolate; a split between a pastor who is canonically blameless, but too accustomed to comfortable living, and the young curate who is full of plans that the older man finds quixotic and inexperienced. Auke's brooding frightens the pastor. He resents the fact that the curate missed a meeting of the farmers' union. It is a harmless thing, childish, even, but that is how it starts. The director takes his complaints to the pastor and remarks that the curate always takes up for the "common people." They call him a socialistic priest who is stirring up the poor. What were the facts? During one of the meetings he had gone to assist at the death of a poor basket weaver. The dying man's

terror disturbs him greatly. The pastor thinks that the basket weaver had been well taken care of: does Auke have no
confidence in the power of grace? "It is hard to answer that,
and you always come back to the same thing: Do you doubt
that grace can do this or do that? I have never doubted
the power of grace and God grant that I never will: but you
act as though grace were like a pocket full of pennies! . . ."
(p. 138) The pastor then labels Auke's ideas "poetic" and
advises him to become a normal man (p. 139).

The young pastor of Ambricourt is not a curate, of course,
and it seems as though he never was one. His practical
neighbors take him to task, especially one splendid Fleming,
the pastor of Torcy, as well as his dean, the pastor of Blangermont. He, too, finds that his younger colleague is a
"poet": "Get this into your head, dear boy . . . at your age
these outbursts are not allowed. In a small community like
ours there is no harm at all in such mutual criticism, and
it would be most unsporting not to accept it with good will."
(Georges Bernanos, *The Diary of a Country Priest*).
"My boy," says the dean in answer to the objection that
hearing the confessions of the rich is of little use, "I'm
afraid that the academic successes of your boyhood might
perhaps have distorted your judgment. The seminary is not
the world, you know—real life is not like that. I don't think
it would take much to turn you into an intellectual, that is
to say, a rebel, systematically in revolt against every form
of social superiority except those derived from the intellect.
The Lord preserve us from innovators!" And when the
young pastor objects: "That's what many of the Saints
were!" the dean says, "The Lord deliver us from saints, too!
Please, don't interrupt me, it was just an idea. Listen to me
first . . ." And he goes on to compare the saints who, while
they were blooming and ripening on the vine, "cost the
vintner no end of trouble, so that they could finally wind

up tickling the palate of his grandchildren." "Isn't the weight of those who have been called saints counterbalanced to some degree by the admirable number of good, zealous priests who devote themselves to the depressing tasks of the ministry?" (*Ibid.*) And the dean who takes Auke to task for having missed the farmers' meeting calls him a rebel, because he thought it more important to assist the dying than to attend a meeting. He advises him to follow the "golden mean" (Dick Ouwendijk, *Das geschändete Antlitz,* p. 142).

It should not be supposed that we use these citations to suggest that it is always tension between Christian mediocrity and the pursuit of sanctity that causes the coolness arising between pastor and curate. The roles can be reversed, and often are. Usually it is a question of the drive to accomplish what has never been done before, and contentment with what has proved to be solid. The young feel that what hasn't been done is something that is essential and, therefore, something that can be done. Or it concerns a mean between ideals ("fancies") and stubborn resistance on the part of the people. This method of compromise is proposed as the right way to do things.

Humanly speaking, nothing is easier than to go along with this offer—even for a young priest, but especially for one who is tired of fighting and worn down with fatigue. The best of them resist the temptation, and the weak among them become confused or unsure of themselves. Or it can be that one allows himself to give in and accepts more than the compromise intended. No one renounces his youth with impunity as long as it is in its day.

3. DEVELOPMENT OF THE ULTIMATE CHARACTER TYPE

The problems which bring about a lack of harmony, however, can lie tremendously deeper. Perhaps it is a case of dissatisfaction with oneself, a dissatisfaction which comes over one who is just about to abandon the gleaming ideal of his youth because of his own weakness. We will have to discuss that presently. But it all amounts to the same thing: the faith that moves mountains is drying up and so is the energy the young priest had when he sprang from his training into the arena of life. That is how it is with not a few. Almost all of them experience some disenchantment. For some it is a painful experience; for others, a process of liberation; still others experience it as the concrete starting point of how they will really have to live. A number of young priests see even in the greatest disillusionment the very fulfillment of their high ideal. The path to this sobering moment is longer for some than others. Or should we say—shorter for some?

Differentiation Sets In

One thing that reflects this development is the yearly reunion. It is a wonderful custom that the priests of each ordination class should have a friendly meeting at least once a year. Many hold these reunions even up to their golden jubilee—until, at the last meeting, the last one takes leave of the next until they see each other again in another world.

The first reunion is usually held about six months after the first assignment. What a happy meeting that is! The friendships that have grown over the years are still strong. Indeed, they are felt more deeply because they were missed through these months. Everyone wants to tell what has happened, and everyone is eager to hear how the other is getting along. They can exchange their first green experiences with each other. They make plans for cooperating with one another and keeping in touch. They think that they still have time for it.

A year later: there's the same old joy at seeing one another again, but it is a little more restrained. Some are already abashed because they aren't doing well; they seem unable to fit in. They are faced with problems they never heard of in the seminary. On the other hand, they have yet to meet a semi-Arian or a Monophysite as far as they can make out. And anyway, what good would the label do them? Their plans were not designed for the circumstances in which they find themselves. Their circumstances seem to conform even less to their plans. The pastor had his qualms. The pious are surprised—yes, even these. This or that one is already "disillusioned." Another is getting along with his "boss" famously. Over there, someone is complaining about the "dragoness" (a play on words for "deaconess," referring here to the rectory cook). Most of them praise their own cooks; they are like good mothers, only a little too overbearing, perhaps. And some of them don't stop at the kitchen door. It will be rare that anyone will complain as Baron Ketteler did as a curate, that the cooking was too good for him. He wanted something simpler. (Franz Herwig, *Der grosse Bischof*, p. 190).

Five years later: the class is no longer of one mind. They still share the same number of years since ordination and they are still very glad to see one another, but it is easy to sense remarkable differences among them. They are changing. They note sadly that they are growing apart from one another. Peculiarities that were fondly regarded in the seminary really mark this one and that one now. One tries one of the old friendly jokes, but meets with a cold rebuff. A process of individuation and isolation has set in that will increase as they get older, although they don't suspect it yet. There is nothing frightening about it. Everyone outgrows the gang life of childhood, and the friendships of youth dwindle to a manly friendship with a few; then these, too, go their way, until there is frankness and freedom with everybody—or total isolation. Then come those years when friends and acquaintances die right and left. This goes on, and the world is filled with strange faces, until each man, as each man must, goes alone for the last roll-call. My first pastor, who was already a priest for forty years when I came to him, had spent most of his life in the same parish. I was touched with a singular sorrow which I was as yet wholly unable to appreciate, and therefore it was almost with fear that I heard him say, while walking between the graves of the cemetery: "I have more friends here than there are outside these walls."

A Preliminary Typology

If you wanted to list the early differences that regularly occur at this time of life and condense them into types, they would go something like this:

a. The old idealist, at first quite vocal, then more retiring, more knowing, wiser. He has preserved the glow of youth.

b. The realists, who know the limits that reality imposes on them as priests and men in their work. They take these limits into cool consideration and have lost the desire of beating their heads against them. They have already reached the point, as they say, of building up their priesthood "as life requires" and reality permits; but within the field that they themselves have determined, they'll do their part. One can rely on that.

c. Those who are resigned or frustrated: "Of course, we do what we can" or "You can't do much." One even says, "You can't do a thing." But he will do his duty.

d. Those who are bitter and misunderstood. Former idealists, they weren't strong, nor hard, nor devout enough to stand up to ridicule or opposition. Their spirits have been broken by years of silent friction with the "boss." Their plans never got beyond the stage of ideas. This fellow had to defend himself against informers. Now all he wants is to be let alone, for the time being, anyway.

e. There are a few who have already figured out how to live as a pastor or curate or lecturer without friction and disagreements.

f. Some no longer attend. There are different reasons. At any rate, their habits of solitude or their individuality is stronger than the spirit of companionship. And even this has almost completely disappeared.

Ten or fifteen years later: the reunion is a wonderful opportunity to renew old friendships. Many find it a waste of time and stay away, or else they haven't the time. The conversation no longer deals with the ministry, and even less with questions of priestly existence. The old idealists still get off their platitudes now and then. But even they quiet down after a while. They don't want to bother anyone. The "Little Church History" of news about this or that one is what they talk about. Priests who have been sent somewhere or other into the country are glad to hear about their friends at these meetings. In the meantime, some of them have already been made pastors themselves and one of them is a lecturer in the city. And they tell about their experiences, and everyone shares them. Their conversation is filled with anecdotes.

Twenty years later: you have no idea what a difference the last five years have made! Personality differences have become more marked. Each one has his own distinct profile. Old friends hardly recognize one another. The first gray hairs start to show. One of them has become a success. Another has been made a monsignor; and if he's childish enough, he wears his red rabat to the reunion. It is rare that his friends congratulate him. "When the man of the world thinks things over, he figures on his chances of success. All right! But what meaning do our chances of success have, what can they mean to us, who have assumed, once and for all, the awe-inspiring presence of God for every moment of our poor lives? . . . figure on our chances of success? What for? You don't gamble against God" (Georges Bernanos, *The Diary of a Country Priest*).

There always were and still are "tendencies" among the clergy. Most of the time these revolved about different ideas concerning methods in the ministry. Even in the same class these are now becoming evident, more so than their old friendships. Anyone who stands up for one side has the others against him. And right in the midst of the joy of getting together again there can be an argument. They are often bitter because this is just the opportunity they have been waiting for. New connections made outside of the class show that they are stronger than old friendships.

After twenty-five years there is a meeting for the celebration of the silver jubilee. A beautiful old custom! The forms have been long ago prescribed, and that's good. This celebration is held even by classes that never met during the other years. The individuality of the different members is now established. Almost all of them have their crises behind them and have found themselves. The chief topic of conversation now—it's the past. They conjure up their seminary and student days. Professors dead for years are imitated and lauded and ridiculed. Yes, in this atmosphere, they all become young again for an hour or two. Then one is chided as in the good old days. Today he doesn't even mind it at all. Or he just doesn't pay attention—not apparently, at least. Who would want to show a sour face to a "comrade of our youth" today? Then some—there are some old gleeclubbers there—have struck up a song, but it sounds oldish and sad. They are all companionably settled and pleasant: one more jolly, another more melancholy. Each one's own celebration is being prepared, in his own parish, by the congregation or the group with which he is working. Or it will be a sad repetition of his First Mass at home. It is rare that anyone is spiritually renewed by this celebration, even when there is a day of recollection added. Or is he? No one forswears his youth and its beauty with impunity.

The Meaning of the First Years as a Priest

There is an external course of priestly development. But behind it there stands the lonely struggle of the individual, the daily, the year-long, the nightly struggle to attain priestly stature. His existence is nailed out upon the cross: its one mighty timber, rammed into the earth, points from earth to heaven; its one horizontal crossbeam seems to want to ignore and cancel the first. That is the line taken by this level world.

The thing that has been essentially produced and decided

in these years is the priestly existence that is ever his own, singularly and personally his own. The usual issues between pastor and curate, between the old and young priest are only the externals of an inner process. The young priest comes from theology courses and his ordination strongly convinced that the world is sighing for salvation, and completely confident of the power of his consecration and his words. It moves and exalts him that God has selected him to bring grace and truth to lost humanity. He accepted this vocation, perhaps after resisting it for a long time. Now he enters the little world of his first assignment with determination and learns of real life as it meets him in that place. He doesn't think that the parish to which the bishop has sent him is a matter of chance; he thrills with a purpose determined from all eternity. Here, within this parish, is the place of grace and of judgment. And it is the grace and judgment which will determine eternity for the people of this parish.

This attitude of the newly ordained priest is justified. It is the only possible attitude he can have. But it is all too vague. Yet against the background of his training, it is the only one possible.

Now everything depends on a number of factors: will his holy faith weary when he meets with the concrete world, its grief and what he takes to be its ordinariness, its anxieties and hopes? And if it does weary, will he refresh it? That depends on the other priests who will enter his life and therefore determine his existence. Will his priesthood, received with such faith from the imposition of the bishop's hands, grow and mature through the work he does in the world, and not be broken by it? For the ideal with which the newly ordained priest enters upon life is not a treasure which can be wasted; this ideal is a design that develops with continued self-understanding and mastery of his duties and only in this way can it be realized. It must pass from the ideas of youth to ever clearer designs until it becomes the full, holy design of the priesthood in reality.

That is what is at stake in these years, nothing less. And there can be no higher stakes. Herein lies the seriousness of these years and their responsibility before the Eternal High Priest.

It would be wrong and therefore unjust to put the whole burden of blame or credit for the young priest's development upon the shoulders of the pastor. The components of priestly existence, as we shall see presently, are so numerous and objectively determined that his life with the pastor is more a test and an occasion than a cause of the individual's developing priestly existence. But what has already been said about the pastor's responsibility for the development of the young priest is not retracted because of that.

The priestly character portrayed by the American Henry Morton Robinson, in his book, *The Cardinal* (New York, 1950) is one of the most splendid in recent literature. This Stephen Fermoyle could teach many a curate how to overcome unjust treatment, and how a young priest can work with two pastors who are so completely different as the brutally-pious and capable William Monaghan, whose nickname was "Dollar Bill," and the saintly Ned Halley, who lives with God in such forgetfulness of the world that he almost forgets his parishioners as well.

There is a timeless freshness and wealth of learning in Canon Sheehan's *My New Curate* (1899). Every young priest ought to read this *Story from the life of an Irish Priest*. The first fifty pages of Carlo Coccioli's *Heaven and Earth* (London, 1953) show that the tensions between pastor and curate are the same in Italy as they are everywhere else. In 1951, there was published in New York the report of a certain "Father X" describing his first years in

St. Rose Parish under the capable and wise pastor Tim Malloy (*Everybody Calls Me Father*). "Father X" had good luck. The pastor greets him as a fatherly friend: "Father, there is nothing I admire more than a new priest. I am proud of you for giving your young life to the service of the great Master. Will you please give me your blessing?" And the newly ordained priest blesses the gray-haired old man, who kneels down in spite of his painful rheumatism. Then the curate asks for the pastor's blessing and that is how their work together started (p. 19). How quietly and paternally he helps the young priest to start his work in the ministry!

IV. THE TENSION OF PRIESTLY
EXISTENCE

The development leading to the individual's final stature as a priest has, as its only source, priestly existence. To describe this in general is to say that it is a "living-in-tension." We want to try to understand that in its plenitude in the following pages. We want to describe it, or at least give its outlines.

In doing so, we are not starting with an ideal that we have previously determined and then show it as it unfolds in its verifications. We are starting with the actuality itself, and that in all its ramifications. We have already spoken of the tension in priestly life, but it is only in the great design—which still remains only a design from the time of the acceptance of the vocation, through the preparation for ordination, ordination itself, and up until the First Mass—it is only in this great plan that this tension will become understandable and generally understood, or rather, sensed.

It is only in the every-day life of the priest that we experience it and suffer it. And at first, it is merely experienced as a fact. It influences the priest daily: he must face it every day without swerving, and make his decision in it. Then, from all of these decisions, as from so many single strokes, his final priestly stature is drawn.

1. SOURCES OF TENSION

Necessary Personal Tensions

There are personal tensions that necessarily accompany the hazard of this vocation.

a. First there is the lack of proportion between the great dignity of his state in life and the actual man who is the priest. This can never be resolved even by the most strenuous effort or by a life-long process of sanctification. It is the holiest priests who suffer most from the difference between the ideal and the reality. St. Alphonsus Ligouri, in one of his books entitles a chapter "On the Holiness Which a Priest Must Possess." Must? Yes, must! But it is a "must" that can never be fulfilled, even though it always remains a duty to try. But what is unreal can carry no obligation. The saintly Doctor of the Church cites witnesses from the whole history of the Church for this clear demand: "It is not through his dignity that the priest is saved, but by works that befit his dignity" (St. Jerome). "Because the priest is given more grace, his life must shine more brilliantly in virtue and holiness than that of laymen" (St. Ambrose). *"Sacerdos ad majorem tenetur perfectionem sanctitatis"* (Thomas à Kempis). And St. John Chrysostom: "For it is unto this that God has called us, that we be at the same time lights and teachers to others, and that we deal with people of earth as though we were angels." "Through major orders a man is raised to the highest estate, through which our Lord Himself is served in the sacrament of the altar; therefore, a more lofty inner sanctity is required for this than is required even for a religious" (Thomas Aquinas). If this was true of the priests of the Old Testament—"Be you Holy for I am Holy!" (Levit. 11: 44)—how much more is it true of the priest in the New Testament!

But St. Augustine looks beyond the command to its fulfillment: "Nothing is more consoling in this life and more precious to men than the office of the priest; but in the eyes of God, there is nothing more difficult and more dangerous" (Epist. 21, n. 1). The Saint knows that men can never measure up to it. Even in the eyes of the all-knowing God it appears to be difficult. That is the one consolation for the one who must endure that difficulty.

The vocation is holy. The man who is called isn't. Daily he hears the demand that he live according to his sacramental consecration and position. And every day he has to experience failure. Not great failure, but necessary failure. It is "only" the fact that he becomes immersed in everyday concerns. And these things cannot be his way of life. The priest is not in a position to bring his life, even if it be the holiest, into any proportion with the holiness of his vocation, yet every day he must try the impossible anew. "Each of us is a man with a body of soft clay, stretched over a glowing cross of iron" (Giovanni Papini, *The Letters of Pope Celestine VI to All Mankind*, New York, 1948).

Petrarch received minor orders to obtain a benefice. When he was asked why he refused the priesthood, he answered that he had enough trouble trying to save his own soul. The priest cannot even restrict himself to the business of self-sanctification. For even the sanctity which is demanded of the priest is inadequate to his state. It is also presupposed for the priest's work. This daily discord, unless it is borne in faith and humility, can wreck a life. Dick Ouwendijk tries to explain this to his brother Auke. He is trying to

attain that impossible equality with gigantic struggles. "It
is God's will," he says, weary unto death, "that we make a
funeral pyre within us, that it should be a wild, uncontrolled
flame that will destroy all the heaped-up selfishness, in-
ordinate passions, and meanness in us. That is the kingdom
of God, the kingdom of Christ. It burns us like the fires of
hell. For what better expression can there be of God's
omnipotence or rejection than fire? But hell sears us, while
this fire, which is the kingdom of God, gives us light and
purification, as steel is brought to its greatest purity and
hardness through the glow of fire. When I learned that, I
became afraid" (Dick Ouwendijk, *Das geschändete Antlitz*,
p. 232). The glowing zeal of the young priest is bound up
with the pious but secret pride of a middle-class family,
whose inheritance he wants to overcome, but still cannot
cast off. Because of it, his fire for the things of God, as he
finds to his terror, has become a danger to souls—his own
and those entrusted to his care, and he does not endure the
tension. Auke is a thoroughly devout and morally blameless
priest. But it is precisely because he takes the matter of
perfect sanctity so stubbornly and seriously, and realizes
his own impotence just as seriously, that his nerves break
under the strain. He abandons the priesthood and writes to
his parents: "I would have to stand at the altar day after
day with a guilty conscience and therefore I consider myself, in the supernatural order, too honest and (I don't
know if you understand this) Christ too defenseless and too
merciful.—It seems to me as though we were being torn
between two powers, by God and the devil . . . by good
and evil. And the tension has to give somewhere. I think
that we'll know only at death which has pulled the hardest"
(*Ibid.*, p. 216).

And yet the tension must be endured. God will never
tempt us beyond our strength (1 Cor. 10: 13) nor judge us.

But we must be responsible according to the strength we have. We are forced to make the same admission as St. Paul, "Of myself I will glorify in nothing save my infirmities" (II Cor. 12: 5).

We are given a great blessing, along with our weakness, and we need it for our work. Only let us not lose our charity. "Now we know that for those who love God all things work together for good, for those who, according to his purpose, are saints through his call" (Rom. 8: 28). Even our weaknesses help. They save us from hypocrisy, from pharisaism, from severity toward the sinner and those who are weak. There are innumerable places in the Gospel that tell of men who violated or forgot the greatest of commandments, that of love, because they presumed, in their self-confidence and the satisfaction they derived from fulfilling the Law, to pass judgment on others (Mt. 9: 11; 12: 2; Luke 11: 52; 18: 11). There is hardly any other sin that our Lord so outlawed from the spirit of His Gospel. Only when a priest realizes that his life is not up to his ideal and cannot be, but that despite all he must keep faith with it and with God, will any blessing for him and his people grow out of his existential need. Charity, trust, and humility are the foundation of his life and work. These alone are capable of supporting him.

b. The most difficult test that the priest must undergo is to try to reconcile the tension between the dignity of his calling and the necessary unworthiness of the priest. For in his daily life, he dare not ignore the danger that he runs, being daily in the most immediate contact with the sacramental presence of God. As terrible as this presence is, *quotidiana vilescunt*, familiarity breeds contempt. "I could not even bear the scrutiny of an angel; how then can I see Thee and live? I should be seared as grass, should I be exposed to the glow of Thy countenance" (Newman).

And yet we face Him every day—eye to eye, from the Consecration to the Communion—every day. "To see God is to die" is the terror-inspired faith of all religions. "No man has seen Him and no man can see Him (1 Tim., 6: 16). "Not that anyone has seen the Father except him who is from God, he has seen the Father" (John 6: 46). That is the only-begotten Son alone. For all of us, "our God is a consuming fire" so that we can serve Him only in fear and trembling (Heb. 12: 29).

That is the fundamental situation in which the priest finds himself as he celebrates Mass every day. *"Cum tuam dignitatem, Domine, et meam vilitatem penso, valde contremisco et in meipso confundor. Si enim non accedo, vitam fugio: et si indigne me ingessero, offensum incurro."* "When I consider thy dignity, O Lord, and my own vile condition, I tremble and am confused. For if I approach not, I am fleeing from Life. But if I come unworthily, I sin" (*Imit. Christi,* IV, vi, 17).

God Himself comes to our help. He lays the veil of sacramental figure over His presence. It is His mercy that does this, or we would have to die in His presence (*Imit. Christi* IV, ii, 6). He does not want His presence to be thought of as one of terror, but as an all-embracing act of love. "Having loved his own who were in the world, he loved them to the end" (John 13: 6).

It is the mercy of God that enables us without terror to pick up our Lord in His sacramental presence, to put Him down, to give Him to others and to receive Him ourselves. Daily! His presence no longer terrifies us. It has become every day. And indeed it must. No man is able to live as he should to be worthy of this numinous fearfulness and the true reality of the Eucharist, despite all the love and mercy of God.

Retreat directors try to bring home the true feelings we

should have in celebrating the Mass by proposing the example of the awe we would feel if we could celebrate Mass but once in our lives. But—we celebrate it daily. And then there was the Protestant minister who confided to this Catholic colleague: "If I believed in our Lord's presence in the tabernacle, I couldn't get off my knees, day or night"—but he would have to get up and pursue his vocation.

The priest can only beg God daily to inspire him with faith and ask Him not to be consumed in the awe of His presence, that the holy liturgy and the forbearance which lies hidden in its quiet, cool grandeur, may not become just a daily job and be spoiled. Then we will have "taken upon our poor lives once and for all the awe-inspiring presence of God." This faith should never become an impersonal "one." "One" never celebrates Mass. The priest offers it, and does it every day. Even at the risk of the dangers we have mentioned? Yes. But he should daily beseech God for faith and mercy.

c. The Breviary, which the priest has to read every day, usually demands about an hour and a half of his day. One of the most frightening priest characters in the modern novels —frightening, surely, in its possibilities—is Dr. Alois Moosthaler, who needs, so he says, only an hour a day. "And then, face puckered grimly, he began to figure out how many hours of his life he had wasted with this book" (Stefan Andres, *Das Tier aus der Tiefe*, Munich, 1949, p. 62). Since about 1500, the Breviary has been growing as an ordered way of sanctifying each day through prayer and reading. As much as individual parts are in need of revision, as a whole it is a work of art that could only have come about through the inspiration of the Holy Spirit. It is a treasure that a whole lifetime will not exhaust.

Even this daily prayer challenges the priest with a daily decision. Happy is the man who still considers it that way.

It is so even from the point of time. The priest who has so much work to do in the ministry must, in the chase of the day, finish his Breviary. Or, as one suspicious expression has it, "get through it." He must try to fit it in between other duties, even on the streets, at recesses in school, or on the street car.

That is why he is faced with an either-or decision that goes to the heart of his existence: either he will "get through it" quickly (you might almost say "get rid of it") or he will read it as a prayer, meditatively. If he decides for the first system, and often it seems that he has no chance to think differently about it, then he is letting a grace slip past him, permitting a treasure to lie untouched. What is more, if he keeps up this practice, he can lose the art of prayer precisely because he is reading the Breviary. And this will happen even without his noticing it. In other words, he can grow to ever greater sanctity from this holy source, day by day, or he can so abuse this genuine means of sanctity, this prayer, so that it has the opposite effect.

And all this can be true without there being any possible objection from the aspect of canon law. And this circumstance quiets the conscience in a way that is in itself startling. It is a very serious problem of priestly life. "We're so prone to swallow graces without chewing them. We lose half of the sweetness, nourishment, and curative power that God has given them. We move on too quickly and violently," Father Faber once said (*The Spiritual Life*). And he hasn't the crass and tragic case in mind that we've been discussing here. What will be the result of this in the long run? What is the importance of neglected graces? "There is never any grace that is forced into a clenched fist" (Reinhold Schneider, *Macht und Gnade*, Leipzig, 1941). Prayer and meditation cannot be sidelines in the life and work of the priest.

They are existential and essential parts of them. And the Breviary is that in a special sense.

Then there's a second point. Every day we read of the examples of the saints in the second nocturn of the day. To what purpose? Certainly, that we should imitate them! Are we doing it? What St. Augustine tells us on St. Valentine's Day (February 14) is true of every other life of a saint in the Church Year: This feast, he says, is celebrated by the Church today. Why? *"Cujus glorificationi congaudet ecclesia, sic ejus proponit sequenda vestigia. Si enim compatimur, et conglorificamur"* (Serm. 44 *de Sanctis*). Just as the Church rejoices in the splendor of the saint, so should the life of the martyr urge us to imitate that life. Only if we suffer with them will we share their glory. Can you read through these lives as you would flip through a newspaper? Can anyone see the daily models without daily imitation? Or without sorrowing daily because of the difference between their lives and ours? Thus the priest becomes responsible. How will he answer for it? Lord have mercy on us!

The Priest and the World

There is a second set of tensions, arising out of the fact that the priest is working in the world. These apply as much to the secular as to the religious priest who also has to work in the world.

What is more necessary for the priest than a secure, victorious faith? And yet this very faith can make him unable to understand how other men can be indifferent or cold toward it. His faith is so strong that the greatest catastrophes in the history of the Church (the Reformation, the Enlightenment, Marxism) only prove to him that he's right.

How much unconscious pride often accompanies faith.

And the people whom he wants and should convert, when they see it, shake their heads and put it down to a lack of awareness. Then they are armed against the man who would be their conqueror even before the fight has started. "Have you ever wondered why so many fiery spirits, so many fearless minds, so many souls that can believe and are ready for any sacrifice do not come and enter your church? Have you ever wondered why the majority of those who listen to your words is composed of women and children rather than promising youths and grown men?" Papini asks through his Pope Celestine VI. These are serious questions. Behind them there are bitter, burning lessons—and dangers.

a. Anyone who wants to win the children of this world to the kingdom of God must be open to the world, and this involves the danger of succumbing to the world. The ideal, or perhaps we should say, the answer, seems at first sight to lie in the by-word of the Redemptorists: "At home a Carthusian, abroad, an apostle" (Johann Hofer, *Saint Clement Maria Hofbauer,* New York, 1926).

It is possible that the very firmness of your faith and the triumphant certainty of your conviction can bring about a closed mind and a lack of willingness to listen to others, even those whom you want so to win. These qualities will do more to repel than attract them. Being open to the world involves knowledge of things as they are, and that requires study of all the problems and relations involved; and you can only derive these from the works of profane science. It is all necessary. There have been pastors who followed their charges into the restaurants, to parties and celebrations, as well as into the secular institutes of learning, but then forgot the way back. So it can happen that a priest, too, could discover that he is tied down by the study of these helpful secular sciences. For the sake of his ministry he might become a beekeeper or a farmer, in order to get near his parishioners and be able to talk to them. But he might suddenly wake up to the fact that he no longer knows what he is himself—a priest or a farmer. The *segregatus a populo*, the man separated from the people, must get back to the people to make contact with them. He has meditated often enough on this during his preparation, and he knows that he hasn't become a monk. But all at once he finds that the people will not let him go. Have the people learned from him, or have the people taught him something?

It is a startling fact that today, in the age of the masses and mass production, there have been no mass conversions. The individual has to be won over by dint of painstaking individual attention and the roundabout method of ridding him of his individual prejudices and weaknesses. (cf. Herwig, *Der grosse Bischof,* pp. 220 ff.) The priest, like Saint Paul, must be weak with the weak in order to win the weak. "For though I was all to all, unto all I have made myself a slave that I might gain more converts" (1 Cor. 9: 19). The Saint could better afford to take that risk. The priest must take it, and he's no saint.

b. This crisis is made easier for him, almost painfully so, because of another tension that he must endure: work in the world requires familiarity with it; and as often as he enters it, he doesn't notice that he's a stranger, but rather thinks that it is avoiding him. He thinks that he is an outcast. Who is unfamiliar with the silence that suddenly ensues when a priest comes in and sits down in a train compartment that was chattering away a second before? That is, until the people recover and start to talk about the weather.

This is not always due to repugnance or hostility. Often enough it is, but even the ordinary faithful want to talk about things that the pastor doesn't have to hear about, and they don't want to be overheard so unexpectedly. And it isn't a question of bad manners, either. They want their own world and time, which "has nothing to do" with the priest. They want to call him when *they* need him. The country priest of *Diary* fame keeps hearing that people in the parish are against him and that the conduct of the count who lives in the parish is an indication of it. So he asks his old sacristan, as he is working: "What does the parish think of me . . ." After thinking it over for a while, the old man says: "A priest's like a lawyer—'e's there if you be needin' him. 'E don't need to go meddlin' with folks" (Georges Bernanos, *The Diary of a Country Priest*). The pastor is supposed to baptize the children who are brought to him, marry the couples who come of their own accord, preach on Sunday, say Mass on time, and give his blessing when someone dies. But beyond that, people don't want to see him coming.

For missionary reasons, there have been many who regret that the priest is set off by his clerical clothes so that he can't engage those in conversation who perhaps need him most. That's why the priests of the *Mission de France* wear the ordinary clothes of their environment. This is in a country where the familiar silhouette of the abbé on the streets was part of the local color. It is a symbol of the transformation of the Church on the mission. For our dress is the costume of our state in life, the last remnant of a long-abandoned society built upon differences in rank. In the denial of that kind of society one can often find the cause of the repugnance to the last representative of the old order.

The rank of the priesthood, of course, goes back far beyond the bourgeois and feudal orders of society. It is of the oldest nobility. As a result, there are priests who are tempted to meet contempt with contempt. "At the beginning of every higher culture, the two oldest ranks, the nobility and the priesthood, set themselves above the tillers of the flat land" (Oswald Spengler, *Der Mensch und der Technik*, p. 64). The things that have driven the priests from this respected position, according to Spengler (*Ibid.*, p. 65), are "theories of a plebeian rationalism, liberalism, and socialism." This likewise expresses the cause of a repugnance which goes beyond the immediate political and religious reasons.

It is detrimental to his work if the priest who lives in this tension fails to recognize and endure his duty: if he tries to shield himself, by way of a sort of substitute, with the trust and devotion of those devout people who often have a passion for compensating for the injustice done him. But if this is not so much a retreat as a massing of forces for victorious attack, then it can be all right.

c. It can hurt even more deeply to have to stand between love and hatred. This hate, called anti-clericalism, is certainly not a product of modern times nor even of the present day. One could console himself with the words of our Lord: "No disciple is above his teacher, nor is the servant above his master. It is enough for the disciple to be like his teacher and for the servant to be like his master. If they have called the master of the house Beelzebub, how much more those of his household!" (Mt. 10: 25) and "if the world hates you, know that it has hated me before you" (John 15: 18).

But that's not so easy. The reasons for this hatred of the clergy were and are quite varied. At one time, it was their luxurious way of life, especially the privileges of their rank; today, it is their political power. That was just as true of the deep Middle Ages as it was of the time just before the modern era (Friedrich Zoepfl, *Deutsche Kulturgeschichte*, Freiburg, 1937, I, 320 ff. 336; Joseph Lortz, *Die Reformation in Deutschland*, I, 50, 95 ff. 119, 227, 280, 307).

The hatred of a Nietzsche distinguishes itself from these old and banal forms of hatred by being one of respect for the greatness of the old rank and its sacrificial life. In the second part of his *Also Sprach Zarathustra* he has Zarathustra say this to his disciples: "Here are the priests—and even though they are my old enemies, pass by them quietly and with a sleeping sword!

"For even among them there are heroes; many of them have suffered much, so they want to make others suffer.

"They are bitter enemies. Nothing is more vengeful than their humility, and he who attacks them, easily sullies himself.

"But my blood is related to theirs: and I desire that my blood be honored in theirs."

That is at least a noble attitude compared to slogans like "Don't believe the papists or the Schlaraffists!" If a poet like Leitgeb wasn't afraid of the injustice and redundancy of the slogan, he might at least have shied away from the bad rhyme (Joseph Leitgeb, *Läuterungen*, p. 38. cf. also the spiteful sketch of the young priest, p. 57).

What is the source of this hate?

It may spring from an unconscious disdain for the last representative of a hated stratified social system. It may be a defense against the power of his influence that is felt everywhere, as a "tool of the capitalists." (The propaganda of a century has yet to take notice of the fact that [economically speaking] the priest is much the worse off for it than all his slanderers.) Anti-clericalism may be directed against "clericalism" as a synonym for oppression, and this extends even to Catholic circles.

The most incontestable and common form of hostility against the priest today, in an age when economics is all-powerful and therefore all-convincing, is, as Spengler says (*Der Mensch und der Technik*, p. 65), the revulsion of the man of action against "the tyranny of pure thought." In his eyes, they are useless consumers, but with some claim to authority. There is also the hatred of pure worldliness for the witnesses of the supernatural, the hatred, often a personal, passionate hate (the detestation of a man personally interested) for those who demand moral rectitude. Even today in this world of license and broken marriages! They hate the one who disturbs their own happiness as a defense against something they can't understand and that can't be understood, a hatred that is felt even in the fold of the church (cf. Sigrid Undset's *Gymnadenia*).

The priest must stand fast between the love of the faithful and the hatred of others. He must not take refuge with the former, and he must redeem the latter from their hatred by charity.

d. There is another difficulty connected with this that can be a temptation to the priest in the world: his vulnerability in the world. He cannot meet the head-on attacks to which he is exposed in revolutions, in the uprisings of those obsessed with progress, in the banal slogans of those who would prepare a paradise on earth, with their own weapons. A Don Camillo appears in the Bassa on the Po apparently only in the fertile imagination of Giovanni Guareschi, and that's why he makes such an amazing and refreshing impression on us (Giovanni Guareschi, *Don Camillo and Peppone*).

Even aside from the persecutions of the first centuries and those of the present day, the orderly preaching of the Word and the sanctification of men does require a certain amount of freedom of movement and security for the priests. The state has guaranteed that to a certain extent ever since the time of Constantine, and not always because of its charity or conviction of the faith. That was the case even with Constantine. "His tactics, which had wonderful success in his own time and during the Middle Ages, consisted in making the first great protector of the Church at all costs an ideal of humanity, in his sense, and especially an ideal for future princes" (Jacob Burckhardt, *Die Zeit Konstantins des Grossen*, Stuttgart, 1939, p. 362). Constantine assured himself of the power of the Church because this power was an apt means of securing his own (*Ibid.*, pp. 393 ff.).

In the East, this developed into an identification of Church and State (Burckhardt, *Weltgeschichtliche Betrachtungen,* 1919, pp. 112 ff.), according to which the affairs of God came within the competence of the ruler of the land, who prescribed for the Church and her work a particular province decided upon by the State. That meant protection and security. But it meant also that the world-revolutionizing Gospel of Christ was hemmed in, if not suffocated. Even the present arrangement in the East, after a mad influx of Western spirit, is a return to the traditional view; but in the meantime, the State has fallen into the hands of powers to whom the inmost concerns of redemption are foreign and apparently dangerous to the "progress" of this world.

In the West, the Church has been freeing herself from this total guardianship of the State ever since the disputes over investiture. She is opposed to the State as a power (something quite inconceivable for the East). She has, as a spiritual power, therefore, done the spirit of human freedom a great service. This Western dualism has more tension; it is spiritually and culturally more fruitful and is especially in accord with the idea of the freedom of the Word, which is for all the people. In this way the preacher of the Word and the plenipotentiary of the mysteries of God are freer, but also more vulnerable. Therefore, they are thrown back upon their own power, which must see how it can hold its ground in the war of the spirit. At the same time, it is still exposed to the power which always has the upper hand in the secular realm. Of course, the free Church comes to terms with the State and tries to guarantee legal freedom for her works. This negotiation can well make one as sad as it did Saint Clement Mary Hofbauer, for the Church must first bargain for the freedom which is her right

(Hofer, *St. C. M. Hofbauer*). But that is the situation between Church and State in the West, and the priests must know its strong points and be able to overcome its weak ones. For even the Western State has a mistrust of a "State within the State," a problem which did not and does not exist for the East.

Now this general situation, at first glance, seems to be no part of the existence of the priest. But it is, and this for the reason that he must endure the tension between Church and State at the uncomfortable point of actual contact. And he must take into account that, because of the tension present in the world, all the external guarantees of his work can be lost overnight—at least for a time, as in Mexico or Spain. The priest whom Graham Greene apparently portrayed from close personal knowledge gives witness to the "power and glory" of God in daily danger of death, despite his own weaknesses. This is a matter of history in Mexico, but it is the present in many other countries and it is a possibility in all (Graham Greene, *The Power and the Glory*, New York, 1946). Overnight, the words of our Lord can be verified in the most bloody fashion: "Behold I send you forth as lambs in the midst of wolves" (Luke 10: 4). And it has always been seen that the wolves had lived until then in sheep's clothing, as harmless neighbors of the lambs. Then these words are true—and everyone must be convinced of them—"do not be afraid of those who kill the body but cannot kill the soul" (Mt. 10: 28).

The Mystery of the Workings of Grace

But there are tensions that lie much deeper, and which can be a temptation especially for the most zealous. They lie hidden in the mystery of the workings of grace.

a. There is the difference we experience daily between the dogmatic certainty of the effect of the sacraments and their apparent fruitlessness when we consider men. All these people who live around us have been baptized; almost all of them have been confirmed; and just look how little they know of grace and how cowardly they are! They have all received instructions in the truths and facts of the Faith, in Christian life, in the sanctifying power of the sacraments— and yet, how little of it is remembered, how little is put into practice, even by those who go to daily Communion, at least in comparison with the plenitude of grace they receive every day. And yet these are powers that are daily released for which we have no other word than "infinite."

The priest is acquainted with the parable of the "growing seed" (Mark 4: 26). And he might be able to go quietly to sleep, "and the seed . . . sprout up without his knowing it." He knows that grace can be effective through or in spite of defeat, real or apparent. The most mysterious thing about grace is the indwelling of the triune God in the soul. It is a mystery that is beyond any experimental proof. But the priest is a man, too, and he wants to see and hear. "The workings of grace are so mysterious that the Church, in canonizing a saint, does not judge according to grace, which is hidden, but according to his deeds" (Otto Zimmermann, *Lehrbuch der Aszetik,* Freiburg, 1932, p. 10). His deeds are external and verifiable. It is something of the external effect of deeds that the priest wants to see. But he is demanding something that was never promised him. It is only in its fruits that grace is recognized (Mt. 7: 6), and it may be that they become apparent only when the one who sowed them is long dead. He knows it and experiences it. He believes in the life-giving power of grace. But the law of cause and effect, which he sees working all about him, does not seem to apply to this case, at least as far as appearances are concerned. Many times, he almost loses courage. He experiences a sense of abandonment and loneliness, and this is the sister of despondency. And that is a temptation to, if not the sister of, despair. Who can tell him how grace works in a particular case? And if it doesn't, whose fault is it? It is painful for a priest to endure, all his life long, the triumphant snickering of the "prince of this world" every night, and to begin anew, every day! To play music for the deaf becomes ridiculous after a while. And it is more than just discouraging. It is a source of temptation.

There are priests who have to drink this misery and its bitterness to the dregs. The theses of dogma, which should be a help to the understanding, can be cited as a consolation in the concrete case. But even these clean-cut pronouncements, which no one doubts—and if they weren't true, even this misery might be illusory—do not make his troubled experience any easier to bear. "I have never doubted grace and God grant that I never will," says Auke to his brother. Those who refer him to the limpid statements of the catechism "act as though grace were like a pocket full of pennies. Of course, pennies stamped with the image of God Himself . . . but as though they are to be counted out by God every time He is asked for change" (Dick Ouwendijk, *Das geschändete Antlitz,* p. 138).

It is not easy to assuage the grief of these hearts. The workings of grace cannot be understood in terms of the laws of the market for gold and produce, nor by the logic of earthly happiness. *Salus in cruce.* Suffering can bring salvation. And what men call happiness can be its downfall. The paradox of the cross is still with us. "Priests (i.e. *those priests with whom he has discussed his spiritual unrest*) like most of all to represent grace to men as an inexhaustible fountain of happiness and inner peace . . . as though God ever repaid our recourse to Him with anything other than more restlessness and deeper sorrow!—He once stilled the storm on the sea, but not without the reproach, 'O you of little faith!'—as though we had never been told that we must be like Christ in all things. That means being plagued with the fear that everything is going wrong, yet all the while having the certainty that we will have paradise here-after as our portion. It means complaining of thirst and being given gall and vinegar to drink. The world is full of those who have *disappointed* the love of God, and do we now demand that we be lulled by the peace of His grace?" (*Ibid.*) Let us not give ourselves or the world a pat an-swer! That means especially not the kind that the world wants to hear. The world could only be deceived that way, for the answer would be deceptive.

All this can be won only from conversation with the One whom it concerns, with God. "If I were being tempted to complain about somebody, the final bond between myself and God would be broken, and it seems to me that I would then enter the eternal silence" (Georges Bernanos, *The Diary of a Country Priest*). To know this and even more, to act according to this knowledge, is something that be-longs entirely to faith, and that, in turn, comes from quiet hours spent with God.

b. The priest must talk to God, and that even though it be possible that God does not answer. That God sometimes does not answer is the most difficult mystery of daily life that the priest has to bear. Just think of priests who are assigned to what they call "abandoned posts." All their en-ergy seems wasted. Think of the priest in dictatorships and the People's Democracies. Every step is watched, every word is suspected and can tear him from his congregation overnight. He has nothing but prayer—and God does not answer. He seems to leave the freedom of His servant and the settlement of the problem of power between Rome and

Moscow (which has to be endured in the parishes) to the politicians. It is a great temptation for the ordinary man. And for the priest!

Rudolf Binding comes back from the first World War and sees what was happening. "It is impossible to pretend any longer that the world is ruled by love. We felt it when we returned home . . . If this world was Christian, and created by the God that Christians call Christian, it isn't like its Creator" (Rudolf Binding, *Erlebtes Leben,* p. 249). And God does not answer the doubter. God does not allow Himself to be tempted. He is eternally true, but this faithfulness cannot be consulted like a faithful watch any time it pleases us. God does not permit us to take Him at His word any time we please. When He keeps His word is something that He determines.

His promises are so clear and certain: "Go into the whole world and preach the Gospel to every creature. He who believes and is baptized shall be saved, but he who does not believe shall be condemned. And these signs shall attend those who believe: in my name they shall cast out devils; they shall speak in new tongues; they shall take up serpents; and if they drink any deadly thing, it shall not hurt them; they shall lay hands upon the sick and they shall get well" (Mark 16: 15 ff.). "Ask and it shall be given you; seek and you shall find; knock and it shall be opened to you" (Mt. 7: 7). "Amen, amen, I say to you, if you ask the Father anything in my name, he will give it to you" (John 16: 23). "All things whatsoever you ask for in prayer, believing, you shall receive" (Mt. 21: 22).

And what if the Christian, or the priest, prays, relying on these words, and God remains silent? Then this silence must be endured in faith, until we reach that place beyond that "whatsoever" of our small hearts where all gifts and evils of this time are pale symbols. God the Father alone knows what is good for us. The fact that we have lost the symbolism of Biblical language and the mysterious transcendence of the visitations of this life gives rise to many temptations. God writes for this time in a mysterious language. That is the only way that the lives of His saints and martyrs can be understood. (Cf. the words of St. Gregory on the Gospel for the feast of Our Lord's Ascension in Eucharius Berbuir's *Das Kirchenjahr in der Verkündigung*, Freiburg, 1949, I, 287 ff.).

These insights overcome the many heavy hours in which it is not only the run-of-the-mill kind of Christianity that is assailed by dark temptations. This is how Joseph Wittig describes the spiritual condition of those who were just about to be driven from their homes in Silesia: "Formerly fairly well-to-do, now beggars who thank their neighbors with tears in their eyes for a bit of bread and a glass of milk, neighbors who own a few acres of land, but whose cows have not yet been plundered from their stalls by the enemy. And winter is coming on, starvation staring them in the face! Ah, the poor children! It is really enough to drive one mad. And no friend can help. Those helpful friends have been impoverished themselves. And no God comes down from heaven; not one of the angels, the messengers of God, who but a few years before consoled our homes and lives, comes to us. Neither a God nor any of the helpful saints seem to exist any more, and they never did exist. They lived only in our pious fancy" (*Roman mit Gott*, p. 13). In this complaint we can see the lack of reflection that always characterized Wittig. It is a primeval quality in this and in other sections of this most recent of his books that betrays the old Wittig. But we prefer to take them here as witnesses of the first attack of temptations, and that often lasts for quite a while.

That is how it is and there is no other consolation than

that faith which enabled Léon Bloy to say to God "O God! You pray for those who crucify Thee and crucify those who love thee!" Just a *bon mot* of French paradox? No. That is how the Son of Man speaks to the "Angel of Laodicea": "Those whom I love I rebuke and chastise" (Apoc. 3, 19). The love of God, which is behind all our trials, becomes clearer with these words.

Herein lies the mystery which is always present and most actual in the Christian life. It is the paradox of Christian, and even more necessarily, of priestly existence. It is the *"salus in cruce"*! Salvation is from the cross! We receive *life* from the *death* of the Redeemer. It is *"sanguis martyrum semen christianorum"*: the *blood* of the martyrs is the *seed* of the kingdom of God on earth. To impress that on us and on all who need it is the duty of the priest. These words apply to him especially and just at such a time: "Take care, then, that the light that is in thee is not darkness" (Luke 11: 35). "In the robes of disaster," says Archbishop John of Salerno to the saintly Pope Leo IX, "grace strides through the years with firm step. When I slept upon the grave of the apostle, I saw a battlefield. It was covered with dead, but they did not have the defiant faces of the Normans. On the contrary, Norman lances and arrows were sticking in their bodies, and many held crosses in their bloodied hands. I also saw you sorrowing upon that battlefield. Clearly I saw your saintly figure" (Rheinhold Schneider, *Die dunkle Nacht*, Munich, 1949).

c. It is only in a special case that the priest has practical knowledge of evil before experience and prayer—both are presupposed—have made him strong and supernaturally wise against this power. The special case is that of the young priest. How straightforward the theses of theological compendia are! But what crooked and confused lines write the story of life! This wisdom of a Portuguese proverb provided

Paul Claudel with a motto for his *Satin Slipper:* "God writes straight with crooked lines." But one can agree with the wisdom and truth of this proverb only after he has experienced it. And that is just what the young priest has to do first.

In Stefan Andres' novel *Wir sind Utopia* a renegade Carmelite is imprisoned during the Spanish Civil War in an abandoned convent. He is locked in the very cell from which he had fled years ago. "He took a deep breath and went over to the high desk over which St. John of God looked at him from an old engraving. (Apparently Andres has forgotten from his own past life as a monk that the co-founder of the discalced Carmelites was St. John of the Cross.) He held his face close to the eyes of the saint and then shook his head, sighing: why did those eyes look out at the world so sadly from under their halo? Oh well, the founder had had to look on from his picture as his son, Padre Julio, stood turned to the door and cried 'un momento'! . . . The saints, lovers and Utopian dreamers keep on turning the world into poetry in their own fashion and they all soon see—the most of them, at least, the best of them, that— Paco, the former Padre Julio, winked at the saint sympathetically—that it is only with difficulty that one can find a place for visions of heaven in this world" (Stefan Andres, *Wir sind Utopia*, Berlin, 1943, p. 19).

It was easier for Andres' Padre Julio to resolve the tension between his ideal (and therefore the possibility of its realization) and the reality that overwhelmed him so suddenly, than it is for the young priest. These tensions must be endured without losing the ideal. It is a long way from the emotion, and the pain of the confessions they hear, to the endurance of pain and its justification that is taken on faith; as the holy Curé of Ars puts it: "M. Vianney climbs up the stairs of his rectory, lantern in hand. It is about midnight. For a moment he feels tempted to think that sinners are well off: they cast their burden into the 'abyss of God' and then there is no more talk about it. But the abyss of God is the poor priest, who keeps all those things in his heart without complaining about them. For he is afraid that if he complained, it would not be so much for the sake of the outrage done to God as for his own sake. If God can put up with so many injuries, he certainly could bear the confession of them" (Henri Ghéon, *Le Jeux de l'Enfer et du Ciel*, 1929).

But the reaction of the young priest is tremendous when he sees this flood of sin, its ineradicability, the ruin that it prepares for even in youth, and his helplessness against that flood. When Auke went into his little room in the rectory, he was delighted with the beautiful view it gave him of the country and the parish, especially at night: "Before, I could hardly breathe for emotion and joy when I looked at this view; I thought that such peace could only be filled with God . . . but now! now I know that it is all false . . . darkness is only the domain of evil . . . the first months when I held Christ in my hands, lifted Him up, I saw Him all shining, without wounds, without bruises . . . the good, holy Body of our Lord. Now I see Him dirtied, beaten, covered with our bruises and sores, and I continue to put Him into the mouths whose wretched stammering I know almost word for word . . . I could almost come to hate my Lord, he whispered" (Ouwendijk, *Das geschändete Antlitz*, p. 40). And it's the same thing, whether it is the poor or the rich, children or adults: "Wherever you find poverty, you can figure with certainty that there is lust . . ." And children! "I consider impurity in children the most sorrowful and terrible thing that there is" (p. 41). Auke visited the side streets of the poorer sections to find comfort. Perhaps that is why they streamed from those sections to his confessional. "Trash, as Pastor de Smet says . . . but what I learned was that the soul is sullied the same way everywhere" (*Ibid.*, p. 158).

It was late, too late, when he knew. "That's how it always goes! If you want to do your work too well, your own zeal trips you up sooner or later and you fall on your face before you know it. I did not know that my priestly work had to be very modest and insignificant. I understood it only after I had given it up" (p. 269).

Omnia instaurare in Christo is the motto that he had heard in the seminary. "And every priest will live up to it with joy in his heart, as anyone can hear in the sermons on feast days: these words are burned into the priest's heart . . . well . . . you must also recall that Christ knew the moment in which He was revolted by the form He had assumed. And in that revulsion we find our task! . . . we desire to do nothing else than to cleanse His countenance of all the open sores and scabs. I might describe the world as consisting of two levels: that of corruption and that of the love of God. Not two levels that lie one on the other without being intermingled, for this corruption is an outgrowth from the healthy flesh of the Love of God, which became man itself . . . Therefore I will never come across sin again, as I did before, with anger or repugnance" (*Ibid.*, p. 270).

That is how one man comes by way of a long detour to a supernatural view of reality. It should never come to a point where evil is made light of. For here, too, familiarity breeds contempt. Nor should it come to a point where the priest breaks down under his experience of the humdrum of his daily experiences and the flood of filth, nor from the conviction that sin is ineradicable. This terror, too, must be daily endured anew. The discovery of the power and universality of sin should not become a danger for the priest himself. "We live cheek by jowl with filth and mire and are supposed to be always clean" (Giovanni Papini, *The letters of Pope Celestine VI to All Mankind*).

Lack of Education

There are tensions which have their roots in faulty education.

a. The first of these tensions throws into sharp relief the disproportion that necessarily exists between the greatness of the priesthood and the man. The priest comes from the seminary into life and does his duty. He is sought out by some and avoided by others, loved by some and despised by others. In those situations where he feels it is his duty to work in the world, everything depends on his ability to make such a connection as a *man*, with strength and uprightness, clearly and openly. He must do it as one whose life is founded on his own personal resources and conscience. It is only the strong, and therefore the bold personality, that is able to master others, even if at first this is purely on the natural level. The vocation is so great that only the strongest human foundation combines with it to form a halfway fitting whole.

We can see from a few examples in the saints what importance a strong personality has for a priest. "Where did Paul get this tremendous influence on men? That was his personal secret, as it is with all the great saints and great men. It was the power of his integral personality, his selfless life, founded on one unified divine center, Christ" (Joseph Holzner, *Paul of Tarsus*, St. Louis, 1944, p. 269). Here Holzner also calls to mind another parallel of clear greatness. Savonarola (cf. Joseph Schnitzer, *Savonarola*, I, 160). Or the great Ketteler! He "said Mass, preached, heard confessions like a simple substitute pastor, but there went out from his personality a power and might that not a single person could escape" (Herwig, *Der grosse Bischof,* 1930, p. 295). Or the simple figure of St. C. M. Hofbauer. He was a simple priest, but where did the power of his work come from? "Hofbauer's sermons were the self-revelation of a hero of the faith who has approached the realm of mystic vision. His sermons are acts of faith of magnetic power" (Hofer, *St. C. M. Hofbauer,* Freiburg, 1928).

What impression must Father Rupert Mayer, S.J., division Chaplain, have made on Hans Carossa in the field: "In the early morning light he was pale yellowish, slender, sharp, with deep-set dark eyes, not without a trace of weariness, but his whole appearance so full of modesty and dignity, so animated by good will, as well as adaptability and cheerfulness, that bodily exhaustion could not easily prevail in him" (Hans Carossa, *Führung und Geleit,* 1943, Leipzig, p. 113). "There are faces that show that the person once stood at the crossroads of many paths and according to the one he followed, the complete man of earth or light was formed. Now here, the result was a combination of priesthood and soldier that was completely new to me in such a spiritual-natural form. You got the impression of a man for whom it was no longer difficult to keep even the hardest vows" (*Ibid.,* p. 113). And when Father Mayer lay wounded, in his own blood, before him, he writes: "The difference between a man who clings with wild tenacity to life and one who has renounced it, who has transformed all his drive into spiritual drive, had never been clearer to me. When one of us died, there was always something left over that was not quite finished or purified; but this man passed away like a sonata by Bach, called out of the darkness, played through in straight, simple lines and completely resolved" (*Ibid.,* p. 23). He was the true representative of an

Order which was always concerned with the complete preservation and employment of his personality. "The ideal of
the Jesuit is modest service, but that is a boundless love of the
magis (of its founder) restrained by the discretion of obedience" (Hugo Rahner, *St. Ignatius Loyola*, Chicago, 1956).

One could multiply examples of strong personalities in
priestly dress at will. The comparison that anyone makes
between himself and these men will always leave him dissatisfied. But if the disproportion in meeting with strong
personalities in the world becomes for the priest a question
of equipment for his vocation, there arises a tension that
simply cannot be resolved. His self-examination takes him
back for the most part to the years of formation which decided him and he thinks bitterly of those educators—pardon
me, those in charge—who saw an ideal in the suppression
of strong individualities and could only put their narrow
consciences to rest when the last one who gave promise of
being a strong personality was shipped out. The priest who
must face his man must be a real, whole man. The human
being must be united with God as a whole, and he must
experience his personal fulfillment from God. That is much
more than a two-legged ghost who does his duty imperfectly.

The experience of this weakness throws the young priest
into doubt and uncertainty. Often it happens even without
this, and that is a worse case. In the matter-of-course manner of a man who determines his conduct according to the
limits of possibility as he has experienced them, he pulls
back to a line that will no longer cause human failure. We
will come across him again in the final types. This is the
meaning for the ministry: surrendering both the victory
and the will to win; restricting himself to the little flock
of those who are always faithful; and helplessness just as
soon as necessity forces him to overstep these boundaries.

An Army doctor, himself a convert and serious Catholic,

who worked with the theologians and priests who were mostly put in the medical corps, had a painful confession to make to me: "I was always distressed to see that the priests and priestly candidates were broken men." He had dealings with other seminarians, of course, but they were the same, too.

b. Another painful discovery, just as bitter, is the fact that the priest's theological preparation leaves him in the lurch.

Examination-theology alone does not last. It is the minimal amount, the foundation, the starting point. It can only give schooling in principles, and the problems that assail us in life need more. They must be met by a man who lives and loves his theology, who has mastered the holy content of his Faith and the moral order as a whole, a knowledge that grows and matures with his struggles in everyday life. Theological preparation cannot go into all the problems that the priest is going to meet on the firing line. But it must at least indicate the direction in which the seminarian can find his further education. It is consoling for him that he never meets those questions of the long-bearded theological ghosts, Gaius and Tiburtius, but it is depressing that there are other difficult questions that he can meet daily, but which were never mentioned.

The order of studies from Rome puts great value upon philosophical preparation. This should certainly not be thought of as a sort of protective vaccination to shield him against infection. It has to enable him to face up to serious questions as a serious and real thinker. The priest can't be an expert in all fields and problems. No reasonable man would expect that of him. But he must be capable of a clear and orderly train of thought where it is a question of fundamentals.

The most painful experience for the young priest in this regard is that he leaves behind him his own proper philosophical domain with its own language and interlocked evidence. Outside of his lecture room and the text books is a world of dynamism and living thought, and he is helpless before it. He must bring with him the openness, the ability to listen, and his training to master the questions that today has for the theologian. It will always be true that it is not every priest's task to be a master of philosophy, ethics, and natural theology. But there must be priests who can do it.

Many hundreds of young theologians and priests who had discussed concrete spiritual and intellectual problems with their fellow soldiers, in the trenches and camps, were returning with a soldierly scorn for the inadequacy of their training and desirous of real priestly formation. A questionnaire about the education of future priests was sent out and then summarized in a general report to the regents of the German major seminaries. There were complaints from laymen: "It is amazing that you can't discuss theological problems with many priests."

Or what is worse: "You can't discuss things religious with many priests!" With whom should this world, plagued with fear and anxieties, discuss its questions if not with the priest? Has the salt so lost its savor?

Suddenly one senses that loss! And happy is the man for whom such a want is still felt as a painful lack. The consequences which accrue to him for his own conduct, and that in a time when we are summoned to recover the lost provinces of the Church, mean loss of ground.

"He who strives for his own and his neighbor's sanctity must actually show solid knowledge, that not only extends to theological studies, but to everything that our time produces by research and technical development," warns the Holy Father (*Adhortatio ad clerum universum*, "*Menti Nostrae*," September 23, 1950).

2. THE CRISIS

Definition

The word *crisis* comes from the medical world and signifies the high- or turning-point of a disease that means life or death. Compared with this definition, our use of the term here is only analogical.

The original Greek κρίσις is closer to the meaning in which we use the word here. In Greek it meant a division, a choice, a distinction or test.

At any rate, we do not take the expression for a turning-point involving the existence or non-existence of priestly existence. It can be this, too. But this would be a rare exception, thank God, that would be described as a crisis for the priesthood itself. In what follows, we are taking crisis as that moment in the development of the priest which, as a high- or turning-point in the tension described above, is a point of departure to the individual forms of existence. But even these must not be competely final.

Further, this *high-point* and this *crisis* must not be perceived as crises. Just how deep the crisis goes and how much it is appreciated differs according to the temperament, the psychological makeup, and the intelligence of the individual. For the most part, it is independent of experiences, events, and disagreements by which the crisis is irritated into its acute stage. The amount of suffering that accompanies it also varies in intensity. Indeed, it is conceivable, and is often the case, that the build-up of the priest's final stature is not experienced as a crisis. It is rather regarded as a process of settling down, of securing and acclimating oneself to the form of life that is finally found to be the proper one.

If the tension, the necessary tension that co-exists with priestly existence, is accepted joyfully and with faith, if it is endured from the beginning as the way to sanctify oneself and the souls entrusted to one's care, then there can be no discussion of a crisis at all.

The Causes

From the religious point of view, one of the causes that produces the crisis is first and foremost the situation summed up in the words of the Son of Man to the "Angel of Ephesus": (Apoc. 2: 4 ff.) "But I have this against thee, that thou hast left thy first love. Remember therefore whence thou hast fallen and repent and do thy former works; or else I will come to thee and move thy lamp-stand out of its place unless thou repentest."

a. The first love is a pinnacle, and there is the danger, according to the drastic words cited above, that it will be a pinnacle of priestly existence after which there can be nothing but decline . . . perhaps decline, and afterwards a life-long, barren mediocrity. That is the danger. Perhaps one becomes conscious of it in the midst of a retreat or else during prayer. That is when the hour of crisis strikes.

It must be noted that in the case of the "Angel of Ephesus" we are not dealing with a bad superior. For the diagnosis of the Son of Man that precedes His warning says: "I know thy works and thy labor and thy patience and that thou canst not bear evil men; but hast tried them who said they were apostles and are not and has found them false. And thou hast patience and hast endured for my name and hast not grown weary" (Apoc. 2: 1).

Our Lord has many good and edifying things to say of the Bishop of Ephesus, but it is not enough to keep up external observances. There has been a transformation *internally:* he no longer has his original love. The fervent union with God, the ultimate source of all self-sanctification and all effectiveness, is no longer found in its old power.

Because of this, the priesthood that once bore him up like an eagle has become a burden that he drags along behind him. The powers that differ as pole from pole become more distant: natural and supernatural, priest and man, dignity and burden. The tension becomes more sensible and is finally simply unbearable. It all forces him into a life that "one can live." In a particular case one can no longer even say what our Lord said in praise of the "Angel of Ephesus" when He called him to repentance: "and thou hast not grown weary"—for he has also tired of his labors.

b. In the light of psychological development, this condition can coincide with or even constitute that critical "moment" which comes when a man turns his back upon the broad horizons of his youth and steps into the narrow confines and the concrete working area of his maturity. For there are not merely three decisive "moments" in the life of a man (cf. the author's *Der rechte Augenblicke,* Vienna, 1948), but five. The fourth is the change from young manhood to real manhood and usually occurs about the age of thirty. The man finally leaves behind him the broad horizons, the stage of life when there is nothing but plans and endless opportunities and the kind of outlook on life that one learns in school, and enters the narrow, unyielding confines of his area of work, in which he must prove himself in every-day life. Then there are two things that are decided: 1. whether what he has brought with him from his preparation for life by way of education and equipment will last in the concrete, sober work of his calling, and 2. whether the man himself is ripe enough for manhood, so that he himself can last in the hard and fast limits of his field of work which are clearly limited locally, temporally, and socially. The crisis that now occurs if either of these conditions is wanting must not coincide with his entry into some position. The "man" will often not leave off the attitudes of his youth, although he has already to play the *man*. The phenomenon observed by Bishop Paul Rusch has its roots in this—"When we reach forty, we usually find that we are different than we were" (*Wachstum im Geiste*, Innsbruck, 1949, p. 265).

c. Before we speak of solitude as a cause and the real sphere of crisis, we must see that loneliness need have nothing at all to do with crisis.

Konrad Leister makes some good distinctions in his beautiful meditation, "Priestly Solitude" (in the collection, *Amt und Sendung*, Freiburg i. B., 1950, pp. 63 ff):

1. There is solitude that is a "romantic fancy," an idyll. To some, the word suggests Carl Spitzweg's pastor in his quiet garden amid the birds and flowers. Another thinks of Dürer's engraving "St. Jerome in His Cell." The harassed metropolitan pastor, when he hears the word, thinks a bit enviously of his colleague in a remote mountain village, or else he becomes melancholy thinking of Annette Droste's verses, "The Old Pastor's Week."

2. Another man, when he hears the word *solitude*, thinks of a friend in the mountains, but it is with a touch of regret, because he is far from all that is going on in the world of culture and sees nothing but farmers and cows and mountains and always the same thing. He thinks that this man's

capabilities are being wasted and that he must be rusting away intellectually in his exile from the world.

3. A third man longs for solitude, away from the world. What he desires is to be alone with God. Fürich's hermit comes to his mind: "As the hart pants for living water, so longs my soul for Thee, oh God!" (Ps. 41: 2).

4. A fourth idea, referring to the priestly life, is spatial: separation from what the world calls "life."

5. The fifth meaning he gives for the word comes closer to what we will say in the following pages: that solitude of the man who is unmarried because of his calling as opposed to a man who, in the companionship of marriage or within the circle of his family, can never be lonelier than the priest, even in a lonely job such as a country teacher. This loneliness, which belongs to his holy state by its very nature, of which he was conscious when he agreed to it, can be a source of temptation in times of crisis.

Because of his weariness and his sense of inadequacy, the priest can get himself into a state of loneliness from which there is only one escape: a closer union with God. But this solitude is often connected with a fear of the demands that God makes: in his weariness he is afraid of being overburdened with a new challenge. He believes that he can no longer carry the ones he has.

Loneliness is a universal human condition, as we must first realize. Every pain, every illness, every risk and decision is surrounded by a circle that no other can enter and in which no one can help. And "everyman" must die alone. But these are passing moments in life. No man can be lonely constantly for a long time. The lonely man has a feeling of abandonment, and anxiety arises from this. The man begins to weep like a lost child and he knows not why. Even our Lord suffered this human loneliness in the garden and the bloody sweat ran from his temples. "Could you not watch one hour with me?" (Mt. 26: 40) He asks His disciples who were sleeping as He cried out to His Father in loneliness, He who had been up until then their leader and mainstay.

Even association with men has its dangers. Let us consider only the religious and moral dangers. *"Vellem me pluries tacuisse et inter homines non fuisse."* I wish I had kept quiet more often and not been so often among men (*Imit. Christi*, I, 10, 3). And going into company is certainly no solution for the loneliness of which we speak here. This loneliness is never felt more depressingly than amid others' loud rejoicing, just as no one can ever be so completely alone as when he is in the crowds of a big city.

There is a life of solitude that the priest lives with God. And that is indispensable for his existence. It must be endured. Its loneliness has a richness and a fullness that no society or good-fellowship can replace. But they lie completely within the individual's power of forming his own life of solitude. "The Bishop rode home to his solitude. He was forty-seven years old, and he had been a missionary in the New World for twenty years—ten of them in New Mexico. If he were a parish priest at home, there would be nephews coming to him for help in their Latin or a bit of pocket-money; nieces to run into his garden and bring their sewing and keep an eye on his housekeeping. All the way home he indulged in such reflections as any bachelor nearing fifty might have.

"But when he entered his study, he seemed to come back to reality, to the sense of a presence awaiting him. The curtain of the arched doorway had scarcely fallen behind him when that feeling of personal loneliness was gone and a sense of loss was replaced by a sense of restoration. He sat down before his desk, deep in reflection. *It was just this solitariness of love in which a priest's life could be like his*

Master's. It was not a solitude of atrophy, of negation, but of perpetual flowering. A life need not be cold or devoid of grace in the worldly sense, if it were filled by her who was all the graces; Virgin-daughter, Virgin-mother, girl of the people and Queen of Heaven: *le rêve suprême de la chair*. The nursery tale could not vie with her in simplicity, the wisest theologians could not match her in profundity" (Willa Cather, *Death Comes for the Archbishop*).

Priestly life in solitude can be beautiful and full to overflowing in varied forms, for example, as it is here, in the love of the Virgin and Mother. It is more than a dogmatic exhortation when the Church repeatedly refers the priest to Mary. "When you feel especially how difficult it is to continue on the tiresome path of sanctity and fulfill your duties, then lift up a confident eye and ear to her, who, since she is the Mother of the Eternal Priest, is also the most loving Mother of the Catholic Clergy. You know well the kindness of this Mother toward you and you have explained the mercy of her Immaculate Heart often enough in your sermons and frequently you have stirred up faith in this devotion of the Christian people in marvelous wise" (*Menti Nostrae*, 128).

But as we heard, Archbishop Jean Marie Latour was forty-seven years old. Old age loves solitude as its element. For a young man it is often an empty realm that causes him anguish and cries out for fulfillment. When speaking of the temptation of our Lord, John George Hamann says something that we should hear in this connection: "All of the advantages which Satan has over men when they are lonely and especially when they are sad, whose arrows no mortal is in a position to ward off, were given to the Tempter here over our Redeemer" (John Hamann, *Biblische Betrachtungen eines Christen*, Freiburg i. B., 1939, pp. 63f.). And Joseph Holzner dares to say that solitude can also be dangerous for the saint. "Without Barnabas, Paul would have been gradually ground down in the mill of his own thoughts. It is good from time to time to be lonely and shut off from the world, but it should only be something temporary" (Joseph Holzner, *Paul of Tarsus,* p. 69).

At the beginning of the last war, a Sudeten-German curate came to me. By a decree passed after assimilation into the German Reich, their priests were deprived of the right to instruct youth in religion and allowed no activity in that regard. They were restricted to the church and sacristy. He said that he couldn't endure the loneliness and inactivity. And as I heard later, he has broken down under it.

The burden of solitude is not even easier to bear when it is "only" a state of psychological depression, and, considered in the light of Faith, unreal. God is closer to those who are more tried than they think. When St. Teresa, after a long stretch of abandonment, asked the Lord: "Where were You during these years?" He answered, "In your heart."

The pious and zealous pastor of Ambricourt, after enduring a long period of spiritual abandonment, writes with relief in his diary: "No, I have not lost my faith. The cruelty of this test, its devastation so like a thunderbolt, and so inexplicable, may have shattered my reason and my nerves, may have withered suddenly within me the joy of prayer—perhaps forever, who can tell—may have filled me to the very brim with a dark, more terrible resignation than the worst convulsions of despair in its cataclysmic fall; but my faith is still whole for I can feel it" (G. Bernanos, *Diary of a Country Priest*). He has found the best way of expressing what the stakes are in this.

The same author reports almost the same thing of the

curate who was later to become the sainted pastor of Lum
bres, to whom harassed and lonely priests would come for
help and advice: "Certainty of his inability to live up to
such a destiny ('whither God summons you you must climb
—climb or fall,' his pastor had said) stopped short the
prayer on his lips. The will of God upon his poor soul overwhelmed him with a superhuman weariness. . . . To himself he seemed ignorant, fearful, lonely, sterile in heart and
mind, incapable of those excesses in goodness, of the glorious foolhardiness which mark great souls, the least heroic
of men . . . Every step pushed him further into the land
of exile; yet he was marked with the mark which only a
little while ago the servant of God had recognized upon his
forehead" (G. Bernanos, *Under the Sun of Satan*).

But all these things are merely tests of the saints and of
the measures they use to attain sanctity in their solitude.
For the simple priest it easily becomes a temptation. To
drown out their loneliness with bowling and card playing
is always inopportune (Emile Marriot, *Der geistliche Tod*, p.
220; Hermann Herz, *Peter Schwabentans*, p. 150).

This emptiness can become a central danger for priestly
existence if it introduces the natural complement of the
lonely man—woman.

But one asks in the meantime—doesn't the lonely priest
have any friends, then? Perhaps. Or maybe not. It amounts
to the same thing in the situation we have in mind. In the
nature of things there is a sort of loneliness for any man
among those of his own sex—and anyone who doesn't see
that should take another look. (Incidentally, that is one of
the difficulties a man finds in confession.) And it is just
in these extreme cases that it has the upper hand. The brutal egoism of man and the involuntary jealousy of women
are only the vicious offshoots of this loneliness. Because of
it, men distrust men and women distrust women.

We must add that this situation has nothing to do with
sex. And it is not the dissolute slattern who will be any
danger to him, but precisely the good, pure, pious woman.

. CELIBACY

Celibacy, of course, does not belong to the essence of the
priesthood, but in the Western Church it has been enjoined
on the clergy, although with many variations and much
opposition, since the first centuries. In the twelfth century
(2nd Lat. Council, Can. 2) it finally became a universal
Church law. Just as wedlock decides the life of the married,
so too does freely chosen celibacy. It is an essential and
existential element of the priestly life.

Nevertheless, we have had little to say about celibacy up
until now. The decision for it in an individual case coin-
cides with the choice of vocation. We have already said
that. We have also said that apparently, in the eyes of the
Church, the willingness of the young man to live a pure,
unmarried life is the touchstone of his seriousness and decisiveness in making this choice of vocation.

What of the agreement on the part of the faithful?
Graham Greene, who traveled through communist Mexico
in the 'twenties as an English reporter, showed how Padre
José, who had married in accordance with government orders, was made a mockery even at that time (*The Power and
the Glory*, London, 1947).

Assumed once and for all with the choice of vocation,
celibacy is not a subject of debate after ordination. But
that does not alter the fact that it is easy for one and diffi-

cult for another to live a celibate life. There is no problem of celibacy when the priest is absorbed by love of the Church and souls, his days filled to the brim with work

But in the desert of loneliness, the priest's single life can be threatened from within. This must be examined. It is remarkable how little consideration is given to this danger

a. There is a danger to celibacy that comes from without. This is not a problem of priestly existence, for it is either a fundamental disaffection in general or it is something that is a source of disquiet or danger in a particular case. Such a danger is not something proper to priestly life but one that any other man would have to face. The personal danger need be mentioned in this connection only in so far as the single life of the priest can aggravate it or to the extent that priestly work can be a cause of it.

We will list first the forms of danger to celibacy which come from without, in order to contrast them to what is really existential.

1. Those which should be mentioned first as obstacles to priestly celibacy would be all objections of a biological, hygienic, national, or social viewpoint; usually all are alleged But they are all one-sided and, therefore, considered as a whole, incorrect. The hygienic objections to it are not at all as recent as one might suppose. We even read in the second nocturn of the Feast of St. Casimir: *"Virginitatem quam ab incunabilis servavit illaesam, sub extremo vitae termino fortiter asseruit, dum gravi pressus infirmitate, mori potius quam castitatis jacturam ex medicorum consilio subire, constanter decrevit."* ("When he was weighed down with illness in extreme old age, he firmly asserted that he would rather die than lose the virginity he had preserved from his childhood, contrary to the advice of his physicians.") The findings of Freud and his school have the most influence in this matter today. But the one-sidedness of this school and

naturalistic determinism can admit the realm neither of freedom nor of morality, much less of sanctity.

In the wake of this biological-psychological sexual theory came a flood of literature that eroded people's minds far and wide with its sticky stuff. One might also include all those novels that treat of celibacy as a mere phenomenon, i.e., simply do not understand its nature.

2. Those who consider women as *the* danger to priests, and women as the instrument of the devil, would point out this as a second form of external threat.

That there are examples which this description fits to the letter no one would deny. But it is incorrect and unjust to form a theory of universal validity out of "cases." In these "cases" you see the defection from a distance, even if they are not as simple as the following examples: Hans Carossa, and one might well believe him, relates in his *Jahr der schönen Täuschungen* a "case": it's the case of Frieda, who is enamored of the curate. He repulses her coldly. So she goes to bed, spits blood, and declares herself to be deathly ill in order to get the priest to call at her home in his official capacity. But he flees from the sacrilegious blasphemer in disgust. No one, however, would think to call that an everyday happening.

It is something that comes just a little bit closer to priestly existence when temptations are considered that can come from the priest's proper work (running organizations, hearing confessions). But he is protected by the seriousness of the situation, by the canonical requirements, and especially by the grace of office.

3. The priestly state cannot permit toying with love, even in its humanly idealistic sense. As harmlessly and affectionately as something like this might start, both can imperceptibly become inflamed with it, according to all psychological laws. And when they do become aware of it, they are

no longer their own masters, until the whole thing ends in a spiritual and moral catastrophe. This has been described with marvelous delicacy in Joseph Weingartner's novel *Castelmorto* (Innsbruck, 1946).

Recently the novel *Goneril* (Vienna, 1947) represented an exceptional case of this type. It relates "the story of an encounter" of a priest who spends the summer in England at a country estate where he falls in love with a young noblewoman, "free of the leaden shackles of sex" (p. 16). Both of them renounce their love with great courage at the end. The motivation is superficial and contestable: "The monk must renounce what for him as an artist is an element of life—beauty" (Introduction, p. 16). The author is Roman K. Scholz, a canon who was condemned as a leader of a resistance movement on May 10, 1944, in Vienna. The surprising thing about this is that a priest should spend the last months of his life in prison where he is faced with death to write down the story of a love that is apparently his own.

The whole thing starts with a polite, sociable familiarity. But Christian is already fundamentally unsure of himself. He recognizes a "prior right of love" (p. 192); he believes in a predetermination of two people for one another "and no one can escape that predetermination" (p. 84). He dallies with his encounter self-complacently as a poet and gives himself to it like a second Goethe: "He knew that his hours with her would one day result in a literary work as tender and lovely as the heroine herself" (p. 115).

A lawn party at Lynton Castle: Christian was present of course. The guests come. Greetings and chatter, thoughtless and unrestrained. "There were innumerable introductions and always the saying of something clever. There were about a hundred and fifty persons invited and they comprised a checkered company—dignified old ladies, slender

entlemen, officers, a whole collection of Anglican clerics
⸱ith their wives, daughters, and fiancées. It was really de-
⸱ghtful, all these brothers in Christ with all their comely
⸱omenfolk. Especially that young fellow there, who looked
⸱o much like him that he might have been a twin. And his
⸱ompanion, a tender blonde and blue beauty, obviously his
⸱ancée. A kind of soft melancholy came over him. He was
⸱ll alone" (p. 140).

It soon appears that he won't be for long. But the both
⸱f them renounce it. "He saw with cruel clarity what his
⸱ituation was. The sweet blindness started to dissolve. He
⸱as one chosen by the Lord and his Lord was a jealous God
⸱ho countenanced no one beside Himself. He sensed the
⸱tigma, the accursed (!) blessing of election and vocation"
⸱p. 192).

One can come upon love in its most attractive form, with-
⸱ut any question of renunciation, and when, to his own mor-
⸱ification, a man is least prepared. But he knows that he
⸱ust keep his word: "Hanna Karcker I saw for the first
⸱ime in the glow of the morning sun. She was coming up
⸱he steps with her brother Peter, whom I knew already. I
⸱ooked at her and in that moment, my breast filled with
⸱varmth. She looked up, Peter said a few words to her and
⸱ could feel the same warmth coming from her eyes. And
⸱t the same time I realized with a start that all that was al-
⸱eady past. I had already been a monk for a year and I
⸱ealized that women would mean nothing to me for the rest
⸱f my life. That sounds improbable, but there are no time
⸱uses on grenades and bombs" (Rudolf Krämer-Badoni
Der arme Reinhold, Hamburg, 1951, p. 111).

b. This would be a proper place to put in a good word
⸱o still all the suspicion and slander of a station that is diffi-
⸱cult, sacrificial, and brave as few are: that of the house-
⸱keepers.

Joseph Bernhart, in his novel *Der Kaplan,* gives a varied and much-documented justification of this position and it hardihood (p. 157) from his own long experience. The type represented by "Miss Theresa" (Federer) and "Hanna" (in Sheehan's *My New Curate,* pp. 11ff.) is by far the most common.

This can really be explained only by "cases." For in stance, there is Rosaline in the rectory of Pastor Camper in Kempenland (Ernest Claes, *Der Pfarrer von Kempen land,* Munich, 1941, pp. 166f.): "In the whole village you could hardly find a more proper person than Rosaline. She was always dressed in black as befitted one who dealt with the clergy. She walked the street with downcast eyes so a not to see anything unworthy such as a male or anything like that; she attended the first Mass every morning, in good weather and bad; she sat right up in the first pew and it was just impossible to expect her to gawk around, even if the saints were to jump down from their pedestals. She be longed to the Sodality and all the other pious organization for women; she cared personally for the altar of our Blessed Mother and that of St. Anthony. In a word, she was a holy soul for whom no one could have a bad word.

"Of course she gossiped now and then a little too eagerly about the doings and the people of the village with Angelica or Finchen Bosmans. And she could speak her mind about everything as well as the next one so that she occasionally forgot the time, and the Pastor would always stare stonily at his soup whenever this happened and his dinner was fifteen minutes late in arriving at the table. But it didn't happen often. And besides, in this way Rosaline got all the news about what was going on in the village and she could tell the pastor a lot of things that he never would have known otherwise.

"The only bad side of Rosaline, if one wanted to take it

at way, was that she more or less considered herself the
astor and therefore easily assumed a tone that many peo-
le couldn't stand. She spoke about things connected with
he parish, the church, and the rectory just as though she
ad a right to be heard. If anyone came to the pastor with
request, then Rosaline knew all about it and had already
iven her own opinion before she got the pastor. It often
appened that she didn't even have to get him, since she
ould take care of the situation herself.

"If someone came in whom she didn't care for, her first
words were, 'Wipe your feet!'; and she just stood there
ntil she was satisfied with the cleanliness of the visitor . . .
he never said *I* nor *The Reverend Pastor*, but always *we*.
And that really meant only *I*. She could put up with every-
hing; nothing was too much for her as long as one was
villing to admit that the rectory—with Rosaline—was the
ead of the community, and as long as they didn't come
n with dirty shoes."

There are many like Rosaline all over, e.g., even in High
Venn, where the villagers nicknamed her "Fritz" (Ludwig
Mathar, *Herr Johannes*, Munich, 1930). For instance, how
loes she receive the students who visit the pastor during
he holidays? "The nearer we got to the rectory with its
lue slate steps, the lower Jerry's former splendid courage
ank. As usual, Snakey rang the bell long and loud. As
isual, 'Fritz' came bounding out. As usual, we pushed serious
Leo through the door as it was torn open, to take the first
ttack. As usual, Snakey forgot to wipe his shoes on the
loor-mat. As usual, Matty knocked over the umbrella stand.
As usual, the 'dragon' only went back to her kitchen a step
it a time, scolding and spitting like a cat" (p. 54). Or,
here's Mrs. Sperber in the rectory at Schrann, overcon-
erned about the health of the old pastor. He feels that this
olicitude for him is degenerating into tyranny. So the pas-

tor, born Count Thalberg, and at one time an energeti
lieutenant in the Hussars, sends her back to her kitchen an
casseroles (Maria Ebner-Eschenbach, *Glaubenslos?*). O
there's "La Pepie," who is able to keep the Pastor Lamott
alive, since he gives everything away, only because she keep
some money hidden under her bed as a final resort. But whe
the wife of the lumberman Bernhard dies, leaving him wit
three small children, he can't find another. So he prays for
miracle. And it happens: La Pepie marries the despairin
widower, and the pastor, who is also almost driven to despai
because of the "miracle," asks God, "What am I suppose
to do—become a saint?" (p. 206).

There's Hanna Holt, who's always concerned about Pas
tor Vogels, with a healthy and natural familiarity and ye
a respectful distance to her master; and with what womanl
silence she takes care of the chores around the rectory
(Anton Coolen, *Brabanter Volk,* Leipzig, 1930). Perpetu
is a different matter: "she had belonged to the rectory o
St. Paul's for years and invariably stayed on with one pasto
after another, for she ruled over these servants of God an
only left them a little authority in the Church." (H. Bor
deaux, *Le Fil de la Vierge*, p. 15).

Of course there are "cases" of housekeepers. Most o
them go about and work more quietly, and many of then
quite unnoticed, in the quiet rectory—much more quietl
than any other woman in a house, and with fewer rights
And they are quite understandably devoted in this position
One Sicilian woman says of herself, and she is a wife: "Wha
is a woman, O Signore? Her foot is so small that she goe
through the world without leaving a trace behind her. T
her husband she is like his shadow. She has accompanie
him throughout the whole of life without his noticing it"
(Selma Lagerlöf, *Die Wunder des Antichrist*, Munich
1905, p. 195). The pastor and the congregation take eve

ess notice of her presence. She knows it and is satisfied and pleasant about it. "The mother of the 'Pastor of Ozeron,' Veronica, effaced herself. It wasn't the submission that the world usually ascribes to the mother of a country pastor, but in the beautiful meaning of the Gospel, where all honor is due the woman who subordinates herself. The Pastor of Ozeron would have been amazed if people who were concerned with etiquette had taken him to task for a lack of attention to his mother, and Veronica herself would have been dismayed if one had made little of her privilege of making herself subordinate" (François Jammes, *Le Curé d'Ozeron*, 1918).

c. The only thing that need really concern us here is not a danger that comes from without for the priest who lives an unmarried life, because it is common to all those who are unmarried. That is easy to overcome: merely by avoiding the occasions and all playing with fire.

We are discussing rather the danger from within that is part of all solitude, in which the two poles of tension in the priest's life are no longer sources of a daily renovation. So it can come about that finally there is at hand a loneliness that cannot be endured, that is a prey for any solution. There is a kind of weariness that the understanding and the conscience can almost no longer perceive. An attack of this loneliness becomes a critical problem for the vocation of Martin Schöpf while he is still in the minor seminary (Joseph Weingartner, *Über die Brücke*, pp. 110, 139). And the fear of it revives as a last temptation immediately before his ordination when he sees the beloved pastor of his home parish die lonely and abandoned. It is this loneliness in the form of emptiness and homesickness that creeps up on Christian and overshadows his priesthood (*Goneril*, p. 74).

The tension which up until now animated the will and work of the priest is no longer felt as necessary and no longer experienced as a grace. He feels as though God has abandoned him, as though he is repulsed by life. It is as though the rope of tension were broken. The tension that was the "both-and" of his power becomes an "either-or." But it is one of escape from both, born of weariness and depression. And it is escape from God, too, at least for a time. But it often lasts for days. Whither can he flee?

It is part of the nature of the priestly state that he is not only deprived sacramentally of any refuge by the indelible seal of his ordination, but he cannot even escape within the community of the faithful. This fact aggravates and deepens the crisis. And this may even become a wound that cannot be healed. But it often ends in a temptation to solve it by compromising. Within his own community and state in life there are forms of existence which contradict the seriousness and depth of this vocation. But to a sort of popular under-standing and to those who are worn out with the fighting these forms do seem to be ways out. Nevertheless, in them the priest takes leave of the everlasting youth which is his portion: "*ad Deum, qui laetificat juventutem meam.*" In the last chapter, we shall discuss these "avenues of escape."

It is obvious that no priest can endure this loneliness who has been forced into the sanctuary without a vocation (Mar-riot, *Der geistliche Tod,* p. 37). But, as we have heard above, it can be endured even by saints only with difficulty when it lasts for a long time. It becomes a danger for celibacy and therefore for the priesthood when "encounters" take place in this emptiness. Father Roman, who is staying in the parish to help out, puts the question to the curate with-out any ceremony: "He asked me what my attitude toward women was; and when I didn't say anything in my embar-rassment, he told me right out that this was the hardest thing that the priest—I as well as any other and including himself—had to deal with" (Bernhart, *Der Kaplan,* p. 108).

d. Let us call to mind the theological basis of celibacy. This shows us the cause of the crisis and the way out of it, the only right way that there is in the objective order.

The reasons for not marrying, as they are found in the Bible, are in themselves formal-psychological; only the source makes them theological as well. One saying comes from our Lord Himself. He said this in connection with a discussion with the Pharisees about the indissolubility of marriage. It seems to have been something new even to the disciples. You can almost see—many of them were married, of course—how they scratched behind their ears and admitted, "If the case of a man with his wife is so, it is not expedient to marry" (Mt. 19: 10). That provides our Lord with an occasion to give his Apostles a decisive word about this: ". . . and there are eunuchs who have made themselves so for the sake of the kingdom of Heaven. Let him accept it who can." ("For the sake of the kingdom of heaven" does not have the meaning here that one sometimes hears, "in order to get to heaven more easily," but rather for the sake of the work in the service of the kingdom of God.)

These words and those of St. Paul on "undivided service" in the kingdom of God belong together: "He who is unmarried is concerned about the things of the Lord, how he may please God. Whereas he who is married is concerned about the things of the world, how he may please his wife, and he is divided" (1 Cor. 7: 32).

Eros, fervent love, this most strong creative love of a man that is ready for any sacrifice is usually devoted to a woman and a family. This fervent love consecrates him "who can accept it" for the kingdom of God, fully and undividedly; it becomes the real power behind his work. It also quite fills up his heart. The command of God, "Increase and multiply and fill the earth" (Gen 1: 28), according to St. Thomas, may be understood and verified not only with reference to the body (*Summa Theol.* 2, 2, 152); for man is not only a creature composed of a body. All other "increase" of man, in cultural, moral, and religious spheres, fulfills this first commandment of God in time and fulfills it on a higher level than the purely biological.

The ability to devote oneself absolutely, that is, free of all earthbound restrictions, to the kingdom of God, is the reason for celibacy. As long as the willingness to devote himself entirely is present and spends itself in the spreading of the kingdom of God, it in turn so fills up the heart of the priest that celibacy cannot become a problem, aside from the weariness and moments of unrest which everyone occasionally experiences.

4. THE DECISION

The crisis is oriented toward the four typical directions described below, although they are a bit forced, as are all typologies.

1. The crisis is a passing stage leading to a priestly youth that is regained and deepened; or

2. It is resolved into forms of life in which "one can live." By this we mean attempts to smooth out the tension of priestly life without betraying the priesthood canonically and socially. We shall see the priestly figures which result from this decision later.

3. The crisis results in a certain stiffness and emptiness. The fight didn't actually end in compromise. It has been left in a state of indecision. The power of the man's love is neither pledged to the kingdom of God nor given to a

woman. We shall treat this case, at least partially, in the last section.

Since that is the case, it would be well to give a brief description of this type here. Karl Rahner, in the collection *Zeugen des Wortes*, wrote a foreword for one of the issues, *Kirchenväter an Laien* (Freiburg i. B., 1939). There he interprets Clement of Alexandria (died before 215): "Even the exterior suffering of martyrdom is not of itself a sign of perfection for Clement. He also realizes that celibacy can lead to a spiritual aridity. Unless he is guided by a holy intention, the unmarried man can sink into the mass of mankind and be bereft of all love." That is what we mean by this third case. It results in an atrophy of the power of loving at all. The consequence is a misanthrope, an embittered spirit, the man with no social capabilities or understanding, reacting against common life and all common work. The inability to lead a common life usually has its origin here. Or there is a naive egoism, a certain oddness. He's an odd fish with the vices that are senseless precisely for celibates, e.g., avarice. Everyone wonders, "For whom is he saving?" He himself doesn't know.

4. In very few of these cases will it be a crisis in which priestly existence in general is faced with a "to be or not to be" decision. The final struggle which now ensues is a burden whose gravity too few realize, and that is because of the peculiar nature of the priestly vocation. And yet it is precisely the reason why the "either-or" of the crisis ends in a reversal that so shocks those outside, leading either to an unpriestly life or even to loss of faith.

Every Christian in the world, regardless of his position or education, can at some time arrive at a point where his faith is severely tested or his moral life badly shaken, and it is his duty to straighten them out. But as long as it may last, he can still fulfill the duties of his vocation conscientiously and without additional difficulty. It may even be that during this time he does his job with even more exactness, merely in order to preserve his peace of conscience in this roundabout way. This conscientiousness can last for a time, or, what is even worse, can continue to be an alibi against the reproaches of conscience, which foretell even more anxieties. At any rate, the layman can allow himself time without fearing an increase of his depression.

With the priest it is different. He too can get into difficulties, religious and moral. But he has a vocation which daily plunges him into more and more unbearable situations when he is in this condition. He must celebrate Mass daily; he gives sermons, religious instruction, hears confessions, dispenses the sacraments, converses with the faithful on religious problems, reads his Breviary . . . All of these are a source of faith and grace. The effectiveness of the reception of the sacraments is guaranteed for the one who receives them (*ex opere operato*).

But what of the man who administers them in this condition! "Behold, whether there are great clouds of mist on the brow of the mountain or gigantic, mountainous waves on the ocean, or blinding sandstorms in the desert, when it is a matter of a critical point at which no one can make a decision, *no choice should be made; nothing should change during such a crisis*. And you should know that at a time like this, no one can force individual ideas or religious customs upon himself. One needs to turn tranquilly to other things, to keep an indeterminate, universal attitude of resignation— to be very humble with oneself and others; so the crisis passes and, indeed, fruitfully." That is the wonderful advice that Baron Hügel gave his niece (von Hügel, *Letters to a Niece*, Chicago, 1955). Splendid advice! But in the dark hours we are describing, what should the poor priest do with it? It is clear that the layman and the priest at such times are in an essentially different situation.

The priest, too, must have time. He must get away from his problem so as to straighten himself out. Otherwise his condition will become unbearable, or, what is worse, sacrilegious, and the danger of further obscurity or even of obduracy is present.

The priest would have to be given a vacation. The case is a rare one, of course, but he must be allowed to rest. The friends of the priest and his confessor would naturally have the right to suggest such a thing to the bishop (obviously without giving any reasons).

There is a darkness and an anxiety in this darkness which immediately precedes that darkness which knows no more anxiety. It cannot be allowed to go that far, and simply because of the fact that it seems as though in this condition the protecting spirit has abandoned the man.

There is a remoteness and a flight from God that is so great that every religious job becomes untrue and ghostly. *Heilige Maskerade* is what the novel of Olov Hartman is called, which tells of an evangelical minister who is unsure of his faith (Frankfurt a. M., 1950). He needs to consider things in absolute silence. And he must have time, a time that stands so still that it might be eternity itself. It must be such a stillness that, because of it, suddenly nothing seems more reasonable than a pure turning to God. Perhaps in the beginning that can only be a quiet turning of the head and a look which at first resists the Eye of God. The priest who would lose his faith loses not only the possibility of praying the Credo. At this moment, the meaning of life and the ground beneath his feet are pulled out from under him.

Religious "duties" can have become so unbearable because there is no foundation there to bear them up. Then a start must be made from the ground up.

There must be another encounter with God as there was on the first day, an encounter in which *you* experience GOD as the only thing that is and the thing that is most important.

For this, a man, a priest, needs time and quiet—and the prayers of his brothers.

BOOK TWO

Modes of Priestly Existence

A TYPOLOGY OF THE FORMS

At the beginning of this investigation we refused to propose a typology of the structural entities of the priesthood with the help of any characterology. A cross-section of the forms at hand and their groupings according to established forms of life do lead to an image that is not without use and therefore could certainly serve as the basis for an examination of conscience. But the categories of the priestly vocation are so peculiarly its own that it would be impossible to completely restrict all of the forms in which they are verified by linking them to one of the usual typologies.

That is why we have tried to show first just what priestly existence is in general and have followed its development in a longitudinal direction, beginning with the vocation and its religious and theological foundations, through the individual attempts to deal with the tensions which determine priestly existence, until that moment when we arrive at a preliminary or permanent integration of the psychological attempts to master it—the modes of priestly life. These are essentially the same, but accidentally quite varied. They are so varied that any attempt to form a typology which pretends to be only empirical and true only of priests can scarcely avoid the danger of being incomplete and one-sided. The borders between the individual final types are at any rate quite fluid. In real life there are both exaggerated and characterless modes of priestly existence. A typology, measuring it by the universal applicability of its norms, is arbitrary and contestable; compared with the convincing concreteness of the individual phenomenon, it is heavy-handed and forced. But we have no other way.

At the beginning of the ensuing typology we have placed the two extremes. They are: the integration of the priestly ideal, i.e., the saintly priest, and its opposite, the case of the fallen priest, one who has abandoned priestly existence. And we've done this in the inverted order.

We remark immediately that both of these extremes, in comparison with the other settled forms, are rare exceptions.

V. EXTREME CASES

1. ESCAPE FROM THE PRIESTHOOD

Canon Law speaks of only two kinds of apostasy: a defection from the Faith and an *apostasia a religione*, that is, a defection from a religious congregation. It does not mention *apostasia ab ordine*, abandonment of the priesthood. But there is such a thing in reality and the Law concerns itself with the canonical consequences of such an abandonment.

Naive Escape

These cases can again be subdivided: we mention first those flights which—from the viewpoint of those who have fallen—are nothing but an escape from priestly existence. It is a naive escape: naive because no one can escape from the ranks of those who have received the indelible character of the priesthood with their ordination. They still belong especially and eternally to God. Canon Law does not take cognizance of this flight, and the Christian community patiently expects that the fugitive will return. Besides, his ordination and years of priesthood have such a determining effect on the psychological life and face of the man that people can see the priest in him as long as he lives. He has that well-known *"oremus* face" the boys in Weingartner's novel *Über die Brücke* make fun of (p. 7).

The flight is also naive because of the fact that those who do flee, whom we are here discussing, do so without the intention of coming into conflict with the Church because of it. They want to abandon their state, but remain at peace with the Church. This is indicated by the request for reduction to the lay state. But that is sacramentally impossible, and it is not provided for canonically when the one in question has received his ordination validly (Can. 211). Exceptions can be made for very serious reasons of the common or private good (Can. 211, 1) either through a rescript of the Apostolic See issued by the Holy Office, the Congregation of the Sacraments, or the Congregation of the Council (Can. 249, 3). Or the priest can be reduced to the lay state by an administrative decree, or, depending on the circumstances, if a legal process has preceded, through a judicial decree. In this case, proof must be adduced to show that the priest was induced by grave fear, unduly and unjustly caused by another (Can. 114, 1). That is the legal status.

The exceptions that we have mentioned take time, however. The decision may take years, sometimes even decades. The consequence of this is that the priest who wanted nothing more than to remain at peace with the Church when he left the priesthood becomes bitter toward her and as a result of that, he might even wind up in real unbelief (according to the laws of transfer of emotions). Another cause is the fact that exclusion from the reception of the sacraments is included in his own freely chosen position.

This flight for many is simply nothing but an escape from the tension that is part of priestly existence. Auke is an out-and-out extravagant idealist. His friend wants to calm him

down. He ought to give up his exaggerated demands on himself. "In my opinion we could be satisfied if Christians did
not refuse to continue to live as Christians in this life of
sorrow . . . we could be content with the fact that men
at least acknowledge Christian teaching" (Ouwendijk, *Das
geschändete Antlitz,* p. 221). But to this Auke replies bitterly, "As though Christ had not bequeathed to us His blood,
His hunger, and His abandonment, along with His teaching"
(p. 222). Later he realizes that it was only his own stubbornness that led him to suppose that he had been called to
protect the face of Christ from desecration. (He had an old
woodcarving of Christ and across the face of it there was a
crack.) "I had imagined that it was my duty and mine alone,
as it were, to close up this split, to repair this desecration . . . As though the desecration of God's face did not go
so deeply that only the suffering of all mankind would be
in a position to make up for it . . . we can only strive for
that with an infinitely humble and charitable patience" (p.
227). But he did not endure the tension between duty and
impossibility. And he deserted. "No, I must first try to regain my peace. Perhaps then I can . . ." (p. 227). He does
not consider himself as a fallen priest. "Don't believe," he
says to his brother, "that I'm a fallen-away priest, as they
are all saying" (p. 221).

The first question asked when a priest deserts is: *"Où est
la femme?"* The pastor in Auke's home parish thought that
this was obvious, too, but it had nothing to do with his case.
He defends celibacy (p. 225) and is so unsuspecting of the
condemnation of others that he hires a girl who had been
seduced and was expecting a child, supporting her as his
housekeeper until her time came.

Here we have an escape from the priesthood that takes
the form of a flight from the distress experienced at not
being able to realize an ideal. He refuses to acknowledge

or accept the advice that friends give him, to take it a little easier. He wants peace and yet he considers himself as a renegade (p. 269).

It is important to study this case and not consider it as impossible, although it is rare.

The more frequent case is the one mentioned above, in which the question that is usually asked is justified, even if the particular one involved at first rejects it as unwarranted or premature.

But even then the woman in the case does not at first appear to be the woman who seduced the priest from his state. As we have tried to show above, the priest is only vulnerable to this temptation when he is no longer fulfilling his vocation, or when he finds himself empty-hearted because of the tension between the demands of God and his own poor humanity. And naturally speaking, only a woman can fill that emptiness.

A Sense of Mission and Escape: The Role of Women

There is another case in which it is his very activity, particularly when he is engaged in it because of a special sense of mission, that can bring the priest into conflict with the Church. This can force him into hopeless loneliness. And into that loneliness steps a woman as the consoler of the idealist.

Here belongs the life of Joseph Wittig. He was one who preached a newly awakened, genuine, untroubled, childlike Christianity. At a time when the young had devoted themselves to the search for a real, healthy life and Faith, they looked upon him as a herald. "O my beloved, healthy, pristine, wild, yet holy faith, that bore me up when the pastor's lame white horse had brought me home from my baptism, thou that didst grow in the poor little cottage my grandfather had built of branches from the nearby trees, thou, my playmate, who first explained and charted the starry heavens and the world of flowers, thou, my guardian angel in the dangers of the world, my light in study and research, the divine power in my striving and work, would that I could preach thee to the world as thou art!" (Joseph Wittig, *Herrgottswissen von Wegrain und Strasse*, Freiburg i. B., 1922, p. 227). And how he could preach that Faith!

But he was at one and the same time a poet and a theologian—a dangerous combination, because one often had to wonder whether it was the poet or the theologian who was responsible for many of his daring ideas. In dealing with the cooperation of God in our actions and especially in matters regarding the conclusions he drew from this doctrine for his ministry and educational work, he got into difficulties with his superiors. Finally, five of his publications are put on the *Index of Forbidden Books* (July 29, 1925). Would he submit? He lived in the belief that it was his duty to preach a consolation of the Gospel that was being neglected in his day. So he did not submit. "I believe that neither fire nor water nor Canon 2314 can separate me from the Love of Christ." That was the answer he gave on May 31, 1926.

His appeal to St. Paul (Rom. 8: 35 ff.) was daring. Canon 2314 pronounces an excommunication on heretics who will not submit. Wittig retired angrily to the house he had just built at Neusorge. He was so rooted and at home in the Catholic Faith that he could only live in it and from it. Now he was excommunicated, excluded from the communion of the Church. The terrible loneliness of an outcast surrounded him. Then the woman he later married appeared. There was a civil ceremony in Breslau on June 22, 1927. It was the twenty-fourth anniversary of his First Mass!

But he still protested that he was not a fallen-away priest. He wanted to remain a Catholic. It was only the "Roman Authorities" that had condemned him. But soon he noticed that more than that had happened. An account of his life, contestable in many details, was written by the aging Wittig before his death under the puzzling title *Roman mit Gott*—God is a poor figure for a romantic novel. He admits what he had confessed before, a thing that his readers noticed with sorrow: "For many decades I had the reputation of being a very active and capable writer about God. The thoughts came to me on wings and they were prettily formed and adorned." And after his excommunication: "For many long months, for an entire year, I could no longer write a single religious story or sketch, and I couldn't even write an ordinary letter for about six months."

On March 9, 1946, in the midst of the storm of the expulsion of Germans from their East German homeland, he received the report that he had been received back into the Church. What great longing, twenty years of long suppressed loneliness, is found in the confession that now follows: "Jesus Christ in the form of Bread and Wine entered our house, the Host, a little piece of bread as thin as a breath, of which I have known and said from my childhood, 'That is our dear Savior, our Lord and our God!' It might be blown away by the wind, so weak and powerless is it, and yet our Lord and our God! The God, Who has given joy to my youth."

According to all appearances, as he himself heard, "he had been reported to Rome as a dying man to whom the communion of the Church should no longer be refused."

The Apostate

Now we will discuss those who form a very small group, considering the long history of the Church. These are the ones who can be characterized as true apostates from the priesthood.

They, too, begin as idealists, as fighters for the Church, in which they either find their ideal already incorporated or find themselves at least at home in it. It is not just chance that the examples we can cite are all those of great minds. Perhaps the reason is that only these are recorded in history. We can suppose that there are others unknown who belong or might belong in this group.

Almost all of them were not only at first great confessors, but also great leaders. This fact already indicates the power of their spirit and fervor, with which they give us an idea of their own interests and those of their age.

The danger lay in their genius. Genius is greatness, but it is seldom that it is not one-sided. This one-sidedness, which blinded and rushed them on, and therefore communicated their conviction to others, was their threat; their temptation is a choice of great success or of failure.

Belief in his own ideas may raise a man's self-confidence to a sense of mission that tolerates no opposition, least of all on the part of the Church, which he wants to serve and believes he does serve. Opposition then forces upon him the crisis when he must decide for the subjective conviction which possesses him, not to say obsesses him, or for the cool, long-considered calm of the judgment of his Church. The heightened stillness of this critical hour is not only complicated by the pressure of his own dynamic conviction, by rebellion against a check or retreat, but also by the noisy appeal of his following. It is part of the tragedy of these spirits that they have raised up waves like a storm, only to be unforeseeably borne away on them themselves, so that in the critical moment of the affair they no longer have the control of things in their hands. Only very cool heads retain their self-possession. Ignatius Döllinger, if indeed we should mention him at all in this connection, says in sober fashion of himself: "I have had only one sleepless night in my life; and that was when I was examining my conscience with regard to the dogma of infallibility."

With regard to our theme here, the same element that can prepare success can also ready ruin. Of course, it was success that was had by those we have already mentioned, a passing success. It only takes a few decades to show it to be sheer error. And those who fail, know that even in their own lifetime, most of them very soon. But most of them do not see where they went off the track; they see only the disfavor which is shown them. Usually these men are not stars of the first magnitude. They, too, thought mistakenly that they were serving the Church and believed that they were at one with her interests. Their failure embitters them. And this embitterment is then directed against the Church for not covering their zealous sally. They feel that they have been misunderstood, abandoned, betrayed. And in the hour of temptation, they fall away. The field of tension of their priesthood narrows itself down to a decision between the Faith in which they have been baptized and ordained and their own faith in themselves and its subjective evidence. The tragedy is that for the most part it is a question of men who deal only in logic, for whom a rational explanation is the only way of solving every problem. They face the decision, divided by faith and human insight. And they don't see it. In the case of the emotional type, they succumb to the love or the hatred that is governing them.

The ultimate secret of this hour in which the powers of darkness get the upper hand are, of course, impossible for the outsider to discover. The priests in this case are different from the ones mentioned earlier because they consciously renounce the priesthood, the Church, and often the Christian Faith itself. That is why it is not just to mention Döllinger in this context. He always considered himself a Catholic, despite the protests of his Church, and he respected the excommunication. He was Catholic and historian enough to keep away from founding any new churches. The old theologian was often seen kneeling in Our Lady's Cathedral, his face hidden in his hands.

But there is one thing that would characterize all those who would be mentioned here: they are always stamped with the priesthood, in their faces, their words, and their minds. They continue to lead a celibate life. They remain ascetics, and are kind to the poor. They are selfless. Their way goes on exactly as before, but in the opposite direction. Their certainty and peace seem to be imperturbable. "The state of infernal grace" is what Emile Baumann calls it (*Exkommunizierte*, p. 80).

Take the case of Félicité Lamennais (1782–1854). Like Chateaubriand, he came from Saint-Malo in Brittany, a country whose native language uses the same word for "religion" and "law." This was a determining factor for him. His influence was tremendous and long felt. There are no important theologians, philosophers, sociologists, or politicians of the previous century who did not align themselves either for or against him. His was a precocious genius; at the age of ten he had read Rousseau and the Encyclopedists; at 16 he was an atheist. He was converted by his pious brother Jean Marie, whose process for beatification is in progress. Then at 22 he received his First Holy Communion. At 34 he was ordained to the priesthood. His first work was a fervent interpretation of the *Following of Christ* for his times. Then he dealt a death blow to Gallicanism (*La tradition de l'Eglise*, 1810), attempted to show that authority was the supreme principle of order (*Essai sur l'indifférence en matière de la religion*, 1818), and soon identified it with a universal human reason (*raison générale*). Revolution as a by-word and the anarchical tendencies of the time were passé. But their effects were felt all over Europe. Within ten years there were eight editions in France, and three translations in Germany alone. Only the Church, with its world-girdling power independent of the State, can fashion the world kingdom of reason and love of the neighbor. That was his gospel. Napoleon had the book mangled for pulp. The grand dream of a world empire with the papacy as the only power equal to the infernal outbreak of those who deny and destroy was not peculiar to Lamennais alone.

The followers of the Enlightenment and Gallicanism attacked him wrathfully and the Royalists enthusiastically misunderstood him. Theologians and philosophers all over Europe reviewed their own theories and agreed with him. He was hailed as a "new Bossuet," as the "last father of the Church" (Leo XII), and the Cardinal's hat was bestowed upon him.

But he saw the revolution coming (*De la révolution*, 1826) and sought to anticipate its annihilating blow at the Church and religion by demanding the separation of Church and State, freedom of the press, freedom of thought, and the removal of the school system from the control of the State —universities included (*De progrès de la révolution*, 1829). The faithful alone should be the mainstay of the Church in this world. He cried out to the prelates, who were disturbed at this change: "Remember that nothing lasts on this earth. If your religion does not progress with mankind, if it does not keep time with the beat of men's hearts, then it must fall behind and be lost. You have ruled over kings—now stretch out your hand to the people; they will support you with their strong arms, and what is more, with their love." What did he want? "We hope to smash the rule of force to the ground and replace it by a kingdom of justice and charity, a kingdom that will produce a unity between all the members of the great human family, in which each one will be a member of the whole and have a share in the common good."

Suddenly the World Church no longer appeared as a distant goal; it was understood as a means of bringing about a World Brotherhood. For this program he founded the first Catholic newspaper, *L'Avenir* (*The Future*) in 1830. All the great and living spirits, not only of France, but also in all Catholic Europe, declared themselves for him. But he did not see what undesirable companions-in-arms they were, even among the liberal enemies of the Church, who were joining him. The ideas of *L'Avenir* became part of the political struggles of the day.

But in that moment when his words were felt throughout the whole continent, there came a rebuff, and it came from a quarter from which he never would have expected it. Pope Gregory XVI rejected the program of *L'Avenir* in the Encyclical *Mirari vos* of August 15, 1832.

This position of the Pope did not take Lamennais entirely unaware. He was conscious of the mistrust his stormy progress had awakened. He had wanted to represent his position personally in Rome the year before, in the company of Montalembert and Lacordaire, but the Pope—then Gregory XVI—did not receive him. That was hard to take. That was the moment of decision for the priest Lamennais, and, as we shall see, for the Christian also. After prolonged struggles, he first signed the retraction required of him "to give his troubled mind peace" and retired to La Chênaie, his family estate, where he had eight years before developed his ideas in the company of his friends. La Chênaie was also the center of the "Congregation of St. Peter." His friends hoped that the fiery spirit had returned to its starting point.

The Church has never made it easy for her fiercest defenders. She represents all that is eternal, lasting, permanent. Her view looks back over centuries, and mistrusts all who think that they have the key to all the puzzles in their puny hands. She is too old and too experienced to charge ahead with every innovator. It is possible that she will later admit that he was right. Regarding the whole situation in the light of today, there are many aspects that we might regret about the way this case was handled. But what would it have meant for the Church at that time if she had endorsed the position taken by *L'Avenir*? (We ignore the fact that she could not have approved of many of his individual political demands.) Revolution! And that on the side of the innovator—open and political? Christianity admits only an inner revolution of the spirit.

But it is precisely this attitude that the prophets and standard-bearers cannot understand. They cannot see that their fervor, their obsession, their influence is a consequence of their one-sidedness. Lamennais' great dream, a great World Brotherhood under the leadership of the Church, seemed to him so close and so feasible. At first he thought he could realize his program with the aid of the legitimate rulers and that of the Church; the former had soon given him the cold shoulder. Therefore he had appealed to the people. And now did the Church also desert him? He was faced with a decision; as a priest he had to choose: shall

I follow the Church or will the Church follow me? His friends trembled for him, and not without reason. At his home he had once dreamed of a world order that had become a religion to him. It wasn't so much his Catholic Faith, which was certainly there, but it was rather the World State which was his dream, and he thought of himself as its herald. He was descended from that Celtic peninsula of France that had but one word for "religion" and "law."

Two years after the condemnation of *L'Avenir* his little book *Paroles d'un Croyant* appeared (1834). Words of a believer—in what? It had nothing to do with what one could call the Catholic Faith. Lamennais projected a prophetic picture of an ideal humanity; it was poetry and vision, with a power of imagery that was schooled in the language of the Psalms and prophets. There were ideal communities of work and noble exchange, in the spirit of a Christianity freed of the Church. "All the restrained passion, all the disciplined fervor, all the tenderness and piety that lived in his soul rushed intoxicatingly to his head and breathed forth in a splendid vision—a very witches' Sabbath of hate and love" (Renan). His hatred was the love of yesterday: for the kings and the Church; and his love—it was for the people. The misanthropic seer had scarcely ever closed ranks with the people before; his love for them was for the idea of the people as he understood it. In exactly the same way, in his later life, his hatred for prince and pope was aimed at a phantom from his past.

The appearance of the book was a psychological earthquake. Three editions appeared in France within the first three months, and about forty refutations struck back in frenzy. The excitement spread into the neighboring countries like a spring flood: there were eight editions in Belgium, seven in Switzerland, and ten translations, five of them in German. The most famous of these was the work of the congenial Ludwig Börne, who had sought out the fascinating Abbé some time before in Paris. At the instance of Metternich, the *Paroles* was forbidden in all the states. It also appeared on the *Index of Forbidden Books* in the same year it was first published, just as did the most of his later works.

Gradually the impetus of his intellectual drive waned. The ideals of his last twenty years were democracy and a "religion" of humanism and a Christianity identified with it. His social aims fit those of Saint-Simon and the "Phalanxes" of Fourier to a T, but he wanted to have nothing to do with them. He retired to an attic room and gave away everything he had to give away, so that he could live as the poorest of the poor, to whom the abstract love of neighbor in his books was directed.

The prayers and love of his saintly brother Jean Marie as well as those of his friends of yesterday, who continued to love him though they had all submitted to the Church, could not win the embittered man back to the Church. Not even the attempt of Pius IX was of any use, so deeply had the blow of 1832 wounded him. This man, who had been an eloquent opponent of religious indifferentism, a fearless proponent of papal authority, and of the Faith over reason, and all that in a critical hour in the history of the world, died in open hostility to the Church and the power of the State on February 27, 1854. Under police protection and through a lane of troops on guard, his body was taken to Père La Chaise. A few friends followed the casket, among them Béranger, Barbet, and Pagès. He had expressly forbidden that a cross be placed above his grave, so that it was soon forgotten and is still forgotten. "Believe or die," the young Lamennais had bidden the skeptic world of his day. He could not then suspect that he would himself choose the "die" of this either-or challenge.

The "Excommunicate" of Emile Baumann also came
from the corner of France that remained most faithful to
the Church when the great Revolution raged through the
land. "In the veins of this Breton there flowed that poison
of anarchy that plunged the Abbé Lamennais into ruin"
(p. 41).

Nor was it a woman that brought about his downfall.
He was a "fanatic of justification"; and when he did not
win the Church over to his way of thinking, he broke with
her, senselessly. His was "a false idea of justification, a
chimera, grown mightier than the certitude of experience,
mightier than his obedience to the hierarchy, and the teach-
ings of the Faith" (p. 28). "The people-god was his only
god. He had sacrificed his priestly duty and social position
to it" (p. 41). He hoped for a future in which "universal
reason would guide the egoism of the individual. Ultimately,
mankind would have to redeem itself" (p. 69).

He came to grief both as a priest and as a man because
of this ideal. Embittered, he retired under the name of Deforis to the cliffs of Clapade and, enamored of his desperate
situation, lived in seclusion as a hermit, with a strictness
that reminds one of the fathers of the desert. There he lived,
his only satisfaction being the fact that he had gone completely astray in his error and had burned all his bridges
behind him, so that he could no longer abandon his evil
ways (p. 23). "No one can force me to serve," he said;
"I am free at least to refuse . . . or if it pleases me, to be
damned, and God cannot prevent it" (p 25). His answer
to his failure is hatred for society, and he wants to be lost
because of that. "Society shall inherit my misery, the despicable world of riches. You must understand, now, that
my greatness consists in my dying abandoned" (p. 40). He
does not want to create the impression that he can be weak-
ened in his stubbornness (p. 85).

Here, too, it becomes clear how plainly even this en lightened apostate is marked by his clerical training: wom anless solitude, asceticism. He lives as a *nycticorax in dom icilio* (Ps. 101: 7), no better than an owl in a ruine building, as he himself quotes. His is an absolute devotion to the opposite of his former way of life. He wants to concea his education. But the way he does it betrays him. "A ru ined chapel—one that seemed to me the image of my sou —though it be robbed of its altar and its windows, it car never conceal the lines of a temple, its lines reaching fo the lost tabernacle; and the holy consecration can neve leave its stones" (p. 26).

Did he die in his stubbornness, in his beggar's pride, and in his cruel misery? A single word gives us the hope that the Angel of God took his hand at the last second. Wher Baumann assures him of his prayers a few hours before his death, he says "Thank you—keep on praying" (p. 91).

Instances of real apostates are rare. It isn't easy to find one like the singular case of the former Abbé Lamennais and it is seldom that one hears of such as the excommunicate o Emile Baumann. The insignificant cases attract little atten tion and the outward indications are something like this: they too frequently begin with a quarrel with (ecclesiastical) superiors. The consequences are dissatisfaction with them selves and their fellow priests, who won't go along with their contumacy. Then follows a certain delight in criticizing clerical practices and ecclesiastical decisions, all in a spirit of selfish, narrow self-justification. There is no longer any joy in their vocation, in friendship with other priests; they prefer association with laymen of an unecclesiastical turn of mind.

The cases of doubters, who are mentally and spiritually disquieted, are similar to this in psychological makeup. So, too, are those rugged individualists and semi-sectarians.

ometimes that is the only way of understanding them.
Iany a man has brooded himself into a corner so that he
imself no longer knows how to get out of it. Then it is that
eaving the priesthood is, for the moment, seen to be a way
f rescuing himself from an intolerable position.

But they have all celebrated the Mass for the last time
—a half-hour full of dreadful mysteries.

scape and Celibacy

'hose who have left the priesthood frequently consider, ap-
arently to their own self-justification, that they have acted
ore decently than those who are just as spiritually adrift
s they, yet remain in the priesthood. It is not difficult to
elieve that something like this can happen, but it is con-
iderably more difficult to prove. But to suppose that these
xistences are frequent just does not follow. Even examples
ke pastor Andra of Welden, whose perverse doings Lud-
rig Ganghofer complacently expands in the recollections
f his youth, are singular (*Lebenslauf eines Optimisten*,
tuttgart). It is regrettable that Ganghofer did not know
aat even such rare scandals can lead people to consider
nem typical of all priests when their doings are reported
o circumstantially, and in book form.

What could persuade a priest today to continue wearing
riestly garb, without leading the life of a priest, or even
rithout faith? Does he want to prevent public scandal?
)oes he still have a mother whom he wants to spare the
hame of having a son who is a "run-away priest," or even
n apostate? Or do his position in life and the worry that
e couldn't get another job keep him back? His position in
fe? There isn't an unlettered workman who would take a
ob for twice the priest's salary, and the priest has twelve

and thirteen years of academic education to fall back on

All of these questions are hard to answer affirmatively

History itself shows, of course, that the fight about celibacy that is really observed didn't stop with the passage of the seventh canon of the Second Lateran Council (1139). The trouble lay for the most part with the ecclesiastically unreliable hierarchy in the individual countries of Europe. So it came about that, in individual countries, and often for a long time, the seventh canon of Lateran II was treated as though it didn't exist, and no secret was made of that fact. For the Christian North of Europe the married pastor was no innovation of the Reformation. Even in Lüttich the heads of the monastery were still celebrating marriages publicly in 1220. The Synod of Bremen (1266) sharply condemned the Bishops' dispensation from the prohibition of marriage, threatened them with excommunication, and punished married pastors with the loss of their benefice. But it was still up to the Bishops to see to the enforcement of these resolutions. And they refused, even though they did not all reason as frivolously as the man that Emperor Fredrich II installed as Patriarch of Aquileia, Gregory of Montelongo (1251-69). According to ancient custom, he also chose a motto at the beginning of his reign and had it set in his coat of arms. He said: *"Si non caste tamen caute"* (If you can't be good, be careful)!

It is well known how soon before the ecclesiastical revolution of the sixteenth century priestly celibacy was forgotten. Secular priests in many places were married, and that with all due form and publicity. Even among the clerics belonging to Orders it was no different. The dossier of visitation for the year 1563 reports that in the well known monasteries of lower Austria a large number of the monks were living "married lives." This situation was thoroughly rectified only by the Council of Trent (session XXIV). This council passed not only a newly enjoined condemnation of marriage for priests and defended its canonicity, but what was more important for putting it into effect, proclaimed requirements for the preparation and education of the clergy, and the priestly way of life, and especially made laws controlling the selection and installation of the Bishops.

But there were still reactions. When St. Clement Mary Hofbauer came to Poland, he found that a great number of the priests were married (Hofer, *St. C. M. Hofbauer*). Willa Cather (1875-1947) isn't merely being fanciful at all in her novel *Death Comes for the Archbishop* when she treats the state of the Church at the time of the incorporation of New Mexico into the United States (1846). She relates that the new Bishop Latour was most solemnly received by a cavalcade of riders, with their pastor Padre Martinez at their head dressed in leather chaps and a broad Mexican sombrero, with much cheering and shooting of rifles. There was only one small incident. Despite all the planning, one little ragamuffin is still standing on the plaza with his mouth open and his hat still on his head. Then Padre Martinez knocks the hat off his head and gives him a sound box on the ears. When the considerate Bishop turns to the pastor and protests softly, this worthy replies in a loud, bold voice: "That's my own son, Bishop. It's about time I taught him some manners." This priest was living in open concubinage. He had also succeeded in becoming the richest farmer in the whole parish, through unscrupulous means. Not only had he patched together a sort of theory for his way of life, but also thought that he could cite passages from St. Augustine to prove his point. The same pastor, with the shoulders of a buffalo, long black hair, fat-jowled, and a mouth full of "unbridled passions and tyrannical self-will," makes the Bishop's hair stand on end, though he is outwardly composed. After dinner he says,

"Celibate priests lose their perceptions. No priest can experience repentance and forgiveness of sin unless he himself falls into sin. Since concupiscence is the most common form of temptation, it is better for him to know something about it . . . the soul must be broken by mortal sin to experience the forgiveness of sin and rise to a state of grace." When Bishop Latour replies that he is determined to put the laws of the Church into effect in the shortest possible time, the Mexican tells him: "It will keep you busy, Bishop. Nature has the start of you here. But for all that, our native priests are more devout than your French Jesuits. We have a living Church here, not a dead arm of the European Church. Our religion grew out of the soil and has its own roots. We pay a filial respect to the person of the Holy Father, but Rome has no authority here. Our people are the most devout left in the world. If you blast their religion with European formalities, they will become infidels and profligates . . . If you try to introduce European civilization here and change our old ways, to interfere with the secret dances of the Indians, let us say, or abolish the bloody rites of the Penitentes, I foretell an early death for you."

That is Padre Martinez. But he did penance for whatever sins he had committed during the year on the same day that our Lord hung on the cross for the sins of the world. Kit Carson's wife told the Bishop about it: "He was tied upon a cross with ropes, to hang there all night; they do that sometimes at Abiquiu; it is a very old-fashioned place. But he is so heavy that, after he had hung there a few hours, the cross fell over with him and he was very much humiliated. Then he had himself tied to a post and said he would bear as many stripes as our Saviour—six thousand, as was revealed to St. Bridget. But before they had given him a hundred, he fainted. They scourged him with cactus whips, and his back was so poisoned that he was sick up there for a long time."

That's how one man overcame the tension of his priestly existence.

No one would suppose that you could still come across a case like this, so unusual in its history and locale. The priesthood of the world has become more unified, stricter, and truly catholic in the sense of a single discipline for the rank throughout the whole world. It is not only the politicians but also the clergy who recognize only one spirit, thinking and expressing itself in terms of the one world. And that spirit is one of eschatological seriousness which is befitting this age, faced as it is with being and non-being.

Priest and Sinner

We must deal quite differently with the "priest and sinner" type that comes up in literature more and more often today. The most famous is the priest of Graham Greene's novel *The Power and the Glory* (New York, 1946).

During the persecution of the Church in Mexico, the author was sent there as a reporter for the London *Times*. Not only his *Lawless Streets*, but this novel, too, can be taken as a report of the actual conditions of Mexican life in the 'twenties.

The "hero" of the book is a priest. He made his preparation just like the others, adapted himself to his people, who were, although after their own fashion, good and pious; he was a good preacher and a correct priest. At least he was correct as the people of his environment understood it. "The good things of life were available to him too early—the respect of his fellow men, a secure job. A pseudo-pious word, a cheap joke opened the way. He knew well how to take advantage of the submission of the people." He had an idea of his calling, as many others might well have had in the simple quiet times of Mexico: "He had imagined that as a priest he would become rich and proud, and that's what it meant for him to have a vocation."

But it turned out differently, very differently. The persecution of the Church awakened him from his dream. He didn't betray his priesthood; he didn't flee the country, as did so many others; and he didn't marry, as the Governor's orders commanded all priests to do.

The priests who didn't conform were arrested and shot. He too was on the list. Pursued by the police and by warrants, surrounded by informers—500 pesos were put on his head—he is chased around the country. He seems to be the only priest who resisted. He starts to go to seed, and soon is in great distress and near despair. Then he begins to drink. He becomes a "whisky priest," despised as a man, but universally longed for as a priest in those priestless days. He falls even deeper. Somewhere in the country there is a child of his. "Anxiety and despair, a half bottle of whisky, and loneliness drove him to a deed that disgusted him." Three times he could have easily escaped over the border, as many had done before him, but each time he did not save his life because some poor sinner somewhere had need of him. He, the "whisky priest," gives his life for his sheep. And it is an ignominious death, not at all like those of the martyrs of which he had read at one time in a beautifully bound book of legends. Slobbering in his fear, abandoned and without consolation, he collapses under the salvo of the executioners' bullets. And his prayer: "O God, help me! Damn me, I deserve it, but give me eternal life!"

The life of this "whisky priest" is one of deeply moving possibilities and modernity. Alois Winklhofer, of course would not agree with that. He traces Greene's intellectual ancestors through those of Bernanos and Bloy back to Pascal and the Jansenism, often unsuspected, of many religious Frenchmen. The existence of this priest is determined by the unendured tension between the sanctity of his calling and the external, as well as the internal, misery of his life. He knows this and doesn't take it lightly, but cannot find the strength in himself to master the contradiction: "What an impossible fellow I am. I've never done anyone any good . . . I might just as well have never lived. Maybe I'm not even worth hell." But the poor harassed priest overlooks his self-sacrifice in helping the abandoned Catholics, at the continual risk of his own life, so that he could bring them the sacraments and the consolations of the Faith. Winklhofer has this to say about his opinion of himself: before the persecution, he was "one of those whose priesthood was only skin-deep." Now? "He became a priest only when he had become a sinner, and the priest in him worked quite impersonally, so to speak." That is the power and the glory even in the poorest, even in the most sinful priest. An interesting example of the theme of "clergyman and sinner," even though it is not about a Catholic priest, but rather a Puritan preacher, is Hawthorne's *The Scarlet Letter*, although it was written a hundred years ago (1850). It all happened three hundred years ago in Boston, which at that time was still a little settlement at the edge of the Indians' wilderness. A beautiful young woman, Hester Prynne, brings a child into the world. But her husband, who is much older than she, has been away for years on an exploration trip. She is not executed, as the strict Puritan law demanded, but she is condemned to wear a scarlet "A" (adulteress) on her breast for the rest of her life. This expiation begins with her two-hour exposition in the market-place stocks, before all the people, before the church and

civil authorities. The sentence is carried out with all harshness and Puritan self-righteousness (although it is unconscious), but with the real seriousness of the time. There in
the market-place she is adjured in the name of the governor
by the young and highly regarded preacher, Rev. Arthur
Dimmesdale, to name the guilty man. "Never," says Hester.
And that's how things stood for the next seven years, during
which she wears the sign of her shame and, through her
repentance and humility as well as through her charitable
works, matures in inner greatness and freedom.

But the father of the child, Dimmesdale himself, suffers
and collapses under the burden of a life of inner reproach
and the greatest external honor on the part of the people.
In continual agony, he wavers between plans to confess his
guilt openly and thoughts of suicide. But it is precisely
this tension between his own heavy guilt and his holy duty
that gives him insight into the tragedy of life and lends his
sermons a mighty power over hearts. "Even during this
time of corporal and spiritual suffering, Rev. Dimmesdale
won ever greater renown in his spiritual calling. He owed
it in great part to precisely those inner and external tor-
ments, which, like a needle, kept all his spiritual and moral
powers in constant tension." The reproaches of his conscience drive him to vicarious acts of expiation. He creeps
to the stocks at night, and there he meets Hester, who is
returning from a death-bed visit. He calls her and the child
up to him. He is just bordering on the insanity that his
physician is fomenting. Unknown to him, the doctor is Hester's husband. Hester wants to save the despairing man by
helping him to escape from the doctor. At first the pastor
agrees to go with her. Then, at the installation of the new
royal Governor, he delivers his most powerful sermon. As
he leaves the church, surrounded by the rejoicing people,
he mounts the stocks and calls Hester and her child to him.

Under the strain of confessing his guilt, he collapses and dies.

One may ask if such a case were possible, despite the credibility instilled by Hawthorne's writing. Alois Winkl-hofer, speaking of a different but parallel case, doesn't hesitate to make this judgment: "This *prêtre* is more of a priest in his downtrodden condition than he was when all the external show of his personality was still gloriously discernible. Then he was proving himself at a time when he was free of all burdens." What do these figures of distress in clerical clothing mean? Certainly it is clear that none of these authors, not one, is trying to belittle the clerical state or cast suspicion upon it.

The fact that the character of the "priest-sinner" is becoming more common in literature, without that intention of vilifying the clergy, shows the seriousness of today's situation.

Sinful man today is timidly and tentatively turning back, since he can no longer see his own way; and knowing that his former life would lead only to destruction, he looks to the priest—more than we think and more than even he will admit. But he has no confidence in the first priests that meet his eyes as he looks over the fence between them. He senses in them the same complacent, self-satisfied Pharisees: the priest and the Levite, who, confident of their justification in the Law, in pious arrogance pass by the poor fellow who has fallen among thieves. A man who dresses and acts like that must be wanting in sensitivity and therefore of no use whatsoever to him. He would even like to spare himself the disillusionment. The poor fellow senses, further, that priests do have, for all that, the "power and the glory," but he is frightened off by their isolated virtuousness. He shrinks from saying the first word, and the priest doesn't say it either. Does this innocent man want nothing more to do with him? The sinner who has been away from the sacraments for years also wants to find in the priest something of his own human fate, something "that takes him down from his pedestal and puts him into the rank of sinners" (Winklhofer). What he really wants is a priest who "can sympathize with the ignorant and the erring because he himself is afflicted with weakness" (Heb. 5: 2). It is in this that we see the soul-saving power which Father Stephan Adrian had at his disposal. At one time, when he was a famous physician, he brought on the death of his wife, because he neglected her in his love of God. He became a monk to do penance and to help others by his own experience. "How tender the soul is! One disarms it when one doubts it, and it is lost when one seizes it too quickly and tries to pull it in" (Paul Regnier, *Netze im Meer,* Heidelberg, 1952). "Even in his priestly office he was still a man who shared in the sufferings of others because he had known sorrow himself. His instructions were not abstractions, but flowed from the source of his own misfortune" (p. 100).

And they do so, not because he wants to be a sinner or even frivolously takes sin upon himself, but because he is a poor sinner. Whoever wretchedly betrays his priesthood out of cowardice is abandoned to the sad laughter Graham Greene reserves for the pitiable figure of Padre José. He had knuckled under the laws of the persecutors, and married. Now, under the thumb of his concubine, he hasn't even the courage to hear the confession of his condemned brother priest, despite the fact that the police officer himself fetches him and is willing to assume the responsibility (*The Power and the Glory*).

This naturally does not mean that priests must become sinners to understand sinners. The only one the priest must imitate is He who became like us "in all save sin" and of whom it is written: "For we have not a high priest who cannot have compassion on our infirmities, but one tried as we are in all things except sin" (Heb. 4: 15). The Lord loves the sinner. That is why those seeming saints of long ago asked, "Why does your master eat with publicans and sinners?" (Mt. 9: 11; Luke 51: 2) And they revile him as "a friend of publicans and sinners" (Mt. 11: 19; Luke 7: 34). But He said of Himself that He had not come to call the just, but sinners (Mt. 2: 17), to call the sinner to repentance, of course (Luke 5: 32); and the Pharisees of the time tried to expose Him as a "sinner" (John 9: 31).

The mysterious and encouraging light that shone in the countenance of the Lord, and made it so attractive to sinners, is also the hallmark of true priestly existence.

I'm not going to give the name or the place where this happened, but I would like to show that the "power and the glory" shines against the dark background of a poor priestly life even today. In a certain town there was a pastor who was a heavy drinker and in his time had given considerable scandal. How often he wanted to pull himself together for the sake of his holy vocation, but the craving for drink held him fast in its clutches. When his excesses had almost ruined him, he pulled himself with one last effort into the pulpit and gave a sermon. His topic was—moderation! With a moving reference to himself, he said, "I beg all of you whom I have scandalized for your forgiveness. I beg all of you not to imitate me in my sin. I pray for all for whom my example was an occasion of sin. I adjure you, my dear parishioners, beware of the craving for drink. You can see in me how it can ruin a man." That church had never heard so moving a sermon, and the grave of the pastor is honored with a sanctuary, even decades later.

It was a much simpler matter for Pastor Peigerle in Lower Tannowitz. Karl Renner, the Austrian president, mentions him in his memoirs (*An der Wende zweier Zeiten,*

Vienna, 1946, p. 61): he was a capable hard-working country pastor. But with the important people of the locality he always played taroc at the inn until the stroke of twelve. In answer to the scruples of his parishioners, he said in one sermon: "Beloved in Christ! Don't act according to my deeds, but my words. For they are the words of God. We are all merely sinful men."

2. THE GOOD EXTREME: THE SAINTLY PRIEST

Against the dark background of all that we have discussed before, let us try to sketch the picture of the saintly priest. As usual, we are speaking of the secular priest or the Religious priest whose form of life and work is similar to those who have to stay in remote parishes, far from their community life. We have said that the apostate is a rare exception. The saintly priest is even rarer. It is distressing to have to prove that. Indeed, one would be tempted to say that the Church had to wait until it was 1800 years old until an exemplary pastor—pastor, we insist—came. That is the holy pastor of Ars, Jean Baptiste Vianney. He was born of poor farmer parents on May 8, 1786, in Dardilly, ordained a priest in 1815 in Grenoble, and served first as assistant to his fatherly friend, Pastor Balley in Ecully. From February, 1818, until his death on August 4, 1859, he was pastor in Ars. In 1905 he was beatified by Pius X and canonized in the Jubilee Year of 1925 by Pius XI. Four years later he was made the patron of pastors.

Within a few decades, the little hamlet of Ars with its 230 inhabitants became the goal of hundreds of pilgrims. In the years from 1827 until 1859 the church of the village was no longer empty. In the last decade there were 120,000 annual visitors who wanted to talk with the saint and make their confessions to him. That was a daily average of from 330 to 400 people; in the railroad station in Lyon a special travel bureau was set up to handle the trips to Ars. There were many private bus companies that were also kept fully occupied. Finally, the saint could only sleep four hours a night. The daily 400 pilgrims came from all over Europe, even from abroad, and at the high point of his work, he was spending sixteen to eighteen hours in the confessional. A wave of moral reformation and holiness spread from the hitherto unknown hamlet over the whole continent, being felt even beyond it. And it all started with the simple priest who could only with difficulty find a Bishop willing to take the risk of ordaining him. Not only can priests believe this, but they must also seriously examine their consciences when we recall what the devil said when pastor Vianney approached a possessed man: "If there were three like you on the earth, it would be all over for my kingdom!"

Nevertheless, his program for renovation was no different from that of the other priests of his day, nor of those of today.

His Existence

What is the source of this effectiveness? The saint is never quite understandable or explainable. He is a miracle of grace, in which he lives and works. He always embodies a realization of the imitation of Christ that far exceeds the usual imitation. He possesses the first of all the virtues, that of divine charity, in a degree still possible to all men. That is the only way of explaining the power of his charity toward his fellowmen. He possesses powers which are special gifts of grace: that of contemplation in the midst of the cares of his daily work, visions, power of miracles, knowledge of hearts, the power of saving sinners and of touching the hardened heart.

1. But these are all realities which his contemporaries hardly even noticed in his way of life. The tension of his priestly life is certainly not destroyed. On the contrary, it becomes harder to bear because he knows the two poles of sin and sanctity with a clarity lacking in the "normal" Christian, especially since his knowledge of these opposites is not in the realm of interesting information, but a matter of practical experience; he sees not only the tension between good and bad, salvation and damnation. His heart is the battlefield of the war between God and His infernal adversary.

2. For that reason the tension between duty and its performance, responsibility and work, are likewise still felt in his life. For the most part, despite the fact that others see nothing but success, he drains that tension to the last terrible drop. Saints see sin, and how fearful it is. They are amazed that this world can continue to exist at all despite its sins (Ida Goerres, *Das verborgene Antlitz*, Freiburg, 1944, p. 433). The holy priests, in whose lives God chooses to reveal that He is working in them, considered externally, are usually clumsy, rarely good preachers, and are often made fun of. This causes them to experience their human insufficiency even to the edge of despair.

Apparently the French novels about holy priests all have Jean Vianney as their model. Father Donissan, the Saint in Bernanos' *Under the Sun of Satan*, was helping the roofers when he was suddenly called to say good-bye to one of his pastor's visitors. This is how the future pastor of Lumbres looked: "His big iron-shod shoes, hastily wiped off, were still white with mortar; his stockings and his cassock were splotched with mud-stains, and his broad hands, half thrust through his cincture, were also the color of earth. His face, the paleness of which was at variance with the tanned redness of his neck, dripped perspiration and water mingled together, for at Father Menou-Segrais' unexpected summons he had hastened to his room to wash. The disarray—or rather the almost squalid appearance—of his daily clothing was made all the more extraordinary by the odd contrast of a new padded winter coat, still stiff with sizing, which he had slipped on in such a flurry that one of its sleeves was laughably tucked up over a wrist as gnarled as a grapevine" (*Under the Sun of Satan*). "The speech of the future pastor of Lumbres was difficult; sometimes it even stumbled over every word, stuttered . . . . He had long suffered from the inability to express what he felt, from that clumsiness which provoked laughter. No longer did he shun this. He plunged straight on." The puzzle of his undoubted power over men cannot be explained by what he said. Even the pastor of Ars, especially in the early years of his priesthood, lost his memory in the pulpit and had to leave. But the way he bore his infirmity had more effect than the most "interesting" sermon.

The saint—with this word we already join the haloed and the canonized saint, although his contemporaries knew nothing about it and he himself would have been frightened to death at it—the saint has no other means in the beginning than everyone else. He is fearful of his own insufficiency. Vianney, who transformed a neglected parish into a holy one, in whose confessional many hundreds of thousands had found their salvation and peace of soul, said this: "You do not know what it means, to come from a rectory to face God" (Francis Trochu, *The Curé d'Ars*, Westminster, 1953). And at another time, the saint complained "I would be the happiest of priests were it not for the thought that

I will have to appear before the judgement seat of God as a pastor."

Considering his tremendous success, his words seem to be exaggerated, perhaps dishonest. But they merely testify to the abyss of evil that he sees and saw, and to the responsibility of the priest who cannot root it out.

3. The holy pastor is conscious that he is exposed to ill will in all its forms and to the meanness that confronts him secretly or openly. He has to struggle with it and gets nowhere. He sees the endless tasks ahead of him and his own poor ability. He would like to escape into solitude, to become strong in God for the fight of life. M. Vianney sleeps only four hours, and opens the church at 4 a.m.; during the last ten years of his life, he opens it at 1 a.m. He rings the Angelus himself. The doors of the church are besieged with pilgrims, even at this hour, who want to go to confession. In his very last years a director from the parish took a great deal off his shoulders. He celebrates his Mass, makes his thanksgiving on the steps of the altar; after he has blessed the religious articles, he returns to the confessional. At eleven o'clock every day, he holds a catechism class in the church. Lunch takes ten minutes. Then he visits the sick. When he finally received an assistant from the Bishop, he was relieved of this work with the sick. Wherever he goes, two men have to open a way for him through the crowds. In the meantime he reads his Breviary. At eight o'clock the rosary is said in common and then night prayers are said by the whole parish. Interviews follow in the rectory. Then confessions again until about midnight.

He did not rest. Vianney was consumed with the longing to become a Trappist. Three times he secretly sought to escape. But all three times he was brought back by the people. The last time he was at the point of death when he was brought back to the rectory.

4. The people loved him: hundreds of thousands came to obtain peace of soul from him. But it should not be supposed that he met with no opposition or that the people of Ars gave in without further ado when, soon after his arrival, he inveighed against work on Sundays, drunkenness, and the dances in the hotels. The little village of Ars had four inns. But gradually they all had to close and there arose great hotels and hostelries for the pilgrims. But that didn't come about quickly. He was baited on the dance floors; the crudest slanders were broadcast about him; his body, wasted by mortification, was reviled as evidence of secret vices. Nothing was spared him: anonymous letters of consummate meanness, attacks printed on circulars, embarrassing rumors. Lecherous fellows sang mocking songs at night under the windows of the pastor. But the thing that most depressed him was the initial cowardice of the good people.

And even more depressing were the harsh judgments of his fellow priests and clerical neighbors. They said he was too highly strung, incautious. The foundation of the "Providence" (a winter school with a building completely unequipped, completely dependent on Providence) was to them "arrant nonsense." The foundation was ill considered. But who dares to judge the ventures of Faith? Despite the miracles which God had performed through his servant, the "Providence" finally had to be given over to an Order of nuns for regular administration, through the insistence of well-meaning fellow priests. His worn and dirty cassock, they said, was an insult to clerical decorum. In the first decades, neighboring priests forbade their parishioners to go to Ars and even went so far as to deny absolution to those who did not heed their orders. The same thing happened when St. Clement Mary Hofbauer started to preach in southern Germany. The Pastor of Jestetten threatened those who attended the sermons of Father Hofbauer with exclusion from the Easter Communion (Hofer). Vianney was remembered for his faulty theological training. He was denounced to the bishop. The investigation, as might have been expected, resulted in the shame of those who had slandered him. The opposition he met disappeared only gradually.

Vianney lived between love and hatred, between scorn and reverence. The latter was often more painful for him. He could not protect himself against the pilgrims who demanded his signature on a little holy card, and he finally gave in. He wrote under the picture his monogram, or the first initials of his name (J.M.B.V.). He refused all artists and photographers. But he could not prevent the more or less successful pictures of him, and scenes of his life, from being sold like hotcakes by the vendors of religious articles.

The canon Menou-Segrais, priest and man of the world, accomplished and devout, says to his saintly curate: "I have believed you, I still believe you, to be marked with a mark, chosen. Enough on that score. This is no longer the age of miracles. Miracles, rather, would arouse alarm, my friend. Such things concern the police. The authorities are only waiting for an excuse to pounce upon us. Then, too, the neurological—as they call them—sciences are all the rage. A simple little priest who reads souls as one reads a book . . . They'd take care of you, my boy" (Bernanos, *Under the Sun of Satan*).

All of this cannot fail to depress the saint. Besides, there is some truth in all of the objections. They are often of the most worrisome nature and feel themselves personally inferior. Weren't they right to shake their heads over Vianney's faulty theology? Father Donissan knew well that because of his own mental slowness he had only been ordained with misgivings and put under the highly gifted theologian Menou-Segrais as pastor for the sake of security.

5. They can even be prey to the temptation to think of

themselves as complete failures. There are notes on the Saint of Lumbres. What do they say of him? "No indication of anything unusual, a man troubled with all the temptations to despair . . . concern for public opinion, a complete lack of self-confidence, joined to a deep, incurable lack of courage" (*Under the Sun of Satan*). Naturally speaking, it is a fearful lot that these saints receive. " 'Save yourself, the hour has struck!' the saintly pastor of Lumbres hears the Tempter hiss: 'Finish the empty struggle and the wearisome victory. Forty years of labor and of little profit. Forty years of tedious strife, forty years in the cattle-shed, among the human beasts, level with their rotten hearts, forty years scaled and conquered!'. .. ... the vast labor, and now this pitiless crowd, night and day packed tight around the confessional of the man of God as though he were another Curé d'Ars; the deliberate severance from all human help; yes, the man of God wrangled over like some bit of prey. No rest, no peace except that purchased with fasting and the rod, in a body felled at last; recurring scruples, the anguish at ceaselessly touching the most obscene wounds of the human heart, the despair at so many damned human souls, the powerlessness to succor them and clasp them through the abyss of flesh; the obsession that it was all time wasted, the vastness of the toil . . ." (*Under the Sun of Satan*).

That is their existence.

His Power

But where does this power over men come from that distinguishes them from other priests? Why did the pious, the seekers, and the sinners go to Ars instead of to the churches near their homes? To Lumbres? To Bebenhausen, to Father

Clement M. Hofbauer? Weren't there any confessionals in their own parish churches?

1. For the first few, it may really have been the unusual piety, the self-possession and selflessness that attracted them. The most abysmal spiritual difficulties, the heavy, often almost unspeakable guilt, or the call of God to grace which demands everything, are most easily discussed with a priest who is near to God himself and therefore has a share of God's mercy and wisdom. These people also made up a great number of the later pilgrims to Ars.

The great influx, or, shall we say, the pious sensation, began when the first answered prayers, cures, and remarkable conversions became known. The mob is always looking for signs and wonders. Even here the disciple is not greater than the Master (Mt. 12: 38; Mark 8: 12; John 2: 18). And the disciple must complain with his Master of the crowd: "Unless you see signs and wonders you do not believe" (John 4: 48).

Jean Vianney would meet a man who had no way of knowing that he was a saint; and although he had never seen him before, he could describe his spiritual condition to a T. Often in his "Providence" school, after a night of despair, there would be bread in the kitchen and wheat in the barn the next morning. The people took these things to be signs, and they trusted him as one for whom God Himself had stood witness. So countless numbers came, hoping to see a miracle. And those who were filled with trust in God were there with them.

So the poor farmer from Forez brought his deaf and dumb son to the saint. The son was not at all unhappy about his misfortune. "He could make himself understood quite well by signs and was the first one to laugh when it didn't work. He could read and write and, especially, think. He could turn within himself and reap profit from that silence in which he had been wrapped by Providence. For silence, too, is a gift. He had no thought of giving it back." But his parents did not stop pleading with God to heal their son. The cures and doctors had failed. They were now relying wholly on God. "No one is ever troublesome to God," the father said to his wife. "That means, woman, that it is even recommended that we be that way." And his son receives his speech in Ars. But he "found little pleasure in being able to hear and talk. He knew the value of silence and loved it . . . but still he submitted himself to the inexplicable favor and thanked Providence with all his heart for it. But he prayed secretly that he would be given little opportunity of making use of it" (Henri Ghéon, *Le Jeux de l'Enfer et du Ciel*, 1929).

But the miracles, these palpable signs of the divine omnipotence that even the crudest intelligence can grasp, were not the greatest things that were done in Ars, or elsewhere. The greater faith, the purer charity when the request for a miracle was not answered: these are the great miracles of the saint. This is what happened to the poor washerwoman Victoire. She begged the saint to pray for the cure of her sick daughter, who lay abed at home pale and hemorrhaging. But he said to her: God could really cure her daughter in a second, but "because God loves her very much and because God willed great happiness for her and her daughter in heaven . . . and perhaps even before . . . and because there are many poor souls in the world who do not believe in the dear Lord and whom we must save . . . the dear Lord willed rather that she did not ask for a cure . . . He prefers that her daughter continue to suffer . . . It is a great honor which He shows you . . . do you understand that? . . . He is taking you to Himself on the cross, you and your daughter." And when the poor woman answers, "My daughter will be very happy when she learns this" (*Ibid.*, p. 580)—

that is when one of the greatest miracles in Ars took place.

And there are thousands of others. But only God and the person concerned know about them, and the rest of us will know only when we shall delight and revel in them at "the revelation of His Glory" (1 Pet. 4: 13).

2. But it was rather with fear that men were struck, a fear which all those who were eye-witnesses shared, when the saint looked through a person completely unknown to him, called him by name, or confronted him. He would suddenly get up from the confessional and call someone to him who was about to give up in despair; he would know exactly those who were in a hurry, and this was so well-known that all accepted it. The return ticket sold in the special window for the trains to Ars in the Lyon station was good for a week. But the crowds around the church were great, and many got to the confessional just before the train was ready to leave for home. The saint knew them. Vianney saw into the hearts in which the battle raged between the tempter who wanted to drive them from the confessional with motives of shame and despair, and God, who had called them to Ars. Saints do not only see into hearts through the eyes: they see into rooms through the walls. Saint Benedict Labre confesses: "I could no longer give the names of the cities through which I have traveled; there must be very many of them. I would also hardly recognize the cities again. Perhaps I could only say what I felt there; I could distinguish still the cities by what I sensed of the men and their souls" (Reinhold Schneider, *Die dunkle Nacht*, Kolmar p. 222).

But the gift of reading hearts is one full of terror and disgust. And it is the same thing whether it is one's own or another's soul: "He saw with his fleshly eyes that which remains hidden to the most penetrating, to the most subtle intuition, to the soundest training, a human conscience. Of course, our own nature is partially revealed to us; we know ourselves indeed a little more clearly than we know another; but each man must go down within himself, and the deeper he goes, the thicker the shadows, down to dark bedrock, the deep *I* where the ancestral shades bestir themselves, where the instinct roars, like a subterranean water-course. And now . . . and now this wretched priest found himself abruptly transformed into the most intimate recesses of another human being, surely to the very point reached by the eyes of the Judge. He was aware of the marvel and was enraptured that this marvel should be so simple and its disclosure so sweet. This burglary of the soul, which someone other than he could never have conceived without thunder and lightning, now that it had been consummated, no longer frightened him" (*Under the Sun of Satan*).

And to a young woman sinner, who cynically and deliberately resists the consolation of Father Donissan, he says: "Don't be astonished at what I am going to say: above all, don't see anything in it to arouse the astonishment or curiosity of anyone. I am only a poor man. But when the spirit of rebellion was in you, I saw the name of God written in your heart." Is that a natural gift, one of reason, or one that can be explained by depth psychology or some other way? "No fire save the divine can bend and melt the ice of concepts. And yet that which revealed itself in this hour to Father Donissan's eyes was not at all a symbol or a figure; it was a living soul, a heart sealed to others." When he was asked later about this gift of reading within souls, he first denied it, and almost always stubbornly. At times, also, fearing he might lie, he gave a clearer account of it: "The charity of great souls, their supernatural compassion, seems to carry them to the most intimate inwardness of beings."

3. With this ability the saintly priest enters a kingdom that is God's, but which God's adversary regards as his

own private field for maneuvering. The saint, therefore, has power over the devil in a place where he seems to be impregnable.

And Satan defends himself. And the means he uses! The saint pushes him so hard he forgets his favorite disguise—incognito. He rages at the saint in forms that are only found elsewhere in the lives of the ancient fathers of the desert. One would suppose that by this time he would have become a social lion or a diplomat or a film star or an elegant woman of the streets. No. Before the brightest of footlights, which he has kindled himself, he disports in the wildest attacks and personally ridicules the man who is still his best opponent in this world, his denier. It seems that all the other priests are uninteresting to him, considering the rage with which he attacks the saint. The saint alone is in a position to disconcert the devil and force him to reveal himself for what he really is. Satan's kingdom is threatened. That is it.

Jean Vianney was exposed to the rage of the infernal fellow for thirty-five years—all night long, in hand-to-hand fashion: noises, shoves, hauling about. And the best he could manage was to make sure that the saint would be beaten and tired when, after four sleepless hours, he would go to the church. These attacks were at their worst when an especially great sinner had come to Ars and wanted to confess to the saint the next day. Vianney knew that, and, under the blows of Satan, joyously looked forward to a soul that was to be saved from even greater danger.

Yes, Vianney is sad whenever "he" lets him alone. It's a bad sign. "What disturbs me right now is the fact that the confessions are becoming more and more monotonous. Nine times out of ten, signs of indifference or tepidity. In the case of souls without any fervor, old 'Clubfoot' only needs to let things take their course. The 'Evil One' has been sleeping too much for some time" (Ghéon, p. 127).

Once a "big fish" got away from him and the saint realized later that he would have had to shake him up considerably to make a saint out of him. He comes back that night to the rectory, depressed. "After he had closed the door, he cast himself on his knees, his arms spread in the form of a cross. Then the thought came to him to impose a severe mortification upon himself. The scourge with its points and knots is at hand. But for what purpose? His poor body has become invulnerable and he has noticed that he gets only proud thoughts from such punishments. And anyway, he had promised his assistant that he would sleep.

"He lay on his large bed, whose extreme poverty was concealed by closed curtains; a paper-thin straw mattress and a pile of twigs. He doesn't even pull off his shoes. He has hung up the lantern so that it will shine on the holy pictures on the walls. Vincent de Paul, John Francis Regis, St. Philomena, the Assumption of Mary . . . If he doesn't sleep, he can meditate on his saints. But he needs the sleep and takes the time for rest willingly . . ." (Ghéon, p. 128).

"But he had hardly lost consciousness when a storm broke over the rectory, which could not have been foreseen at all. The rectory shook from attic to foundations; the shutters banged, shingles flew from the roof, window panes fell out and shattered in the yard in the midst of a rustling of dry leaves and dry branches . . . At least it sounded like that. Even the bed was rattling.

"M. Vianney wakes up and understands. He makes the sign of the cross and says softly: 'That is he.' He wants to go to sleep again . . . but suddenly the storm stops and immediately afterwards, regiments start to march past. At first the marching feet of the infantry, precisely in time, unabating, one thousand or two thousand feet stamping simultaneously; then the clatter of the cavalry in a walk, trot, then gallop, whinnying, jingling bridles, hoofbeats—

and the horses storm the doors. Finally the artillery like a thundering storm, with the rattling of a collapsing wooden house, rumbling gun carriages and munitions wagons, grinding wheels, snapping whips, curses. Now it seems as though the three kinds of wagons are vying for the street and are racing for the house. They crash the gate of the garden, stream in with wild confusion and screaming like Cossacks, start to make themselves at home. It is a genuine invasion and the noise is enough to split one's head. M. Vianney casts a look at St. Philomena, his little saint. Silence.

"A little rustling of a mouse on the roof. A pause. A grating door. The flame of the lantern moves . . . good, he's here. He whispers in his right ear: 'Vianney!' He whispers in his left ear: 'Vianney—you won't sleep!' He laughs. 'No, you're too old . . . I'll leave you alone.' But he doesn't go. He is a rat again and chews for a long time on the foot of the bed.—Suddenly he becomes angry; he races through the room like a drunken ape; he throws the chairs around and they really fall over. He lifts up the bureau, the table, the bookcase three feet above the floor and lets them fall again with all their weight; he plays a drum roll with a key on the water pitcher; he makes the pictures dance on the wall; he hangs on the bed curtains, he acts like a dog, a lion, a cow, and screams at the top of his lungs, 'Vianney, Vianney, you truffle eater! You aren't dead yet, but I'll get you.' M. Vianney's blood runs cold. He looks at his crucifix and says: 'I love you, my God.'. . . then the one whom he calls Clubfoot grabs him by his big shoes and shakes him. Once. Twice. Three times. 'Blessed be the holy and undivided Trinity!' says M. Vianney. The other seizes him by the shoulders and throws him on the floor. M. Vianney answers, 'My God, I thank Thee,' and lies down in bed . . . he thinks that the whole affair is a sign of tremendous fear in the kingdom of darkness. Apparently it will be a good day tomorrow. There will be no more tepidity—'Well, my poor friend,' he says to his persecutor, 'you haven't let me sleep; what more do you want? It's time for me to go to work again.' Clubfoot has a sense of the comic and laughs aloud. He laughs little, but he laughs. And then his laughter is heard no more. The séance had lasted for two hours. M. Vianney gets up. He is exhausted" (Ghéon, pp. 129, 132).

In the last years, the men of Ars established a watch. In turn one of them slept every night in the room next to the pastor's bedroom. In his difficulties, Vianney took comfort at the nearness of another. There were hours in which even the saint had a horror of being alone. This was his Gethsemane. He consoles his fearful heart that even the Master asked the disciples, "Could you not watch one hour with me?"

Father Donissan, the future pastor of Lumbres, had the same kind of experience. On his way to help out with confessions in Etaples, the black fellow confuses him for the whole night with false trails because he fears and hates his absolution in the confessional. And that always wins, it seems to him. It is his hate-filled ambition to make the saint despair by facing him with his apparent defeats. "Your past life, your useless, yet touching toil, your fasting, your scourging, your slightly naive and vulgar loyalty, humiliation within and without, the enthusiasm of some and the unjust mistrust of others, and certain utterances packed with poison. Oh! all is but a dream and the shadow of a dream. All was but a dream apart from your gradual ascent toward the real world, your birth, your release. Clamber up to my mouth, harken to the word where abides all knowledge" (Bernanos, *Under the Sun of Satan*). "He" succeeds so far as to make him ask God for a visible sign of the victory over the prince of this world. But he dies on the cross of his holy vocation and life, beaten like his Lord, on the battlefield of his struggles and victories, having had a stroke while sitting in his confessional in his church at Lumbres. "The aged athlete, pierced by a thousand blows, bears witness for the weaker ones, names the traitor and the betrayal. Oh, but the devil, the other one, is surely a skillful fellow, a wonderful liar, this wayward rebel in his lost glory, full of scorn for the heavy and human cattle which the thousand courses of his guile arouse or subdue, according to his wish, but his humble enemy faces up to him, and beneath the forbidding hue and cry shakes his stubborn head. With what a tempest of laughter and shouting does joyous hell acclaim the artless speech, barely intelligible, the confused and maladroit defense. What matter! Still another hears it, whom the heavens will not forever hide."

What a world! It's only worth a head shake, worth a deliberate smile of the one who, from the eminence of the last three centuries looks back on the enchantment of the dark centuries, ready fodder for parapsychologists and depth psychologists, even now good enough material for dissertations with which bright boys and girls earn their doctorates. Psychotherapists are hunting for such phenomena, but they can't find them. Too bad—they would have just the cure for them, all set.

"O you who never knew anything of the world except colors and sounds without substance, soft hearts and lyric mouths in which harsh truths would melt away like sugar candy—small hearts, small mouths, this is not for you. Your deviltries are proportionate to your weak nerves, to your mincing minds, and the Satan of your strange daily round is merely your own image, distorted for the devotee of the carnal universe, is Satan unto himself. The monster watches you with laughter, but he has not laid his talons upon you. He is not in your driveling books nor is he in your blasphemies or in your silly curses. Yet Satan exists" (*Under the Sun of Satan*).

And the holy priest knows, experiences this monster, and is his conqueror. And what if his victory appears to be the same as that which his Master won, dying on the cross? Can it be different? The rules of the victory were given with the beginning of the triumphal procession.

The Source of His Power

From what source does the saint draw his power?

1. The first source of strength by which his power is supported and determined is the complete and absolute supernaturality of his existence—his mountain-moving faith. Vianney, in the eyes of his professors, was hopelessly unfit, was refused by his own Bishop, and was ordained by another only with reservations. He relied upon God and the help of his saints for all his strength. His preparation had robbed him of all self-confidence. "God, only you . . . ! " When he had been a priest for three years and came to Ars, he cast himself on his knees when he first saw the hamlet and called upon the guardian angel of his parish. That was how he began. There was no procession and no welcome. The people were indifferent. They thought, though, when the bells sounded the Angelus on the evening of February 18, 1818, that there must be a new priest in the parish.

He composed and meditated on his sermons before the Blessed Sacrament. He wrote them in the sacristy, as close as he could get to the tabernacle. Formally considered, he was a bad preacher. At first he learned what he had to say by heart and, as a young pastor, often lost his memory. And yet his goal was as high a one as could be set; he wanted to make out of neglected Ars a parish of saints. The shelter that he characteristically called "Providence" he had fully entrusted to God. And God was faithful in every desperate situation, as always.

2. Above all, the saint was driven on by his love of souls. To this love he sacrificed his greatest inclination—solitude. How else can we explain the fact that a poor and sickly priest sacrificed every hour every day and three quarters of the night for the saving of souls? He wanted to save souls! He wanted to send saints to heaven. And he took all opposition into the bargain.

3. One might suppose that for the poor, untalented young man it was easy to be humiliated. He started his humanistic studies when he was twenty. But his previous lack of training made this almost impossible. He couldn't get Latin into his head. Abstract thinking was foreign to him. The many younger students laughed the old blockhead to scorn. "My poor head," he complained every day. A disgust for all knowledge came over him. The greatest temptation of his life beset him: back to the farm! It was a pilgrimage to the grave of John Francis Regis that set him straight again. When he was twenty-eight he began the really scientific preparation for the priesthood. As an "extremely weak student" he was received into the seminary, but soon sent home again as a hopeless case! He had little self-confidence. But the persistent pastor Balley finally succeeded in getting him ordained.

His humility never left him in the days of his public success and fame. In 1850 he was, as they said, the most famous priest in France. The Bishop appointed him an honorary canon (Trochu, *The Curé d'Ars,* Westminster, Md., 1953, p. 388). The investiture, because of his discomfort and sense of humor, was almost a comedy. He wanted to put the *cappa* on the curate; it would fit him better, he thought. When the "celebration" was over, he sold his purple conceit to get money for the poor. He did the same thing when Napoleon III made him a Knight of the Legion of Honor. He never wore the cross.

Whenever an ancient form of Christian sanctity appears in the Church, the forms and manners of the infant Church re-assert themselves as a matter of course. In this following of the Holy Spirit it automatically becomes clear what is true and real and what has a comic effect in such an atmosphere. Vianney was surely quite humble, but he could not abide having his priesthood made ridiculous by any kind of wrappings or titles.

And the pastor to whom hundreds of thousands came to confession, among them many bishops, including his own, was troubled about his poor work. "It is terrible, to come before the judgement seat of God as a pastor."

And how little the saintly pastor of Lumbres thought of himself! (*Under the Sun of Satan*).

4. Both of them were penitents because those who should have been were not. And penitents to a shocking extent! Both of them had taken the words of the Lord very literally and seriously when He said that there was a devil who could only be driven out with much prayer and fasting (Mark 9: 28). In the moment immediately before his death, when there were no witnesses, pastor Balley reached under his pillow and gave the young Vianney his own instruments of penance. No one else was to see or use them any more.

With penitential chains, hair shirts, and scourges he belabored his "cadaver"—the "old Adam" as he said. Later he confessed, as did St. Aloysius, that he had gone too far. But a lack of moderation is the moderate virtue of the saints.

Unconscious from excessive penance, Father Donissan lies on the sofa of his astounded pastor, the Abbé Menou-Segrais. He has to open the curate's soutane—a horrible sight confronted the polished, accomplished, yet pious Pastor of Campagne: "From the armpits to the base of the loins the torso was wholly encased in a rigid sheath of the coarsest horsehair, loosely woven. The slender thong which held up the front of this frightful undergarment was so tightly drawn that Father Menou-Segrais undid it only with difficulty. The skin then appeared burned by the unbearable rubbing of the haircloth as though by the application of a caustic; the epidermis, in places destroyed and in others swollen into blisters the size of a man's hand, constituted one great wound from which oozed a watery liquid mingled with blood. The filthy gray and brown hairshirt seemed impregnated with it. And from a deeper wound in the fold of the flank, bright red blood dripped, drop by drop" (*Under the Sun of Satan*). But Father Donissan regained consciousness and, as though by a miracle, continued to live. And he did not give up penance and the scourge.

5. A thing that further determines the holy priest is his *absolute* selflessness and his poverty. That poverty is an essential rule for the full imitation of Christ is not unknown. The law has a profound result. God entered the world in poverty, and poverty is the only fit dress for the representative who wishes to stay in His company. "Is not created poverty in this world the true dignity of the man whose riches are uncreated?" asks Father Frederick William Faber. "Can even the thought of comfort approach the Almighty without dishonoring Him? Silver and gold, diamonds and pearls, houses and estates—all these things in truth would seem to be more of an insult to God than the trafficking on Sion or the cruelties on Calvary" (*Bethlehem*, Philadelphia, 1955).

The Curé of Ars, the businessman would have said, promotes outside trade. New enterprises sprang up; the need for transportation, accommodations, and shelter became ever more and more necessary. The people are making money.

Vianney had the greatest difficulty, and he only half succeeded in bringing those around him to live by the law that guided his own life: selflessness and poverty. His first income was 500 francs a year; his dwelling was bare; his bed, twigs covered with paper. Madame Bibast, who had already taken care of the needs of the student Vianney, did not have an easy time of it; as a matter of fact, of course, it was very easy. For the pastor ate only eggs and potatoes all year. "It isn't easy to serve a saint," she often complained (Trochu). Whatever he received he gave away.

6. Every saint has his secret which distinguishes him from other saints; his individuality. Saints are always strong personalities, but the secret of their power is always supernatural. The natural-personal singularity he possesses is alloyed with the supernatural element of the saint, and holds all that it meets in its sway.

Even the saint's effectiveness has its secret: its apparent and many-sided power of miracles which finds no chronicler and can find none; the gift of helping, although he himself has nothing; the power of discerning spirits; the power of reading hearts; above all, the strength to hold on throughout a troubled life on the raging front of opposition to Satan. Besides that, the power to fill everyone with peace, while he himself must endure the most difficult inward trials.

The wise and experienced pastor of Campagne knows this way, even though he cannot bring himself to travel it. He is concerned for his beautiful carpets, but he sees clearly, and he speaks clearly of it to his curate, Father Donissan, who of course knew nothing of it, but was living it. (Maddened by "the possession of so many souls by sin," he had offered his life and all the consolations of the Holy Spirit which might be his to God for the salvation of their souls. He even offered the salvation of his own soul for them, "if God will it.") "My dear young boy," said the old priest, "what perils await you! The Lord summons you to perfection, not to peace. Of all men, you will have the least assurance in your life, clear-sighted only for others, passing from light to shadow, fickle. In some fashion your rash offer has been heard. Hope is almost dead within you, forever. Of it there remains only that last glimmer without which every task would become impossible and every merit vain. This extreme poverty in hope—here is what matters. The rest is nothing. Along the road you have chosen—no!—into which you have hurled yourself!—you will be alone, definitively alone, you will walk alone" (*Under the Sun of Satan*).

But the saints have their secret in this loneliness. That of the saintly pastor of Ars was his charity and his deep devotion to St. Philomena. She was not known until recently. She was a saint from the era of the catacombs. Perhaps the report of the finding of her body in the catacomb of Priscilla in 1802, or perhaps her life, richly adorned with legend, made a deep impression on Vianney. At any rate, next to St. John Francis Regis, she was his saint. A mystic friendship bound the two lives together over a gap of 1600 years. He took his great sorrows and most heartfelt pleas to her. She was "his Beatrice, his ideal, his sweet star, his consoler, his pure light" (Trochu). He had a relic of her and took it with him when he attempted something very dangerous. And she never failed the poor priest. What meaning there can be for the priest's life, that each has "his own" saint!

7. A saint always is a puzzle. So is the holy priest. The means that he uses are the ordinary ones. Many things that we think are absolutely necessary for priestly existence suddenly appear to be what we consider of suspiciously relative importance. Such inferior theological training joined with such effectiveness! We find nothing easier to understand than that the Bishop of Lyon refused to ordain Vianney.

And it seems perfectly logical that the Bishop, who was finally found willing to ordain him, would do so only under the condition that he would not be allowed to hear confessions for a year. And yet all that—we need only to mention it—is not only ridiculous, it is to be understood as a smile of heaven at the things that we think indispensable.

There are two kinds of theology: one is learned and the other is lived. And the latter is the theology of the saint, which, of course, does not exclude the possibility that the others may know it equally well. But that there is such a knowledge is certain. "He knows so many things, poor pastor of Lumbres! which the Sorbonne knows not. So many things, which are not written, which are scarcely said, of which the avowal is torn from within you, as from a wound healed and ripped open—so many things! And he knew likewise what is man: a great child full of vice and boredom.

"What is he to learn that is new, this old priest. He has lived a thousand lives, all alike. No more will he be astonished; he can die. Brand new moralities there are, but never will you put a fresh face on sin.

"For the first time he doubted, not God, but man. A thousand recollections surged upon him: he hears the bemused wails, the shamed stammerings, the pained cry of passions which steal away and which a word rivets to the spot, which words of simple clarity bring back and flay alive . . . Once more he saw the poor distraught faces, the eyes which would and would not, the conquered lips as they fell limp and the bitter mouth uttering its no . . . So many sham rebels, eloquent indeed before the world, whom he had seen at his feet, laughable! So many proud hearts wherein a secret rooted! So many old men like unto dreadful children. And towering over all, coldly staring at the world, the youthful misers, who never forgive" (*Under the Sun of Satan*).

The saint scarcely knows the definitions and distinctions, but he has seen good and evil and has the gift of discernment of spirits. And that is more and more decisive than all else. "Finding an excuse in an affectionate upbraiding delivered by Father Menou-Segrais, he began to annotate and write a commentary on the *Treatise on the Incarnation*. You should with your own eyes see this volume—in a rather rare eighteenth century edition, one of the jewels of the pastor of Campagne's library—the margins of which were crammed with Father Donissan's big handwriting! The awkwardness of these notes, the naive pains the poor priest took to relate the author's words to the texts of the Gospel by means of references slightly comic in their preciseness—all this, even the blunders in his rudimentary Latin, gave proof of so great a labor that even the most cruel would not dare to poke fun. Moreover, we know that these memoranda were no more than the outline of a much more important work surely just as ineffectual—now lost and probably moldering away at the bottom of some drawer, tragic and stumbling witness to the aberrations of a great soul . . . The pastor of Lumbres was ever a poor metaphysician and experience alone can convey to you the meticulous torture which the obstinate struggling with an obscure text can inflict upon an intelligence lacking in the requisite elements of understanding." He did not see through the pedantry of distinctions in the books, for they seemed to him a waste of time and senseless. But he did see through hearts and had power over them. He saw by the gift of grace how the soul was disposed toward God and where its danger and hope lay. That was more.

The Saints and the Others

Today we see the saint. His contemporaries saw him as one of them, a neighbor from the same section of the country. They didn't see or understand his sanctity, or at least, not as such; they took it to be his oddity, his strangeness. The kindest way of putting it was that they admitted that he was a real character. They thought that what he said was extreme and what he was doing, extravagant. Gradually, at first, some began to see, then more and more. But even that is not always the case. It is just the way the Dean of Blangermont puts it: saints are like precious wines which in their own time cause the vintners no end of trouble and concern, and their excellence is appreciated only by the next generation (*Diary of a Country Priest*). His contemporaries can't do a thing with him—because they are always more advanced than he. The kindly and shrewd Canon de la Motte-Beuvron knows how to explain it to the Pastor of Ambricourt: "You see, my dear child, these people don't hate you for being simple; they're on their guard against it, that's all. Your simplicity is a kind of flame which scorches them. You go through the world with that lowly smile of yours as though you begged their pardon for being alive, while all the time you carry a torch which you seem to mistake for a crozier" (*Ibid.*).

Yes, the uncomfortable and really unpleasant manner of the saint can take tragic forms and have tragic consequences. Jean Baptiste Noulleau (1604-72) carried on a thirty years war with his Bishop de la Barde. The latter "did not have the spirit of bravery with which this apostolic man spoke so frankly to him, and in 1647 he forbade him to preach." "The saints are not always easy to get along with and one can imagine without difficulty that the possibly excessive zeal of Noulleau angered the Bishop of St. Brieuc" (Henri Bremond, *La Métaphysique des Saints*, 1939, p. 112).

Noulleau is not canonized, possibly because of this conflict. But how does Bremond describe him? "His writings are not those of a fanatic. Perhaps he is unyielding, stubborn, but always disciplined, humane, supernatural to a high degree and of perfect wisdom"; and he quotes an eyewitness of his life: "He was so poor that his room contained no more than his manuscripts, books, his Breviary, his desk, and a supply of writing paper. He never had two cassocks, since he seemed to think that the words of the Gospel obliged him literally. He never owned a coat, collar, or cuffs. He gave whatever he earned to poor students and his inheritance to the beggars. His Mass stipends sufficed to keep him alive. He neither drank wine nor any other intoxicating drink, ate only the plainest and most ordinary of food which he always took in the company of two of the poor. He took the discipline daily and slept in a hair shirt. His shoulders were always bruised and bloody" (*Ibid.*).

And they all died, wholly surrendered and devoted to their God, but not with the sweetness portrayed in the ostentatious Baroque or the idealized Kitsch of their pictures. Bernanos composed a prayer for his dying saint and that has much more verisimilitude: "You have cast us like a leaven into the lump. The universe, of which sin has stripped us, we shall recover, inch by inch, we shall hand it back to you just as we received it, in its order and in its holiness, on the first morning of the days. Reckon not the time for us, Lord! Our heedfulness falters, our mind so quickly turns aside. Constantly the eyes espy, both right and left, no possible way out; constantly one of your workers casts aside his tool and goes away. But your pity, your pity grows not weary

and everywhere you hold out to us the tip of the blade
. . . We are not at all those rosy saints with blond beards
which the good folk see in paintings and whose eloquence
and sound health the philosophers themselves would envy.
Our portion is not at all what the world conceives. Compared to it, even the compulsion of genius is a frivolous
game. Every beautiful life, Lord, testifies for you, but the
saint's testimony is as though torn out by iron" (*Under the
Sun of Satan*).

That, of course, is the reason why sanctity is so much ad-
mired and so little imitated. That is why one wavers on the
borderlines of devotion described in the familiar rhyme:
admirandum, non imitandum.

The saying, "There is only one reasonable cause for sadness, the fact that we are not saints," comes from the pen of
Léon Bloy. In these vales of tears and tragedy which we
have just described, this is not one of the sources of sadness. Indeed, it is scarcely the lot of the most immediate
companions and students of the saints, and even of the
saintly priests. It is symbolic to learn what the chronicler
has to say of the day immediately after the death of the
saintly Curé of Ars: until the day of his death, the Angelus
was rung at one o'clock in the morning. With that, the saint
began his day's work and so did his assistants. On the first
day after his death, the Angelus was put back to dawn, as
was the custom before the arrival of Vianney in Ars.

Every-day life and its requirements quickly reclaim their
old "rights," even after the death of a saint.

The Type Modeled on St. Francis de Sales

By way of supplement we must discuss another type of
priest for which we can produce not one canonized example

from the last century. But there is such a man. Winklhofer cites him as a contra-distinction to the Vianney-type mentioned above. It is the man who has followed in the footsteps of St. Francis de Sales.

We meet him in the novels about priests today. He is not just a product of the author's imagination. He may perhaps be intended as an ideal for those readers who are priests. But the features and outlines of these priests described as saintly derive from an actual example.

This man is a consummate theologian, even though he has been educated in other fields. He moves with a certainty that is both natural and God-given, in the salons of the rich as well as in the homes of the poor. In his person, the tension between the world and heaven, nature and super-nature has become a perfectly balanced and unified whole. This is the life that he lives before the world, which can find in him the image of Christ. However difficult and hard the way to this form of existence may have been, he conceals it behind the clear calm of his face.

There is nothing common about him. Perhaps there is a touch of it in his family background. But because of it, he must live no less poorly and despise the world no less. He has polish and modesty. In his description of Ignatius Loyola, Hugo Rahner puts it this way: "Restraint, noble self-possession . . . A love of good manners, even to the extent of being a martinet, a mistrust of all extravagance. Breeding loves tradition. A feeling of distance . . ." and he quotes as an example for this that the saint's love of poverty always preserved a noble finish. Father Benedetto Palmio relates of him, "The preparation of the table was certainly conspicuous for its love of poverty and simplicity. But beneath it all there was an indefinable air of 'gentility.' There always had to be two or three at table, especially when externs were occasionally invited. On such occasions the drinking glasses were first tasted and then presented to the guest with such an elegance that it could not have been done with more finesse in the most noble courts" (Rahner, *Ignatius Loyola,* Chicago, 1956).

The element that fully animates him and opens hearts to him is his boundless charity, even toward the sinner, especially toward the sinner. He lives in the faith in "the God and Father of Our Lord Jesus Christ, the Father of mercies and the God of all comfort, who comforts us all in our afflictions, that we also may be able to comfort those who are in any distress by the comfort wherewith we ourselves are comforted by God" (2 Cor. 1: 3-5). He cannot send anyone away unconsoled, even though, as a priest, he be at the limit of his authority, or faced with the difficult, impassable wall of despairing circumstances, or the helplessness and unwillingness of men. He can arouse the trust and love of God in the most hopeless and abandoned of sinners, relying on the words of St. Paul, that "for those who love God all things work together unto good" (Rom. 8: 28). Even sin? Even sin. Naturally, not in itself, but through the liberating moment of terror that accompanies it. He never slams the door and is far from uttering the self-satisfied *"dixi et salvavi animam meam"* (I have spoken and saved my own soul), which brings despair to the confused and hesitating sinner.

His model is the Good Shepherd, who leaves the ninety and nine and goes out to seek the one lost sheep. And he does it out of love, as a brother, a shepherd responsible to God, and all this, out of a real attachment to those who are lost. The mystery of the Good Shepherd is not wholly the "mystique of sin." The characters of the priests in Gertrud Von le Fort's *Der Kranz der Engel* are not known to us by their lives, but only by their words and opinions. They even contradict one another, but both are marked with this seal of generosity and sympathy. "Because he is far from God, you may never separate from him (the fiancé), for God Himself never abandoned those who were far from Him. In fact it was these, precisely these, whom He sought and loved in Christ!" (Le Fort, *Der Kranz der Engel*, Graz, 1948, p. 209); and "love still joins us with God when every other bond has already been destroyed."

In the same way, Father Angelo writes to "Spiegelchen": "The faithful must embark upon a full sharing of love with those outside the Faith. They must leave behind their own devout security and share their heavy tragedy, and then those without the faith, too, will win a share of its blessing" (*Ibid.*, p. 124). "There is a natural disposition to meet this hostility (of the present-day world to Christianity) and there is a supernatural one. The first cuts itself off from the Godless, to preserve one's own soul; the supernatural attitude decides to remain at their side. The natural one is perfectly understandable, but most will find the supernatural incomprehensible" (*Ibid.*, p. 282).

But the dean of Heidelberg had a different opinion. And he had solid pastoral tradition on his side, too. But he knows how to express it, not only in correct ecclesiastical terms, but also as a humane priest: "You are a rare case, my child. I notice, as a matter of fact, that yours is a religious problem. Don't think that I am mistaken in that. Your case is quite different from others in the same situation. But nevertheless let us not be blind to the dangers which threaten you. Your fiancé desires marriage, not as a sacrament, nor does he dream of administering it as such to you. The desire for a holy marriage will rest entirely with you—do not rely too much on your own strength" (*Ibid.*, p. 136).

These Francis-de-Sales characters meet us in the old priest in Graham Greene's novel *Brighton Rock*, in the protagonist of *The Cardinal*, by Henry Morton Robinson, in

Abbé Donges, in Ouwendijk's *Satanische Trinität*. Even Don
Ardito in his middle period as president of the Academic
Club in M. should be mentioned here. These are priests who
have a harmony still possible to men, priests of natural nobility and natural perfection in mental and moral respects, and
perfect likewise in grace and in the love of God. "The perfect Christian, the saint, can be the most cultivated of men
at the same time. The heights of divine love are splendidly
compatible with the most active intellectual interests, with
the highest scientific education, with the finest worldly polish, with the most exacting business activity," says Arnold
Rademacher (*Das Seelenleben der Heiligen*, Paderborn,
1916, p. 228); and the reports that we have of this noble professor of theology at the University of Bonn tell us that he
himself personified the ideal he outlined here. We in Vienna,
in considering this ideal, think of the Spiritual Father and
later Regent of the Vienna Major Seminary, Karl Handloss.
He lived this ideal before our eyes when we were theologians
and young priests.

The Imitators of "Sebastian vom Wedding"

In Le Fort's *Der Kranz der Engel* we read that it is the understanding of Father Angelo, in view of the tremendous
power of today's unbelief, that salvation can come only
"with the sacrifice of one's own safety and with the utter
risk of charity" (p. 138).

This is the risk that the priest in Franz Herwig's *Sankt
Sebastian vom Wedding* assumes (Munich, 1921).

The monk Sebastian is sitting in the peaceful garden of
his monastery. As he reads the words of our Lord in his
Breviary, "Behold I send you forth like lambs among the
wolves," he has a vision. He sees how men fall upon one

another like wolves and devour one another. "Why am I sitting here on a peaceful island, seeking my own soul's salvation, selfish man that I am?" He is no longer willing to wait for the wolves in a well-protected confessional. He wants to go to them. In the solitude of a hermitage he comes to know God's will. "At times he had the vision of incalculable swarms, pouring over the cross of Christ like a tremendous destructive flood, whose confusion continually renewed itself, only to plunge into the eternal darkness of a black gorge" (p. 13).

Then he dons the dress of a worker and betakes himself to the Wedding, the poorest slum section of Berlin. He comes to know hunger and unemployment and the abandonment of the shelters for the homeless. In this world of hatred, avarice, and envy, he wants to offer the love of Christ. One man is uncomfortable with him; another thinks him a fool. But by degrees many see in him and his life a world wholly unknown to them, and they gather around him. In an uprising of the poor he tries to preach the love of Christ. A policeman, whom he rescues, dies with a curse on his lips. A priest comes to him. Sebastian says to him, "You have a suit of fine cloth; put on a dirty work shirt! You've got white hands—get a job that will roughen them up. You should look no better than those you love" (p. 66). A prelate comes and warns him: "The Church mistrusts you. You are making a mistake." And to him he says, "We are spearmen who are aiming at the future, and we are running to the attack. Some day, after a long time, you will bring us back with a blessing" (p. 68).

Two monks from his monastery have followed him in the meantime. He preaches and announces the love of neighbor as the fundamental law of human society. The sick are healed at his touch. A new community composed of those outcasts of the city who have been reborn gather pleadingly around him. With these men he finally offers the Holy Sacrifice.

An outbreak of hatred. "The green light from the predatory eyes of Satan streams over them." And they strike Sebastian dead and tie him, like his saintly namesake, to a lamppost, to pierce him through with bullets.

"Lord, let my blood be fruitful!" is his last prayer. Then there ensues a great silence. The crowd sneaks away. The murderers run like madmen from the courtyard. And out of the catacombs there echoes the loud prayer: "Saint Sebastian, pray for us!"

Franz Herwig's legend made a tremendous impression on religious youth after World War I. It expressed what many had been thinking for a long time. This and that detail in the model which had been given them led to new attempts to approach the men lost to themselves and to the Faith. And even though it was done at first only by example, there were many priests who followed, unknown, in the footsteps of Sebastian.

Over all the individual experiments one stands out in the great, organized *Mission de France*.

Up until the second World War there was a striking difference between the German and French clergy. The Germans were the organizers, the heads of societies, practical men, close to the people. Often enough most of their work was done outside of the church and sacristy. In Germany the priests were educated in the State universities. They even gave religious instructions in the public schools. In France, with the exception of the University of Strasbourg, which received its charter in 1871, there was no theological faculty. After heavy and devastating skirmishes, there resulted in 1905 a hostile separation of Church and State. The public schools, hostile to religion, dominated the field for decades. A paganizing influence spread from the cities far out into the villages. The clergy retired to the sacristy and church. They were forbidden to enter the schools and even the hospitals, unless the patient had expressly asked for the priest. A mass defection resulted, not due to outside pressures, but to a falling into indifference to God and His kingdom. This was especially true of southern France, and not merely in the cities, but even in the country. The North and the Northeast remained staunch. The closer France was to the Swiss, German, and Flemish borders, the better things were.

This situation aroused the best minds to action. France today, religiously speaking, is a country of the most extreme contrasts. On top of the mass of a religiously arid people, there arose an upper crust of high religious culture and intellectuality. France boasts of the most important Catholic literature in the world. Even if Heinrich Schrör was right fifty years ago in his criticism of French theology, the deficit has long been erased. Indeed, France has continued to be the country of exemplary saints even until the present day.

With the separation of Church and State, the most terrible problem that beset France was the lack of priests. And that in a two-fold sense: the small number of candidates for the priesthood and the economic distress of the priests. It was only forty years ago that France had so many priestly vocations that it could take care of the domestic clergy as well as one third of the missionaries. Now there are cases where a pastor has to look after five or six or even more parishes.

That is the background for the *Mission de France*: it is an ambitiously designed experiment with methods that are new, especially for France, of trying to win the country again for Christ from within.

Its precursors are the priests in the sections of Paris most neglected in the ministry (Pierre Lhande, *Christus in der Bannmeile, Gott regt sich*). The spiritual founder is the Abbé Henri Godin (born 1906, burned in his bed 1944). In his book *France pays de mission?* he asks the question whether France is a mission country, and gives an affirmative answer: there is ignorance of the Faith among the masses, lack of understanding and ineptitude in the priests who approach them. ("The priest must leave his bourgeois world, his official position, and become a brother of the worker.")

Godin's daily prayer was: "Holy Virgin and Queen! Keep me from becoming a bourgeois priest! Keep me from forgetting how poor, how very poor I am!" There is a new type of priest developing in France, and, as we have said, it is an excitingly new thing for France. For it is in a country where the familiar silhouette of the Abbé with his Roman *chapeau*, soutane, and the bands, which survive today only in France, is part of the street scene (to an extent, even today); it is in a country where a priest appearing outside the rectory without the cassock was punished with suspension in many dioceses. It is in this country that the priests put aside their clerical dress during the week and settled among the poorest slums, labored with stevedores and shared the work and needs of the day with them. Here, in this milieu, they first wanted to live Christianity themselves and give an example of it before they dared to preach, according to the model of their Master, "who took the nature of a slave and was made like unto men and appeared in the form of a man" (Phil. 2: 7).

Ecclesiastical authorities at first looked the other way. There was room for a sort of Gallican freedom and magnanimity. The increasing distrust, even delations to Rome, were side-tracked by the intervention of the great Cardinal Emmanuel Suhard. Cardinal Suhard realized that the Church

was no longer contacting the greater part of the baptized
with the methods used up until then. It was from him that
the soberly worded confession came: "Of the five million
in my diocese (Paris) there are almost four million without
any connection with the Church." And he acted accordingly. Henri Bordeaux takes even a dimmer view in this
book, *La grande misère du clergé en France:* he estimates
that only five million at most of the forty million French
are practicing Catholics. The most important undertaking
is the *Mission de Paris* (under Abbé Hollande). Those who
cooperate in it (from the secular and regular clergy) are all
volunteers, without any vows. They can also retire at any
time. An absolute mutual confidence is a prerequisite.
Sneaks, creeps, and schemers are all undesirable, and everything that is not human and genuine is turned down. They
wear the soutane only during liturgical functions; otherwise they wear ordinary clothes and live in poverty with the
workers. They never work singly, but there are at least a
pair together (*collège sacerdotal*). They recruit lay helpers.
Their work, at first, has nothing priestly about it, and they
only go after those whom the ordinary ministry does not
reach. They must endure openly and with dignity the suspicion of Communism ("The Vatican's Fifth Column,"
"Paratroopers of the Church").

The *Mission de Marseille* was controlled by the Do-
minican Father Loew from the beginning. For years he
wrestled sacks as a dock worker, and lived for five years in
a slum among the last of the ragged proletariat. (On the
right of his "apartment" lived a rag collector; on the left,
a prostitute.) He worked with the members of the *Jeunesse
ouvrière catholique* (JOC) and formed cells of Christian
families among the poor workers. After five years, at the
request of the Bishop, Father Loew founded a "mission parish" among these neo-pagans. He was offered a beautiful

old villa with a front garden, but in a section where there was not a tree to be seen far and wide! Father Loew refused it, because "the thirty steps from the garden gate to the house would set our work back as many years," as he said while visiting Vienna in July, 1947.

For the central *Mission de France* a special seminary was founded, with Father H. Gray as its regent, by the Franciscan Bishops' Conference in Lisieux. The aim of its training is the "incarnation of the spirit of Christ" in this faithless world; it had 160 priestly candidates for the year 1948-1949. The ministerial aim of the training is this: "the evangelical witness of charity" among men. Personal training is aimed at independence and initiative (*"liberté d'engagement"*) and it is built upon trust (not mistrust); the moral formation is based on conscience. The method is unusual because of its worker groups (*"équipe de vie"*) of six to eight seminarians who are assigned to each other by the director. Attention is given to truthfulness, fraternal cooperation and correction, all with reference to the future work they will do together (no more of the *"curé solitaire"*!). Theology is taught with the motto: "Freedom from all that is mummified: Christianity is not a theory but a message of good tidings."

The form of life: poverty, simplicity, prayer, generosity to one another, and, outside of the seminary, happiness and trust. In their free time, the seminarians help out the poor or the sick that they have looked up somewhere themselves.

What is being tried out in France on a grand scale is going on everywhere in large and small beginnings, even in Germany. Of a Sunday after Mass, Father François goes to the "Sport" café, because he meets the men there who don't go to Church (Robert Morel, *Le Satisfait*, p. 27). It is natural, of course, that during the summer the students go to the places of work, not just as working students among others, but so as to share and know the life of those to whom they will one day have to preach the good news of the kingdom of God.

The thing that first interests us in this connection is that we have here a kind of priest that we have not seen for centuries, a type that takes upon itself the tension between familiarity and distance to the world, the tension between an order of rank and its hostile environment, a life between love and hate, in a daring hazard of utter defenselessness—that of the "sheep in the midst of wolves" (Mt. 10: 16), that of Brother among Brothers—and seeks to make that tension fruitful. For he cannot totally destroy it, since it is an essential part of his existence, according to the words of our Lord: "You are not of the world, but I have chosen you out of the world, therefore the world hates you" (John 15: 19). But these are and will continue to be the words of the commission they receive of Christ! "Do not go in the direction of the Gentiles, nor enter the towns of Samaritans; but go rather to the lost sheep of the house of Israel" (Mt. 10: 5). Here the internal mission is declared superior to the external, obviously, since the latter depends for its power on the former.

Already a novel has appeared dealing with the priest-workers of the *Mission de Paris* (it seems the novelist is keeping step with his times with a stop-watch on his wrist). It comes from Gilbert Cesbron, a layman, and is called *Saints in Hell* (New York, 1954). The locale of the plot is Sagny, an imaginary slum of Paris. The "hero" is Father Pierre, who seeks to master the difficulties and opposition of his ministry (hatred of the worker, mistrust of the employers and the local pastor, as well as the police, and finally of his friend, Henri, the secretary of the local Communist cell). He has a run-in with the archiepiscopal ordinariate and is transferred to the industrial regions of northern France.

The real priest-workers disdain the novel. They have no need of publicity, propaganda, and even less of the literati and their misunderstanding. The author himself confesses in his foreword: "I had no right to write this novel, since I was never poor, nor a priest, nor a worker." Bela Just's *Mission de Paris* portrays the life of a priest, a fugitive from Hungary, who at first takes up the laborious life of a loader in a Paris warehouse, merely to be close to his poor brothers in his homeland. He becomes acquainted with the priests of the Mission and joins them.

Léon Morin hasn't exactly taken off the soutane like the priest-workers, but it is so spotted and dirty that it soon amounts to the same thing. Even his appearance is the existential contradiction of the bourgeois priest of yesteryear. He is completely inept in society, but that doesn't bother him. He has a sense of humor and is always self-confident, even in the most hopeless situations; he is completely independent, a man of disarming cheerfulness. Whoever attacks him is beating the air, for he is no one's enemy. He's far from all show and talk. In his ministerial methods he is foolhardy and often dangerously naive. But he knows how to take care of himself. He pours a bucket of water over the head of a girl who takes a fancy to him, and consoles her with the assurance that she'll soon dry off (Beatrix Beck, *Léon Morin, Priester,* Frankfurt a. M., 1953).

"Freely you have received, freely give. Do not keep gold or silver or money in your girdles, nor wallet for your journey, nor two tunics, nor staff; for the laborer deserves his living" (Mt. 10: 10). Poverty and a life of confidence in God are part and parcel of the priest's existence. And "behold, I am sending you forth like sheep in the midst of wolves" (Mt. 10: 16). Defenselessness and weakness are both presupposed for genuinely religious and effective evangelizing.

The new experiments trying a *permanent* Home Mission such as that of the Capuchins in Zürich (Father Wick) seek out men in their own homes. The poverty of the discalced monks ridicules the trumped-up charge that they are the allies of the capitalists. And, "for reasons of honesty," they do not take off their habits when pursuing their mission. In the city of Zwingli, with its Swiss state religion, that is a risk already. Such a risk would have to be taken, even though the mission itself were in many cases made suspect because of it, and even though, by their visits, those very people were mocked and despised who most need their help. There has to be a scale and hierarchy of values. If the whole world is not as important as one human soul (Mt. 16: 26), one can also confidently suppose that of one Capuchin.

VI. THE GOOD AND DEVOUT PRIEST

We are really telling the truth when we say that the type of priest mentioned here is by far the most common of all the priestly characters. In fact, they outnumber the representatives of all the other types put together. One should not get the impression that the kind of priests who are most written about are found in the same numbers in real life. This impression would be false, since it does not fit the facts. Yet it may seem to be established as a fact, because the unusual cases interest us far more than the ordinary ones. The devout and zealous priest, both in the cities and in the country, represents by far the most predominant type of the Catholic priest. This is true in all the Catholic countries of the world, at every time and place, even though there are different shadings in their variety and dress. That depends on the particular country and its history. There may also be differences in the way the priest lives and in his social acceptability, but they are all of equal dignity. Indeed, this predominant type is well on the way to a kind of uniformity. The earth has shrunk in size; continents today are less distant from one another than the valleys on either side of a mountain, used to be. This also colors the behavior of the priest throughout the universal Church.

All this amounts to saying that this is the type of our

century and that of the immediate future. Many of the characters yet to be described here are the somewhat ghostly descendants of a form of life that was once the predominant type. There may even have been times when, at least in some countries, a very dubious kind of average priest brought the whole calling into disrepute. This would seem to be the case, if a serious historian can put the blame for the decline of the life of the Church on the priests of the fifteen-hundreds (Joseph Lortz, *Reformation*, I, 249), or when Savonarola complains of the same period that it is just those— the priests—who are the cause of the ruin (Joseph Schnitzer, *Savonarola*, Munich, 1923, I, 236). Alois Schrott (*Seelsorge im Wandel der Zeiten*, Graz, 1949, p. 56) cites a popular saying reported in Tacchi-Venturi's *"Storia della Compagnia di Gesú in Italia"* that was current in the 1500's: *"Se vuoi andare all' inferno, fatti prete"* (if you want to go to hell, become a priest). *Corruptio optimi pessima*, as another proverb has it. The corruption of the best is the worst of all. "The mediocre Christian is more despicable than all other mediocrity, for he falls deeper, falling with the whole imponderable weight of the graces he has received" (Bernanos). And first of all, the priest!

1. HIS LIKENESS

Shall we describe the characteristics of this good and pious priest? It is something most difficult to do, because his likeness is taken as something for granted, so that it is consequently rarely described. Because he takes so many forms, it is hard to reduce him to a common denominator. Then again, in his simplicity he is so common and well known that it is not easy to write about him. That is also the reason why many biographies of men who were good priests can be so deathly boring (e.g., J. B. Buohler's *Charakterbilder aus dem katholischen Priester- und Seelsorgerleben,* which was even brought out in a second edition by Father Augustine Maier, Regensburg, 1889).

The same old story is just told and retold in different words. It is only when one can sometimes feel the essence of a real author (e.g. Beda Weber) behind the empty sentences that one can keep on reading.

1. At the risk of the danger just mentioned, let us try to describe the character of the good priest. He endures the tension which he has freely assumed, between the sanctity of his vocation and the weakness of his humanity. The basic law of his existence becomes the basic law of his life. But it differs according to temperament: child-like simplicity or unsparing demands on oneself; crucified or joyful; humorously or with a holy fierceness; but always faithful and loyal, without any heroic self-deception, matter-of-fact and brave.

2. He doesn't merely endure. It is the very tension that he experiences daily that becomes his path to a real, mature humility, not just something he's been talked into. It makes him alert for the people who come to him for help and advice. His holy "life" is also a continual temptation to Pharisaism. The priest is schooled by his own struggles and becomes understanding and compassionate. Priestly existence is a mighty determinant of the existence of the man who is a priest.

3. He has kept the spirit of the newly ordained priest fresh within his soul. But it's not as rosy as it used to be, just true and without illusions. That is his secret. It is the eternal youth of a bent, white-haired priest who prays every morning, as naturally as a newly ordained priest: "I will go

unto the Altar of God, to God, who gives joy to my *youth*." This is not just something that moves us deeply; it gives us an intimation of that state of grace which no longer knows the succession of youth and age. Something of the eternal becomes transparent. He still has his "first love," even though he had to preserve it through struggles and hesitations. The holy Eros has continued to be the strength and grace of his life. It is a fact, not a delusion. That is why he experiences no disillusion. He does not think of this love as a sacrifice, though it grows and grows. He has a vocation which, as no other, gives him insight into souls. He knows what St. Paul means when he would have his followers unmarried, to spare them distress (1 Cor. 7: 26). "It had not been easy for him [Father Smith] to become a priest, of course. It had not been easy to give up the soft comfortable things of the world which were not sinful in themselves. Girls, too . . . but nowadays, when he saw and heard the women he might have married yattering in public places, he did not think that God had asked such a tremendous sacrifice of him after all. And then, when he had seen a few of them all wet and dripping in their bathing dresses, the practice of chastity did not seem quite as difficult as some of the saints had made out" (Bruce Marshall, *The World, the Flesh and Father Smith,* Boston, 1945).

It is priestly Eros that fills his life to the brim with work for the kingdom of God. He smiles over the struggle for the eight-hour day and forty-hour week, and over the strikes to work less and get more. From his own viewpoint, he might misunderstand and rage at the life-struggle of the rest of men, if he were not faced with it every day in a thousand different forms. He knows about boredom only as a word in the dictionary. He never has enough time, scarcely enough to get the rest he needs.

4. He loves his books, theology and asceticism, too. He's

sad that he has so little time for them and that he's only able to follow them in the dribs and drabs of periodicals on theology. With what an experienced heart he could now fill up the meaning of those polished, ivory-tower definitions of the manuals! What wonderful examples and interpretations he would often have liked to discuss with some real professor, if they weren't such a rarity.

Then I think of the old pastor, Ignatius Wenzl (Vienna, XVIII). How often he came up to my room with a passage in the Bible of which he wasn't sure, or to ask whether his comment when explaining the Canon of the Mass last Sunday was permissible: he'd said that the priest after the Consecration was like Moses, who had been forty days alone on the mountain with God. Far away and below him were the people. Then suddenly he remembered the people and, turning aside a little, said half-aloud: *"nobis quoque peccatoribus . . ."* Or whether you could say this: they were preparing for confirmation. Previously, the choir had always done a Mozart Mass during it. But in that Mass, a soprano sings the *"qui tollis peccata mundi,"* as it was written; this year he wanted to have a Mass by Anton Bruckner. Ah, that sounds quite different. He asked his audience if they had noticed how the vineyard workers really labored when they had to haul the buckets loaded with manure to the vineyard? The manure, that was the sins of the world, and our Savior really had to labor under them, to carry them away. In the Mozart Mass, a thin woman's voice sang the *"qui tollis peccata mundi"* (and he imitated it a bit), so he told them there couldn't be much in the tubs. But with Anton Bruckner! Then comes the heavy bass: the Lord is almost collapsing under the weight. Bruckner knows more about the burden of sin that our Lord had to carry . . .

5. The pious priest suffers under this world just as his Master suffered. When he sees how distant it is and how

hard of hearing even the good can be, and how even the
best are often hard to capture, then he would like to weep
with the Lord, who wept over Jerusalem. But he's no pessimist; rather, he's a bit of an eschatologist, to his comfort,
in the sense of "the little while" (John 16: 16). "Amen,
amen, I say to you, that you shall weep and lament, but the
world shall rejoice; . . . but I will see you again and your
heart shall rejoice, and your joy no one shall take from you"
(John 16: 20 ff). Oftentimes he thinks to himself like Father Smith: people aren't as bad as they seem: "It's what I
call the new hypocrisy. In the old days people pretended to
be better than they were, but now they pretend to be worse.
In the old days a man said that he went to church on Sundays even if he didn't, but now he says he plays golf and
would be very distressed if his men friends found out that
he really went to Church" (Marshall).

6. His life itself is his most convincing sermon; and it
makes no difference if this sermon is a little roguish or very
bumpy or really original and quite idiomatic, and certainly
not at all if it has humor. It is his genuinely human quality
and healthy individuality that makes up for everything.
Anyone who goes around like a lithographed sample of all
the virtues convinces no one. He may even seem comic. Only
what is genuine in nature and grace has a real effect. His
life, his prayer, his Mass are the source of that power his
words have. *Agere sequitur esse.*

7. And the thing that is decisive: every day he places
himself in the field of tension proper to life and especially
to priestly life, with every Mass he celebrates, and every
sermon ,he preaches. He confronts himself every evening,
and examines both sides and submits himself to the judgment: with simplicity, honesty, and inflexibly. In his novel
Der Kaplan, Joseph Bernhart paints a likeness of this priest.
But the most precious portrait of the pious priest is painted

with much experience and humor by Bruce Marshall in his *The World, the Flesh and Father Smith*. The priests described by the Irish Canon Sheehan all belong here. His stories should never be forgotten. Most recently A. J. Cronin gives us a realization of independent priestly character in his *The Keys of the Kingdom*. The depth of Father Chisholm's faith lay in his love of the poor, in his work in the disreputable parts of the city where he got fleas . . . He was never comfortable, never at ease except at the bedside of those who were crippled and outcasts of fate or when looking into hopeless eyes. He is an independent character who does what he thinks is right before God. And it is a matter of complete indifference to him what his fellow priests say. Cronin has the Bishop give him some rather dangerous words of praise: "For me you are not a failure but a howling success. You can do with a little cheering up, so I'll risk giving you a swelled head. You've got inquisitiveness and tenderness. You're sensible of the distinction between thinking and doubting. You're not one of our ecclesiastical milliners who must have everything stitched up in neat packets—convenient for handing out" (Cronin).

2. THE DEVOUT PRIEST

Out of the great number that we have described here, one could pick out a group that the people would call "devout." They represent a type halfway between the canonized saint and the pious priest. If the people could determine who was to be revered as a saint by their honoring of them, as they once did, there would be more "sainted priests." Untold numbers of them have deserved it.

And yet not in the same sense as the pastor of Ars. Helene Haluschka introduced her account of the Pastor of Lamotte with the words: "There have been greater saints on earth than our Pastor of Lamotte. But none, I think, so full of human understanding and compassion." And she adds: "He was certainly no saint; he loved his rose garden, his glass of Neuchâtel wine and his bacon bread too much for that. But no one took exception to it, because his weaknesses brought him closer to men's souls than his virtues." This latter fact is quite frequent and makes one think. The door of the rectory in Lamotte is open day and night so that wanderers can help themselves at any time of day or night to the bacon bread and the jug of cider that was always ready for them on the kitchen table. The Pastor of Lamotte can certainly take his place in the ranks of those we are discussing here, despite his liking for a glass of Neuchâtel and bacon bread. He's not a saint in the sense of the Church. And he would laugh loudly in his own way and with real humility, to hear that he was mentioned in such a connection. Yet, when his housekeeper marries a widower out of sheer sympathy for his brood of children, and the old pastor stands there abandoned, he argues a while with God: "What am I supposed to do then—become a saint?"

There are priests whose piety and charity and compassion can't be missed. There are priests who are never forgotten by anyone who meets them, priests whose effectiveness is only felt in a place long after the name on their gravestones has become illegible. We could all give examples of such men. Here we have to rely on written witnesses.

There is the pastor in Adalbert Stifter's *Kalkstein* who lives in complete poverty in a lonely mountain village in order to be able to build a bridge over a treacherous stream for his school children. There is the selfless, deeply devout old man, afflicted with gout: Don Evaristo in Stefan Andres' *Das Tier aus der Tiefe*. His cassock is soiled; the sacristy smells of rabbits and chickens which are stalled next to it, and of fish, too. But the Savior, who always liked fishermen when He was on earth, wouldn't be put out by that. He shares the poor life of his people in the old Città Morta. Then there is the mountain pastor in the story by Franz Jantsch, whose door is open to welcome anyone who comes to him.

There are the two pastors described, or rather set to poetry by Francis Jammes: the saintly pastor of Abrecave, at whose grave a miracle takes place, and his pupil, the pastor of Ozeron. With the matter-of-factness of a devout youngster, he chooses the priestly vocation: "Actually, religion seemed to this soul in the midst of the unfolding secret of life like a mountain that towered toward heaven, and no doubt could underlie its existence at least. Such a life was itself already an answer to the question of the creature" (*Le Curé d'Ozeron*, p. 21). The great model of the old pastor of Abrecave accompanies him throughout his life. Like him, he too wants to be devout, gentle, and kindly, and belong entirely to his holy vocation. How wise and understanding he is in allaying hostility! How simply and convincingly, and yet how considerately he wins over the old sinner Poli (pp. 88 ff); he becomes a steady man. The *Novel* is a poem in prose on the pearl necklace which a young countess gives to her uncle, the old pastor of Abrecave, on the day when the future pastor of Ozeron says his first Mass. The proceeds of this necklace's sale in the hands of the pastor of Ozeron become a pearly chain of good deeds which give promise of continuing to produce good. No one departs from him without a blessing. And no one can forget him. The rascal Poli goes through the countryside as a junk dealer, singing his pastor's praises: "The old chicken thief had received only a dew-drop of the pastor's blessings, but that drop was a pearl, too, the pearl in which the heaven of poor wretches was mirrored. He felt how his heart overflowed in the midst of the overshadowing splendor. And in order to show his joy in his own way, he blew on his little horn, the way that street peddlers do" (p. 221).

There is no doubt that the saintly pastors mentioned here were not made up by the authors, but were drawn from life. It may be that traits seen in different persons are attributed to one. We could all of us name priests who are like these, whose characters are unforgettable. It is a real service that is done us when Pastor John B. Buohler collects his *Charakterbilder aus dem katholischen Priester- und Seelsorgerleben*, even when his talent as a story-teller isn't considerable. Many of the men mentioned there have even been forgotten by their own fellow-priests. It is unjust, but unavoidable, that those only are remembered who were Bishops, such as George Michael Wittmann (Regensburg) who is mentioned in the book, or Clement August Count Droste of Vischering (Cologne) or that others are remembered in a particular place, such as the Cathedral Canon in Vienna, Franz Schmid (died 1843). It is an injustice to the others, if you will, if only those are mentioned who had a place in history as authors or intellectuals. But this injustice, too, is unavoidable. Their lives do have a universal meaning. Their lives are written in a book of eternal importance—in the "Book of Life" (Apoc. 3: 5).

There is the case of John Henry Newman, not only a very great thinker and theologian, perhaps the greatest of the last century, but also a deeply devout, saintly priest. After a night spent in prayer, he put his confession of Catholic Faith in the hands of a Passionist priest on October 10, 1845 (almost at the same time that Ernest Renan, after a long crisis in his faith, abandoned the Seminary of St. Sulpice).

Newman took the same step as he, but in the opposite direction: "to be converted means to devote yourself unconditionally and unreservedly to God and forget yourself wholly in Him," he says. This decision is not one of unalloyed rejoicing. "The joy one feels because of the present grace and the fear of the judgment to come" are quite possible and even matter-of-course in the heart of the convert. The necessary tension of this life is only raised to a higher level. "Let us therefore be the living paradox as we are said to be in Scripture" (M. Laros, *Kardinal Newman,* Mainz, 1921, p. 78).

This great theologian was surrounded by suspicion at the peak of his productivity that would have disheartened other men, but he endured it with the greatness of soul and devout silence that this paradox demands. In his strong faith, and in the belief that God's love would try him, he overcame all bitterness of heart and, thus purified, he lived the lonely prayer of the last years of his life: "To be misunderstood, that is my fate . . . That has always turned me more and more into myself, and driven me to an even more intimate union with God. I came to understand that my only consolation is the Most Blessed Sacrament" (p. 97). Alienated from the world, he welcomes the gradual extinction of his earthly life as a delivery, as a liberation from the images and likenesses of time in exchange for the vision of eternity. He composed his own epitaph: *"Ex umbris et imaginibus in veritatem"* (Leaving behind the shadows and images of earth, I go to the Truth).

Or take the case of Newman's friend, Frederick William Faber. How moving is the leave-taking of the pastor from his congregation in Eton, when he had finally decided, after years of struggle, to profess his faith in the Catholic Church. He stands in the pulpit and tells his unsuspecting and shocked parishioners, "What I have preached to you up until now was all true. But today I know that it is not the teaching of the Anglican Church. Therefore I must leave it for the sake of Truth." He descended from the pulpit, let his cassock drop, and went to the rectory. There they besought him to stay, saying that they would accept what he had preached before and whatever he would preach later. But he leaves, and all cry after him, "God bless you, wherever you go!"

In the Oratory at Brompton (London), he now lives his rich, devout life. He hardly ever goes out. He suffers much, prays, reads, and writes. The fact that he captivates everyone, even in the best society, by his consummate courtesy, kindness, unselfish consideration, wisdom, and gracious conversation, numbers him among the imitators of the holy Bishop of Geneva.

The death for which he had prepared so well was long remembered in the Oratory. His consolation was the prayers of Saint Gertrude, whose intercession he constantly besought in the last days of his life. He died, as he had advised others to do in his book, *All for Jesus:* "Serve Jesus out of love, and even before your eyes are closed in death, before pallid death spreads over your countenance, even before those who surround your deathbed are sure that this last sigh they hear is your dying breath, ah, what a surprise will be yours! You will stand before the judgment seat of your dearly Beloved, your Love Himself; the songs of the heavens will sound in your ear and the glory of God will shine from your eyes, never again to be extinguished."

This example should stand for all the other devout priests: for an Alban Stolz, whose beatification, I hear, is being readied; for the less well-known, but no less holy priest, Andreas Faulhaber, who was hanged in Glatz, a martyr for the secrecy of the confessional (on December 30, 1757, by order of Frederick II); or for the well-known social worker, Father Adolf Kolping, whose beatification is also in process.

3. TYPES OF THE GOOD AND DEVOUT PRIEST

Now we come back to the simple, devout priests. It is impossible to describe this great throng more accurately than we have done already. But it is easy to distinguish not only strong personalities among them, but also determined types, even if this difference depends only on the kind of work in which they are principally engaged.

The Silent Sufferer

There's the case of the silent sufferer, the man whose work is hidden. The world about him is convinced of his piety, of course, but because of the secrecy of his effectiveness he always presents a problem, if not a puzzle. This is where Father Mathias, in Elisabeth Langgässer's *Unauslöschliche Siegel*, belongs. Even the "Jansenistic" cross on his desk brings him into sharp focus. "It was a terrible and shocking piece of work, which came from a French branch of the Mathias family. M. Henri Matthieu, as his distant uncle was named, had willed this cross to his clerical nephew." M. Bellefontaine is surprised to find something like this in his pastor's house. "These closely pressed arms, which embrace but few, according to the doctrine of Port Royal, and which restricted the fullness of divine love within His breast at the moment of the Redemption . . . the head, thrown back in pain with the tense arching of the throat, which prolonged His cry to His Father in that hour of greatest need into horrible seconds . . . All this was without consolation or compassion; it was a sign of wrath and of justification, yes, even more, it was the irrevocable condemnation of predestination" (p. 89). What was this cross doing on his desk, on the table of this pastor so well known for his kindliness, who at this very moment was being badgered by an insistent farmer in the garden? At midnight he comes out of a house of ill repute and is seen. Bellefontaine, shocked, asks him: "Your ignorance—please, Father, don't take me amiss—in all the affairs of daily life is truly pitiable. Haven't you ever even given a thought to the consequences to yourself, to come here all alone?" And the pastor answers: "Well, I believe it is my fate to have to give scandal. Or has that escaped your acute mind up to now?" (p. 188)

Yes, his kind of ministry was a scandal even to himself: "I was their shepherd for twenty years," he says of the farmers, "and even now these poor fellows' faith is not self-sufficient. It is I alone who stand in their way. A wonder-worker, but not one to wake the dead. One who deprives them of their Faith, instead of helping them on" (p. 99). Not a rare case at all. But with Father Mathias it is different. He can arouse men to faith, and does it, plainly and stubbornly, when it comes to a showdown (p. 224). And he is not afraid of taking the round-about way, no matter how long it is. He is the sower who resolutely went out to sow his seed, but he sees nothing but weeds growing. His greatness lies in his loyalty, which is unconsoled, but remains firm. For his loyalty trusts in God.

This is exactly the kind of life Bernanos' diary-writing priest lives: "Should one want to judge us according to our so-called deeds," he writes, "it would be just as vain as if we were to be condemned for our dreams" (p. 109).

Simple and Unassuming

There are the unassuming, simple, and pious priests. Their number is legion. We have all met one. Their lives preach more than their words. They are disregarded and silent witnesses of the omnipotence and splendor of God. They are noticed scarcely any more than the daisies of the field, yet both of them bloom not only in the summer, when God's sun makes it easy, but in the winter, too. It is rare that anyone realizes it; only their most intimate friends know them. It is rare that their deaths are noted outside of their own parish.

There are Father Malachy in Bruce Marshall's *Father Malachy's Miracle,* and Father Smith by the same author. There is the throng described by Father Buohler so simply, perhaps precisely, because their lives were no different. There is the lonely mountain curate whose death Beda Weber describes so movingly in his *Charakterbildern* (Frankfurt a.M., 1853, pp. 69 ff. In Buohler, pp. 192-215). "The habit of his devout life and work became even more vital and spiritually transformed in him, the weaker his body became. All those present felt deeply that they continued to live on with his spirit, and that they would meet with the most beautiful fulfillment of heaven, so that one could truly say that his deeds followed him. Each one understood in this splendid image of death the importance of preparation and lifelong habits on earth for a happy life later in heaven" (pp. 214 f).

Their virtues and their humanity work harmoniously together. There's nothing tremendous that one can see. It is much like their restricted field of work, as in the case of Don Evaristo. The great Dr. Moosthaler took objection to everything he met with; he had "touched his vestments as though they were rags. They were certainly poor, but not particularly out of place in so poor a church" and "turned up his nose, because it smelled of hares and fish. But how could it smell differently in a place where fishermen, miners, and day laborers live and raise rabbits and go fishing?" (Stefan Andres, *Das Tier aus der Tiefe,* p. 160). And yet these poor priests are like crystal and precious stones; they do not glitter only because they are never brought out into the light from their concealment and darkness.

Inspired by Love of Neighbor

There is the great throng of those who, kindled by the love of God, love His creatures, men, especially the poorest and most abandoned, and to a most improbable degree. And yet this sheer improbability is a reality in their lives, as it was in the case of the pastor of Ozeron and his model, the pastor of Abrecave. There is the pastor of Lamotte, kindly and compassionate to the point of despoiling himself. Day and night, every day, his door is always open to welcome the traveler. And on the table there waited bacon bread and a jug of cider for anyone who was hungry or thirsty. "La Pepie," his housekeeper, no longer dared to hang up the torn linen of the pastor to dry publicly, because he had given away all his good shirts. In the winter time, the windows of the rectory frosted over, because all of the wood had wound up in a little house at the edge of the village. Ignoring the giggling sales girls, he himself buys a poor woman the most beautiful hat he could find in the smart shops of the city, so that she could go to church. And well he understood how to instruct his people in love of neighbor in his sermons (pp. 34 ff).

There is Ludwig Mather's *Herr Johannes* (Munich,

1930), the father of students and pastor of Kaltenscheidt in Venn. He doesn't seem nearly as pleasant as he really is. He is brusque, short. "A powerful, wrathful giant. A square skull, as sharp-edged as a *Vennwacken*,[1] with terrible, raven-black Holofernes hair" (p. 9). But he has a heart of gold. And he doesn't even give up on Jerry, when his former model boy finally becomes a frivolous worldling. Then there is Watzlik's *Pfarrer von Dornloh,* who shows his tremendous charity to his congregation at a time of extreme necessity, and so preserves Dornloh for his people.

The Social Reformer

One group represents the great and hidden *advocates of social justice* and love of neighbor in priestly dress.

The Pastor of Harassenwyl is known to his fellow-priests as "Radicalinsky." But he did provide work for his poor parishioners: a great brush factory ("from top to bottom all the corridors and holes were stuffed full of pig bristles and plant filaments"), with whose products still others were going from house to house; a great herb apothecary thrived on flowers and weeds that used to dry up unnoticed; an extensive snail nursery provided for the fanciers of this Lenten delicacy for miles around; a knitting mill kept the formerly starving and unemployed tenants occupied. The people live, cooperate, and produce what they need themselves. They built the church themselves. There are never any *collections*. "Of course it's built on the lines of a barn and much too small," "the shrine-gothic of the altar, the saccharine statues, the gingerbread of the sober decoration of windows and walls, cold as a November day." The pastor helped his con-

---

[1] *Vennwacken,* a common type of bread for this area (German-Dutch border), large and rectangular.

gregation economically, in his own fashion. There was much to criticize and some cause for compliant. The parish was "a horrible mish-mash of village and city." But that doesn't bother him (Herz, *Vikar und Presshusar*, Regensburg).

They are the small and well known social reformers and helpers in priestly dress. There are others on a grand scale, however. Bishop William Emanuel Count Ketteler: even as a curate in Beckum he was supporting the needy and the poor. As pastor of Hosten (1846) he was stubbornly trying to raise the moral—and economic—level of his parish. He was elected to the Frankfurt National Assembly in 1848. Half-forced by his friends, he accepted the appointment. He, the Count, sought help in his fight to help the workers by joining the left. That often put him on Lassalle's side. But a lasting fight in company with free thinkers was impossible. He founded the "Catholic Club." It was not easy to bear the tension of priest and parliamentarian. Even then he wanted to remain all priest. It is not at all surprising, then, that the most important announcements of his plans for social reform were sermons. Such was the series given in the Mainz cathedral on "The great Social Problems of the Present" (W. E. Ketteler's Writings, edited by John Mumbauer, Munich, 1911). Or he utilized episcopal letters which he published when bishop of Mainz.

Among the greatest who should be mentioned here is Adolf Kolping. Since his beatification is already in progress, his name is mentioned in one of the earlier sections.

He was born on December 8, 1813. He came of modest circumstances, but the pious family from which he took his origin led him to consider the family the educational institution given by God Himself, which one must necessarily imitate but never can replace. He became a shoemaker, and as a journeyman learned the distress, the misery, and especially the dangers of the worker looking for a job. He loved his days of travel all the rest of his life. For him, travel was a symbol of our life. After the death of his mother (1834), he decided to act upon an old longing, and after careful consideration, he became a priest. He started his humanistic studies at the age of twenty-four. He was poor, often in great distress, and frequently ill. An old chronic cough set in. Nevertheless, and despite all warning, he found the time to nurse a poor shoemaker, abandoned in an attic room with smallpox, until his death. In 1846 he was ordained in Cologne. Then as a curate in Elberfeld, he called his former fellow-workers together. In 1848, there appeared an appeal for members of his union with the motto: "Active charity heals all wounds; mere words make the pain worse."

He wanted to found a great family of those who were wandering around looking for work, separated from their parents and families. Everywhere, wherever they went, there were to be houses ready for them, in which they would feel at home. All of these houses would be under the patronage of St. Joseph, the artisan and patron of the family. They would not just drop out of the Christian family as uprooted men; religion, virtue, industry, professional honesty, charity, and peace would be the stars of this great family. Joy and good humor would reign in all the houses. As cathedral vicar in Cologne, he founded the first "Catholic Workers Union," in the modern sense, in 1851. Now Kolping pleaded for his ideal in long journeys and in all of his writings. In 1862 he became rector of the Minorite Church in Cologne. Then he, who was always sickly, though ever unwearied, died on December 4, 1853, and was buried. But his work prospered. In 1853 the first workers' house was built in Cologne. In Germany and Austria alone there are 300 workers' homes. There are many others in all the countries of Europe, in North and South America. Millions of workers since their foundation have known the blessing of a home that tried to take the place of a family until they could start their own. The number of members in the best years was about 150,000.

And all that was the work of a single priest who devoted his life to it. And his disciples and his spirit lived on, and spread a blessing wherever it breathed. They are all included in this section. Adolf Kolping created an enduring type of priest with his own life, and it is still among us.

Priests with Magnetic Charm

Now we are discussing those priests who by nature and spirit exercise an almost magical influence on the world about them. They are like magnets to which everything is attracted as soon as they appear, and yet the secret of this power is not in their wills, but in their great and holy personalities. Complete priests, complete Christians, and great men they are, often gifted with an unusually rich mind, yet withal guileless as children in their temper. For that reason they are often misunderstood and misinterpreted. Such a man was John Michael Sailer. Georges Goyau once called him the German Francis de Sales; and he could well be enumerated among those followers of his described above.

He too came from a family in poor circumstances. He was born November 17, 1751, at Aresing in Bavaria. His father was a shoemaker and his mother was not only a woman who educated the child, but all his life she was his model of the ideal Christian mother. Much later, in his book *Erziehung für Erzieher*·he wrote, "Thank you, dearest Mother! I will ever be in your debt. As often as I considered your look, your bearing, your way of life, your suffering, your silence, your giving, your work, your blessing hand, your quiet, continual prayer from the earliest years, eternal life and the feeling of religion were then born anew in me. And afterwards no doubt, no suffering, no depression, not even sin could kill this feeling in me. This eternal life still lives in me, even though you left this world of time behind you forty years since."

This is the source of that inmost, unshakable peace of this priest, even in the years of the hardest trial. Here too lies the secret of his sure, balanced humanity, a gift of nature and grace that made such an impression on all. He was ordained in 1775 at Eichstätt; and by 1777, he was a lecturer in philosophy and theology at the University of Ingolstadt; by 1780, professor of dogma. The most fruitful years of his life, in intellectual productivity and priestly work, were the years 1784-1794, in which he was lecturing in popular and pastoral theology at the University of Dillingen. These wonderful ten years ended in 1793 with a humiliating disciplinary reprimand and his deposition in 1794.

Even the documents of this reprimand, which long served to found suspicion and slander against him, and whose untenability was proved by the research of Remigius Stölze, show us Sailer in all his priestly greatness and power. The chief reason for his deposition, of course, was the envy of some of his colleagues who could not stand his influence on his students. "The chief sin of Sailer was his tremendous influence on the students—a title of honor and a proof of his intellectual superiority. This it was that angered those less influential colleagues. It was this that they could not forgive" (Stölze).

Because even students of Kant came to him, he was labeled a follower of the Enlightenment; he was reported to have undermined morale and discipline. What truth was there in this charge? The kindly Sailer had often interceded successfully for disciplined students, and it happened that students cut obligatory lectures to attend his. The "Regulativ" which his opponents wrung from the weak Elector and Bishop Clement Wenceslaus on September 16, 1793, forbade Sailer's private lectures (for these were always filled to overflowing), forbade any discussions after a lecture (after class he was always besieged with questioners), forbade his work unions ("Forest Sermons"), since his free time belonged to the students, and the same thing applied to his hikes. The theologians now were to have him for only one year instead of three, and lectures for the students of all other faculties were forbidden him. He was to be put on the shelf.

And how did he take it? On August 1, 1793, in the midst of the attack, he writes in his diary: "This was a year of bitter suffering, and so, as Christ teaches us, a year of great blessings. What else can we do but praise the Lord for it —to recognize our nothingness in His eyes—to do good with His grace—to suffer evil as we must according to His providence—and await complete refreshment from His good graces?" And later he writes: "Lord, suddenly you cast me into the sea, without a purchase under me, without heaven over me, without shore to right or left; all is lightless, groundless, shoreless. Health, peace of soul, honor, possessions, and friends you threaten to take; you destroyed everything to give me all. That means what can, what else ought I to do but put myself and all that is mine wholly and unconditionally in Your hands and heart."

Under the spurious pretense of economy (the complaints did not suffice to have him dismissed from his office), his chair was discontinued and in the most galling way he was transferred to Asylingen as Beneficiate. In 1799 he again returned to the University, this time Ingolstadt, for moral theology, homiletics, and pedagogy.

Now for the first time his influence spread abroad. But even here there was no lack of suspicion. He reveals his true greatness in the manner in which he answered his friends who pleaded with him to defend himself; "I would rather suffer ten years in innocence than spend one day in the defense of my innocence. With me it is not a virtue to forget the injustices I have suffered; to remember them is a source of disquiet, and peace of conscience is so dear to me that I would rather not live without it."

There were no important Catholics in the Germany of the beginning of the nineteenth century who were not Sailer's pupils or who were not at least decisively influenced by him. He isn't mentioned much in the history of theology, since he was far from the revival of Scholasticism. But he is the most read theologian up to the present day, and many of his works still appear in new editions. There have been about twenty biographies written of him. There are two works which deal only with the great number of his pupils and disciples: Berthold Lang, S. J.'s *Bischof Sailer und seine Zeitgenossen* (Regensburg, 1933) and Philip Funk's *Von der Aufklärung zur Romantik* (Munich, 1925).

The story of his encounter with Melchior von Diepenbrock is characteristic of him: Diepenbrock was a hero of freedom in the struggle against Napoleon, a repulsive, haughty Junker who always got himself into a rage whenever he learned that Sailer had returned to his father's castle. To avoid meeting the priest, he always went hunting. Once, in 1817, he was persuaded by his mother to at least make a courtesy call. The call resulted in a short walk. And after that, this problem child of his parents decided to return to the sacraments. He began to study theology with Sailer; and when Sailer was appointed Bishop of Regensburg, he became his private secretary. He was the later great Prince Bishop and Cardinal Diepenbrock of Breslau. From him, long a friend of Sailer, we have a testimony which reads: "I have observed him in times of sickness and health, in hours of joy and sadness, in moments of the highest honor and again in bitter disappointment. I have seen him deal with the most varied kinds of men, great and small, friends and enemies, patrons and those who envied him, enthusiastic admirers and cold observers and eavesdroppers—and I can assure you before God that I have always found him to be never petty, never unlike himself, never proud or small-minded, never angered, never put out of spirits, never irritable or morbid; and even though he was deeply hurt and saddened on occasion, he never lost control of himself, was never moved by passion, but always worthy of himself. He was a man by whom one was lifted up, edified, and taught how to be a man and a Christian."

This testimony is also the answer to the question of the source of the tremendous personal and intellectual influence of this priest, and of others like him. It would be difficult to find another priest of his greatness, however, despite the fact that he may be of the same stamp.

The Organizer

Priests whose chief characteristic is their talent for organization form another group. Mostly they are clear-sighted, masterful characters. The tension between the openness to the world that the priest must have, and the danger of succumbing to the world as a priest of the world, for these men becomes a particularly keen temptation. They tend to try to defeat the world with its own feared means and methods. The warning of Saint Paul, "Be not conformed to this world," they think not meant for them, as far as their methods are concerned.

The founders and organizers of the great Catholic alliances belong here. They have something of the general about them. They fit in well with the organizations of the Church, and she recognizes that. It is well known that the Catholics present the greatest religious united front, even though they are outnumbered by some other confession in a particular country.

You can come across these types in many of the north and northwestern parishes of Germany. We have already met them in the foreword. Here we think principally of the Dutch pastor: he has his parish firmly in his grasp. The confessional school, the help of the State and that of rich parishioners give him the possibility of laying a sound foundation of Catholic life and making it secure. Here too belongs the pastor (and even more, the Bishop) in Ireland. He is not only a spiritual leader, but even outside the church he is an important man in the community, as is quite understandable from the history of Ireland.

Related to these, and fired with the enthusiasm of the matter-of-course freedom of movement that he has in his country, is the North American "Father." Even sports and physical well-being were developed in his seminary training. His theological course aimed more at producing a pastor who is prudent, practical, and able to lead the people. For he is not only a minister in the ordinary sense, but, as a pastor, the parish school is also under him and, in larger places, also the high school. And since in the United States charity is still left to a great extent in the hands of the Church, he may also be in charge of a hospital or sometimes an old people's home. Of course, he also takes charge of all the Catholic organizations and their works, either personally (as moderator) or through his assistant priest. His importance in the parish is unquestioned. He is also respected by non-Catholics, who are always being impressed by the organizational ability of the Father.

Even that title of "Father" testifies to his position. After his ordination he is called "Father" by his own family, and even by his mother. He is the Father of his congregation. Therefore, he can address all his parishioners, even including women who are older than he, by their first names. And the Americans want to see him respected. The poor *prete* of Italy, the starving *cura* in Spain, even the poor *Curé* of France who is beginning to find a following everywhere today, with his worn-out soutane—pastor, curate, sexton, and housekeeper all in his own person—is not according to the taste of the northern New World. They would consider it a disgrace if their Father could not live as a regular citizen, if he couldn't afford a car and hire a housekeeper, which is considered much more of a luxury in the United States than it is in the Old World. A sample of this type is Father William Monaghan, pastor of St. Margaret's in a suburb of Boston. Because of his ability in raising money for his church and school, the people call him "Dollar Bill." "In other times and places, had he not been a priest, William Monaghan might have been many things; centurion under Pompey, the master of a clipper ship, or the general manager of a Bessemer steel mill . . . he ran the parish of St. Margaret's as a veteran conductor runs a crack train, responsibly and hard, along the steel tracks of pay-as-you-go discipline" (Henry Morton Robinson, *The Cardinal,* New York, 1950).

And yet this type does not represent a priest who lords it over the people. Kühnelt-Leddihn distinguishes him in his study of the priesthood even from the clergy of the other Anglo-Saxons. The American does not want "a pastor who belongs to the poorer class, but not a high-born Anglo-Saxon with a Harvard accent, either; nor do they want a bookworm, but just a jovial fellow like you and me. One who is different from them, not in essence, but in degree, so that they have to look up to him. That is why even the seminary does not set too much store by separation from the people, and the seminarians enjoy earning their own bread with a 'summer job' during the holidays."

The organizer type is personified on a grand scale in Dr. Karl Sonnenschein (born July 15, 1876, in Düsseldorf; died February 20, 1929, in Berlin). Before the first World War he was the organizer of the SSS (Secretariate of Student Social Work) in the People's Union for Catholic Germany (Munich-Gladbach). Within a few years, he had educated thousands of students to responsibility for the people as a whole, where before they had spent their lives in arrogance of social position, student pranks, drinking bouts, and drinking songs. Many of them may only have taken an inkling of it all with them into life. His publication was *Sozialen Studentenblätter,* and in his programmatic book, *Die sozialstudentische Bewegung* (Paderborn, 1909), Sonnenschein projected gigantic plans. There was no question of higher education that he left untouched: university training, dormitories, textbooks, libraries, study halls, health insurance, scholarships, student government, freedom of assembly, education for popular solidarity; "leadership is not inherited, but won"; psychology of the worker, metropolitan problems, the question of sex, right of unionization, strikes, surveys, instruction courses for the workers, Vincent de Paul work, study of the social question, summer jobs, settlement, "Student and Alcohol," "Student and Waitress," student and the rest of youth, cooperation with other peoples, especially those of neighboring nations and their students, welfare work for and by the students. In gigantic numbers, pamphlets went to all college towns with news, information, and pleas for further membership, and in all the college towns, students' social study groups were founded.

When the first World War was over, the active Rhinelander disappeared for a time. "Where will he start next?"

people wondered. Suddenly he popped up in Berlin in 1918. Here he created the type of the metropolitan priest on a grand scale, "the modern apostle with telephone connections and a checking account." He had set himself a terrific program (on his own initiative, with the subsequent approval of his Bishop): he wanted to educate the 400,000 Catholics of the capital (10% of the whole population) to form a solid Catholic bloc with strong self-consciousness. He had the seeds of his death in him when he went to Berlin. He went to a doctor: "How long do I still have?" "Ten years." "Ten years? Good, I can do it by then." He lived through the last ten restless years of his life with a watch in his hand.

First he prepared the groundwork. He committed himself to no one direction. The canonical framework was, for him, too narrow, not bold enough, too old and outworn.

His ministry, at least at first, is not strictly sacerdotal. He knows it, but brings the men on whom he was to rely, not into the Church, but to his offices and conference rooms. He again sets up the SSS (Secretariate of Student Social Work), the AAA (Universal Labor Office) and the KKK (Catholic Artist's Union), for he was partial to them by his very nature. In these ten years, he became the organizer of the Berlin Catholics.

He himself lived an extremely poor life. No one really knew on what he was living, nor where he got the money to run his offices and pay his employees. He lived without any order, day and night, so to speak. Often he had nothing to eat. Then he would just up and go to some family he knew and invite himself for dinner, or he would consume a pie someone had just given him. His was an artistic nature, with a touch of the *littérateur*, the Bohemian, the party-goer and fellow worker, intelligent, uprooted, with an amazing sort of gushing intelligence. He is a keen observer: he waits and can wait until the moment to strike comes; then he strikes brutally. It was thus that he finally wrested the *Berliner Kirchenblatt* for himself after long planning, and he made it over in his own spirit and format. It became his organ, with which to extend his influence.

He set all his media into continuous attack on all fronts: pulpits, monster files, telephone, cars, offices, telephone poles, the press, consultations, pamphlets. All of them got to work and he with them, almost day and night. An army of volunteer workers stood at his disposal. He himself was a brilliant speaker and editor (the ten volumes of *Notizen* that came out after his death are mostly from his *Kirchen-blatt*).

And the success? He had called the Catholic minority of Berlin to life, to be Christians in big city style, to be the Catholics of the German capital, and that without any spite toward others. He wanted a spirit of Catholic awareness among students, workers, athletes, immigrants, foreigners. A city of the world listened to him, far beyond the realm of the Catholics.

But his work was one-sided. His methods were unconsidered. His opponents were especially the representatives of the hierarchic, the sacramental methods of ministry, the pastors. His importance was recognized more and more by the official Church and his methods of work tolerated. He knew that he would still have to come to an understanding with the official ministry. But for a man of his type, that could only mean one thing, and that was to take the controls into his own hand. It didn't work.

He was already a broken man, marked for death in 1928, when he tried to justify his methods before the Magdeburg Catholic Convention and seek support. That was a year before his death. The theme of his speech was "The Ministry in Heavy Industry and the Metropolis." It was a partial failure, or was it a total one? "He spoke without finding any echo of his sentiments; he went awry in stating the problem, but took over control of the problem at the same time, an exaggerated control; he was laughed at, and people sensed the overweening pride that blinded him, and realized the tragic beginning of the great struggle against the collapse of all moderation" (Ernest Thrasolt, *Dr. Karl Sonnenschein: Der Mensch und sein Werk,* Munich, 1930, p. 386).

But it was clear to all how important Karl Sonnenschein was and how far the radius of his work reached when he was buried. There had not been such a funeral since the last Kaiser was buried. The Government was represented by all its ministers, and the diplomatic corps; among the mourners hundreds of thousands marched in the procession which took hours to pass through the black-flagged streets of the capital. The newspapers of all parties wrote long farewells. All the religious bodies, Catholic and non-Catholic, grieved at his grave. A Communist confessed, "That's no funeral; it's a migration." And someone answered him, "That is a priest who got no salary and fed and clothed thousands." He was a great priest, and in his way, inimitable, a personality that was great to the point of being autocratic.

At his grave, Wilhelm Deling said, "Sonnenschein lived like a beggar and died like a king." And that is the best judgment of him.

The Lord-Pastor

Born rulers on a small scale are those lord-pastors without whose permission not a cock can crow in the village. They

are a race that has been sorely reduced in number during the course of time, but their almost universal sway lasted until late into the nineteenth century and in many places even into the twentieth. "The conduct of life, marriage, and morality were still unchallenged . . . The names of girls who had fallen were unrelentingly read from the pulpit, and the Spanish cane of many a pastor was much feared by the young. When the inhabitants—so we read occasionally—prolonged their Mardi Gras celebrations into Ash Wednesday, the pastor would appear in the dance hall and smash the musical instruments in righteous indignation" (Franz Schnabel, *Deutsche Geschichte im neunzehnten Jahrhundert,* p. 45). They lived then and today without a stir of opposition. That made them autocratic. The only time anyone ever made a fist against them, it was in his pocket. The will of the pastor was final.

There is Pastor Campens from Kempenland. He directs his congregation right from the pulpit on down. "Everyone found that a man such as the late Pastor Campens had the right to tell him the truth to his face; that he had the right to come up to him on the street and give him a good dressing down. If there had been a quarrel in any household, then the late Pastor Campens could go there forthwith to tell them what he thought about it. Oh yes, the pastor could do that calmly and no one would have looked at him twice for doing it. . . . One day Jan Seppes, the mason, had disported himself shamefully when he was reeling drunkenly through the village. A couple of fresh kids had pulled his pants off—this didn't prevent Seppes from staggering from one pub to the next; then the late Pastor Campens burst into his house that same evening, and fetched Jan three or four mighty slaps in the face right in front of his wife and seven children. Suddenly Jan was as sober as a judge and saw stars dancing before his eyes. As the pastor went out, he left with the warning: 'And now you just show up for confession, you hear, Jan, and you'll find out what a binge like this costs . . . shameless fellow that you are!' And Jan Seppe's own wife and seven children were agreed that Father Pastor had really pulled him up short for once, for he hadn't a word to say" (Ernst Claes, *Der Pfarrer von Kempenland*, Munich, 1941, p. 7).

But his power was not always seen so obviously and argumentatively. "There isn't a sorrow in the village that did not somehow leave its scar on the pastor. He is always a willing helper, the wise counselor to whom one can tell everything, of whom one can ask anything. For Father Pastor, of course, knows everything, and to whom else can they go, anyway? He can read in an embarrassed gesture or in a timid glance what they could not express in words. You don't need to say anything; the pastor hears it without a word. He divines the avarice in the shrewd eyes of Dorus Dahm, and feels the misery in Rosa Braun's coughing" (pp. 30 f). But there's a modern man there now, Jef Leirs. He is easygoing, good friends with the pastor. But he has socialistic tendencies and doesn't let himself be told off so easily as the others. Pastor Vogels acts exactly the same way, only not quite so roughly, in Anton Coolen's *Brabanter Volk* (Leipzig, 1933). He rules with kindness, and everyone responds to it. He not only reforms their souls, but also the cow barns and chicken coops. And when the farmers get their backs up at the innovations, he wins them over by his own model example.

Then, too, "Lord John" is "laird" in his Kalterscheid. There comes Karo the Spitz, racing out and barking, but he stops at the edge of the street out of respect for the "laird." Here comes a little girl running up to the pastor without timidity and gets a little pat on the head. There stands a farmer in the doorway, thick-set, with a black patriarchal beard. Numbskull, rumbles the pastor . . . an old farm wife beams with pleasure when she spies the laird: "Praised be Jesus Christ." "For ever and ever amen!" thunders the laird across the broad road . . . (Ludwig Mathar, *Herr Johannes, Der alte Pfarrer von Hohen Venn*, Munich, 1930, pp. 79 f).

The pastor of Hopsten, W. E. Ketteler, can also manage to have himself invited to dinner by a farmer who has turned away a beggar. He comes all right, but brings the knight of the road with him. Then he leaves (Herwig, *Der grosse Bischof*, p. 214).

This Kempenland and the High Venn are still to be found here and there, but no longer are they so untroubled. And this type of autocracy was well fitting for the most of these places and countries, for it was the power of a blessing, as it was in Ozeron or Lamotte and in many another pastor. The pastor and dean of "St. James," who was addressed as "Reverend Father," lets his good Catholic community feel the weight of his displeasure because they did not elect him to the House of Representatives; he thinks he can allow himself this in his parish (Emile Marriot, *Der geistliche Tod*, Berlin, 1924, p. 35). Don Camillo stays on, despite the fact that he has Communists in his congregation with drastic and inimitable means; and his only sorrow is that he has to share his autocracy with the Red mayor Peppone.

There are two levels of the good and devout priest which must be examined on their own merits: extremes of his existence which tend in the opposite direction, the fanatic and the introverted man, who has broken down under the weight of the world.

4. DECADENT VARIETIES

The Fanatic

Are fanatics and fanaticisms determined by a man's constitution? The Latin proverb, *"omnis pinguis bonus,"* all fat men are jolly, has been established to some extent by Ernst Kretschmer's studies of the characteristics of the pyknic type (*Körperbau und Charakter*, Berlin, 1944). There would have to be a separate investigation to determine whether the fanatics among priests are thin and tall, and so owe their fanaticism to indigenous factors. The objection that is always thrown up to Kretschmer, from the clinical point of view, is that his typology is not 100% accurate; consequently, at best it is heuristic (serving to discover or stimulate investigation) in one direction, but does not allow of a certain diagnosis in a particular case.

We can set aside, as far as our case is concerned, the experiments which seek to prove that the body influences the soul, even if it is only in the manner of its expression. In fact, we would be inclined to ask if it is not the soul which determines (*anima forma corporis*) the body, and not the other way around.

There are also fanatics among religious men, even among priests. The derivation of the word (*fanum,* a shrine) even gives rise to the suspicion that fanaticism is a genuine religious phenomenon and the term, when applied outside of the religious sphere, is only used analogously. That is certainly credible. The religious world represents that which is inmost, the ultimate source of what determines man. It is something unconditioned that admits of no further reference or comparison. Fanaticism is not *actio;* it is *passio,* a *passion* which is not its own master; it is a blind zeal, a kind of obsession with an idea. You cannot reason with a fanatic. He admits only the absolute, or what he takes to be such. The only thing you can do is give in to him. Or better, he is obsessed with the one absolute that drives him on. He will not admit the validity of a distinction between idea, ideal, and its realization. He does not see the weakness and wretchedness of man, and he will not admit the possibility of error in good faith. He can't do it. His colors are black and white. He knows only the saved and the damned and consequently presupposes that there is a final condition which simply does not exist in this life. He suspects that he is running into a stone wall and curses the wall. He is only aroused by opposition, only strengthened by contrary reasons; and to tell him to try to understand is to put him into a rage. That rage is his ruin. The Puritan preacher Jonathan Swift (died 1745) stormed against the total depravity of mankind all his life long with fanatic fervor. And when his preaching bore no fruit, "he threw himself down to die in a fit of rage like a poisoned rat in a hole."

For him, psychology is diabolic knowledge, insofar as he is able to make any sense of it at all. For as far as he can see, it is psychologism, which understands everything and therefore admits the justice of everything and excuses everything. Understood in that sense, he is surely right. It is also true that with an understanding psychology, hard times have come upon fanaticism, and that the fanatic in certain circumstances can also be analyzed psychologically —and understood. To write him off as a psychological abnormality would be as little to the point as admitting that he is determined by his body. What would that explain, anyway?

Fanaticism is an ethical category. It must be considered

morally, and eschewed. It should not be equated with the
zeal of faith. It is not consonant with understanding and
charity. Its impatience is not one of yesterday; it was yesterday and is today still loveless, and therefore sinful.

And yet when one knows priests who have been condemned as fanatics, this fanaticism may seem, at first glance,
to be a fervent love of truth, based on evidence that no
longer allows him a glance to left or right. Yes, this love
of truth can be joined with a great charity, which urges
him to preach to erring men and save them that way. But
this kind feels its own helplessness and therefore strikes out
blindly in all directions. It can become rampant and lose all
deliberation, when error comes forward frivolously and dazzlingly, winning all the scoffers to its side with mockery.
One can call the blustering Pastor Wolf in Handel-Maz-
zetti's *Jesse und Maria,* a fanatic merely because of the way
he heckles the arch heretic of Grosskrummnussbaum from
the pulpit, for "the son of Satan is spoiling my parishioners,
man by man, house by house." But when the people of Vel-
dendorff are miserably led astray, and all those who used to
kiss his hand now want only to give him their foot, Wolf
becomes compassionate and wonders how he can be of help
in the trouble that has come to the castle. Wherever love
breaks forth, any former fanaticism was only apparent.

Fanaticism is the inability to sense what is going on in
another's mind. And for that reason it is the inability to
minister to the countless numbers who have questions, who
are still seeking, who are wandering in hopeless error. And
their number today is great. The fanatic has no patience
because the way, that long way to another man and from
him to the truth, is unknown to him. Just as he only recognizes error as the result of ill will, so he only understands
conversion as a short circuit. Timmerman's *Pfarrer vom
blühenden Weinberg* is a thoroughly kind man, and no one

would take him to task for being a fanatic. He knows that faith is a grace, and yet he cannot quite understand why Michael, the fiancé of his niece Leontine, does not believe, since faith is so simple. It is really difficult for a man whose faith and pious life have never known a tremor since his baptism to understand how another man, also baptized and breathing the same air of faith in the Brabant country, which Timmerman describes so convincingly, does not find the faith.

Since the fanatics in priestly dress are not really genuine, there are also conversions among them from fanaticism. Hermann Herz tells in his novel *Wandlung* of the pastor, Joseph Abrogast, who thunders against even the most harmless pleasures, until he so alienates the people that they no longer listen to him. His own dying mother finally has to tell him that he will do more with insight and patience, and so completes his transformation.

It is different if the fanaticism has nothing to do with religion. The political fanatic among the clergy was a much condemned figure among the writers of Liberalism. Such was the pastor in Peter Rosegger's *Waldschulmeisters,* who deprives the teacher of his job in an ugly fashion. The model for this man was Pastor Plösch of St. Catherine's in Hauenstein, with whom Rosegger had been acquainted as a curate in Krieglach. But Rosegger later realized that he had done the pastor an injustice. In the last edition, he had that chapter on the *Kulturkampf* eliminated. In *die goldene Jubelmesse* he composed a splendid tribute to the old pastor Plösch. The first pastor of Winkelsteg is a former Jesuit who had once driven a sinner to despair by his strictness in the confessional. Now he does year-long penance, living as a recluse in a remote mountain valley. The woodsmen call him "the hermit." Now as a pastor, he wants only to be "a helper and friend to the poor in spirit" (Rosegger, *Die Schriften des Waldschulmeisters,* Wien, 1950, p. 221).

The Abbé Martureau is a fanatic adherent of the Bourbons. In the memento of the living, he always slips in a prayer for the royal family, that ends with the words: "My God, you know your irreconcilable enemies. Destroy them!" (Emile Baumann, *Der Exkommunizierte*, p. 30).

We are acquainted with political fanaticism. It is a terrible thing when a priest is consumed with it. The aggravated case, aside from canonical considerations, is a betrayal of the priesthood. But it does show how blind fanaticism is. For Baumann must admit that otherwise the Abbé had character, and such ridiculous tendencies were only one element of his personality.

The struggle against evil, when that struggle assumes the form of fanaticism, is unchristian. It reveals, by its paradox, its impossibility on the level of Christian existence, and consequently, also priestly existence. By fanaticism, the fanatic himself falls prey to the evil he would uproot. Fanaticism is always bound up with a lack of charity, a lack of spirituality, or with a more obvious crudity, with a cruelty which feels itself justified, and with Pharisaism and cant. Evil can only be overcome with good. That is the teaching of Christ (Mt. 5: 39; Rom. 3: 8; 12, 17-21). It demands charity even toward our enemies, and prayer for them, even in the martyrdom and death that they prepare (Luke 23: 34; Acts 7: 60).

Fanatics are often idealists, selfless ascetics of a headlong credulity. But in their bitter fight against evil and error the devil has them by the neck. Since they cannot bear the paradox of our existence and do not want to admit it, their defection is so much the worse. They do not want to admit that there is any mystery or tragedy in our freedom; charity seems to them to be weakness, or at least uncalled for here. And yet it is the fundamental law of Christian life. There are fanatics of freedom who are capable of the meanest misdeeds. We can only bring them to their senses by a defenseless and boundless charity. They will be shown up by their own fruits, but that can take a long time. Christian charity can spare them this delayed knowledge or at least shorten their time. "Christian" fanaticism against that of anti-christ seems to many to be the obvious and only effective way, but it is a detour and a betrayal. And it shows in a lightning stroke how far we are from the freedom of the children of God and His love. It is a helpless deterioration into the methods of evil. *Passione interdum movemur: et zelum putamus (Im. Chr.,* II, 5, 5). We are sometimes moved by a passion which we mistake for zeal.

The "Passivist"

At the opposite extreme of the good, devout type of priest stands the "passivist," as Bishop Paul Rusch calls the resigned, frightened, retiring priest (*Wachstum im Geiste, Ein Buch priesterlicher Betrachtung,* Innsbruck-Vienna, 1949, pp. 307 ff).

Here, too, we may ask how much constitutional determination is at work. Actually, K. Jaensch has discovered nothing new in his I. i-Type, which is an internally integrated man, as opposed to other external forms of being (*Grundformen menschlichen Seins,* Berlin, 1929), nor is C. G. Jung's distinction between the introvert and the extrovert anything new. (*Psychologische Typen,* Zürich, 1925).

There is such a type, even among priests. But in the case of the secular priest he is, so to speak, out of order as an extreme. Perhaps he should rather be in the cloister. Mostly there is a blending of natural and supernatural integration of this type into one. St. Joseph Cupertino, "who called himself Brother Ass, was a powerful and modest creature, yet he showed himself to be limited to the extent that people pushed him all over the place. So he went through life with an open mouth; he gave offense everywhere and was sent from one convent to the other in constant confusion. He wandered around and was incapable of taking care of the smallest jobs. He was, as they say, a real blockhead. He broke everything he touched. Once he was ordered to bring some water, but, sunk as he was in constant thoughts of God, he forgot all about it. And then, when everyone else had forgotten about it, he brought the desired water four weeks later" (J. K. Huysmans, *En Route*, 1926).

Of course that is a crass example. But when one reads it, who does not remember some good friend whom he has met in life, even among good, pious priests, withdrawn into themselves, frightened of the world. But they are almost useless in the ministry. They are harder hit by life in this world because they are constitutionally more sensitive and defenseless. If they teach in a school, they easily become the martyrs and sport of the pupils, and in the eyes of adults, they are more deserving of pity than reverence. They would have been honored as saints, perhaps, in a more childlike and pious age. But unfortunately, their time is past. The "rush of centuries" (Jos. Kirschweng) overwhelms priests whose youth is even more hardy and zealous. They shyly avoid it and draw their courage from prayer, atonement, penance, and freely accepted suffering. All of these are tremendously important, as many a man had thought when he became a priest, but the priest must face the world.

"The distress of the times had schooled the weaknesses of all sternly, and a man like Sabbas, the deacon, had not entered upon the clerical life to spend his life more quietly and in retirement. By taking a more decisive part in it, he wanted rather to atone for sin, the sins of which his time and his race had become guilty. The blood of martyrs was the seed-matter in which his strength and decision were rooted. He became a Christian by profession, so that he could consecrate all his strength to the affairs of Christ. And that did not mean the same thing to him that it did to Father Seraphim, to deepen one's understanding of the nature and dogma of the Church by meditation; for him it meant caring for souls and bodies, for everyday people, less for resurrection by means of words as for redemption by means of deeds. Without knowing it, these men of God had become champions and voices in the wilderness when the storm of the time had swept away the Russian Church, which had been sunk in itself and withdrawn from life. And with it went the secular power which had been loaned it by the State; all that was left was splinters, of which they were one" (Edzard Schaper, *Die sterbende Kirche*, Leipzig, 1936, pp. 34 f).

That is the situation of the Orthodox Russian clerics, hard on the border of Russia in the years after the first World War. They are depressed by the increasing shabbiness of their houses of God, which become for them a symbol of the dying Church. They become even more and more isolated. Everyone is living with a rope around his neck, and no one knows what innocent word could be the reason for tightening it. The inner world of all that is holy becomes not only the refuge they choose themselves, but the last resort of their existence.

What in these areas is daily distress can become necessity, and can also be a fate half-chosen and half-suffered in others. There are priests in places faced with opposition they cannot master, perhaps because they are not up to it. They go to pieces under their vocation and so their vocation goes to pieces with them. They cannot bring themselves to

decide to resign. Recourse to the ideal of the monk is no
permissible for secular priests as long as they want to re
main in that state, but that is the consequence. They ca
find no way to approach the men who have become secular
ized in this world. The saints in their church stand ther
on their pedestals as they did centuries before in gesture
of ecstasy, and the little constant light flickers and cast
its beam on the tabernacle in which God is silently present
Outside, the grandchildren of the men who built the churc
go by and know nothing about it. The attacks against th
priests have ceased, but they were the last connection wit
the children of this world.

Now he is left alone, the last one praying in the church
He examines his conscience: is he wanting in energy, in edu
cation, in the grace of his vocation? He would like it muc
better if he could answer yes to these questions, so that h
would have some reason for his retreat from the front line
where the assigned place of his work was. Perhaps they ar
doing penance for the former matter-of-course and ofte
misused power of their predecessors. Perhaps their lonel
misery will go so deep and their penance last long enoug
to make them recognize the fact that it was their one-tim
painless authority which was the cause of their penance
and that external power is not any longer worthwhile. Fo
power is always a temptation, even for those who must us
it in the Name of God. In no other Name is there powe
worthy of note, which of itself does not soon lead to cor
ruption; until the life of sheep among wolves is finall
welcomed as the existence our Lord and Master preache
and therefore as something to be considered genuinely exis
tential.

Then a successor can start all over again. But he will no
be able to be a "passivist."

The perfect example of this type is portrayed in Henr

Morton Robinson's novel, *The Cardinal,* in the character of Father Ned Halley, pastor in Stonebury, now nearing the end of his life. In the eyes of his Bishop, he was both "a conspicuous failure" and "the gentlest spirit and poorest administrator in the Archdiocese of Boston."

White-haired, emaciated, almost toothless, with sunken lips, but brilliant, lively eyes; always rather absent-minded and withdrawn: when he meets his new curate in the rectory, which is always open, he hardly asks his name and lets himself be served a cup of tea in the damp, cold kitchen —that is Father Halley. The next morning, the curate serves his Mass. A moving experience: "Flesh of earthly defeat became radiant as Ned Halley humbly united himself with the victim in the mystical reenactment of Calvary."

Father Ned Halley is a boyhood friend of autocratic Cardinal Glennon, who turned out quite differently. That is the reason for the Cardinal's exceptional solicitude. He sends Halley to St. Anselm's in Stowe. But he fails, under the huge mortgage on the church. Then he had to leave Needham, a parish with a heavy bank account, when he runs it into debt. Despite the remonstrances of his friend, the same thing happens in Malden, then in Taunton and Ipsfield. Finally the Bishop gave up. He assessed his pastors according to their success—economic success not the least of all. Now he "works" in the northern edge of the diocese, in a Protestant city. Shut off from the other large cities, it has only a small, poor settlement of French Catholics in the gorge of L'Enclume.

The only reason his church does not collapse is that it is built of granite blocks, "but its very durability gave it the sadness of sub-eternal things." But there were leaks in the walls and roof; panes were missing from the windows, an arm was off the cross on the steeple; cascades of water streamed from the broken gutters. The whole edifice needed

repairs. The carpets were worn out. The poor wooden sta
tions of the cross hung askew. The altar linens were in ur
gent need of replacement; the sacred vessels were tarnished

The rectory stood open day and night, for there was
nothing there to steal. When the curate arrived, it was
empty; and no voice answered his call. The rooms were un
aired, the windows without curtains. Now he knew that
there was no housekeeper at work here.

And yet there would have been money available: the
curate discovers that a forest belongs to the parish—Ned
Halley had quite forgotten it—and he figures that $10,000
could be made from the lumber alone, provide work for the
needy parishioners, and see to the needed repairs. When he
presented the plan to his pastor, he replied, with his "self-
naughting serenity," "Thank you for the suggestion
Father." No more. "Just the placing of a period at the end
of an impossible proposition." Ned Halley knew nothing
of these problems. His curate saw "that this obscure priest
possessed a serene and literal trust in goods that thieves
could not steal nor rust corrupt."

And the curate gave up the idea. "Ned Halley's fearless-
ness made Stephen fearless, too. After that supper of bread
and fish he stopped worrying about money."

When Ned Halley lay dying, the almost ruthlessly powerful Cardinal came roaring up in his Daimler and himself
administered Extreme Unction to the friend of his youth.
When Ned says, "I did not deserve your remembering," he
confesses, "Gentle Ned, you deserved more than I ever gave.
I should have made you my confessor and lighted my path
by the shining circle above your head"—a tribute from
the lips of a priest-dictator to the greatness of the devout
"passivist."

VII. MALADJUSTMENT AND THE
FORMS OF COMPROMISE

Under this title we bring together in the following pages the men who make very heterogeneous attempts to live as priests. We will divide these into separate groups. In them, we will again compare forms of life that have a fairly similar basis of existence. That is for the most part a pure formality, so that the following section is a somewhat loose collection. Their common denominator is that which is negatively expressed in the title.

Those represented in this group are not tepid, or at least should not be. If they are, then that circumstance will not be considered in this connection. Exceptions and extremes will be treated separately. An individual will usually be fully understood only when he is considered as belonging partially to several of the types dealt with here. Still less are the men we are considering faithless or apostates. They are all, or mostly all, in good faith, either forced to it or from conviction. Their characters have developed gradually out of their abilities, prejudices, and education, or from untenable presuppositions. And the fact that this does happen by degrees, and as a development, is a source of conviction by itself.

Whether one accepts, understands, or even discards these forms, we are proposing them in accordance with the task this work has set itself, and will attempt to explain them genetically. Those who are represented in the forms of life mentioned are calmly convinced that they are going about things in the right way. Or they are at least convinced that they could not do otherwise. Externally, considered canonically, as it were, everything is in order, for the most part, at least. In these forms we find men who are justly held in high honor in the Church. At different periods, some of these forms of existence were predominant. That convinced them not a little of their justification.

They all develop because they will not acknowledge the life-in-tension that is necessarily a part of priestly existence. They are either concerned for a security without tension, or they see in such security the attainable ideal form of priestly life and work. Or else they ignore or do not put up with the tension; they want to coexist with it. But their vocation is necessarily heroic. It countenances no evasion of this essential law, not internally, and not even externally. The former has already been treated, and the other has its place in the following discussion.

The attempt to find a peaceful coexistence with the essential law of the priesthood brings about a long and scarcely noticeable development, in which interest has been lost. Such priests have forfeited the ability to meditate on themselves. That is often the case in old age. But the process of development can often have been decided long before. It can even come about that the border situation which is part of the last years of a man's life can open his eyes—either for the first time, or anew.

1. THE MEN OF SECURITY

The Priest-Politician

We first mention the attempt to banish by socio-economic means the insecurity of the priest in this world which is necessarily part of his "not-of-this-world" character. If this becomes a factor existentially determining the priest, we have the priest as a politician.

The Old-Time Statesmen.   Let us first distinguish from our own era those times when religion (in our countries, the Christian religion) was considered as the most essential support even of the civil order. The civil protection of the priests and hierarchy, their support, the security of the ministry and the preaching of Christianity were of the most intense interest to the State itself. Within the State, there was no difference of opinion about that on the part of prince or people, even in places where parties shared the government. Party politics in the present-day sense, with programs that differ on this point, were unimaginable, just as was any separation of Church and State. Of course there were clashes in the West between the officials of the Church and the governments of the States. But the reason for this often was that both of them wanted to secure the support and influence of the priests for themselves.

To consider the Pope-Emperor conflicts of the Middle Ages through the eyes of modern man is an anachronism. Nothing shows this more than the fact that the Emperor who still seems to us to be the most modern, not to mention the most free-thinking, passed the strictest laws against heresy. That was Frederick II. Ostracism followed upon the ban, and on this point, too, there were no differences of opinion. Indeed, the conviction that the State cannot be ruled without the religion of its citizens, and that religion can thrive only under the protection of the State, was considerably solidified under the Reformers and still endured in some states even until the nineteenth century. The view that "the State cannot be ruled by paternosters" (Schnitzer, *Savonarola,* I, 209) is quite modern. Only under the presupposition that the State, and each state for itself, has to protect the religion of its citizens can the unconcerned acceptance of the supremacy of the deliberations of power politics be explained in the case of inter-state disagreements.

This pre-eminence of power politics it was that enabled a pope to ally himself with the enemies of the Emperor, who had all he could do to preserve the Catholic territory in the German Empire; it was this, too, that made Cardinal Richelieu take sides with the Protestants against the Catholic Emperor without a second thought. How the political enemy verified this maxim in his own realm seemed to them to be none of their business. (Instances of this pre-eminence of politics over religion can be found in Lortz' *Die Reformation in Deutschland,* Freiburg, 1938.)

We must completely pass over priests like Charles Maurice Talleyrand in this consideration, who traded his bishopric at Autun for the role of a politician and unscrupulous diplomat, essentially political and irreligious character that he was. There are some who acted much in the same vein, but not many. In the character or even in the work of Richelieu, as it has been handed down to us in history, one will seek in vain for the rules of life governing priestly existence. His priesthood may have been blameless, but, obscured as it was in the purple of a Cardinal of the Holy Roman Catholic Church that he "earned" by his political accomplishments, it is overshadowed by the politician. Even his conciliatory attitude toward the Huguenots and the establishment of religious peace in France were only determined by political considerations. The Cardinal of the supra-national Catholic Church had no voice in this: the same religious peace that he cared for in his own land he sought to hinder as an ally of the Protestants in Germany by all possible means. According to his own desire, he did not want to appear on his tombstone in prayer, as was the custom. A figure, symbolizing religion, *supports* the torso of His Eminence.

One can understand that a Bismarck can say: "There is no altruism among nations." Every other politician has acted according to the same norm. And unfortunately, the priest-politicians did the same. One might regret that the maxim of Soloviëv, which contradicts all that—"Thou shalt love other nations as thine own"—has never in the past two thousand years been the platform of a great statesman, not even when he was a priest. The only statesman whose national politics were fully determined by religion was Mahatma Gandhi. It had been said by this man himself that he owed his political attitude to the Sermon on the Mount. Unquestionably this is true: "It is a prerogative of the Christian religion that it does not exist to support political institutions" (Burckhardt, *Die Zeit Konstantins des Grossen,* Stuttgart, 1939). And Leo XIII acted accordingly in magnificent fashion.

The Party Politician. When we speak of "religion and politics" today, we are thinking of internal politics, party politics. And so we mean to speak of the priest here as a party politician. More exactly, we are considering the priest whose existence is determined by party politics. Strictly speaking, we ought to exclude from this consideration those priests who are sent to the legislature as representatives, without their new duty becoming a determining factor.

Those, too, should be excluded who accept their appointment as a sacrifice and who suffered or still suffer in the conflict between political work and their priestly attitudes, as did Bishop Schoepfer (Cf. Klotz, *Dr. Aemilian Schoepfer, Priester und Volksmann,* Innsbruck, 1936).

So, in the following we are speaking of the priest whose priesthood and work take their character from the fact that he is a politician. Since in our case it is not the occupation but the personal attitude which is the deciding factor, we must consequently number in this series those priests who do not actually have a political appointment, but who expect to solve the question of Church and State, and that of their own effectiveness, largely or only by civil guarantees. And we have those especially in mind who, sharing that same conviction, subscribe to the new powers after every political upheaval. In his stimulating book *Les grands Cimetières sous la lune,* Georges Bernanos has subjected to an unsparing judgment this political tendency of the Spanish Bishops with regard to the dictatorship of Primo de Riveras, the abdication of Alphonse XIII (1931), and the victory of Gil Robles (1933), until the regime of General Franco (1936). As much as one may regret the tone of this critique and many of its expressions, no one can deny that it comes from the sorely wounded conscience of a man who was devoted to the Church with every beat of his heart until his death.

Christian Party Politics. There is absolutely no doubt of the necessity of Christian politics and therefore of a Christian politician. The time is past when governments feel themselves to be in power "by the grace of God," with the consequent obligation of caring for the religious weal of their citizens. It is rare that any treaties or laws are passed today in the Name of God. There is no One Church in the West since the Reformation; with the Enlightenment there set in, on many levels, a de-Christianization and a spiritual decadence. The system of democracy hands over to the people, who are split in their outlook on the world, their own government. But to govern always meant, and means today still, to have come into power.

Should Christians desire to realize their ideal of the State and order within the State, they must enter upon the civic struggle for power. Indeed, Christians today must in many places strive to guarantee themselves the minimal amount of religious liberty. Herein lies the relative necessity, not only of politics with a Christian outlook, but also of parties deriving their character from the Faith, because these parties alone—at least at first glance—can engage in the struggle for political power.

The Priest as a Party Politician.   Must these representatives of the Christian people be priests? Or—can priests be among them? That is our question. The Church's attitude to this is primarily negative. Canon 139, 4, of the Code says: "In order that clerics accept a legislative position, they need both the permission of their own Ordinary as well as that of the Ordinary of the place in which they are to be elected. But should there be a prohibition for any particular place imposed by the Holy See, then only the Holy See can give the permission." On April 25, 1922, the Code Commission explained, in connection with this, that such a permission was to be given rarely, and not without consideration (A.A.S. XIV, 313). So, too, the Bishop has the right, even the duty, of forbidding political activity to clerics, if they do not conform to the norms of the Holy See. He can even impose ecclesiastical penalties on his clerics if his instructions are not followed (Reply of the Code Commission, March 15, 1927, A.A.S. XIX, 138).

The Church obviously has good reasons for, as well as bitter experience behind, this ruling. She wants to see her priests engaged primarily in their spiritual ministry. But there have been, and still are, depending on the different countries, priests who, with the permission of the Bishop, are elected to be representatives of the people.

The only thing that concerns us here is to analyze the existence of the priest for whom politics has become a vocation.

He will soon find himself in difficult straits, if he is a real priest. The parties of Europe are primarily those with a particular internal, social, and economic policy as their platform. Only secondarily are they concerned with a distinctive moral outlook, if at all. Even the parties that are generally considered as non-Christian, and those, too, who are hostile to the Church and irreligious in their principles, still allow their members to choose their own religion for the sake of expediency, or as a matter of principle. On the other hand, even parties with a Christian platform are not Church parties. In the political arena they, too, represent vested interests and have their own idea of the proper economy. Their view may seem to other Christians excessive or even inimical to their own interests, and so they align themselves with those who defend *their* vested interests. In a secularized world, this struggle is fought to a finish with that fervent devotion that once was proper only to religious faith. There have been and still are "religious socialists" who are such out of religiosity. There have been and still are "Biblical socialists," who see in the classless society of the future that brotherhood and community of mankind preached by Christ. At any rate, by far the largest number of adherents to those parties characterized as "unchristian" are baptized Christians. Many may no longer be very active as Christians, and they are consequently so much the more endangered by the agitation in their own party. But at least they have not abandoned the communion of the Church.

Now if these men see priests in the ranks of their political enemies, men whose vocation it is to save them for eternal life, what effect will that have on their already shaky faith? This is a very serious question. There is a psychological law of the transfer of emotion, for example, from a person hated to the thing that he represents. And what if this rising anger, such as was the case between the two World Wars, is still fanned by the freethinkers; and what if, because of the fact that a priest is foremost among the political opposition, there is agitation for apostasy, or actual apostasy? One may debunk this propaganda as a political trick, but political passions, like other passions, are not dispatched from this world by ready reasons, by hushing them up. What priest, who remains a priest, would want to be responsible for that? He is faced with the decision of being either a priest or a politician. He must choose between two things of infinitely different value. If the salvation of *one* soul cannot be compared with winning the whole world—and that's what the Lord said (Mt. 16: 26)—what reasons can still be so weighty that he can remain in politics? *Salus animarum suprema lex*. The salvation of souls is still the supreme law.

The dean of St. Jacob's, turned down by his own farmers as a candidate for the legislature, can afford to show his "embittered irreconcilability" to them—so it seems—because they still have so much faith that they can distinguish between the priest and the politician (Marriot, *Der geistliche Tod*, p. 35). It would be a gross self-deception to presuppose the same condition today.

It comes to this, then, that the political struggle takes place under circumstances in which it is best that one not see a Roman collar. When is a priest really at home at any of these meetings, even if they don't degenerate into a battle of beer mugs and furniture breakage?

But there is more involved than clerical decorum. "Behold, I send you forth like sheep among wolves," says the Lord (Mt. 10: 16). This touching and disarming defenselessness is the power with which the priest must meet the world, according to our Lord's will. The political struggle is the struggle of wolves. *"Homo homini lupus"* (dog eat dog) is the general rule in the political arena. Of course it should not be overlooked that older democracies conduct their struggles in a more decent fashion; even in the most bitter confusion of election time, they still do not lose sight of the common good. And neither should it be denied that a priest may see exactly in this his vocation as a politician, as one who can make the deportment of politicians more humane and more according to the Gospel. But experience shows that precisely because political hatred turns especially against him, he will put aside the "requirements of etiquette" in political contests.

A thing that touches the existence of the Christian and the priest even more closely is shown by another consideration. The Church has always proclaimed several rights as inalienable. Most recently, in the World Congress for the Lay Apostolate (Rome, October 7-14, 1951), she reiterated them: 1. the right to religious education and upbringing; 2. the right to public worship of God, including the works of Christian charity; 3. the right to the performance of ecclesiastical marriage and to marriage and family life; 4. the right to a job that will support a family; 5. the right to choose one's state in life freely, including priestly and religious life as well; 6. the right of free access to material goods within social boundaries and limitations. In addition to this, there is the demand for freedom for the ministry and for the preaching of the Word of God from every supervision of the State. At least a minimum freedom of movement is a relative necessity for the work of the Church. And the Christian politician must secure that minimal amount.

We should not tempt God. But this minimum has always had to be won with a struggle: at one time a struggle against a hostile State, at another against a paternal State. But the work of the ministry must go on even in times of persecution. The risk and the uncertainty are only greater. Insecurity in this sense is always there, and the daring is always necessary. Indeed, it is essentially proportioned to the existence of the Christian and the priest. If it ever falls off completely, then it will be a danger for the priest and his ministry; often this is a danger that is seen, but most often a creeping danger. We do not escape the tragedy of man's works; neither do we escape the paradox of our existence. It is part of the platform of all Christian politics to guarantee the freedom of Church and ministry. But history teaches us that security makes them careless and slack. It is only an alert desire for penance and sanctity that can protect us from being more impoverished by the most ideal freedom than by persecution. *"Salus in cruce!"*

Political priests, as we discuss them here, then, are often much less legislators who are priests, than priests whose whole interest is absorbed by politics and who seek to base the security of their existence on political means. The fight against what is unholy and evil must always be fought and conducted in the soul of the individual; it can never be replaced by any institution. Souls in drowsing security are more endangered by far than the souls of men in whom there is that essential, God-given *"insecuritas humana."*

Examples. We would like to cite a few examples to illustrate what we have said.

Ignatius Seipel can serve as an example of those priests who were politicians fully devoted to their duty, but who remained priests wholly and without changing a whit. He hadn't much to say about himself. But it seems that he suffered under this double position. He himself had real scruples about the subordination of the priest to the necessities and laws of politics (Cf. Rudolf Blüml, *Ignaz Seipel, Mensch, Christ, Priester* [Diaries], Vienna, 1933, p. 135). He was conscious, however, that he had his obligations as a statesman and apparently knew no one else who was up to them. So he endured his lot, and his political accomplishments are great enough to deserve the recognition of history. But his priesthood was beclouded by the tragedy of Seipel the politician, a tragedy that he sought to overcome in lonely self-examination. He was a man of sober common sense and a careful ascetic, so that he treated himself and others unsparingly, according to principle.

In ten years after the first World War, over 100,000 people left the Church in Austria. In the year 1927, the year of the July rebellion, during which the Palace of Justice in Vienna was burned, about 30,000 apostatized. As head of the government, Seipel had to hand over the arsonists and murderers to the courts. But the wild seed sown against the "prelate without mercy" and the "chancellor without pity" had a tragic harvest: some ten thousand turned their backs on the Church of the prelate in rage and disillusion. The agitation was mean, party-inspired, and unfounded. Their scandal at the "pitilessness" of the chancellor was properly assessed by the cool moral theologian and labeled *scandalum pharisaicum*, pharisaic hypocrsy, and he acted accordingly. But this theological judgment fit only the few instigators, not their sacrifice. And there were tens of thousands. In his diary he wonders if he should have taken the agitation to apostasy because of him as a person more seriously (p. 119). But he stills his own fears.

No one would simply blame the few ten thousands of apostates on him. In the case of so earnest a priest, the same warning of the Lord applies as it does to any other: "*Nolite judicare!*"—Judge not (Mt. 7: 1). Subjectively this conscientious priest and sober moral theologian had been able to justify his conduct in the situation. Objectively the simultaneous apostasy of the 100,000 from the Church is still a fact of history. It is also true that there was a causal nexus between this subjective conduct and the objective result. It was not the only one. But it was one. We can suppose, without going into it any further, that the agitation for apostasy would have found other reasons if Seipel hadn't been chancellor of the republic. But he was. It is also historically certain that his double position as priest and responsible statesman was the express (no matter how expedient) reason for the agitation to apostasy. The law of the transfer of emotions from the man hated to the thing that he represents is an actual law, and a power that cannot be ignored with impunity in a consciously responsible attempt to resolve a conflict. Those who think in pure principles often suppose that the only laws are those of rational understanding, logic, and the moral order. But the laws of psychology are no less existential in life and are generally mightier than those of the syllogism.

Again we must objectively recall the words of Our Lord: "What does it profit a man if he gain the whole world . . ." (Mt. 16: 26). The great historical achievement of the statesman still endures. But even if he had saved the whole world, and not just Austria, would that have been equivalent to one soul, according to the words of our Lord? And there were tens of thousands.

Ignatius Seipel had surely secured the agreement of the Church for the length of his stay in office. That was apparently the ultimate reason, too, for staying in office until he was recalled. For the priest as a politician not only needs the permission of the Church to accept his political appointment; he is still a priest in his work as a politician and therefore answerable to the Church. And she can recall him if she finds it good, and she does it in such a way that the process often looks not unlike a dismissal.

So it appeared in the case of Don Luigi Sturzo. In the signing of the concordat with Mussolini on February 11, 1929, both he and his long and successful political activity were brushed aside as though they had never been. For the final section of Article 43 of the concordat read: "The Holy See takes this opportunity to renew the prohibition for all clerics and regulars in Italy against enrolling in any political party or participating in their works." The bold Sicilian had to try to get over the border as quickly as possible. It was a sixteen-year banishment.

Was this just another case of the footman having done his duty, and now being free to go? As pertinent as the judgment seems to be, it is false because it judges only from the outside.

It is true that there is an authentic and obligatory concept of the State, described in the encyclical of Leo XIII *"Immortali Dei"* of November 1, 1885, and Sturzo had abided by it. It is further true that there is a doctrine preached by the Church dealing with the civil law in the encyclical of the same Pope *"Libertas praestantissimum"* of June 26, 1888, and another on the nature of democracy in the encyclical of Leo XIII *"Graves de communi"* on January 18, 1901. And it is just as true that Don Sturzo derived his program for his Populari party from this encyclical, and that he had the not so common energy to devote his life to the carrying out of the papal directives. Then came February 11, 1929, and Sturzo had to make sure of his life by escaping as an emigrant.

But this is how things are: the priest is still a priest even when he becomes a politician. And he is still, as he knows, subordinate and responsible to his ecclesiastical superiors. The government of a kingdom that is not of this world, but which has its citizens in common with the kingdoms of this world, has no political power, at least it hasn't for a long time. It is therefore unjust to speak of an alliance of the Church with Fascism when the concordat of 1929 is discussed. The only thing the Church had in mind was to guarantee at least the minimum of that freedom that is necessary for the ministry so that its one concern, the salvation of souls, does not suffer. And she cannot always, indeed seldom, demand that freedom from a State which sees things as she does. She must secure that freedom by treaty with that government that happens to be in power actually. Concordats usually do not mean only guarantees, but also sacrifices. And the State concluding the concordat demands them. As deeply as one may share the grief of St. Clement Hofbauer that the Church is forced to secure for herself the freedoms which are rightly hers, nevertheless she is forced to it.

And in this distressful situation the Church, too, must demand sacrifices; and from whom first of all if not from her priests? These sacrifices are not always as bitter as Don Sturzo's sixteen-year banishment, but during the bitterness of those sixteen years, the great Sicilian considered the difficulties in which the Church, whose priest he was, found herself, and he submitted.

The political life of the priest Joseph Tiso was more daring: daring because of the fact that the good to which he devoted his life was a lofty one, but, compared to his duty as a priest, still of secondary importance. Tiso was a child of a people among whom the priest was not only a cleric, but also a political leader. This was a consequence of centuries of independence, somewhat similar to the conditions in Ireland which make such a thing matter-of-course. The independence of the Slovaks, a political by-word for twenty years, was made possible by a massing of powers, and he realized that combination for six years. Although not many knew of it, as long as he was president, he was still every inch a priest, or more accurately, a pastor. For every Sunday he left the residence in Pressburg and was a simple country pastor in his parish, a political idealist and priest, beloved by his people, who hailed him as a national hero. When he was lying in prison in Pressburg, four hundred people, all independently, took it upon themselves to bring him food every day, so that the painfully emaciated man would not suffer from the prison diet. He was condemned to death by hanging, by judges who had no respect for an idealist and even less reverence for a priest; unmindful of how they besmirched the love of their own people by their verdict. He was a tragic symbol of how the priest as a politician can come to ruin. If a priest is destined for martyrdom, it should not be a political one.

The Political Priest.   The times when politics were automatically assumed to be more important than religion are past. We are no longer living in the Renaissance, when there was confusion in this regard, confusion notable for its extremity and for those in high places who were led astray by it. And it is no longer taken casually, as it was in the first decades of this century, that the clergy take part in party politics. The newly ordained Peter Schwabentan, on his arrival at his first assignment in Monstad, becomes involved in a political association of pastors, which the dean was running with such adroitness and elegance that the new arrival was struck with envy. It is taken as a pure matter of course that the city pastor is installed as the head of the elective committee of the "Christian People's Party." And the new priest, just as casually, is elected as secretary and parliamentarian. The parishioners are neatly sorted into "ours" and "opposition," depending on suspicion or evidence.

And with that they are off (Herz, *Vikar und Presshusar,* Regensburg).

Anyone who wants to know the type, and how such a priest thinks who is fully concerned with politics, should read the diaries of the prelate Joseph Scheicher, who was a politician for many years (*Erlebnisse und Erinnerungen,* Vienna, 6 vols., 1906-1912). He was born in 1842 in Lichtenhof, Steiermark, and died in 1912 in Vienna. He became a professor of moral theology in St. Pölten, and in 1894 was elected delegate. That was the topic of his book, *Arme Brüder* (Stuttgart, 1913). He was also the founder and for many years editor of *Kleruskorrespondenzblattes,* and did a good job with it. His writings are rich in information about the incidents of a long priestly life and are a valuable contribution to the history of the times. But his book *Arme Brüder* is worth reading for the portrayals in it, even in his treatment of a character such as Martin Deutinger. There are conflicts of priests with Bishops, intrigues, denunciations, and matters of principle; there are priests disciplined and transferred without fault or trial; bishoprics which became the bailiffs of the secular courts; abandoned and ostracized priests; "lack of charity in one's own camp" . . . One asks in vain for facts and reasons. What is essentially priestly is banished to the side lines, or is simply not recognized at all, and therefore not even mentioned, even in a case where a priest suffers under the tragedy of his existence or comes to grief. It is vested political interest behind Scheicher's pen that stamps the characters he describes, or takes to task, like a journalist. We suppose that he did it all in good faith, but it is not always according to historical verisimilitude.

The duty that he felt was his for decades: of obtaining legal guarantees for the necessary liberty of the Church; the willingness, often called upon, to protect persecuted priests by his intervention; preserving the traditional position of the pastors in their parishes and their committees, and all this with the means available to a political office holder; the consciousness that he had influence where even the power of the hierarchy was helpless; the daily association with party politicians; the speeches in the hotels and the applause —all of these things together left their stamp on the priestly type, a kind of man at once knowledgeable and empty, affable and presumptuous. Scheicher had to hear and see many things, and it was rare that the priest or theologian in him was called upon to help. It was always the delegate, who had to hush up some shady deal or suppress a scandal. They shouldn't be judged harshly, those clerics who have become politicians existentially.

The fact that the politicking pastors of Monstadt were always "playing their little game" at every opportunity makes them suspect of trying to guarantee a comfortable life by winning an election.

The Priest Overshadowed by the Theologian
Securing Intellectual Existence

If the politician is seeking to avoid the risk of external existence—the priest who is primarily or only a theologian is the one who is trying to avoid the threat of insecurity that is an essential part of priestly existence, an insecurity that is indissolubly and essentially rooted in the supernatural and in mystery. And that in a twofold direction: on the one hand, by reducing the mystery of the faith and the *tremendum* of God's presence to pure concepts. "Even when its claim to supremacy is unchallenged, dogma is the most exalted form of being armored against revelation." We cannot simply endorse this saying of Martin Buber fully (*Dialogisches Leben,* 1947, p. 156). But woe to the theologian who overlooks the danger it points out! The other threat consists in his attempt to secure the position of theology among the other sciences at a sacrifice of its supernatural character. The folly of the Cross, which was nonsense to the heathen and a scandal to the Jews, has become a stumbling block for him, too.

The Dialectic of his Existence. It may be that the reason why theology has become the basis of his existence was already determined by the kind of vocation he had. Or more exactly, by the thing which impelled him to become a priest.

When the young John Joseph Ignatius Döllinger (1799-1890) was alone at home with his father, the famous anatomist of the University of Wurzburg, or with his pious mother, or when he went with them for a walk, the precocious child was always full of questions that far exceeded his mental age. (At the age of five he had learned Latin; and Greek, when he was seven.) Children from the ages of three to six are always full of questions, and more questions, which soon lead up to the ultimate question. And whenever the father, who restricted himself to his own specialty, said to his truth-hungry son, "There's no answer to that"; or his mother said, "You'll only understand that when you are able to read learned books about the Dear God"; and when he heard that these books were not available in the medical faculties, but only in the theological, it was already decided for the young Ignatius that he would study theology someday. And the reason was so that he could give his honest father and pious mother the answers to the questions to which they had confessed their ignorance. It wasn't a desire to be a priest, but to be a theologian that drove him on, even when he first studied a few semesters of jurisprudence at his father's wish. It wasn't only the empty dryness of his professors that repelled him; theology attracted the old questioner.

And that was how it was throughout his whole life. He wanted to have concrete and solidly documented results, established by theological investigation. When he was excommunicated in 1871 for refusing to admit the doctrine of papal infallibility, he took it with the matter-of-factness of his own father. The sober Church historian kept himself far from experimenting with an "old catholic" Church and was still a tireless theologian and researcher, remained unmarried, and continued to live as an ascetic. A single meal during the day and a glass of water at night were enough for him. The theologian in him was and continued to be the determining factor in his existence.

There is an existential dialectic within priestly existence which can be mastered only by a clear ordering of the facts of existence. In this hierarchy the first place is held by the sacramental, ordination, mystery; in second place is the religious, relation to God, the call of grace and the proffered "abundance of redemption" (Eph. 3: 20); and only in third place do we find theology; and its position by no means belittles it.

The priest who is only or even predominantly a theologian reverses this scale of values. That can only mean disaster for his priesthood. It becomes a temptation for him. This is the basis for the mistrust the Oriental monks felt toward theology.

In Döllinger's case, it was theology, and not religion, that determined his choice of vocation. There certainly are men, too, who become believers by meeting a theologian or by reading a theological work. But the thing that usually determines conversions is the meeting with a religious man whose religion is lived, not just something he knows. But God's grace is supreme. The mysterious, paradoxical words of our Lord in John 3: 21—"he who does the truth comes to the light"—decide faith and salvation. Every logician and mere theologian would have to conclude that there is a want of logical nexus here, since the only thing that can grasp the truth is the intellect. One knows the truth; he doesn't do it. Of course! But all the same, the fact is that it is not knowledge of the truth, but grace and a life lived according to the truth that decides our salvation.

The History of the Type.   Teachers of theology who are not first Christians and priests, but essentially theologians, are quite rare today. But there were times in the history of the Church when they were so numerous that they almost represented a type. Personally, they were often men who were highly regarded, somewhat like the noble Bernard Bolanzo, whom no one less than Edmund Husserl called "one of the greatest logicians of all time." After his death on December 18, 1848, the Prague "Bohemia" praised him as the "most perfect man of our generation." In the eighteenth century of the Enlightenment they constituted a large percentage of the professors of theology. Why? They were all hard pressed by the tension between the old attitudes of theology and the disdain for it on the part of the Encyclopedists and followers of the Enlightenment. So they solved the conflict by speaking as little as possible of the supernatural, or by making light of it. It is not by chance that France provides the most examples of this: the radical Abbé Gabriel Bonnot Mably (1709-1785), Abbé Etienne Bonnot de Condillac (1715-1780) who finally abandoned theology for empiric philosophy. Then there is Abbé Emmanuel Joseph Sieyès (1748-1836), former vicar general of Chartres and a later revolutionary leader. But the Germans, too, had their free-thinking theologians—the characterless Eulogius Schneider (1705-1794), follower of the Enlightenment and professor on several faculties; he handed a number over to the scaffold until he himself was beheaded. Then there's the

Viennese canonist and enemy of the Church, Josef Valentin Eybel (1741-1805), and Franz Berg of Wurzburg (1753-1821), who denied the revealed character of Christianity.

We wonder if there was then no *missio canonica*. Yes, but even the Bishops were partially children of their times. The regents of seminaries and the professors of theology often had to preserve the teaching of the Church against their bishops. And that lasted into the nineteenth century (Franz Schnabel, *Deutsche Geschichte im neunzehnten Jahrhundert*, IV, Freiburg, 1937). The faithful and the clergy of the country often had to hang on in spite of the prelates and theologians (*Ibid.*, p. 44). Bishop Wessenberg, intellectually and morally, represented a type of highly placed prelate that could still be found in the German territories as late as the first half of the nineteenth century.

The Present?   Is there such a type as the mere theologian today? It is not a question of idle curiosity, but one of conscience. This type will indeed be found here and there in isolated instances. It just so happens that those French novelists who have made the concern of their lives faith and salvation through the grace of Jesus Christ always confront their holy priests with those abbés who are theologically polished, ecclesiastically correct, but cold in faith. They ridicule such men's teaching and show their spiritual helplessness in a decisive religious crisis. Apparently these have all been sketched from life. And the fact that the authors occasionally protest that their novels are not to be taken as *romans à clef* betrays the temptation to model their characters on persons more or less well-known.

There is the pastor of Luzarnes, the "future canon" Sabiroux, in *Under the Sun of Satan* by Bernanos. The decisive "Father of the Church" for him seemed to have been Descartes, "who by an expert compounding of mathematics and wit made out of the problem of being a pastime for gentlefolk." He never had any real doubts of faith because he had never doubted his own judgment. In the rectory of the pastor of Lumbres, who is nowhere to be found, he meets the celebrated Antoine Saint-Marin, member of the Academy (Anatole France?). Bernanos always calls him the author of *Leuchte Pascal,* and Anatole France did not write that, at any rate. But he attributes quite openly to the "old comedian," the frivolous cynic, every idle self-revelation, including the abuse of Pascal. Anyway, the pastor of Luzarnes is quite taken and delighted by this singular opportunity of meeting the great master, and fawns all over him, excusing the excesses of the holy pastor and calling his penances dangerous means and a scandal. But the surfeited wit "could only be reached through the senses." The wall, red with the bloody scourge of the pastor, disgusted him, but the subservience of the sycophant pastor he despised.

The holy pastor of Lumbres had tried to frighten his neighbor, the pastor of Luzarnes, into a realization of the supernatural nature of his vocation, but apparently without success. The pastor of Lumbres put his finger on the forehead of the future canon and said slowly and hoarsely, "Wretched are we who have here only a little bit of brain and the pride of Satan! What have I to do with your prudence? . . . mind you remember, Sabiroux, that the world is not a cleverly built machine. Between Satan and Himself, God hurls us, as His last rampart. It is through us that for centuries and centuries the same hatred seeks to reach Him . . . Oh, our ignorance is deep! To a learned, well-mannered, prudent priest what is the devil, I ask you? Hardly do they dare utter his name without a smile. They whistle to him like a dog. What then, do they think they have tamed him? I tell you! I tell you! It's because they've read too many books and haven't heard enough confessions. All they want to do is to please. They please only fools, whom they reassure. Our vocation is not to induce sleep, Sabiroux! We are in the vanguard of a struggle to the death and our little ones behind us."

These Sabiroux lectures always keep coming up in stories when it is a matter of life and death. There is the yielding Abbé in the novel *Vor dem Grauen* (about St. Benedict Labre) by Reinhold Schneider, and the Genevan Bishop Abbé Marinier in Antonio Fogazzaro's *Il santo* (1906).

It is in this connection that I would like to mention "the most frightening priestly character of modern literature," as Winklhofer calls him. (I would restrict that: on literary grounds!) He appears in Stefan Andres' *Das Tier aus dem Tiefe* (Munich, 1949). He is Dr. Alois Moosthaler, who says of himself: "I'm a bit of a dogmatist; I teach pastoral theology and am besides a censor of books as well as spiritual director in a boys' boarding school" (p. 48). The novel is a singular travesty (and half-genealogy) of the collectivist dictatorship in which National Socialism and Bolshevism are seen combined. The German theology professor comes to Città Morta at the moment when Olch, the confessor and prophet of the new Model Man, has just announced him. Moosthaler takes over the role destined for him. ("One Model, one party, and one flock," the professor explains to the Bishop of Città Morta, Cherubini.) Olch soon realizes that "this Moosthaler is an intruder and a traitor; because he keeps silence, Olch likewise becomes a traitor because he (with his prophesying) did not want to make himself ridiculous, and because he wanted to share in the product which would result from the multiplication of two lies and two traitors" (p. 159).

Moosthaler becomes "the great model." Brutal and crafty, he is an unscrupulous psychologist and hater of mankind.

Power has him, and he it. He is only interested in what it can do for him. "The powerful man shows himself to be worthy of his name precisely by the fact that it is a matter of indifference to him how he gains his power" (p. 130). He himself is crude, flabby (even bodily so: "300 lbs. of theology"), and he becomes a "theological tyrannosaurus" (p. 85), an all-powerful model, an I-the-Savior and Patriarch of the collective man of the masses and the future state of the masses, a Moses of the working generation for fifty thousand years (p. 184). He purifies the old Model Program of the confessor Olch of all atheistic and anti-cultural tendencies (p. 135), but his theism is dictated purely by his goal, since "he would not like to think that no use was made of God for purely pragmatic reasons, despite the miserable results" (p. 139).

For his future society he discovers a smooth theological formula, despite Bishop Cherubini's scruples: "Since the man who is dependent is lifted to a level, without his noticing it, where sinning becomes difficult for him, not only a social, but also a religious problem is solved. The AFTW ('All for the Worker'), and that says everything, is nothing more nor less than Divine Providence reduced to practice, *Custodi nos Domine, sicut pupillam oculi tui!*" (p. 184).

But Bishop Cherubini's fears are still not dispelled.

To fill in the other details of this theologian, consider these facts: at a banquet he performs a baptism with a glass of whisky; he laughs at the terribly realistic crucifix in Don Evaristo's sacristy and jokes about the "size of the shoe" for the pierced feet; he tells the Bishop that as Model he would "naturally" have to be laicized, and besides, he denounces Don Evaristo as a Jansenist (p. 187), and this the Bishop seriously considers a catastrophe.

The chief complaint against this book of Andres, that the

political theology of the Church would offer collectivism the principle and bases upon which it could exist, is a misunderstanding which we cannot go into now. What concerns us here is only the priest and the problem of his existence.

The clearest portrait of the kind of theologian we mean here is given by Henri Ghéon in his 'novel' *Les Jeux de l'Enfer et du Ciel* (1929). In this book he describes the work and effect of the Curé of Ars. On a bus, which is going to Ars, almost every type of person can be found. Among the pilgrims there is the Abbé Sauvaire of the diocese of Paris. He was coming in order to investigate the mystery of this remarkable pastor. He had fought all his life long against "all that is miraculous, for which he had never had a palpable proof in his hands" (p. 174). Now he has come, to unravel the cause of all the excitement about the theologically untrained Curé of Ars. But he had bad luck: shortly before getting to Ars, the horses take fright, the carriage overturns, and he has to spend part of the precious days he had planned to use in solving the mystery of this puzzling man in bed. There had already been a discussion in the carriage, egged on by three suspicious looking characters, about the devil. But he didn't join in it "because he only talked about things where he could shine" (p. 170). No one there wanted to believe in the black fellow except the Abbé, and he only *par distance*.

The devout farmers, in whose home he had been forced to rent a room, arouse his mockery—"he had the habits of life proper to an ascetic. He would be willing to deny his body, and in necessity, even his soul, everything, but not his wit its opportunity to make his puns and pointed remarks" (p. 349). Just how is it, then, with the dependence of these simple people on their pious pastor. He asks them questions. What is the result? "As for him, little was wanting for him to believe that the saints, the real ones, were rebels, people who wanted to make their own dogmas" (p. 350).

He uses the time, since he cannot leave the room, in looking through the printer's proof of an article, "The Contradictions of the Saints. Attempt at an Experimental Apologetic," which is intended for *Studienblatt für geistliche Gelehrsamkeit*. "In it he develops the subjective origin of faith which for the elite among the faithful always takes on such an intimate and new form that one may well ask if it is not the product of 'character'—to whose help a special grace of God comes in a supernatural fashion. This 'supernatural help' for him is just a phrase he stuck in to ward off an excommunication, and the *Index*. He lacks little to believe that faith is one of the most beautiful discoveries of man; indeed, the most beautiful, and indeed for the reason that it goes beyond its discoverer and leads him to a world that is inaccessible to science and even philosophy, of which he never spoke without deprecation" (pp. 350 ff).

It has gotten late. Then he recalls that he has not finished his Breviary. "And since he kept to the form, he took it up—without the slightest profit. At midnight he closes the book; he is squared away with the Church . . . In the bosom of the Church he is all the more able to undermine her and he is therefore that much more content. His most dazzling paradox is that of his life and position" (p. 352).

Half-asleep, he thinks some more, just as one does when he has been turning over some problem before going to bed and now wants to put it to rest forcibly. "His thought . . . lay entangled within him, like a worm or a snake, yet formless and insoluble. But then—as though at the whisper of an adjuration—it stretches itself up and slithers away. It winds itself over him and lets all the colors of its scales play in the light of the spirit. It chose the theme: *Die Idee des Wunders* . . ." (p. 353). He had been in a state of war with miracles for twenty years (p. 430). Now one was to happen: the boy who was mortally injured when the carriage over-turned was cured by the pastor.

And with the logical consequence of those hard, toilsome, logical dreams of thought in which one doesn't quite know whether one is awake or asleep, and from which one awakes the next morning racked with headaches, his thought con-tinues, undisturbed by the light of day and his world:

"If this thing isn't a miracle, then why were the others, that we know now only by hearsay? . . .

"Miracles don't happen any more today. Then why was there one yesterday? Why the day before? Why ever at all? What if the world is ruled by the same laws? . . . The holy pastor of Ars works no miracles. The saint works none; no one does!

"Christ? Not Christ, either, if He were merely a man . . . Yes, but Christ was God. What do we know about that? Did he really say it—and prove it? And who has handed His proofs on to us? And His words? (Textual Criticism!) . . . If He was really only a man like us, He did nothing that we cannot do. . . . If we cannot work miracles, Christ didn't work any, either. Or did he . . .?" (p. 354)

"Here the thought of the Abbé Sauvaire stopped. He is frightened by his deductions. He has already gone further than he wanted to. He forces himself to curl up. But he curls up, only to stretch out again . . . He sees that the beautiful snake, which had crept out of him, is now upright over his bed, hissing at him with its head cocked off to the right side. It is just at the same height as the crucifix, which hangs opposite him."

When he is halfway cured, he goes over to the Church to say Mass. He chooses the time so that he cannot meet the holy pastor. He fears his power of reading souls, of which one hears so much. "His faith—he has faith—is in his opin-

ion different from the naive belief of the holy pastor, and
the holy pastor would not understand him. It is better to
avoid a dangerous encounter which wouldn't be interesting,
anyway" (p. 429). Abbé Sauvaire goes to Mass "like an
official to his office. He wants to check in. The higher-ups
won't have anything on him, that way" (p. 429).

He is angry because he gets the miraculously cured peasant as server. He is angry because he is sent to the altar
of the "little saint" of the pastor "who is not an historical
person, anyway" (p. 431).

But by the grace of the place and the sobbing of the man
who had been cured behind him, he himself is cured, the
poor, too-intelligent Abbé. For how long? "He hardly had
risen from his thanksgiving, which he had made in the dark-
est corner of the church for as long as he could, when he
felt that his past was again coming over him. He shook his
rather curly head, slipped his collar into place. Is it all over
already? . . . He would like to stay longer, but he is afraid
to meet M. Vianney—and he leaves" (p. 434).

No one will suppose that the cases of such theologians are
frequent. Nor that they are always so crass. But we had to
show what kind of man we had in mind in describing an
extreme case of this type.

2. SECURITIES

Under this title we introduce a number of forms of existence
which are not only considered by those who live them as
justified, but also as valid, if not ideal, guarantees. Such a
security in this world of dangers can be for a time and in
some places the predominant situation, perhaps even for

centuries. And that can establish the right to validity and permanence of these modes of existence in the conscience. Any scruples about them are accounted to be subversive, ignorant, and even unecclesiastical.

Priest and Man of the World

Dick Ouwendijk once heard his brother say: "God would have abhorred becoming a man in an environment of well-situated people" (*Das geschändete Antlitz*, p. 9). Whatever one may think about that, let us leave the idea in its subjective indifference: at any rate, it is certain that the "Son of David" came into the world in a stall and, when scarcely born, barely escaped the sword of Herod, then led the life of a carpenter and went around the country as a preacher of the kingdom of God. In that country, where the foxes had their holes and the birds their nests, He knew not whereon to lay his head (Luke 9: 58); it is certain, too, that He died on the cross, ostracized by His people; that his disciples traveled about the whole world in proverbial "apostolic poverty"; that early Christianity was persecuted for over three hundred years, even if not continually, until —yes, until it became at home and secure in this world.

With this there begins not only the dialectic of Christianity—but of every Christian, of every priest. Emperor Constantine's edict of Milan and the privileges which he accorded the Church were received by the early Church as a liberation that we today can hardly appreciate. But it was accepted by the best with fear and trembling. What will become of the heroic Church of the Martyrs if it no longer means risking one's life to be baptized? There began a rush to baptism and the clerical life. The prohibition against such numbers (A.D. 320) was hardly effective, and was often circumvented. And before we know it, we already have prince bishops who are so perfect in their species that one would think that they had had hundreds of years of development behind them. And among the sons of Constantine they are the most submissive bearers and opportunists of the Arian heresy.

And a few decades after the last martyrs died under Diocletian, even the others, the best, the holy bishops have an attitude that is notably different from that of the Martyr-Bishops. There is food for thought when Augustine, who was paying his respects to the Bishop in Milan, reports that he received him *"satis episcopaliter."*

This is the existential dialectic which now sets in: His kingdom is not of this world! But it must endure the world; its citizens must live also as citizens of this world's kingdoms. In order that His kingdom can work, it needs at least a minimal freedom and a relatively necessary security enforced by the powers of this world. This security, and the blessing with which salvation illumines even this world of time, create regard and prestige. The world itself gets a Christian face. A new culture based on the Faith springs up, imposing, powerful, singular. This itself is understood to be a gift of God and a permanent ideal, indeed, as the ideal of a redemption of the world in faith: not a flight from the world, but rather a mastery of the world! The Church waxes great, becomes powerful, grows rich. The work of faith in this world becomes itself a part of the world. The churches and the splendid edifices of the monasteries become objects of all histories of art. The boundaries between heaven and earth are erased, perhaps consciously erased, as in the ceiling paintings of Baroque churches. Those who flee the world retire to hermitages and the cells of their monasteries. Power, esteem, and wealth become a danger and constant temptation to the Church and to all of her representatives. It becomes not only a threat to her own soul, which is worth more than all the riches of this world, but also a threat to her pristine effectiveness.

That is the existential dialectic of the history of Christianity. The type of priest, of which we speak here, was born at the pinnacle of Christian culture—perhaps not quite at the pinnacle any more. It is the type which was cultivated after the peak of the Christian impression on the world, the esteemed bearer of the Christian culture. This is still an ideal in the eyes of many, even though the high noon of Christian mastery of the world, historically considered, has already been lost in the past. There are already cracks in the beams of the huge edifice, but he is still sunning himself in the setting sun of a great era. And just as the evening light is often reflected in the east, he frequently enough confuses east and west when the whole heavens are suffused with a puzzling fire.

Josef Weingartner has given us a sample of this type in his solidly historical novel *Der Kardinal* (Innsbruck, 1947). It is that of Ypolito de Ferrara, and the evening of his life at his ornate castle on the rim of the Campagna. "Yes, his beautiful garden and his splendid villa! All his colleagues had always envied him this possession, even though most of them knew themselves what the beautiful Villa Surburbana was . . . even Julius III and Pius IV. How many prominent guests, how many princely personalities, how many countesses and princesses had he not already led proudly through these arbors and flower beds. He had shown them the select and rarest trees and bushes, the intricate water fountains, the classical sculpture which gleamed by the dozens in the extensive work. And now he couldn't walk around his own garden any more; he could only have himself carried around in it with difficulty" (p. 6).

The Renaissance prelate is, of course, an opponent of the

reforms, which, sad to say, are not only being preached by bullying monks, but even by those wearing the tiara on the chair of Peter. Life depressed him in a world that was no longer his own. His relatives were already arguing about his will. He preserved his dignity and nobility in the face of their meanness. "The Cardinal had to look on as his people, so to say, pillaged his living body, and witness the naked greed with which the most trusted men scuffled about his estate. It filled him with such repugnance that he finally cared nothing for what happened to him and let things take care of themselves" (p. 80). When the doctor told him, upon being ordered to do so, that his end was drawing near, he said, "Thank God! You could have told me that immediately. You wouldn't believe how weary I am of this miserable life" (p. 82). He wills a few houses to the work of Philip Neri and dies in the consciousness that he has also contributed to the reforms that will come. At his deathbed, only his confessor and faithful servant Giovanni are kneeling beside him.

Even the contemporary of Ferrara, Archbishop Johann Blankenfelde of Livonia is a man of the same stripe. His passion is more for power than for splendor. But he is less of a Renaissance prelate and even less effeminate. But he is of the same nobility, which in him showed itself in chivalric and military traits. "The archibishop made no secret of the fact that he prized his ecclesiastical dignity principally as a possession by means of which he could serve his one great passion: to form men and events. And in that, he set more store on the constant attainment and impression of power 'than on administration" (Werner Bergengruen, *Am Himmel und auf Erden*).

That, of course, was the type which failed miserably when the great storm of the sixteenth century roared over the Church (Lortz, *Reformation*, Vols. I, II).

And yet there is something about this type that is time-lessly valid. Even the holy Bishop Ignatius of Antioch, and so a quite unimpeachable witness, desires that the bishops impress the heathen (*An die Kirche von Tralles*, 3). Why? "In your bishop I received a copy of your love and have it with me. His whole bearing is a mighty sermon and his humility is power. Even the godless, I believe, must respect him." He wants them to impress by the ancient strength of Christianity: charity and humility.

One of the most stirring scandals that we still give the world after twenty centuries is the nonsense that it is not the men of force and those who have power, but the meek, who inherit the earth (Mt. 5: 5). One almost has to add that the believing Hindu Mahatma Gandhi had understood this better and had made it the kernel of his political creed. He confessed in his memoirs also, that the source of his re-ligious-political attitude was the Sermon on the Mount.

The Renaissance is past. But its great monuments, man-sions, and monasteries are still standing. They breathe a spirit upon the successors of those prelates of three hun-dred years and more ago, to which they may succumb in the long run. Hermann Gohde tells us in his novel of a critical moment for the world, *Der achte Tag* (Vienna, 1950) that the victorious leaders of the armies of the last World War were given splendid Baroque castles as a token of gratitude. But these have made the old soldiers com-pletely effeminate, simply because they lived there, even though in a completely transformed world.

The future drawn by Gohde (in the year A.D. 2074), which is very much present, seeks to burn out Christianity by all means, because it disturbs the balance of this world through its most logical representatives, the priests, and introduces an uncontrollable element into this completely rationalized, "self-contained life" (Paul Tillich). Collectivism cannot permit that, since it runs life by planning and calculation.

The time when the bishoprics were almost without exception taken over by the younger sons of the high nobility, whether they had a vocation or not, is past. That was a time when those who aspired to a position as cathedral dean had to display their gymnastic ability (Lortz, *Reformation*, I, 84). But their type disappeared only very gradually from the stage. "Higher Ecclesiastics" for a long time did not mean, as one might suppose, a sacramental or hierarchic position; by this term was meant the upper crust, which was separated from the "lower," composed of simple priests, by a wide gap. (Cf. Franz Schnabel, *Deutsche Geschichte im neunzehnten Jahrhundert*, IV, 10). Today we speak of that with as much emotion as amusement. Pastor John B. Buohler, who apparently wrote his pious *Charakterbilder aus dem katholischen Priester- und Seelsorgerleben* for table reading in seminaries, praises, for instance, the devout John Julius von Moll because he, although he was a canonist, dean, consultor to the consistory, and general visitator to the archdiocese of Salzburg, "among all his honors and dignities, never forgot that he was a priest" (p. 23). "He showed to all the honor which befitted him, indeed, often more than their rank or his rank and dignity would seem to have permitted!" (p. 25) And Graham Greene, the sober reporter of reality, can still report of a priest who —just imagine!—was a monsignor, but still was involved in the Mexican persecution. Contrary to his expectation, he was shoved up against the same wall as the simple clergy: "he really despised the lower clergy and right to the last he insisted on his rank. Only at the very end did he think of saying a prayer" (*The Power and the Glory*). For the convert Graham Greene that is apparently not just an amusing anecdote in the midst of a moment not at all amusing. He also intended to point out wherein the "power and the glory" of the priest is rooted and where it is not. "The rush of the centuries" was too fast for some people. They haven't got the picture straight. In the *Münchener Illustrierten* (December 22, 1951) Greene describes the life of the Holy Father Pius XII under the title of "The Pope Who Stayed a Priest." As flattering as the title intends to be, the article misses the point. But even so, there is a serious and general concern involved in this.

We believe "that the possession of episcopal domains, of extensive monasteries and capital goods no longer provides a fruitful ecclesiastical life" (Schnabel, p. 18). For that's what it comes to. But the type that believes in the necessity of these goods still lives among us. And he has his own good reasons. And he has no idea of changing his mind. And it would almost be too bad for him, I may say. So thinly disseminated among the others, he had his duty. Even today. When we give examples, we distinguish: 1. those who do not betray their priesthood by being men of the world; 2. those who do betray what is essential to the priesthood thereby; and 3. the "bourgeois priest," who has such a bad press today.

Being a Man of the World without Betraying the Priesthood. There are the uncle and nephew Schöllhaas in Werner Bergengruen's *Das Beichtsiegel* (Innsbruck-Vienna, 1947). The uncle is a chaplain and confessor of the family of the Margrave Thann-Ballenstein, and in the eyes of the princess, he "made little distinction between himself and the courtiers of her father. He was a part of her traditional court life" (p. 55). And so were the things he taught and demanded; all had become parts of the whole which was courtly life. Then his nephew Martin Schöllhaas, a curate in Corpus Christi, came to help out in the castle. What was he like? "He was no man of the world in clerical dress. A priest, painted as though by the colors of legend, he stood before her. There was none of the uncouthness and awkwardness or the coarseness about him that one felt could be detected in priests from laborer or farmer's stock. He was slender, handsome, spirited, and moved by the passions of the intellect." Then there is a characterization that could serve as a typology, at least superficially: "He wore his soutane, not like a woman's dress nor a night shirt, but like a toga" (p. 55). And so he is a man of the world! He is, but only in that respect and to a certain extent.

We suppose that this is where the nattily dressed American Father sight-seeing in Europe fits in, whom Joseph Bernhart meets in an art store and regards with the jealousy of a poor curate (*Der Kaplan,* p. 164). And I suppose that that famous preacher and canonist also belongs here. He was the one who rhapsodized on the camel-hair clad John the Baptist before a huge audience, mostly women, with delightful organ music and pathos, waving his carefully kept hands and flashing his gold cuff-links (*ibid.,* p. 177).

Here we also find Don Antonio Zei, pastor of San Sebastiano in Campo: a solid priest, almost envied by his neighbors because he has such support from his congregation (Carlo Coccioli, *Heaven and Earth,* London, 1953). He lives a comfortably untroubled life. He is unfavorable to everything new and unusual. He goes hunting, doesn't examine his conscience. He is on his guard against his curate Don Ardito, who sees in the parish only indifference and "half-hearted adherence to the usual tradition." "They come to church in the same way that one gets out of a hail-storm." He sent his restless curate to a remote mountain parish.

There is the serious and self-confident Canon de la Motte Beuvron in *The Diary of a Country Priest.* The shy pastor had confidence in him and would like to have spoken freely with this man, who was every inch an aristocrat. "But these miserable socialites are afraid of being disturbed." His cool self-possession and unimpassioned manner freezes the young Curé. The Canon does not think it proper for the pastor to go up to the chateau to see his nephew, the count, who wishes to speak with him. "Nonsense, my dear child, you can see him here. You go on as if you were their private chaplain." In the conflict between the pastor and his nephew, the canon does not side with his nephew, who wants to have the pastor dismissed and to this purpose plans to lodge a complaint against him with the Bishop. "His Grace is so simple that he takes him for a person of real importance." The old, independent judge of events dissuades the shy country pastor from allowing it to come to an investigation of his case by ecclesiastical authorities. "You don't know the bureaucratic mind . . . you'll never be able to speak their language. Even if you tell them that two and two make four, they'll still class you as hysterical, a kind of lunatic."

"Well, receive my nephew and say just what you want to him. But remember that he's a fool. And don't be impressed by his name, title, and the other twaddle which I fear your generosity has made too much of. There's no longer any aristocracy, my friend . . . The aristocrats of today are only shamefaced bourgeois." So spoke the proud count and Canon de la Motte Beuvron, and then took his leave.

There is the old Abbé Menou-Segrais, canon and pastor of Campagne. As a young priest, he believed that he was meant for higher things. "His spirit of fierce independence, a common sense which might be called irresistible, but the application of which not infrequently involved an obvious cruelty all the more apparent to the sensitive because of his refined courtesy, his scorn for abstract solutions, his very

lively taste for the highest spirituality—a taste hardly satisfied by speculation alone—had at first awakened the bishop's
distrust" (Bernanos, *Under the Sun of Satan*).

When on top of all this, he favored the election of the
liberal candidate, who was defeated, he himself fell into
disfavor and retired to the desirable country parish of Campagne. "He was heir to a great fortune which he managed
with wisdom—intending that the whole of it should go to
his Segrais nieces—living on little, but not without distinction, a great lord in exile who brought into the very heart
of the country something of the ways and customs of the
court, curious about the lives of other men and yet the
least of gossips, skilled at making people talk, groping for
secrets with a glance, a haphazard word, a smile—then the
first to request, to enforce silence—always admirable for
tact and spiritual dignity, a delightful table companion and
through politeness a good trencherman, on occasion talka-
tive by reason of kindliness or charity, so perfectly polite
that the simple pastors of his deanery, caught in the snare,
always viewed him as the most indulgent of men, in inter-
course agreeable and confident, perceptive without being
sharp, tolerant by taste, even skeptical, and perhaps a bit
suspect."

Assigned to this cultivated man, concerned about the
spotlessness of his Smyrna carpets, the awkward peasant
Donissan comes as a curate. He had even chosen him himself, "so as to be able to form him according to the best
of his ability for the ministry." Menou-Segrais is a real
priest and devout enough to confess to his curate: "It is
the other way around . . . it is you who are shaping me
. . . It is God Who names us. The name we bear is only
a borrowed name . . . My child, the spirit of strength is
within you." And then this man, who had been ready to
send his crushed and boorish young priest back to the stalls

and pastures from which he had come, is the first one to recognize the mission of the future saintly pastor of Lumbres.

With Betrayal of the Priesthood. The other Canon, Jacques Le Roy, whom we meet in the company of his old confrere at the Notre Dame Cathedral in Paris, is cut from another bolt of cloth. Filled with amazement, he looks at the fine stone work on the towers and sighs: "Beauty—that is what has made me a servant of the Church and one of her mystics. Not her moral beauty; not that beauty which one sees for the first time on the death masks of the saints —no! It is rather such beauty as results from the harmony of all masses, the intermingling of tones, the flowing unity of color, the classical perfection. Ah, what peace; with what perfect content these trees bend over the bank toward the rippling water . . . Certainly, the kingdom of heaven suffers violence—but that, as everyone knows, is on an entirely different level" (Elisabeth Langgässer, *Das unauslöschliche Siegel,* Hamburg, 1946).

The old and obviously weary confrere with whom he is staying is for him a rebel with "a beggar's sack full of theology which does not even stop at the doctrines of the Church." He has written a book—one would not believe that that is any longer possible today—*Apparitions of the Devil in the Lives of the Saints,* in which he not only believes, in the real sense of the word, but he also proves that "the perfect antichrist will only be recognized with great difficulty, since, being ubiquitous as God is, he is already become familiar to the majority of men to a shocking degree; in fact, he is a favorite custom" (p. 197).

That is as far as as the Canon could read the book—no further. Now he has come to the old fanatic. He wants to know if he has handled M. Bellefontaine correctly, as a priest. He had met this man during the war when he was pastor in a God-forsaken little village. "He had no companionship, no stimulation, not a man with whom he could share his library with its priceless first editions of the Encyclopedists, and his collection of tropical butterflies . . . Contentedly he contemplated his well-kept fingers with their carefully cut nails" (p. 192). He had known that Bellefontaine was leading a double life. Mysterious thing, that! But the old man shouts at him: "Stop it! Sheer formulas, mere generalities, ha!" Was he sinful in his treatment of M. Bellefontaine? "What a question! Of course you're at fault. Everyone is responsible for his neighbor. You for Bellefontaine, another for you—I'm thinking, for instance, of your teachers, who gave you that 'theological armour,' as they call it so exaggeratedly, that looks more like rusty iron."

But Le Roy admits he is no Curé d'Ars. "Anyway, I'm unfortunately not the man who can give a decisive no. And I don't want to. I shy away from any form of harshness, from strictness, from inflexibility. No, no, I'm cut from different cloth. And certainly not from the kind that could be used to make an ascetic. I'm good-natured, that's all" (p. 194). All he wants from Bellefontaine, in whom he suspects a double life, is "nothing more than a companion, a man with whom one can chat and play duets on the piano" (p. 194).

Others play taroc or go bowling on certain nights with the fellows, or have their nightly pint of beer with the liberal Philistines of their little city (Bernhart, *Der Kaplan*, p. 192). And with them, they would never in their lives discuss the problem of Gretchen in Goethe's Faust. They are like that personal physician of King Maximilian of Bavaria of whom Hans Carossa tells that he daily played Schach with the king, but one morning couldn't see His Majesty—because he was sick (*Führung und Geleit*, Leipzig, 1943). When it is all over with their companions at Schach and poker, the game is up, too. They never notice that they have neglected anything with their partners. What has become of the priest now? They have relegated him to the ranks of mere good company.

The "Bourgeois" Priests. You can't quite say that of the priest in Robert Morel's *Le Satisfait*. His name is Tolerable:—*nomine et homine.* Or is he?

Pastor Tolerable has two brand new curates, restless zealots. They even want, he has heard, to turn the altar around and celebrate the Mass facing the people! The pastor is against it, not because they haven't the right to change the liturgy, but because a Mass like that would bother him. He doesn't want to see the people. He celebrates the Mass and lives with his back to the people, who spend their Sundays with their backs turned to their pastor. He "doesn't want to confuse the parishioners" (p. 24). "Besides, the pastor is collecting reasons for clipping the wings of his curates" (p. 25).

On this particular Sunday there is a special service for the soldiers who have returned. This gives the pastor an occasion for a solemn sermon on the Maid of Orleans. Oh well, the sermon was no better and no worse than all the others given on a patriotic occasion, that is to say, it had nothing to do with the written word of God and little to do with religion. And what was said of the holy shepherdess of Domremy could have been said at any military assembly. What Morel has to say about the sermon I cannot repeat out of good breeding. But that should be taken symbolically, as far as the sermon is concerned.

Tolerable likes to be invited to dinner (p. 27). At noon he eats at the home of Mme. Komfort; in the evening, he dines with M. Soustrait, the Notary, whose wife makes a fuss over him. He likes it. On such occasions, of course, he meets all sorts of people who don't come to church. But he doesn't offend anyone. He is against all immoderate piety. His god is Moderation. Once there was a young fellow present at coffee. He had read Léon Bloy. "Ah, Léon Bloy!" says the pastor, "that is poison. He is much more a man of the Old Testament than the New; by his exaggerations he causes a good deal of harm and confuses souls. The thing that is most against him is that he has always tried to cause scandal" (p. 180). But Tolerable doesn't contradict the young chap who contradicts him, but gives a conciliating answer to his objections. "Pastor Tolerable knows well how to influence every atmosphere so that all can feel at ease" (p. 181).

On his way home late—"a delightful afternoon!"—he meets Mlle. Bartholemy. She is the leader of the Catholic Girl Students. They are very serious about it. In youthful exuberance she can already see "a generation of saints" in the future. That is not exactly the case with the pastor, and he warns her: "People forget too often that saints are men who get out of line. Jesus, however, the God-made Man, Who took upon Himself our daily sufferings, never stepped out of line as a man. He is simply a man, and that is why we, too, can imitate Him. He knew all our needs; and that is why His first miracle was to turn water into wine . . . He became a man without arousing any great interest, almost, you might say, without being noticed. Our Catholics must think about that a good deal, and especially the young girls who want to turn things upside down" (p. 204).

On this day, Morel introduces a coward, a man without faith, a lecher, a murderer, a venal man, a magician, an idolater, and a liar into *Le Satisfait;* the scene is a French provincial town, which is just like any other town of the continent on Sunday. And late that Sunday night, the pastor Tolerable comes home, tired from his big sermon and two invitations out. After he has had himself served a cup of coffee and a roll, "he gets through" the rest of his Breviary. "In his favorite deep easy chair, with his feet on the electric radiator . . ."

"Cum invocarem . . ." He reads the awe-inspiring songs of the Psalmist with their burden of faith and vital fear. "It is his duty to read it, all of it." And he reads it. "He reads as quickly as he can, so that he can get to bed the sooner." He "knows the psalms by heart. He knows what is in them . . . His Latin flows like water." He was even a model student, once. "The night surrounds the pastor. It makes him lethargic; he says yes without saying it—as his custom is; he smiles; he is agreeable; he gives the night his blessing, and has already drifted off into his reminiscences. They have nothing to do with an examination of conscience" (p. 232) . . . "The pastor pulls himself together again. When he has said his Breviary, he will be able to dream and take it easy. The Sundays are always the most strenuous days. The sermon . . . My sermon was a real success, I think . . . I said everything without stepping on anyone's toes . . . Many must have realized that they think as the Church does . . . Certainly next Sunday there will be more people than usual in Church . . . The Breviary! Oh, yes, the Breviary!" . . . *"Non accedat ad te malum* (Let no evil approach thee!). He doesn't listen to it; he knows everything, absolutely everything! he reads his Breviary out of a sense of obligation; he also feels himself obligated not to distract himself by attending to the meaning of what he reads" (p. 234). "But psalm 90 cries out *'And let him behold my salvation!'* at the very moment that the Breviary falls to the floor, because it is no longer grasped by its owner, and thus disgorges a heap of holy cards.—And it is night" (p. 235).

The "novel" has as its motto a sentence by Charles Péguy: "I must tell the truth with the emphasis that belongs to it, sad when it is sad, harsh when it is harsh, and joyful when it is joyful."

The Official of God with a Fixed Income

These are late descendants of a race that is dying: Already something rare, but still there. Where did they first appear in Christian history? We can only say when their ancestor tried to appear. He didn't quite make it. That was when Simon Magus got the idea that in the vocation that came with the laying on of hands by the apostles and is full of supernatural power, one could live quite nicely and make some money (Acts 8: 19). But he went to the wrong people with his proposition. Later that was not always the case.

His History. Apparently the hour in which this type was born is the same as in the preceding case: when it was no longer a dangerous and daring thing to become a priest, when the priestly estate became honorable and, in certain circumstances, lucrative. That is why the atmosphere becomes a little thin for this type, in the measure that the risk and uncertainty again begin to mount.

He was predominant in a time when an historian can say, "The number of men becoming priests was large. Many parents regarded the priesthood as good hunting ground" (Friedrich Zöpfl, *Deutsche Kulturgeschichte*, Freiburg, 1931, I, 566). In that time, the Bishops were first vassals of the king and only second, pastors of souls; they had abbeys and parishes to bestow on their subordinates; secular lords bestowed benefices and were paid for them. Whoever had come into a benefice by purchase sought to make up the price he paid by high stole fees for baptisms, Masses, Communions, official duties and consecrations. Even absolution was often given for money (*Ibid.*, I, 191). Since one foundation or benefice did not always suffice to support them, many priests sought out several. In that way, one could get by.

When the deluge burst upon these priests in the sixteenth century, they were less concerned about the true Faith than they were about their jobs. Joseph Lortz even tells of one who was minister in the Lutheran town of Rod on the Weil (1536) and a pastor in Catholic Hasselbach. "He tried to please both, there by preaching, here through the Mass. During a Lutheran visitation, he put the blame on the parishioners; they had forced him into his double role. At any rate, he was left undisturbed in his evangelical office" (*Reformation*, II, 220).

But the type did not disappear. In Gallicanism and Josephinism he stands before us again in an altered form. These State-Church tendencies saw in the priest first an official of the State. The State assured them of their support. Even the French Revolution in this respect signified no break with history. It merely demanded of the priests that they take their oath of allegiance to the new State (*Constitution civile de clergé*, 1789). To their honor it must be said that only a third of them acceded to that demand. This constitutes proof that, at that time, the type we are discussing here embraced only one third of the clergy of France. But it wasn't to the new Republic that they swore their allegiance so much as to the one that paid their salary. The idea of security, understood as a guarantee of the means of living, drove the same men into the service of Absolutism after the Revolution.

And herein lies the historical fault of this type: despotism not only guarantees the priest his salary; it also demands of him that he declare himself unreservedly for the one who provides his daily bread. (Despotism today is no different. It plans on using state endowed priests.) The memory of the terrors and cruelties of the Revolution were still so vivid that this *quid pro quo* of the clergy could have a convincing basis. But the clergy had to agree to the fulfillment of desires that brought upon them the hatred and the apostasy of the forces that were rapidly gathering. They wanted to save their lives, and thus lost them. That is the fundamental law of Christian, and therefore priestly, existence (Cf. Mt. 10: 39), that cannot be ignored with impunity. Even more: it was the conduct of these priests that gave a foundation to that mistrust which in many cases still cannot be overcome today, for a scandal given in a critical moment of history is not easily forgotten.

His Basic Attitude.   What is the basic outlook of the kind of man we are discussing? Perhaps one can express it like this: the real priest lives for his vocation; the priest-official lives on his vocation. That is the circumstance that characterizes him. It is not the fact that he draws a salary that is the decisive factor. That is understandable, or at least it can be. But the fact that the secure life is guaranteed by his salary is something that decides his existence. The concern of his existence is to establish an "existence" for himself and to make it secure, just as a business man makes his own "existence," or just as an official guarantees his "existence" by means of his appointment and makes it secure, i.e., his salary, the economic basis of life.

We must also number among those of this type the man who is not exclusively concerned only with his economic welfare—for that is rare indeed!—but the man for whom that interest comes first and foremost. When he attends a pastoral conference, he lets all references that deal with ministerial problems go right past him and only comes to life when, and for as long as, the point at issue is one of daily life, dealing with stole fees, salary, promotion, bienniums, and matters like that.

There is nothing one can hold against him. He fulfills his "duty." He goes to the church like an official to his office and dispatches what has been assigned him. And he does so conscientiously, for that is why he has the job. It would be wrong to accuse him of unbelief or even of indifference in matters of faith. He has solved all his problems of faith once and for all by an all-embracing act of *fides implicita*. Problems of theology and the ministry are his concern, he knows, but only in the same way as the ticket agent in the railroad station is supposed to know about coal consumption and horse power. They aren't his job. He is very strict in insisting that everyone take care of his own job which is assigned to him and is therefore expected of him. That's the only way the whole thing is going to click.

Needless to say, neither can he be taken to task like the hireling in John 10: 13. He has hired himself out, that is true. But he won't desert in the moment of danger. Why? Because he has obligated himself to it. He will stay with his flock, but he leads them to pasture so that he can fleece them.

Of course, everything will be done within the limits of the prescribed stole fees and legal admissibility.

Like all officials he is ambitious. He wants to get ahead. He is always out to win a "better" parish, understood to be one that has a more lucrative benefice than the one he has. The "world" around him thinks that he is completely justified. And obviously so.* Why not, he asks; or he does not ask at all.

---

* According to this point of view, one could divide the authors who write about priests into those who know what priestly existence is and those who haven't the slightest inkling of it. Thus, Emile Marriot considers it a virtue in the best priestly character of her *Geistlichen Tod*, Joachim Perkow, that he is eager to "get ahead." And the affair becomes amusing when the novel has him "advance" by getting a position in the court of the Archbishop of Salzburg, and then with the Cardinal in Vienna. Or when Maria Ebner-Eschenbach has Curate Tipps given the position of visiting consultor for a career.

Because he is essentially a pusher, he is resolved under the proper circumstances to use improper means to further his plans. He lays the greatest value on the fact that he is the superior's fairhaired boy and that he is canonically—and dogmatically—in the clear. He is not troubled about that at all, and no one should be bothered for his sake. He has learned that the sacraments work *"ex opere operato"* and he sees to it that, in administering them, he at least has a *"virtualis saltem implicite determinata"* intention if he can't manage an *"intentio actualis."* No one is going to get into trouble here or in the next life because of him. That is part of the regimen of service that he has adopted.

There is no existential dialectic in the sense that we have used it before for this type. For him, "existence" means the economic guarantee of life. Any other meaning of this word is alien to him. Once more, this type is not found merely because the priest receives a salary, but only when the question of his salary and the securing of his means of livelihood are the only thing, or the thing that most determines his interest in his way of life.

Today?

Until the eighteenth century, the Church took care of the expenditure of money for her priests and officials from her own possessions or from the free-will offerings of the faithful. It was only with the great secularizations around 1800 that she had difficulties. These seemed to be taken care of at first by the obligations which the princes assumed when they took possession of former ecclesiastical properties.

The problem of the support of the clergy was solved differently in Austria. Emperor Joseph II with the decree of October 30, 1781 (and more followed that one) ordered the appropriation of those monasteries which "make no visible contribution to the common good," and that meant all convents of contemplative orders. By this decree, 738 monasteries in Austria and 135 in Hungary were affected. From the proceeds of the sales of these properties, several hundred new parishes and ministerial positions were founded, and the "Religion Funds" were endowed from which the priests were supposed to be paid. (Their salaries were called *congrua*.) But these funds were appropriated during the Napoleonic wars when the State fell into monetary difficulties, and were covered by a certificate of national debt, according to which the States undertook the obligation of paying out the salaries of the clergy. It was a painful situation in later years when the obligations for the *congrua* were debated every year in the parliaments of the States. Before World War II, the Church declined the payment in Austria, and introduced Church taxes, which were handled by each diocese through its own finance official. There is a similar regulation in most of the States. That gives a sort of security, but it has its dark side. It is different in France. With the separation of Church and State (1905) and the confiscation of Church property by the Republic (1908), hard times fell upon the French clergy. The priests of France live even today on the free-will gifts of their people. It is a difficult state of affairs in a country where there are few active faithful, or none at all.

The diocese obliges itself to see to the sufficient support of its priests when they are ordained (according to Can. 979, 2). There is also a canonically guaranteed quasi-contract between the priest, who enters upon the service of the diocese by his ordination, and his bishop, who assumes the duty of providing for his means of livelihood in return for the services he renders (*titulus servitii diocesis*). This matter-of-course and anything but luxurious guarantee, which will free the priest for his work in the kingdom of God, becomes for the type we describe here the express or implicit existential fact of his life.

All this amounts to saying that for him, the ministry is of secondary importance. Or should one say that the ministry is a means of getting a job as a priest? In his sermon on the words of our Lord, "Saul, Saul, why persecutest thou me?" (Acts 9: 4), Saint Bernard says: "Now they have received sacred ordination . . . They show themselves exceedingly pious in receiving it, or even more in the acceptance of the duty of the ministry, yet they are not in the least concerned about this, and any thought of the salvation of souls is their last. Could there ever be a more bitter persecution for the Redeemer of souls?"

This type has his time behind him. And that would be the case even if the reason for his being were not destroyed from within, by the intensification of the priestly vocation which began with the reforms of Trent. In a time when the salary of a priest scarcely reaches that of a worker's helper without any profitable training, the motivation of taking up the priestly life for reasons of economic support is negligible.

Joseph Scheicher (died 1924) supposed even in his time that this was rare (*Arme Brüder,* p. 186), even in this short time things have changed considerably. This calling is scarcely ever chosen without a real vocation. Its burden is a "sweet burden" only for those who are chosen; otherwise it is too great to be undertaken in anything but the "good faith" as understood in the decision of June 26, 1912 (A.A.S. IV. 485). And so difficult is it, that the thought of merely making a living vanishes before it.

The Old Pastor-Idyl

Their "Existence." Undeniably, and in spite of everything, the priestly vocation, especially in its most proper form, that of the pastor, is one of the most beautiful of vocations, even today. Not for nothing has it found so many who praise it, set it to poetry, and paint it. And there are still wide landscapes in the great kingdom of God on earth where the noonday sun in its luminous splendor pauses over comfortable rectories with a blooming garden in their midst. When they hear the word *pastor,* many immediately get the picture of a white-haired gentleman who is reading his Breviary in a too-sunny garden, or working in the flower beds, or sucking on his pipe in the arbor, while around the garden wall, with its wild vine, there pervades an infinite peace. Just behind him is a beautiful shepherd dog, who trots along all the paths and waits until his master gives him a look or gently scratches his head.

There have been times and countless examples then, and even now, when the life of a pastor seemed to unite all the paradoxes, all the discords of this life into a single harmonious accord. Even on entering the rectory one can sense the peace and quiet. The pastor's simple humanity, his hospitality, his helpfulness is only an expression of it. Nature and the super-nature meet in one man. "Whenever my father sent me with a message or something like that to the rectory, and I came into the very simple dining room, I always thought that it must look something like that in heaven," reports Propst Weingartner of his childhood in Dölsach (*Unterwegs,* Innsbruck, 1951). The cheerfulness, minus the tragedy, of this life has an almost transparent effect here, and that transformation derives from eternal life. These rooms are penetrated with a special atmosphere; children cannot understand why they are so happy and at home there; and it is there that a man, distracted, can regain his peace, or the most troubled can find security again. Just as the Church is God's dwelling among men, the rectory is an expression and an image of how a man's life appears in the presence of God. In the rectories, according to Anton Coolen, there is a smell that is peculiar to them alone (*Brabanter Volk*).

The type of this priest was not a product of the Middle Ages; or if it was, we know little about it. It comes from the time when the struggle was waning which had broken upon the Church in the sixteenth century. There then ensued that peace and quiet that alone could produce these generations of pastors, after the consolidation of parochial boundaries. There seemed to be little need for ministerial work as we understand it today. As a matter of course, the people came to church faithfully every Sunday, made their Easter duty, and to gain indulgences, came to confession and Communion. A peaceful, untroubled comfort was the foundation of this leisurely pastoral life. The congregation itself took care of difficult cases of disorder by its own healthy atmosphere. Any hostility to the pastor as pastor was not even known, even when there were anti-clerical tendencies perceptible in the villages and remote valleys. And that lasted until late into the nineteenth century.

The people granted that the pastor "had it better" and was a "gentleman." When I was a child of eight years, and in a strange town, I said "The Pastor"; . . . a man interrupted me and said, "Look here, sonny, you say *the pastor* for sheep, but *Father Pastor* for the priest." The people made a fuss over him and kept him free of disturbance. They were glad to see the pastor's hospitality and the beautiful fraternal companionship of the pastors among each other.

These get-togethers of the pastors had something relaxing about them which we simply cannot appreciate today. This being together had its own culture, its own language, and its own jokes. Franz Spirago (Prague) has edited the most extensive collection of these, *Heiteres aus dem Religionsunterricht und aus der Seelsorge,* but there are others. And even in this collection the best jokes aren't included. It was in this climate that original characters developed, of such singularity that we who model ourselves according to our duty and schedule cannot understand them. Father Hocke-Wanzl was one, and it is a shame that his life wasn't written by his contemporaries. For he was not merely the mad practical joker that a non-Catholic pastor described him to be. For from him there derives an expression that could be used as the introduction to the most serious priests' retreats. When a visiting bishop asked him how much his new parish brought in, he answered, "As much as your bishopric." "How's that?" "Heaven or hell." When I was a newly ordained priest in Kirchberg on the Wechsel, I saw for the first time all the pastors of the deanery sit together around a long table. I stared: they had the real, devout, amusing individuality of peasants, each one different, and yet how they stood together! And how they tore into each other—in brotherly fashion—when there was a difference of opinion!

The first thing to decline was the gentility of this existence . . . by degrees, but irrevocably. The pastor who had baptized me in my home town still had two horses and a fine carriage and of course his coachman, on occasion, when he went to a celebration or to a *"Läitz,"* as the people used to call the pastors' get-togethers. His successors had only the carriage; and a farmer drove it, when he had time, with his horses. The coach became more and more shabby. The present pastor goes *per pedes apostolorum* if someone doesn't happen to be going the same way and pick him up. Or he goes on his bicycle!

Now there are motorcycles. But the tranquillity of the old pastors and the dizzy pace of today are as different as a calash behind a pair of comfortably trotting horses, greeted in friendly fashion by all who meet it going through the countryside—and a motor bike that roars over the highway, with its smell and dust and exhaust chasing the terrified people it passes into the fields. When they have pulled themselves together and dusted themselves off, there is no more than a speck to be seen of the cyclist. Only then do they suspect that it may have been their pastor. Of course it's too late to wave hello. But that's not the only reason why the pastor is greeted less frequently today.

Examples and Illustrations. Annete von Droste-Hülshoff portrays such an old pastor's life in seven poems, *Des alten Pfarrers Woche*. Of course, even in bad weather, he has to go to see lame Friedrich, "to say a Christian word to him." The housekeeper, Anna, is already looking out for the old gentleman with the greatest concern:

> *The doors are shut; she pauses, then,*
> *To clean her glasses once again,*
> *And survey the cozy nest:*
> *The fire crackles, and the lamp's bright beam*
> *Lights the Sunday wine with a ruby gleam;*
> *The chair where the pastor loves to dream*
> *Invites to cushioned rest.*
> *Slippers—nightshirt for the pastor's wear,—*
> *She looks again, but he is not there . . .*

And that is only Sunday.

Johann Heinrich Voss tries to conjure up the idyl of the Evangelical pastor of the eighteenth century in his *Luise*.

But in spite of the good coffee and the long-stemmed pipe, the enlightened pastor chatters too much and becomes disapproving of those of different persuasion. Eduart Mörike, however, left a timeless monument to his own rectory idyl in Cleversulzbach, in his *Alten Turmhahn*.

Der grüne Heinrich, by Gottfried Keller, portrays the pastor's life at home in bright colors: "The splendor of the aristocratic government spread itself most at the pastor's home. The Reformed clergy of Switzerland were no poor, humble rascals, as their brothers of the Protestant North were . . . They were often born rich and their country rectories were more like the country estates of great gentlemen; there were also a number of pastors of noble birth whom the peasants had to address as *Junker-Pfarrer*. Now the pastor of my native village was not such a man as this, much less was he rich. But for all of that, he was descended of an old city family and united in his person and in his way of living all the pride, spirit of caste, and jollity of a comfortably situated city life. He indulged himself somewhat in being called an aristocrat, and combined with his clerical dignity a slight touch of the rough noble-militarist. But he did it quite naturally. There was always a noisy and happy time at his home. His parishioners gave him sizable donations of whatever the fields and stalls provided, and his guests themselves brought hares, woodcocks, and partridge from the forest; and since the chase was not yet a custom in that part of the country, the farmers were invited to large sociable fishing parties. That always meant a big feast, so that the parish house was never wanting noise and enjoyment. People hiked through the country roundabout, paid visits to one another in large groups, set up tents and danced under them, or spread the canvas over the brooks so the Grecian ladies could bathe under them. Or in gay groups they would descend upon a cool mill, or row on the lakes and streams in crowded boats. The pastor was always at their head, with a duck gun over his shoulder or a heavy Spanish cane in his hand. Intellectual requirements weren't much in evidence in these circles. The secular library of the pastor consisted, as I saw it, of a few old French pastoral romances, Gessner's *Idyllen,* Gellert's comedies, and a much-thumbed copy of Münchausen. There seem to have been two or three individual volumes of Wieland that were loaned out in the village and never returned . . ." (*Der grüne Heinrich,* I, 1).

The life of the Catholic pastors seemed much less aristocratic and less taken up with social events—celibacy brings that with it—in such a solidly Catholic country, for example, as Flanders. Ernest Claes' *Der Pfarrer von Kempenland* is a unique eulogy on the good old days of the pastor idyl. There is a touch of sadness about it because, even though it hasn't completely disappeared, it is on the way out. "The late pastor Campens liked a little sip of wine; he found it a divine drink because it was so often mentioned in the Gospel, and because it tasted so good. It was really a drink for pastors. And was there anything more wonderful than this transformation of simple water into delicious wine? Didn't our Lord want to show us by this that this was the drink of His disciples and their successors, the bishops and the good pastors . . . A pastor without wine was no pastor; the two belong together like the two weights of a grandfather clock. Wine was something for which people should have reverence. Whenever they met anywhere, the pastors of the surrounding parishes could beam at each other with a glow of contentment in their eyes that came from the wine glasses before them on the table. They could talk for hours with one another about this or that brand and its properties, and this or that vintage, or this or that purveyor. Then they would tell stories about the late pastor Van Reeth, the former pastor of Scherpenheuvel, who could tell you blindfolded not only what he was drinking, but the vintage . . .

"Ah, the late Father Van Reeth! Pastor Campens stood still for a minute to think of him with regret. What a good man he was! When it was his turn to entertain them at a little party, no one missed it. They just let everything wait and take care of itself, for that would be a real feast. The pastor of Averbode had his old 'Nuits' that he had inherited from his uncle. Among them they called the delicious beverage 'Averbode's Good old Uncle.' The pastor of Testelt . . . Liebfraumilch, which they had christened 'Madonna Wine' and drank from tall antique glasses. They closed their eyes with delight when it trickled down their throats . . . The Medóc of the pastor of Testelt was nothing compared to it, almost insipid, and they thought it tasted like holy water, although none of them had ever drunk holy water . . . That had been a wonderful time!" (p. 156)

Felix Timmerman's *Pfarrer vom blühenden Weinberg* is set in the same country. His wine cellar could almost be called a state of mysticism. But he never entered it during the holy season of Lent, just as during the long weeks of penance there was never any meat on the table and his long pipe stood cold in the corner. "But no sooner was the word *Easter* painted in the skies than he hurried to the cool cellar with a burning candle" to his wines. "He wanted only to enjoy their life and richness and savor their mystic meaning, just as a scholar can stand before his books, lost in thought, touching the books, which, though closed, have already been read and reread. For in the pastor's eyes, wine is a symbol of the blood of Christ . . . And when the wines came from France, Germany, or Portugal, from Turkey or Italy in their little casks, the pastor himself poured them into the bottles; like little monks in the monasteries, they gave up their baptismal names and received different ones, full of Christian symbolism that awakened heavenly thoughts and emotions" (p. 10).

"No, he couldn't enjoy drinking wines if they had names as banal as Pommeröl, Bordeaux, Port, Vermouth, or Mosel . . . His wines' names had been changed. One was called 'Tributary of the Jordan,' a white wine, with a yellow-gold tint and the humble fragrance of a violet; another was 'Vein of Christ,' a dark ruby, almost black, as soft as silk, whose taste, as clinging as incense in a church, lingered on the palate" . . . Another kind: 'Smile of Our Blessed Lady': a bright golden liquor, brilliant as the sun. Another: 'Dew of Heavenly Fields,' yellow and gravely shimmering as the yellow stone prelates wore on their white gloves.

"And then 'Rainbow of the Promised Land,' a sparkling red liquid that took on a rosy color through long 'lagering.' Its noble flavor thickened the blood and brought on a longing for faraway places. Another, 'Mirror of the Angels,' a bright liquor of white grapes with a shy tint of meadow greens waving in the wind. There is one that is called 'Delight of Assisi,' a golden brown wine, and one sip of it made one close his eyes in delight, while it soothed the restless heart like oil upon a burning wound. Another, 'Liquid Paradise,' that spoke convincingly of the sanctity of its grape with an aroma that outdid balsam, and a savor that went through the body like a benediction, soothing the nerves like music . . . And many, many others.

"Finally he tore himself away; he selected a bottle carefully here and there and held them to the candlelight that shone darkly in them with a ruby or golden glow. He murmured their names reverently, pondered on the flavor and aroma, made fanciful comparisons that exalted his thoughts to heaven, where the music of angels enchanted the rainbow; and then, as complacent as one who had leafed through a volume of poetry, he meditatively laid the bottles back in their dark repose."

Then the portly maid Sophie might call him to eat and poison herself with the thought that her precious veal had grown cold in the meantime (p. 11). He wasn't disturbed.

And this mysticism of wine ran through his quiet life and his sermons. He knew all the passages of Scripture by heart, and every word the saints had said about wine.

The first thing he would do with each guest was to lead him to the splendor of his cellar. Only then "they would sit together in the blossoming fruit garden at a table, on which there would be afternoon coffee, with some colorful radishes, and cheese from Holland. The garden is white as a lamb. All the fruit trees are laden with blooms, luxuriant and thick as cabbage, and the tender scents drifted and flew about their heads" (p. 41).

An idyl it was, in the midst of a land replete with the all-pervading presence of the living faith (pp. 126 ff.).

And yet, all this beauty is only the bright background for the dark tragedy of a pure girl, the niece of the pastor, Leontine, who may not marry her beloved because he does not have the Faith and cannot find it. They are crushed by the tragedy; but not in vain, since Michael finds the grandeur and grace of the Faith in the death of his loved one. And the old pastor saw none of this coming, in his happiness!

And the pastor prays: "Blessed be Thy Name, O Lord, for the new grape Thou hast destined for thy divine chalice! O true vineyard of Jesus Christ!

"The heavens fill their soul with wine; the heavenly wine cellarers sing amid their casks and flasks. And behind the land, the hill reaches in solemn stillness for the moon, like a great white host" (p. 186). The idyl has a crack in it, hidden as it is in a bottle in the sand of the cellar.

But even in the midst of the idyl of the "late" pastor from the Kempenland there stands a harbinger of times that will be less idyllic—Jef Leirs, half good-humored and half mocking, perhaps a little cynical.

The idyls look a little different today. For wherever true humanity and true priesthood are united in one human life, even if this is not in England, that life will always be a thing of beauty: something like the life of Father Smith in the diaspora of (apparently) Glasgow, with the splendid priests who are his brothers, and all characters. They are all "servants of the forbearance of Christ and the day laborers of the Lord." And yet, what a beautiful life this is! He consoles himself, going on his bicycle from one Mass to the other through the rain, praying for the conversion of Scotland in his own way: "for all the intercession of the Blessed Virgin, Caledonia, stern and wild, continued in 1908 to remain as unimaginatively Presbyterian and unsanctified as before. What could even God and all His saints make of a country which preferred the metrical version of the Psalms to inspired English or Latin, and whisky to wine? Was it not Hilaire Belloc who had written:

> '*Where'er a Catholic sun doth shine*
> *There's always laughter and good red wine,*
> *At least I have always found it so,*
> *Benedicamus Domino*' " (pp. 1 f.).

Of course that doesn't mean that they get drunk there. Even in the abundance of wine of the Kempenland and the mysticism of wine in the Blooming Vineyard there was nothing like that. The most priceless character in Father Smith's acquaintance, Monsignor O'Duffy, warns in a sermon, "My dear brethren in Christ, it begins with a thimbleful and ends with a bucketful, as all good Kartholic drunks have had to avow in the Holy Sacrament of Penance."

Too, there is a world that is quite different and yet an idyl—the author calls it correctly "mondo piccolo"—where Don Camillo on the Po fights it out with his Communist mayor Peppone. A robust fighter, this pastor, maybe one would even call him a fanatic, but it is all watered down by his humor and practical humanity (G. Guareschi, *Don Camillo and Peppone*). These are the idyls of today, and they can be so tomorrow.

•

3. FORMS OF ESCAPE

Escape in "Work"

Every priest who takes on an assignment also assumes clearly defined duties, and he must fulfill them; he has to do his job. In a large parish with many assistant priests, anything that is foreseen or foreseeable, the work that presses on them every day, must be done without complaint and according to the time schedule that is made out exactly for each priest. The established services, the sermons and religious instruction, the administration of the sacraments and the willingness to take sick calls, and everything else must be taken care of. The "burden" has to be divided, and each one should also have his time off for recreation.

This is what is meant when we say that the priest in the ministry has his job to do. But that alone does not constitute a priestly type. Consequently, that is not what we mean here and it is by no means belittled when we speak of an "escape in work." What is it that we mean?

The Existence of Escape.   The existential dialectic which leads to what we mean here by escape is as follows: the presence of God which is part of every sacrament, indeed, in every word "that comes from the mouth of God," and especially in the Most Blessed Sacrament of the Altar, not only signifies grace; it means also fear and trembling. It is a fear that must be endured for a whole life time. It is not the dogmatic mystery that we have in mind, not even principally, but rather the reality of the presence of God in our lives.

Can one "get used to" this Presence? It is a terrible thing to have to answer yes to this question. And the priest first realizes how used to it he has become when he sees a complete lack of realization of it in others. When I was a young priest, I often had to carry the Blessed Sacrament to the sick, who were often hours away. Then everyone I met knelt; waggoners stopped their teams and often knelt in the mire of the road. When they saw my white surplice from the farm house, the people all ran up and knelt at the edge of the fields and lofts so that I could bless them with the Blessed Sacrament. But when I had my first sick call in the big city (again in surplice, with the host on my breast, but all covered up with a black coat) and threaded my way through the streets between pedestrians, errand boys, and cars, no one took any notice of Him Who was their Redeemer and Judge "on the day of wrath," and a chill ran down my spine. They couldn't realize it, since I had myself covered the Mystery with my coat. But how about myself?

What is the experience of others? "Pastor Cawder got up from his knees and made the sign of the cross. He looked at the altar. He stared through the darkness at the glimmer of the brass tabernacle. Behind that weak reflection, behind metal and cloth, hidden in a tiny container, lay God. An incomprehensible humiliation. A God, who had submitted himself to time and space. The Holy One of Israel, Emmanuel, the Lion of the Tribe of Juda, the Anointed One. My Jesus, mercy! Lord, have mercy on us! It was a disconcerting and awe-inspiring mystery. The anointed Messias of the Jews, born of a Virgin, as Isaiah had foretold, He lay here, locked up in this wooden shrine a carpenter had put together. His Flesh and Blood were present here, here on the corner of Rozier Street and Winter Boulevard. The Savior of Christians and Jews, of heretics, Communists, and atheists was confined in the dark. No one saw him. A few steps away no one even paid the slightest heed" (Crawford Power, *The Encounter*, New York, 1950).

And it is possible that pastor Cawder and all of us ten feet away from the place, of which the Church says *"terribilis locus iste"*—terrible is this place—may have lost the consciousness of the terrible presence of God.

To be a priest means to live daily in the scorching Presence of God. Anything that happens every day becomes everyday. Can the Presence of God become something everyday for us? This is a question full of terror, since it can be answered with a yes. "Everyday" in the sense of no longer being exciting, something that loses more and more of its wonder for us and therefore is no longer taken into account, therefore unnoticed, therefore—unimportant? A grandeur, made casual by its every-day occurrence, a light to which we no longer advert like the light of day? We don't look at that because it blinds us. And do we no longer take any notice of it? God "dwells in light inaccessible, whom no man has seen nor can see" (Tim. 6: 16). That is natural and understandable for us men. When the Lord slew seventy men of Bethsames and fifty thousand of the common people, because they had looked into the Ark of the Covenant when it came from the land of the Philistines, the people cried in terror, "Who can serve the Lord, this

Holy God?" (Sam: 6: 20.) And what is the Ark of the Covenant compared to the tabernacle and the sacramental presence of God?

It was because our Lord was mindful of our weakness that, in His mercy, He hid His Presence in the Eucharist under the form of bread and wine. That is how we can bear His Presence and His being among us.

But as far as our ordinary consciousness of them is concerned, these forms become a screen that not only conceals the Presence of God, but shields us from it. The *Tremendum* is still there as an object of virtual faith, an object of the prescribed and standardized devotions.

But for the consciousness and the rest of life, even for the immediate life of the priest, the Holy Mass, the dispensing of the sacraments (*ex opere operato!*), the reading of Scripture and the Breviary, it is put into parenthesis. It is as though it didn't exist. In a certain sense, it becomes impersonal—and we with it!

Objectivized Person.   A second source: each priest is the representative of the Church. Each is an official, the pastor, the curate, the dean. How? "The dean [in Heidelberg] expressed himself a little differently [than when he was Pater Angelo]. He was more stiff, cooler, more sparing. But the content of his words was exactly the same. While he was speaking, a change came over him: the determined attitude and the somewhat self-important set of the mouth vanished together. It was as though everything personal in his face had receded to make room for a great, simple objectivity. Suddenly I had the feeling that I was speaking with a strange priest, and that it wasn't an individual at all who was facing me, but rather the Church herself" (Gertrud Von le Fort, *Der Kranz der Engel*, p. 132). And this dean as pastor was the one, in the name of the Church, who gave Enzio's fiancée the answer.

That means greatness, certainty, for everyone who asks a question about the attitude of the Church, and not the attitude of so and so who may happen to be the pastor in Heidelberg. But it is patent that there is a danger here too, not indeed for the sacraments and their validity, but for the priest himself and all the priestly work which demands the intrusion of the person. The ministry is always an intrusion. Anyone who thinks that the answers to all the problems of the present and future can be found, timelessly valid and ready for anyone who will take the trouble to look them up after he has given them the right catchword, is bound to fail. Every question is asked with the burden of distress behind it that the questioner is living, and the only answer that will meet the need is one that the priest, too, brings forward from a heart that beats for the questioner. Even those answers which are timelessly valid, if they can be dignified with the name of answer, must still meet the particular need of the particular person in his own time of necessity. That is the other *Tremendum* of the priest's life.

Fate [*The Danger*].   The care of souls, since it is *care,* is therefore something which by its very nature can never be mechanized, but it can become just a "job." The *Tremendum* is still in the priest's consciousness, but, as it were, in parenthesis: a potency—what am I saying! *the* potency, simply, that is not reduced to act. And with it the necessary tension of priestly existence no longer exists, to the eternal loss of the priest and also to the detriment of his effectiveness. He does his job. He is faithful. But his faith is not alive and loses the power of arousing faith in others. The *"territus terreo"* (since I am terrified, I can awaken terror in others) of St. Augustine and the *"qui non ardet non incendit"* (he who is not afire will not enkindle others) of St. Gregory are no longer there. What was it that the Lord wanted? "I have come to cast fire upon the earth and what will I but that it be kindled?" (Luke 12: 49.) The air that moves through our churches and chapels is quite cool.

Because—and this is *equally* essential for this type—whoever withdraws from the fire of God forgets that this fire must flame up anew at every moment in the history of salvation and in every priestly life.

Each one does his job, conscientiously. Does that mean that he fulfills the duties that are assigned him? That means much more than "getting it done." Everyone does his job—that also means that there are times when he has no job, in which there are others "doing" the job. At those times he is a man. He is free. At one time he went bowling; another had his evenings of taroc, which were held as conscientiously as his job was done. Today he goes outdoors or to the movies. He "has no job." But has he no obligation?

Thus this type can easily be confused with the type that we described in the last chapter, the "official of God." But the difference between them is that for him, salary and a secure life are not the determining factors. His way of life arises from a real priestly necessity, as we have deduced above. It has developed by degrees or at one leap. In this way of life he feels free and comfortable: that's the way to live a priestly life.

And so it is that this attitude can flow into forms of existence that we have yet to treat, and these too can have their formative influence. A habit is something that has developed over a period of time. It is something that has grown. It has the toughness and resilience of all growing things, and it also has its own laws. You can do a job by the time-clock. But the care of souls isn't something you can turn on and off like a radio. But in this case the "care of souls" becomes just a job, and the priest does a job just like the postman on his route. But the spirit that renews the face of the earth isn't something on sale at a window, like stamps and tickets.

He does his job, and does it so conscientiously that he has hopes of being made a "consultor" or a "Monsignor."

From the point of view of the history of religion, this type is associated with the priestly caste which had the exclusive right to offer sacrifice. The sacrifice was their right and their job. The theologians (those learned in the Scriptures) were another caste. The Catholic priesthood does not admit this distinction. Ordination creates a dignity and a mission, a mission that is always fresh and always faced by new decisions. One does not become a Mass-priest by ordination. He assumes with it a threefold duty: he is a priest, a prophet, and a shepherd, with all the cares of his flock.

The classical period of ecclesiastical job-holders begins with the time of the Carolingians, when it was not only a Church obligation, but a civil one as well, for the faithful to attend Mass on Sundays and feast days, to hear the sermons, to receive the sacraments; and all of these, as civil obligations, could be enforced by physical punishments or imprisonment. Then the pastor—apparently—had no other care and no other obligation than to provide the pastoral functions which were assigned to him by the chapter. The care of souls—apparently—was taken away from him by the ecclesiastical and civil law and their sanctions. When he had done what had been assigned to him, he had no other job. No one could reproach him with anything further.

This matter-of-course participation in divine services and the regular reception of the sacraments lasted far beyond the times when they were civilly enforceable, preserved as they were in the conscience of the people. Wonderful times! Or were they? They were a danger for the zeal and the missionary power of Christianity and shared the guilt of the blindness on the part of those priests who overlooked their duty in hours of decision, so decisive for our present situation. This type also produced a type of Christian who was in agreement with him, which wanted none other. Remember again the old sexton in Bernanos' *The Diary of a Country Priest"*; his answer to why the people were dissatisfied with the pastor was, "A priest's like a lawyer—'e's there if you be needin' him. 'E don't need to go meddlin' with folks."

But in the earlier Christian community there were soon not only Christians by custom, but also non-Christians by custom. These especially must have become so, who were tormented by the distresses and woes amid which the most recent times were born. They sought their salvation where one was promised them and where they at least felt that they were understood: they turned their backs on the unfeeling clerical job-holders, and in that, also on the Church.

Decadent Type.   Even in the face of this fact, it is frightening to see that there were innumerable priests who opened their shops as usual and did their job as though nothing had happened. And is it less frightening that this type could last even up to the present? He's again just "doing his job." He lets nothing throw him off. "No one," he says, "can demand more of me." He has a good night's sleep; he's at the altar at the prescribed times and shows up in the pulpit or goes to the confessional at the times announced in the parish bulletin. The priests who want to stir things up beyond that are agitators and quixotic. For anything extraordinary, there are the missions for the parish prescribed every ten years, and he really listens with interest when the preachers give it to his sheep "straight from the shoulder."

He sees no problems in the ministry; *problem* is a foreign word to him. And even if there are any—he holds to his consolation unshakeably—the theologians of the Church have solved them long ago or have exposed their senselessness. With an expansive *fides implicita* he adheres to these and all other solutions that the theologians think up. The final examination he took at the end of his studies is now taken literally: for him, theology is finally over and done with. He can make very witty comments on the alarms raised by the newspapers or by diocesan officials. This type has a sense of humor, one has to grant him that, and his joke usually hits off the weak point of the alarmist perfectly. That comes from his untroubled slumbers.

And anyway, he seems to be a model of equanimity, peace, and confidence. He grows on you. He has generous doses of work and recreation spotted throughout the week. Both canonically and in the light of moral theology, everything is in order—that moral theology, that is, which is almost identical with canon law. There is a casuistry—I wouldn't exactly say that it produces this type—which is congenial to this proved man of clerical jobbery. In it he seeks and finds his justification and the last quieting of his otherwise not easily troubled conscience.

But night is falling on these equable representatives of yesterday and the day before. They sense that. The prognosis looks bad for them. "The good old days" are on the way out, when the people came to the pastor and they all did come; when the pastor of a Sunday only had to do "his part"; when all those who were born were also baptized; when all the children received religious instruction in school as an obligatory thing; when the church was full every Sunday and holy day; when civil marriages were rare as comets and every Christian wanted to be buried only as a Christian: yes, they were "the good old days," so one sighs as he shuffles his deck of cards for another hand of taroc—and he is really right, at least in a certain sense. Today they're not nearly so well off as they used to be, when they could always find time for their favorite study—a hand of four kings. They even become a little melancholy and irked. In the meantime, the earth has given a couple of mighty turns—not at all to their liking. This type, like all the forms of escape, is condemned to die out.

It used to happen that this type actually helped foster vocations. The young man who decides for the priesthood today, does so in spite of it.

Escape in Activities

Representatives. Who doesn't know these men, these much-occupied pastors? What are they occupied with? Wherever they are assigned, they have already decided by the second day what has to be renovated and what has to be rebuilt, in the church, the rectory, the annex, the roads, the grounds and garden. He's never finished. If the rectory is in perfect condition, the workmen are already shoving their ladders and braces up against the walls of the church. And if the church is finished outside, including roof and steeple, they'll work on the inside.

There is no stopping the pastor. The generosity of the people, who are at first amused by this, falls off. But he knows how to fire them up again. And if there's nothing to renovate, then something will have to be bought. In my home town we had a pastor who had this problem. So he had a priceless Baroque altar, bought many years before from a church in Vienna, torn out and replaced by a simple wooden one from Grëdnertal. All the misgivings of the farmers were misinterpreted as a lack of understanding of art and a fear for their pocketbooks. The gigantic statues of St. Clare and St. Francis terrified unsuspecting visitors for years afterwards behind the stable door of a farmer. One of the woodworkers who took out the old altar asked for permission to scrape the gold from the gilded columns, which were wound around with vine branches. Of course he was allowed to do it, since the twisting columns were going to be chopped up for firewood. What he took with him was worth more than the whole Grödner altar. New side altars would have been added, but for the lack of money. Otherwise, the old ones wouldn't still be there.

Then there are those who have a passion for building. A clubhouse (even though there are no clubs), a kindergarten, an old folks' home . . . The most satisfactory part of all this is the preparations: the appointing of the committee, no —committees—for *one* group can no longer manage and direct all the projects—the many meetings, the collections, the arrangements that are necessary to bring in money. Half of the parish is continually on its feet behind the pastor. Now that's really living! And the drive never stops. Already the less energetic are looking forward, if not to rest, at least to a breather. But the non-stop-whirlwind doesn't slow down until the pastor packs up his grip and is off to start all over again in a new field of work.

There is the clubman. Any kind of organization that the parish can possibly sponsor is founded. Consultations, meetings, inauguration ceremonies, social evenings, concerts with his "cock and hen choir" (Bruce Marshall), theatrical presentations with their innumerable practices beforehand, lectures with and without lantern slides—in all this he's in his element. But he is likewise a consultor in the Farmers' Union, presiding member of the Building and Loan, the Bee Keeper's Alliance—a pity that there's not more doing in such a nest.

Now the "parish principle" has become the only one, even though there are a few loop-holes. He can take care of himself. Here, too, there is an occasion—it always comes to this —for lectures, concerts, family nights, parish feasts. He doesn't miss a trick.

Then there is the "joiner." No possible meeting can be held without his being in attendance. He's always there. He has the knack of making friends. Somebody once said to me, "It is certain that Mars is uninhabited. For if it were, then the inhabitants would be sure to have meetings, and so-and-so would have been there, sure as death!"

There is the man with a passion for starting pilgrimages. Whatever can be reached in the neighborhood is visited; once upon a time it was afoot, then by railroads, and today —this is a real discovery!—by busses.

I hope no one thinks that I want to ridicule the things listed here. I admit that I have exaggerated the case. It frequently will not be the case in real life, but only the extreme clearly shows what we intend to say, and no one would deny that there has been and still is a type like this.

Its History. It even has an honorable history. For a hundred years in Europe, for instance, we have enjoyed freedom of union. And that Europe, incidentally, ceases whenever there is no freedom of opinion, press, information, and the freedom to form societies. All tendencies—left, right and conservative—have utilized these freedoms since 1848. It would have been a very dangerous spiritualism if the pastors had not joined in and won members, unionized, held together, i.e., organized. The great societies, especially in Germany, have a proud past. And they have accomplishments behind them, despite the drawbacks of this system, which no other can show. If one wanted a proof of it, it would be the fact that the dictatorships of all colors first dissolved the Catholic organizations and banned them.

Since approximately the same date, the Church, stripped of her former means, was put on her own. She had to fashion the things necessary for her coordinated work herself, preserve and renew them: the churches, their parishes and meeting halls. All that was not some hobby of inconstant planners, but a necessity.

The priestly form of life which we are examining in this section is comprised only of those who occupy themselves with the production of the means, but never enter upon the ministerial use of them; and those—this is where the question of their priestly existence comes in—who find an alibi for their conscience in this activity, and who do not find time for work that is more important and more essential. What work? "But now it was to become clear to Father Seraphim with fearful clarity what a curse was involved in the practice of his Church, which first built mighty houses of God and then began to look for souls with which to fill these havens of Faith" (Edzard Schaper, *Die sterbende Kirche*, Leipzig, 1936).

Of course one ought not overlook the fact that a failing Church is also a symbol of a failing Faith (Southern France!). The novel of Edzard Schaper treats of this situation in a community on the border of the Soviet Union in the years after the first World War, at a time when the Christian people are already so weak and abandoned that they cannot rebuild dilapidated churches. We mean here the priest to whom the external activity has become the be-all and end-all of his activity. By preference? And so predisposition? Or as an escape? Or are there other causes?

Its Existence. We must be clear about this. There is, you see, the man who can do nothing else but do, do, do. He is afraid of the moment when there will be nothing more to build, to repair and organize. That will never happen, he tells himself.

Would that be a condition of boredom? Boredom, says Nikolai Berdyaev, is "a satanic condition." "The soul is afraid of emptiness. If it has no valuable, positive, divine content, it will be filled with false, negative, satanic things.

If the soul senses the condition of emptiness, it will sense its loneliness" (*Von der Bestimmung des Menschen,* Bern, 1935). But boredom is a satanic condition: "an idle mind is the devil's workshop," as the proverb has it. Is it the fear that this proverb could be verified in him that drives the busy man on?

Aristotle names a vice, the vice of "doing too much," and it is the enemy of reflection. Are we on the track with this idea? Is this activity an escape from reflection?

Or is the much-occupied man merely caught up by the activity of the world about him, only, as one might say in excuse, "a child of his own times"? Or does he sense in reflection and silence a reason why his own times disown him? The "practical man" and the "man of action" today hate the man of thought. They rebel "against the tyranny of pure thought" (Spengler). It is the tempo, the tempo of a world fleeing reflection, that no longer wants to think about itself. With regard to this world, the restless Apostle of the Gentiles warns: *Nolite conformari huic saeculo* (Do not be like this world—Rom. 12:2). Is that not the *really* satanic condition of the world which has fled God, which, in its flight from God, does not want to be confused by silence? The flight which the priest must oppose? The "sacrament of work," which according to Thomas Gregory (*The Unfinished Universe,* 1938) was discovered by St. Benedict in addition to the other seven, has become the only valid sacrament of the present time in opposition to the other seven. It would be a terrible thing if the priest were to become the administrator or victim of this "sacrament."

Existential Dialectic.   In the life of a priest there is a tension between external and internal, between center and periphery, between contemplation and action, between the *ora* and the *labora,* between the mean and the means. This tension is essential for the existence of the secular priest. He cannot exist without it. It must be endured. It is harder to endure it today than it was in the other times we can think of. The priest can only preserve his priesthood by an in-this-tension perseverance, the secular priest, that is, and every other who must live and last as he does. If the tension is cast off in favor of contemplation, then the priest ceases to be, existentially, a secular priest. He becomes a contemplative monk. If it is action that holds the upper hand in his case, then he ceases, essentially, to be a *priest*.

An escape into activity, on the part of one with no contemplative talent, can be a result of his anxiety about Satan's boredom, or his fear of loneliness, and therefore completely moral. But it is still an escape from priestly existence.

For this existence cannot last without quiet, without contemplation, without the *"solus cum Solo."* It becomes a flight from the Presence of God and can become a flight from the Living God. The reality of God is still in his life, but it is shunted to one side, put in parenthesis. It is an escape from his conscience, which gradually forgets how to come into that Presence. Or it is an escape into a state of conscience that can proudly say each night: "Well, we got a lot done today." The life of the priest becomes an empty round of activity, and its necessary quiet is drowned out by the hammering of the builders and the crashing of trumpets. He is lastingly blinded in his search for the mean.

We are purposely describing the extreme case. No one can ever be certain in saying that it is verified in a concrete case. Every secular priest is a secular because he is obliged to work in the world. And all of them must undertake jobs, or direct jobs, which are this side of the sacramental life and have absolutely nothing to do with the spirit of their mission. So where does this particular type begin? How do you recognize it? Who is one of this type? It is that man who no longer finds that necessary external work a cross, especially when it assumes and can assume an importance that can only be given to the priest. That is the man who is in danger of making his activity an escape.

Listen to what St. Bernard says in a letter to the prior of the Carthusian Monastery at Portis. It is a cry that comes from the distress of his soul. He is answering a question the monk had sent him; but then his distress gets the better of him: "Now it is time that I think of myself. My impossible life and troubled conscience cry out to you. I am the chimera of my century, for I lead neither the life of a cleric nor of a layman. I have put aside the life of the monk long ago, even if I still wear the monk's habit. I have no desire to write about what I am doing, for I believe you have already heard from others how hard I am laboring, what I am studying, and to what painful disputes in the world I am devoting myself, nay more, to what depths I am driven. If you have heard little about all that, you can ask and send me your advice and prayers accordingly" (Epist. 250, Migne, PL, 182). For it was the fate of the holy abbot to be summoned from the quiet of his monastery to take part in the secular, political, and extra-ecclesiastical disputes of his day. And what a cross he found them!

This is where we can distinguish between those who are faced with the necessity of rebuilding their churches and erecting clubhouses, and the others. For these men combat their distraction from what is essential through their quiet and recollection, even if they have to get it late at night or in the early hours of the morning. It is the others who build as a passion and found societies and make their pilgrimages, and the more unrest there is, the more they are in their element.

Examples.   Since it is difficult to draw the dividing line between the true and false cases, even within the soul of the particular persons, there are but few clear-cut examples that we can mention. They can be seen at their best when it is not a case of an either-or decision between one's personal recollection and professional distraction, but when the choice is between the necessary external works of the ministry and mere activity that is extrinsic to the priesthood.

In the tragic tension between Pastor Cawder and his zealous curate Father Moran it is more the concrete example of the object of our discussion that is illustrated than the clear case of a personally differentiated existence. The curate's head is full of plans: for the women there ought to be a Mothers' Guild and in it an active group to help those who are expecting; he wants to buy a strip of woods and a saw mill so that the poor Negroes can have free firewood; he wants to build a hospital that would accept those whom the public hospitals turn down as not having a sufficient cause; there ought to be some study clubs for the papal encyclicals and a course in active social work, a cooperative farm, a credit union to lend money without interest or security . . .

But the pastor is no man for activities; on the contrary, he is so retiring that it is questionable whether he is within his rights as a secular priest. The only thing he has to say to all these plans is that the curate seems to fear capitalism more than sin. "I don't see what the need of organized social assistance is here. That is exactly the opposite of what I have been thinking" (Crawford Power, *The Encounter*). The pastor wants to leave it up to personal charity, as it was before.

Even that is not a clear case: I knew a pastor who saw to it that after twenty years of activity all the roofs were repaired, all the walls decorated, all the doors freshly painted and all the windows puttied and the panes replaced, but of the 1200 souls in his parish, he knew only about half. This is not a clear case, because at the same time, he was a quiet, interior priest.

For the management type, everything has to be business-like, even to the most modern methods available for the care of souls. Once a pastor showed me his card file for the parish, the neatest and most reliable, I'm sure, that I had ever seen. But out of sheer joy in his model file system, and because he wanted to keep it always up-to-date, he never got around to using it in the ministry. He could just as well have kept a canary.

I know a man who, in one three-hour period, was directing a club meeting, teaching French and English in different rooms, performing baptisms, and reading his Breviary all at the same time. And of course he had time to talk with any-one who wanted to see him about something, too.

It doesn't work out as easily, of course, as the curate Auke supposes. He goes to the other extreme. What does he plan to do if he ever becomes a pastor? "Then the devil with all societies. I'll put a couple of fellows in charge I can rely on —there are always a few in any parish—and tell them: 'You just take care of things yourself; I haven't the time; then I'll just look in on you now and then. Say a prayer when you start and conduct the meetings according to the ten commandments and the eight beatitudes . . .' And in general, I'd pull up a chair wherever I'd be welcome, and be grateful for any little thing they might give me to eat. It wouldn't bother me to sit down and dunk my potato in the gravy dish with them; now they whisk it off the table in embarrassment whenever you have dinner with them. I'd be right behind them like a 'hound of heaven'" (Dick Ouwendijk, *Das geschändete Antlitz,* p. 173).

He has had his fill of this club business: "I know of no work more senseless than this. It takes up most of your time and the soul can only look on to see how the rest is coming along . . . We are getting so organized that sooner or later it will get to the point where the Mass will start at the rap of a gavel: 'May I have your attention for a moment for the Lord Jesus Christ in His Sacrifice?' " (p. 173)

That is exaggerated, of course, and he admits it. But what he intends to say is correct, and even in such an exaggerated form it would be a salutary consideration for the man who, with his energetic activities, wants to escape the one thing necessary.

Escape in Side Lines

Usually it is a real hobby. Once a pastor laughingly confessed to me, "You know, I'm a professional photographer and an amateur pastor." Here we have reduced our case to a clear formula. The fact that Pastor Francis Xavier Semelhofer, as far as I could see, was also a genuinely apostolic priest, gives us cause to hope that the others mentioned here are too.

Their Genesis.   In itself, this third form of escape is another step down compared to the former. For the activity of which we spoke before was at least something that could be considered as a preparation for priestly work, or very close to it. Here we're dealing with an escape into profane occupations.

It is not easy to keep the life of a priest, day after day and hour after hour, on the level that we call clerical.

All professional work, even clerical, is tiring, and therefore it puts the worker in a psycho-physical condition of diminished efficiency which even the best of will cannot remedy. This condition is merely a physical result of the bodily processes and accompanies the onset of fatigue. Even the strictest Orders have their times of recreation, freedom, and relaxation. Recreation is always distraction, always a getting away from the cares of one's calling. One might even say that the greater the distance between one's professional work and his recreation, the more effective it is, all of this, of course, within the limits of the moral order. The organs in the nerve centers, in which the energy used up in specifically priestly work are stored, must be given a rest so as to refresh them, and that is best done by not using them for a while.

So it is understandable that a reasonable recreation is recommended even to students, even determined forms of recreation. In peaceful times, no one took it amiss that a priest spent his free time with a good hobby. That is how many occupations came about and still do come about, which can be a great help to the totality of the plan of his vocation. Often, however, they have been disassociated from that totality, have become independent, and even got the upper hand in one's whole life. The incentive to this development is the fact that recreation is always more pleasant than work. And the more pleasant it is, the more frequently one falls into it. And instead of being recreation that enables the priest to do his work better, it becomes a second life next to the priestly one.

Is it the immanent temptation that is part of all earthly things? Is it Satan, who perverts the necessary rest and recouping of forces to a means of power over the priest, a means that is attractive, harmlessly inviting, and therefore really a lulling and dangerous means? When once there is no more tension, the priest can no longer return to the tension that determines his existence. In fact, these tensions, under the necessity of relief from tension, can even unconsciously become an evil. From the dissolution of that tension there arises a splitting of his life. That life of tension becomes a see-saw life: clerical-secular, secular-clerical.

Suddenly there no longer is any tension as a source of that vital priestliness essential to the spiritual life. Because of it his priestly work becomes poverty-stricken, and however correct it be, a mere performance of duty. It becomes a life alongside another life, which has gradually assumed *equal* importance merely because it appropriates more of his time, not in the belief or the will of the priest, but in its reality and its power. There results a life with two sources of power: then the circle which had one center becomes an ellipse with two foci, at least in the extreme case.

A hobby can demand *all* one's attention: the real professional photographer and amateur pastor! Or it may be the transformation, which at one time was easier to find, from pastor-farmer to farmer-pastor. Such a man would be hard to find anywhere today, but Joseph Bernhart met him frequently: the man who was quite a model economically, but as a minister he was much less the diligent village pastor (*Der Kaplan,* p. 26). But there are modern forms of it; I must confess immediately that I haven't met any of them around this part of the country: "I've met priests who were more enthusiastic about banking and hunting than they were for their own duty, who thought more of a good kitchen than a good reputation; and others who were more devoted to politics and economic problems than they were to keeping track of the salvation of their flocks" (Giovanni Papini, *Letters of Pope Celestine VI to All Mankind,* 1948).

Cases. Literature has much less to say about this type than it has of the former type. It is uninteresting. Why? Because this type presents no problem. Slipping into some sideline would at best be illustrated as the spiritual analogy of gravity. But it would be hardly worth more than the observation.

As a curiosity we may mention the case of a pastor who was simultaneously an innkeeper in the same town; finally the duties and cares of his side line became so demanding that he could easily be an innkeeper who was incidentally a pastor. "Have you already heard, Brother, that a pastor is an innkeeper at the same time? The owner of a very respectable tavern? That he puts out the best wine in the country and runs a kitchen that is famous among all the connoisseurs? A joke? Unfortunately not! I was there myself" (Hans Wirtz, *Ein Laie sucht den Priester,* p. 52).

The case is hardly worth mentioning since it could happen only rarely anywhere. Or could it? In Latin America? There, it is often said, one can find pastors who are much interested in business as innkeepers, and also in all other branches of business. I can't check on what has been said. And it would be scarcely more worth mentioning that Hans Künkel, in his novel *Schicksal und Liebe des Niklas von Kues* (Leipzig, 1936, p. 54), reports of a pastor, in the fifteenth century, that he played for dances. Or when Friedrich Zöpfl in his *Deutsche Kulturgeschichte* names priests who had public houses or public baths. For in the Middle Ages it did happen, especially in Slavic sections, that pastors, upon assuming their office, would oblige themselves to the lord of the manor to take upon themselves at the same time the job of herdsman, and take care of the breeding cattle for the community. But even then such things were exceptions and were regarded as an unseemly abuse. So they are not within the limits we are considering. More to the point would be a pastor I knew myself, who developed several patents through long and difficult years of research, for example, a mechanical trolley signal and secret formulas for making liquor.

Others collect beetles or butterflies or stamps, or what seems more clerical, prayer books and holy cards. That doesn't demand much of their time, but it does demand their interest.

Some years ago I went on a priests' pilgrimage to the Holy Land. There was one priest with us who hardly gave the holy places in Gethsemane or Emmaus or Bethlehem or Bethany or Kiriath Jerrim a second glance, because he looked under every other stone to find rare beetles for his large collection. But this made no noticeable inroads on his priestliness and devotion.

Others make sports their passion, or raising fruit, or keeping bees, or raising medicinal herbs. The pastor of St. Magdalena's in Gries was "famed and beloved far and wide-as a country doctor, and all of those who were tubercular in Brixen, or any other sickly Fathers, were sent to him as assistants and he always cured them," reports Propst Weingartner (*Unterwegs,* p. 53).

There are researchers among the clergy of such an intensity that it would put any university professor to shame, so much the more because they are not concerned with coming to a correct result. For them, science is a sport.

When the Curé of Ozeron visits the successor of the saintly Curé of Abrecave, he finds a hospitable priest in his place. At his first visit, the Curé talks for a long time with his guest about the advantages of the new telescope which he made himself; then he proposed his own theory of how duels should be fought: both of the duellers should be lodged in a hospital for contagious diseases and there try to outdo one another in their self-sacrifice until one of the contestants dies of infection and disease (François Jammes, *Le Curé d'Ozeron,* p. 129). When he visited him the second time it was impossible to speak with him on the topic about which he was calling, for the Curé of Abrecave had in the meantime discovered a new method of deep-sea diving. "He thought that he had so perfected the diving apparatus that the diver, without being attached to the boat with air lines, could go up and down with ease, and he could eat, drink, and even sleep" (p. 176).

It seems to be a clear case with Abbé Calixte Merval: he is a mystic painter of light and of its miracles in nature and only incidentally pastor in St. Paul in the woods (Henri Bordeaux, *Fil de la Vierge*, Graz, 1952). Priest or painter, sanctity or beauty are the questions of enduring importance in his life. The old cook Perpétue rushes out when the new pastor arrives with a black dog, a white cat, an owl, and a bird cage. And the parrot screamed three times "God wills it!" The pastor commits one folly after another, but is a lover according to the "new commandment" (John 13: 34), and so he accomplishes more in the obdurate parish than his predecessors with their strictness and learning.

Other priests have assumed major professional duties that were not clerical; there are professors on secular faculties, librarians, actual researchers and scholars of secular sciences. All honor to them! But there is a danger to their priesthood in this, even if there is no threat to their faith, as even St. Augustine realized (Conf. V, 3, 4, 6).

Don Ardito Piccardi has escaped from his lonesome mountain parish Chiaratorre. There have been amazing conversions and miracles performed at the hands of this pastor, honored as a saint. He is afraid that he will be driven into the arms of the Evil One by the reverence they show him. He had challenged God Himself. Terror had gripped him when he stood in the midst of the mysteries of which he was no longer in control.

He takes over a "club" in the large city of M. for Catholic students and those interested in intellectual things (Italy apparently has so many priests that the Bishop, in spite of his distrust of this undertaking, can spare him for it). He wants to serve God, no longer in the poverty and sanctity of a mountain parish, but in the clear knowledge that leads to God through logic (Carlo Coccioli, *Heaven and Earth*, pp. 170 ff.). He is no longer the poor pastor who was ready to answer every call of God; when he arrived at his rectory, he had sent off the rude Corinna Malvini, cleans things up himself, does the washing and cooking and ironing, and scourges himself, spending day and night in prayer. Now he has a comfortable dwelling, and as the countess Michelacci tells the frightened fellow, he is not only a priest but also a cavalier! (p. 214)

Don Ardito knows how half-secular his new apostolate is, no matter how entirely priestly his intentions in it are, and agrees with the Bishop who says to him, "I don't quite trust this amalgamation of heaven and earth. There's a danger in it. At any rate, I know that you are a real priest, and that reassures me" (p. 228). And that is the only thing that can be assuring in all similar situations.

Side Lines in the Service of the Ministry. The "sporting curate" Robert Simon is a real athlete, with trophies to prove it; and he dives from the 50-foot tower in an elegant jackknife without so much as a splash. When he comes up, he is enthusiastically received by his parishioners. Since 1944 he has been pastor in Sâone near the Swiss border. The church was falling down, the congregation tepid. With the consent of the Communist mayor and school commissioner, he organizes games and sports for the children. A glance at the trophy he had won in a swimming meet gave him the idea. A few days later huge posters announce a sport competition with the chief feature *"L'homme planeur"* —the human glider—"Benefit of Church-building Fund." The "glider" was the pastor himself. When he climbed out of the rather unsuitable swimming pool with a bump on his head, he was the most highly regarded man in the village. His athletic contests won a name for the village. The renovation of the church could then be taken in hand.

Here is one man who put his hobby in the service of his parish, although in a most improbable case. Worth imitating?

We don't want to add anything to the fundamental notions that have been suggested, but neither do we want to take anything away from them.

Escape in a Substitute

As a young student, I was once a guest of a pastor. There were some relatives of the pastor present and at the lavish dinner the company was expansive and hilarious. The pastor suspected, and indeed also secretly wished, that I would want to be a priest. After dinner he said to me: "You know, we priests haven't much of life. We have to make up for it now and then with a good dinner."

Why did he tell me that, I wondered. Did he want to excuse himself to a young idealist? Or was it that he didn't quite trust my idealism and really wanted to tell me: even though the man who chooses the priesthood has taken upon himself a life of sacrifice, he can console himself with the thought that there are opportunities of which he can avail himself, completely unobjectionable, both morally and canonically?

The Reasons.   He may have been referring to celibacy when he spoke of a life of sacrifice: celibacy, understood as the surrender of the comfort and joys of family life, and, what is even harder to bear, humanly speaking, the loneliness that is a part of it. It might consist in all the other obligations which this last remaining rank of a former rank-conscious society assumes as laws to preserve its honor

(*Codex Juris Canonici,* can. 138-142): the dress proper to his station, which lifts him above his environment, to the indignation of some; and the limitation of his freedom insofar as going to the theater, concerts, hotels, vacations, trips, participation in sports and hunting are concerned. He is limited as to his political activity (can. 139). The lack of freedom consists, to a great extent, in the fact that both priest and pastor are always on display; by their position they are constantly subject to the observation and judgment of those about them, and this is not always indulgent.

The ingratiating Lower Austrian-dialect poet, Ferdinand Bruckner (died as pastor in Aggsbach on the Donau), once had to go to Walkenstein to take the waters there as a cure for his nervous condition. He was immediately welcomed into the brotherly circle of other priests taking the same treatment. "Lord," said he after greeting them, "you don't know how glad I am to be rid of giving-good-example for three weeks!" That's it! Of course he had no idea at all of living any differently those three weeks than before, or of giving bad example. But the restrictions of giving edification by profession fell from him like shackles. He just wanted to be a man again for a little while. "The Pastor of the Blooming Vineyard" walks through his garden and looks at his beloved flowers, sighing: "Ah, to be a flower like that, without quarrel or mistake, just content to send forth its flowered happiness in its scent!" Hans Carossa once wished he were an animal, "just to be a creature in the world of created things." So too Richard Billinger (*Die Asche des Fegefeuers,* p. 9) and many others. The priest, too, is overcome with the longing to be a simple man. He wants nothing more.

Existence. The faithful suspect something of this. Many seek to offer him a substitute. Many take the best of their home and garden to the pastor. They pamper him. No one does that more than nuns in their treatment of the house chaplain, whom they would like, on the other hand, to be as devout and ascetic as possible.

But despite all understanding for the situation of the priesthood, every attempt at a substitute for his indubitable sacrifice is an escape that endangers his nature. It is not without reason that we mention this form in the last place. Considered axiologically, it is the most fundamental of the four named.

Priest and man, loneliness and familiarity with the world, the words "Remain in me" (John 15: 4) and "Behold, I send you" (Luke 10: 2), ideals and their realization, are all related to one another in tension, in a tension that cannot be eased, and which is therefore life-long. In this crucifixion by the vertical that goes from heaven to earth, and the horizontal of his humanity and his time, the priest not only grows and perfects himself, but from the endurance of this tension there flow into him those powers that make his work blessed. Neither of the two arms of his cross can be missing, not even the horizontal. For this it is that supports the priest's strivings for holiness and all the sanctity that should and must flow from him, vital and fruitful, that sanctity which brings him near to men, and opens his eyes to the need for redemption in his time. Neither arm of the cross must be missing. For the fundamental law of our redemption is planted on Golgotha, and all the days till the end of the world say but this: *salus in cruce*.

It may be well that the escape from this law must be often considered as a mere psychological phenomenon, and not at all ethical; it may be that this aberration is just an expression of emptiness or weariness—but the priest must always pull himself together again and dare what has been impossible up till now all over again. Otherwise he has abandoned the means of his existence. An escape into a substitute is the desertion of his post. By a mixture or a succession of sacrifice and recreation, the only life that can be his, a life of tension, becomes instead a see-saw existence and a schism: first a priest, then a man; then priest again, then a man.

He must shrivel in a life like that. His work becomes empty and hollow, if not a continual scandal. And his care of souls only becomes fruitful from the tension of nature and grace. Don Ardito faces a thorough skeptic: "An ineffable compassion overcame me. How I would have liked to say something human, that would have been suited to his human distress . . ." (Coccioli, *Heaven and Earth*). He couldn't think of anything to say, because the situation was completely foreign to him.

We are not thinking of a double life here in the ordinary and bad meaning of the term when we speak of scandal. There's no question of anything like that here. What we are thinking of is something, externally at least, that is completely within the framework of Church law. Even less are we concerned with the ordinary, necessary recreation of the priest.

Its Tragedy. We must speak out clearly, in what is to follow, because of the degree of tragedy which is often involved in the individual case. It is a tragedy that is part of life in our era. There are Orders which are founded to realize the idea of the following of Christ by example. And they succeed. And a century later, or even sooner—the holy rule is still around and everyone appeals to it—the ideal of the Order is abandoned and a start has to be made all over again. New Orders try it, and the result is the same. Reformers rise up within the Order itself and wrest a number of their brothers to themselves. But soon the Order they have abandoned is in a better condition than the sons of that reformer. The history of each of the great Orders is an individual proof of this. Is it not shocking in itself, and yet no one takes offense at it; and if no one is bothered by *that*, what can possibly bother us?—that Orders whose professors have praised holy poverty, and who therefore wanted to be free of the thorns and thistles of this life (Mt. 13: 22) suddenly come into possession of huge tracts of forests and estates, mansions, houses, and farms, and have to govern them! All gifts of the faithful, who once wanted to guarantee support for the poor monks and be sure of some merit for their own poor souls! But that alters the life of the monks and must change it, in spite of the holy rule.

And how quickly that happens! At the end of the eleventh century there are the Benedictines of Cluny, who have called upon all the preachers of the pristine sanctity of the Church and her servants. But already at the beginning of the twelfth century, Saint Bernard is casting reproaches upon the monks of Cluny, again in the name of St. Benedict and their common holy rule, because of their meals, their bedrooms, their dress, and their luxuriously decorated churches. And he does it with a vigor that can only come of the conviction that such accusations could never be made against his own monks! But wait a minute! The sons of Citeaux are also in for a trough in the waves of the centuries, and the best among them only have the hope that the mercy of God will again raise them up on another crest.

Wherever we look, we find the same phenomenon. The first missionaries of northern New Mexico were driven off by the Indians or murdered. But their successors were much more comfortable. Father Balthasar "seemed convinced that the pueblo of Acoma existed chiefly to support its fine church, and that this should be the pride of the Indians, as it was his own. He took the best of their corn and beans and squashes for his table and selected the choicest portions when they slaughtered a sheep, chose their best hides to carpet his dwelling" (Willa Cather, *Death Comes for the Archbishop*). And Père Latour had to start all over again.

So it is with many a priest's life that might be mentioned here, and there is no excuse for it; it is just a little touch of realism in the corner of the gigantic painting that portrays the puzzling journey of the Church through time. Everyone has to fear assuming the role of judge because he knows not whether he himself will be brought before the bar tomorrow. For even though heaven and earth pass away, these words remain: "Do not judge that you may not be judged" (Mt. 7: 1). And these others: "Watch and pray, that you may not enter into temptation" (Mt. 26: 41).

The Failure of All Escape. But there is one thing that must be said of all the forms of escape on the part of priests. On the basis of experience and observation, and not from any prejudgment or aversion, I would say that the real tragedy is their failure in the care of souls, and indeed in that ministry which has to deal with a world distrustful of the faith or alienated from the Church: they have failed in their fight for the kingdom of God. Their type belongs to the past, and even in the past it was a figure of degeneracy. They have no understanding of what is at stake today; and if they do understand it, the figure they cut is itself a proof to all who are suspicious and hostile to the Church that their distrust and fears are well founded.

There can be no doubt about it: Wilhelm Busch is no Father of the Church. But the fact that he (as all so-called humorists) is a bit of a pessimist, but still an unusually able judge of men and a debunker, is certain. How did he see the priests who met him, and, as we hear, whom he asked his questions? We don't want to go along with the malice of his mockery by any means, but we would like to examine ourselves in the mirror of his verse and ask honestly whether there was and is such a type (*Kritik des Herzens,* Munich, 1911):

What a shame I'm not a priest,
That would really be my field.
I'd just bum from feast to feast
With mind and heart to troubles sealed.

Of all life's doubts, why, I'd be free,
For peace of soul I'd never lack,
And all would be so clear to me,
All the answers white and black.

And then, because no demon haunted,
I'd soundly sleep and never dream,
By all well-fed and highly vaunted,
I'd grow fat on steak and cream.

He sees the priest as one who loafs through life, who has no problems and sees none. What is such a man to say to some poor, tormented soul, when he has all the answers at his finger tips, once and for all? And there was no encouragement to try to talk with that priest about the doubts that tortured him and robbed him of his sleep, when he saw that fat silhouette, even though such a priest need not necessarily fit into one of the escape-types already mentioned.

4. FORMS OF ARRESTED DEVELOPMENT

We would like to sketch in advance what is common and essential to all of the forms which we will treat in this section. The individual types can then be described more concisely. This group is represented by the smallest number, so much so that many traits are only true of individuals.

The Phenomenon. Who doesn't know the phenomenon? You come to the rectory and you are met with a silence that tells you immediately: that's not the quiet of rectories which tells of the presence of God; it isn't that silence that speaks of long preparation for sermons, where prayer seems to cling to the walls; it is not that refuge to which all who are plagued by the world might come for help. What is it? It is the silence of old ruins or of an abandoned house; not the quiet of repressed conversation, but the speechlessness of a mute; not a refuge, but isolation and alienation; not recollection, but emptiness.

A grumbling housekeeper has opened the door, and then the pastor comes and his look says only one thing: "I wish you were out of here." And so he gets through with the whole affair as you stand there, without even asking you to sit down, although there might be a few dusty easy chairs around.

The rectory stands in the midst of the neighborhood as though it were not there at all, and were it to disappear overnight, the people wouldn't miss a thing. The church is bare and unattended. The saints are frozen in their Baroque attitudes and have a comic effect. In front of the statues there are paper flowers in the old vases. The housekeeper before the present one must have forgotten them. There are churches that give the impression of being houses of prayer, and others that feel like barns.

And yet everything goes externally according to schedule. The pastor says his Mass every day. And there are always a few old people there, but only as if by chance. There is no community with the priest at the altar. He preaches every Sunday, but that is so perfunctory that the men go to the tavern after the "service."

These cases are not frequent, but they do exist.

Their Development. How do these forms come about? Where do they come from? Are they perhaps the result of old age, and calcium in the veins and tissues? It cannot be just that. For there are many more priests with white hair and trembling hands who are still young in heart and enjoy a wonderfully purified priesthood. They have a vital inwardness and a joy that must have grown in the daily experience of the grace and mercy of God. "For all who were with him were amazed at the catch of fish they had made" (Luke 5: 9). They have had that experience repeatedly. Amazement is a sign of youth. The daily encounter with God "Who gives joy to their youth" and the daily response to the summons of the Lord, "You therefore are to be perfect, even as your heavenly Father is perfect" (Mt. 5: 48) has not made them perfect yet, but it has brought them to follow God cheerfully. And this cheerfulness has been contagious for all of those whose pastors they were, and all who came into contact with them. They know that it is not easy, even if they couldn't say it as beautifully as St. Augustine: *"Inhorresco in quantum dissimilis ei sum, inardesco, in quantum similis ei sum"* (Conf. IX, 9)—"I am seized with fear inasmuch as I am unlike Him, but I am fired with love inasmuch as I resemble Him." And the words of Kierkegaard, "One can never be a Christian, but can only become a Christian," are something that they have been living, even though they have never heard of them, and so they can hand this experience on to others. Another fact that contradicts the statement that the condition described above is a result of old age is that it can be found even among relatively young priests. Bishop Paul Rusch once said, and he based this on long observation, that many had lost much of their original zeal when they were forty (*Wachstum im Geiste,* p. 265).

What is it that happens in a case like this? In this section we set aside all the other reasons and forms that we have previously discussed. We are trying to find the first causes from which these arrested forms can develop. Of course, these can coincide with and be part of the other forms that we have discussed. We are proceeding typologically, for how else can we arrive at a general picture? But the "cases" are all individual and defy any typology, no matter how neat its distinctions are.

There is one thing that we must insist upon especially in this section, and that is that we are giving a typology, and so we are seeking forms of life and their genesis; we are not giving an axiology, which would consequently intend to evaluate them religiously and morally. Any one can point out the lack of logic in such a procedure, but it is unavoidable. Why? Because both the final forms as well as the causes that bring them about are moral and religious concepts and assertions. Therefore, we must also say that we are by no means treating of the faith or the good conscience of the arrested forms to be mentioned later, neither are they questioned. And this, not because we refrain from passing judgment, but because no one can judge the individual "case." For as disreputable as the origins and paths may be which lead to these final forms, no one can say in an individual case what the condition of that man's soul was, who decided on such a course, or who was forced in that direction. Both in the beginning and in the further development of this form he can be in good faith and therefore not reproached by his conscience.

That is why we are not concerned, or not very much so, about the moral bases, but with those which are presupposed in the exclusive reality of priestly existence in all its relationships, possibilities, and shadings. These are the same for all. We refrain from passing judgment as to why they have led to arrested forms in this or that case. Behind this investigation there are decades of observation and exploration of the things involved in each concrete example. But even so, our attempt is a daring one. Nevertheless we will risk it. Why?

The reason for this, of course—and again we meet the same

old lack of consequence—has nothing to do with the typology: it is that we might help one another, so as to prevent us from becoming that way insofar as we can possibly control it. And it is to help those, especially, who still have their high ideals and the design for their realization before them.

Its First Causes.   The reasons are many and most varied. And these reasons are not causes with a necessary effect. We should have spoken earlier of occasions, occasions, that is, which are good and necessary in themselves, but which have led to faulty development and have ended in a dubious self-realization, because of the contingency of the moment, or for reasons that have to do with the particular moral condition or character of an individual. If we said above that we are ignoring the subjective guilt involved, we should now add: even objectively, there is no cause which would be "guilty" of this development. For the same situation for another man becomes a blessing and a help.

And so we are speaking of first causes or situations in which the development took its beginning. Moreover, these situations have been even more of an occasion, insofar as they were good and necessary in themselves. For it is precisely this goodness and necessity that is a camouflage and cover for one who, as he thinks, is planning his life on the basis of them.

There is the established form of our converse with God in the holy liturgy. God's mercy with us who would otherwise be consumed by the fire of His Presence, has given us this. There is no prayer and no gesture that we ourselves choose that can be adequate to what the liturgy should express. But now there is a form that is offered to the priest in the liturgy of the Church: or better, he is obliged to one form. He is spared the distress and concern of creating forms of association with God himself. He cannot be spared the duty of not forgetting the *Tremendum* of the Presence of God; and he himself must see behind those symbols the thing that is symbolized. Otherwise—and there is the beginning of a faulty development—the symbol is enough for him (though he receive it in faith); he acts as though he can dispense with the duty the Apostle lays upon him: "Work out your salvation with fear and trembling" (Phil. 2: 12); he loses the feeling of transcendance in the reality which is still a tremendous fact, which is present and at work in the symbol. He does not receive the form with gratitude, as a favor of divine mercy, but as a substitute, as an occasion of setting his watchfulness at rest. He knows and believes that mysterious effects do proceed from the sacraments that he administers; he utilizes the matter and form as he learned it; he knows that the real minister, the *minister principalis*, is Jesus Christ Himself. He is only His instrument (*causa instrumentalis*). What a staggering fact! But he is well on the way to becoming a dead instrument. A person can never be just that. That is where the faulty development begins. The form, which is grace and mercy, for him becomes rigid adherence to form.

He completes the form . . . daily, for years. Always the same form! A development starts which the psychologists call automatization. Things are done at first with full advertence and with the intention of doing what they mean. The constant repetition brings on a readiness in doing them. Finally they flow on without any conscious control and, one may almost say, without any personal participation at all. Even that attention can finally be wanting which takes into consideration the effect of such an attitude on others. In fact, the attention can be turned completely to other things; then one grinds out the same words at the grave that he has "prayed" a hundred times before, while he eyes the mourners curiously, wondering just who followed this particular "corpse" to the grave today. People notice that he is sizing them up. Ah, to think that even these rites, these moving rites in the face of death and judgment, can be tossed off in wooden routine!

Or: what a grace, what certainty there is in the doctrine of the *opus operatum* in the administration of the sacraments for the one who receives them. The grace produced by the sacrament depends on the power with which it is invested as an instrument by Christ Himself. When the matter and form commanded by Christ are united, the effect takes place. And so it does not depend on the *opus operantis,* that is, on the worthiness of the minister. All that is necessary is that he will to administer the sacrament; but even here, an *"intentio virtualis"* suffices, that is, the intention which was once made as an act *(intentio actualis)* and is not retracted.

Yet this very blessing for the one who receives them can be a danger for the minister of the sacraments. The priest who baptizes produces a holy effect, one which is determined for all eternity: original sin is forgiven; the demon flees and divine life overflows into a poor human child; it is then born for heaven. Tremendous responsibilities are laid upon the child, and the hand that does this should tremble. But all of this, even should the priest feel it as keenly as might be, can never even approach the reality of the grace that is imparted. And none of that realization is necessary for the validity and effect of the sacrament. The acts may be mechanical but completely valid, yet the priest can suffer increasing damage by this familiarity. He stops short at the form. That is how it is with everything *automatic,* e.g., the good intention once made, endures.

"Getting through" the Breviary has already been touched upon as a danger. The question so much discussed in moral theology of *materia gravis,* that is, what is necessary to constitute an objective serious sin, can easily induce a rascally kind of morality and an even immoral attitude, which seems to say that it is really a matter of indifference how many

Psalms one wants to steal away from God. Such priests forget, furthermore, that it is a matter of prayer, which presupposes a reverence that must be shocked at such casuistry. They are exact in making distinctions and restrictions with regard to vocal prayer, which always degenerates into labial, but how little they heed the complaint of our Lord (Mt. 15: 8), "This people honors me with their lips but their heart is far from me."

And yet all of these prescriptions, and even in a certain sense, the casuistry that comes along with them, are justified and have their meaning. But if lines are not drawn beyond those norms, into the depths and the heights, they can lead such priests into the emptiness of the desert.

Or the Latin language of the Breviary! Is there any bond more obvious in the community of priests which extends beyond all peoples and continents than this one? And yet it is unavoidable that the priest often "gets through" difficult passages, because for the moment he hasn't the time to translate, and perhaps even the means to help him are not at hand. What a danger that can be, if he accustoms himself to it!

For life is constantly under the summons of the living God. That is true also of the priest, and to an eminent degree. He has placed his life in the immediate Presence of God: "Behold how the eyes of the slave is on his master's hand and how the eyes of the maid is on her mistress'; so our eyes look to the Lord, our God, till he have mercy on us" (Ps. 122: 2). His hand gestures for us to approach. Even in the night He can call His Samuel, and He need not call him thrice. I took it as a grace, when as a young priest taking leave of my first assignment, I was told that as far as they could remember, I had had most of the night sick calls. That often took hours of travel in the mountains. There is no more beautiful recollection in my priestly life than these walks at night with the

Eucharistic Savior on my breast, with the one who had come to get me walking ahead with a lantern.

Our only salvation is constant watchfulness before God, and a conscience that is always ready. No fulfillment of mere written prescriptions, which are naturally necessary, can provide it. No mere regulation should replace Him on His Throne, upon whose hand our eyes should rest. Our conscience and its ever-watchful decision cannot be replaced by a table of objective conditions to be fulfilled, as though all we had to do was trace their outlines into the pattern of our own lives and those of others. All that would require merely a sharp eye and a steady hand.

No, our eyes are not fixed on the letter of the law, but upon the Lord, and that at every instant. For every moment is in the scale of God, and not one has ever been nor will it be again.

Otherwise everything becomes formalism and routine.

The life of the priest is not an easy one to endure. His eyes are directed toward the Lord, but they also grow weary and would like to sleep. And many things intrude themselves between our eye and the hand of God during the day. The priest is stretched out, as we have said, crucified both on the vertical beam of his God-given vocation and on the horizontal beam that the world and the man in the priest lays athwart the other. His eye is raised to the Father from the sixth to the ninth hour . . . all his life. The sun may dim; the mob may jeer, "Come down from the cross!" Even if he cry out with His Master, "My God, my God, why hast Thou forsaken me?" and "I thirst," he can only do it with his Master and only in His words. It seemed senseless to the disciples then to hang upon the cross, and often enough the disciples of today, and of all times, ask "Why?" But salvation is still in the fullness of the grace of this existence, and no other, both for the priest and for his congregation.

The point at which the dissolution of the tension is manifested as a faulty development is when the priest is unable to carry out the last commandment of Christ: "Go, therefore, and teach . . ." His life is introverted in the bad sense, and loses the power of fighting for the kingdom of God. When we use that term "introverted," which is taken from the typology of C. G. Jung, we would like to indicate to his credit that one can speak of a psychological predisposition in this development. His internal and external life seem to have little relationship to each other. Religious people are shocked at his unreliability, and those who are still seeking come to despair at his hands. He has lost his ability to listen and therefore cannot give any answer.

We must call again to mind the undecided crisis (p. 134 above). It resulted neither in a renewal of the "first love" (Apoc. 2 : 4) nor in defection; it ended with a crippling of his ability to love at all and, with that, in an arid condition of soul. Psychologically considered, this is the cause of formalism and of all its expressions.

The Workman

The Phenomenon and its Origin.   Mass flows under his hands smoothly and tirelessly, in buoyancy or boredom, but always like a well-oiled machine, automatically and impersonally . . . mere gestures. That is the external impression. The same is true with the other sacraments. The same form of advice in confession, and always the same five Our Fathers. The blessing is just something he says. Whenever he says anything else, one gets the impression that he is reading it. When he says his Breviary in the trolley car, it is a real *oratio labialis;* the people used to laugh at his flickering lips at first, but now they know him. They also notice in passing that he has the gift of hearing everything around him. Or is he listening to the conversations and only incidentally reading his office? It is impossible to decide.

His sermons, too, are impersonal, and the same trend of thought is expressed again and again. Even the sing-song tone, and the somniferous preacher's tone, are his. The parish office is like the post office and like the office of the local magistrate. That is where one gets certificates and reports weddings and baptisms. No one comes to ask him about his religious problems; and when some unsuspecting person does come, he doesn't even hear them out, and they get a consoling talk that sounds as though he were reading it from a card. If they should happen to come again, they hear the same talk. He has one for all situations. If you ask anything beyond that, it's as though he didn't hear you. He has lost the ability to listen.

How did he get that way? It was the same or something similar to the way described in general above. He did and still does abide by the rubrics, the directions; all his previous and subsequent education has become frozen gestures. He is like a lifeless shell. Perhaps there were crises that he left unsolved. He escapes from them into formalism. His character has probably developed and become fixed unconsciously. Maybe he fought it. But at any rate the result is fixed. Maybe a good deal of it is the appearance of old age.

Seen from the outside, he seems lacking in faith. But one would do him an injustice to suppose that. At any rate, he is unapproachable and out of contact with the needs of the hour or the needs of the people who come to him. In his own way he may even be devout. But his religious life is devoid of all that is arousing, alarming, demanding. There is a devotion of habit, of custom, and it is all-embracing. There is something about it that is solid, lasting, above crises. It inclines one—

and this is its only vital aspect—to consider everything new and alert and vital as suspect.

His Many Forms. Is it a "holy masquerade"? * One should reflect a good deal before supposing something like that without more evidence. But the appearance gives it credence.

We cannot afford to overlook the fact that daily duties always become matters of habit. The greatest part of our activity runs on tracks already laid, without our really being conscious of it. We mention this fact only to point out that it is not a consciously cultivated habit that we have to deal with here. Dare anyone let his holy duties degenerate into routine? "Habit impairs the zeal of the man who prays, and that of the man who loves or serves, and it hinders him from doing his duty aright. It is habit which degrades the object of meditation and the heart that contemplates, spoiling the colors, dampening resonance, ruining the form, and because of habit, the blessing and prayer seem to become empty gestures" (Paul Regnier, *Die Netze im Meer*, Heidelberg, 1952, p. 56).

Even vitally religious men can suddenly find themselves on the tracks of routine. Even Auke, whose life is the most extreme opposite of routine, once says to his brother "Remember our last conversation? Strike it from your memory! Don't forget that I've become a routine priest in the meantime . . . Ah, even reverence becomes worn out by repetition sooner or later" (Ouwendijk, p. 92). But he was soon cured of that. He knows a kind of priest of whom he says: "They are the ones who've been hollowed out, who are satisfied with their emptiness; with every word they say and every gesture they make

* Olov Hartman, *The Holy Masquerade* (in Swedish, *Heilig Maskerad*, Stockholm). The novel treats of the problem of the contradiction between the faithlessness of an evangelical minister, Albert, and the hypocrisy in which he continues to hold services as a pastor, along with his passably Christian sermons. It is in the form of the diary of his wife, who wants to expose the hypocrisy.

you can feel what a chill comes out of that emptiness" (p. 276). It is suspicious to note that in the word *ceremony* there is an undertone of *empty ceremony*. Even a holy ceremony is not exempt from the law of banishment to unconscious performance. But in this case it becomes a scandal, because the contradiction between gestures and that to which these gestures refer is most unfathomable.

Gestures, we must admit, are also a matter of temperament. And the temperament of peoples is very different. They can easily misunderstand one another. When the Scottish Bishop brought the nuns who had been expelled from France from the station to their new home, he asked the Reverend Mother if she had ever been in Rome. "Yes," she said, "but she hadn't been impressed as she had imagined and that she was sorry to say that some of the princes and high prelates of the Church hadn't seemed to have very spiritual faces and had hurried through even the holy mysteries of the Mass in a distraught and irreverent manner." But the Bishop had an explanation for that: "that was perhaps because the Saxon mind could only think of one thing at once, whereas the Latin mind could think of several, so that it was possible that an Italian Cardinal's eyes and face might reflect the worldly thoughts of half his mind, whereas the other half was really and truly thinking about our Lord and all that He had done for us."

But the Reverend Mother wasn't satisfied with this explanation and thought "there was perhaps something in what the Bishop said, but that His Lordship must not forget that she was a Latin and no Saxon and that in spite of that fact she had been considerably shocked by the scurried ceremonial and the slothful thought of some of the higher clergy in Rome" (Bruce Marshall, *The World, the Flesh and Father Smith*).

One would do well to let the kindly interpretation of the

Bishop stand as a warning that no one of himself or from the standpoint of his own people should misunderstand others without further consideration.

But the scandal can be great. It can be a misunderstanding. But the other scandal is worse, and more important for the case we are treating. Routine no longer reminds us of the mystery; it rather conceals it and exposes it to mockery. It slanders it. It gives the unbelief that comes of relativism and psychologism the most convincing of arguments. The "work-man" ceases to be an advertisement for the kingdom of God. In a parish subsisting on a Christianity of Routine, he is at best taking the place of one at whose hands the fire of the Holy Spirit will again become manifest in the rites of his sacred functions.

The Arrested Theologian

Is there such?   "There are so few priests with whom one can have a theological conversation," the laity was complaining, as we learned through the questionnaire circulated by the directors of the seminaries.

There is an increase of interest in theology and theological training. There have been many hundreds who have gone through the two-year theological course—"The Layman's Year"—during the last decade in Vienna alone, and they have done well in the examinations, too. The study of theology by the laity in the theological faculties is also becoming more common. The reluctant attitude of many priests arouses suspicion against them. But they may be merely thinking of the dangers connected with it. The priest is also not just there to "have theological conversations."

But he does need enough theology to answer everyone who asks for help and every doubter, with that accuracy demanded by the question he meets. This it is which might give rise to a theological conversation. I cannot believe that there are many who are not up to that.

But there are cases when people, young people especially, but adults, too who suddenly feel the need of certainty when they find themselves tortured by their consciences. And then they come to the pastor, because there is no one else, and, as Peter said to our Lord, they ask the priest, "Lord, to whom shall we go? Thou hast the words of everlasting life" (John 6: 68).

And what if they have to go away disillusioned, because the man they wanted to question, even before he had listened to them, had given them a few ready answers from the catechism they already knew, answers that had little or nothing to do with their personal question? They could even have asked their children at home about it, since they've got the words of the catechism by heart, too. Also in their hearts? That is the point. For men who are driven to the priest by their spiritual difficulties do not all come with questions already printed in the catechism, and consequently the answer that is printed there is not the answer to their question.

His Development.   The paths that lead to this kind of rigidity are numerous.

Some of the fault may derive from the presentation of theology which they heard during their years of preparation. Theology, like the Faith itself, which it reduces to clear concepts, cannot be a dead science. Just as the great theologians who lived a thousand and more years ago had to answer the questions of their day, so, too, the theologians of today must be able to answer the problems of today from the same theology: and the answer must be theological, clear, and convincing.

Or is it sheer examination theology, that minimal amount of fundamental information about that science, sufficient to show its relationships to the present, if it is not to remain a dead load that is to be simply handed on?

Is it a lack of further theological training, a failure to deepen their knowledge, which necessarily leads to an unworthy primitivism? Are they mere theological formulas, taken along like uncracked nuts, as sheer shells of knowledge, without ever making the holy contents one's own? That is a danger that is present especially in concepts and definitions formulated in Latin, unless they are developed in all their rich content.

The layman, no matter how pious, is often helpless in the face of a theological work. "Now and then, when I read certain treatises which point to perfection as though through a thousand stumbling blocks, my poor small mind quickly tires, and I close the learned tome that is breaking my head and drying up my heart and pick up Holy Scripture," writes St. Thérèse of the Child Jesus to the missionaries in 1897 (Ida Fr. Goerres, *Das verborgene Antlitz*, Freiburg, 1944). The little saint had a right to slam these books closed; the priest does not. It is his duty to push on through the necessary schooling to the sweetness of the kernel. But he must be guided in doing it.

The arrested theologian perhaps only knew the dry externals of theology, the shell of thought, not the thought itself. And now he has only answers ready-made, at best. But these are an article little in demand.

But there are also theological primitives, whose simplicity and childlike devotion have an edifying effect on religious men, even educated ones, and disarms all criticism. Strictly speaking, then, they do not belong here. During their lifetime they have lived among simple people, men who had their faith and superstition, their well-worn prayers, their sheep and beef and their sins. They never heard a thing about theologians; all their lives they only knew about the pastor. Naturally they knew nothing of theology, and they never felt any loss. And so it came about that their pastors, too, forgot all about theology. And they, too, never noticed that they had lost something. Do these pastors belong among the arrested forms? We mention them only on the margin of this chapter. Their life has often been praised by simple story-tellers who themselves were simple men (Hans Schrott-Fiechtl, *Das linke Pfarrerle*, 1926; Peter Rosegger, *Die Ehrmesse*, and many priest-characters by Patrick Sheehan). Don Evaristo is one of them: devout, even saintly, among the poor of the old city of Cittá Morta (Stefan Andres, *Das Tier aus der Tiefe*, p. 160). And Thomas Gouvernec is one right from the beginning (Henri Queffelec, *Island Priest*), and the Bishop of Quimper ordained him anyway and sent him back to his countrymen on the rocky isle of Sein. (Why the famous picture left out this fact, which is the high point of the story, I cannot understand!)

The Ineffectual Type

The Phenomenon.   This type is not to be equated with the lonely man, and not with the "passivist" with whom he has the greatest similarity, considering only the phenomenon. He is the most obvious example of the type we described right at the beginning.

He lives in retirement. He neither hears nor sees what goes on around the rectory. One gets the impression that he has even forgotten that he has a congregation of which he is the shepherd. Of course, he comes when called, but he is uncertain and shy. He startles easily. He shrugs his shoulders. He obviously knows that he has no strength to master things. To excuse himself, he says that the people who talk like that are often deceiving themselves anyway.

The phrase *segregatus a populo*—separated from the people—was once used in the seminary as an explanation of the priesthood. This phrase he has subjected to a tragic misunderstanding.

His sermons are monologs without one vital "you." Therefore, they are also without concern and without charity. At least so it seems, since charity, even charity for the flock, is meant for the neighbor, the man next to a person, and not just for men in general. Words without a "you" in them are just spoken to the air, over nodding heads, without love, but also without hostility: almost with the fear that the people in the benches down there may wake up and ask him a question. A haunting half-hour, that!

Whether there are many people or only a few, he never seems to notice. He does notice it, though, and will try to find out the reason for it. And he may find the reason, but of all the suggestions that are made to him, he'll take none. He gives his sermons and reads the Mass the same old way he always did. This ordered repetition does him good, and he finds protection for himself in it. The order that one can predict from the time when men first started to think is the empty realm of his life.

He is devout. He is full of faith. Most of all, he is turned within himself and tired. At least that is the impression. Is this weariness physical or psychic? Perhaps it is both. Or is it really religious? Is it the expression of a tremendous confidence in the power of grace? It is certainly a distrust of activity, and that from a gradual incapacity for it. Who can any longer say in this benumbed condition what is a cause and what is an effect? He has one favorite parable in which he puts all his trust: "Thus is the kingdom of God, as though a man should cast seed into the earth, then sleep and rise, night and day, and the seed should sprout and grow without his knowing it. For of itself the earth bears the crop, first the blade then the ear, then the full grain in the ear" (Mark 4: 26-28).

His Origin. How did he get this way? Perhaps he is naturally shy, reserved, and distrustful of men who are different from him, what C. G. Jung would call the introverted type. It is always likely that he will become a determined pessimist who lets things happen as they may. Perhaps he should have been a monk instead of a secular priest. One of the most noble characters drawn by Joseph Weingartner in his novel of seminary life *Über die Brücke* is Sylvester Wörg. To the surprise of his friends, he enters an Order when he is still in his years of preparation. Why? Because he says that he is afraid of the ministry and wants to save his own soul (p. 198). Is that it? For those outside he remains a question mark. No one can say that he really knows.

Perhaps he is tired of the struggle. At one time he was quite determined and full of hope. But one disenchantment followed another, and he saw little success despite his hardest labors. The sinful were not converted and the devout live on in satisfaction with their own goodness. Perhaps he had some particularly bad experiences. He worked along for some time, and pulled back by degrees to the line of least resistance. And finally he gave up resisting at all. He felt that he could never master the disintegrating and hostile powers that daily assailed his congregation. Places of refreshment and recreation, movies, radio, papers and politics, even if they aren't immoral or contrary to Faith, are daily dinned into the ears of men. These greedy people, hungry for self-satisfaction, have an entirely different logic. He cannot and will not compete with buffoons and honky-tonk atmosphere. How are these people still to hear the voice of God and their conscience? He gives up the fight.

And what is his attitude? That is not even important, for the type portrayed here is not merely represented by the pessimist. There is also the ingenuous, laughing kind of resignation. Just listen to this example. Father Johannes, who is staying in the parish to help out, says to the young curate: "Keep this idea well in mind: people are both as good and as bad as you can imagine. So the best way to get along is to gather strength from the one to enable you to put up with the other. You can't hope for more" (Bernhart, *Der Kaplan*, p. 99). And the pastor of Abricourt says of his parish to his confrere at Norenfontes, "The good and the evil are probably evenly distributed, but on such a low plain, very low indeed! Or, if you like, they lie one over the other; like oil and water they never mix" (Bernanos, *The Diary of a Country Priest*). And the splendid pastor of Torcy tells how the nun who helped him thought she could do away with dirt in the church once and for all with her frenzied scrubbing. But finally she contracted rheumatic fever; "her heart gave way and—pouf! —there was my little nun before St. Peter." And he applies that to the inexperienced idealist before him: "The mistake she made wasn't to fight dirt, sure enough, but to try to do away with it altogether. As if it were possible! A parish is bound to be dirty. But a whole Christian society's a lot dirtier. You wait for the Judgment Day and see what the angels'll be sweeping out of the most saintly monasteries!" The brave pastor of Torcy was no passivist, anything but. The distinction that one must combat evil without the intention of rooting it out completely gives him his splendid courage, his sense of humor.

His devout neighbor is more resigned. "The face of my parish! The look in the eyes . . . They must be gentle, suffering, patient eyes. I feel they must be rather like mine when I cease struggling and let myself be borne along in the great invisible flow that sweeps all of us helter-skelter, the living and the dead, into the deep waters of eternity."

No one, not even I, can say that these "examples" really

describe the type that is intended here. They only point out the direction of the path upon which he is entering. He is in the midst of his parish; and the parish is like a village snowed under and cut off from the world of the good and the bad. The murmuring brook that runs through it in the summer is frozen over. All the roofs are covered with snow, and so is the roof of the rectory. The lonely finger of the steeple reaches out of the white shroud and points to heaven.

The Embittered Type

This type has had the same experiences as his predecessors, but he does not fall into the same resignation, but rather into its opposite, senseless opposition, and has become frozen in that attitude.

He had ability and zeal. Perhaps the latter was too self-centered. He wanted work, lots of work. And he thought that it was about time that he succeeded. He thought of the ministry as a unified and mighty attack, but he was so interested in the attack that he forgot that the Son of Man had not come to fight and defeat those who are lost, but to "seek what was lost" (Luke 19: 10). He forgot that publicans and sinners were attracted to Him (Mt. 9: 10), and that it mattered not at all to the Savior that the pious people of that time pointed the finger of scorn at Him and asked His disciples, "Why does your Master eat with publicans and sinners?" and "Why is He their friend?" (Luke 7: 34) And the answer that He Himself gave was that He had not come to call the just, and so attract them, but the sinners (Mark: 2: 17), and, of course, "to call them to repentance." Why did our Lord act that way? "For even sinners love those who love them" (Luke 6: 32).

This love is wanting in this type, and, what is worse, he doesn't miss it. And yet that is the heart of the Gospel and of all care of souls. He wants to protect and secure the kingdom of God in his own field of work. What Grillparzer has Cardinal Klesl say to the Archduke Ferdinand in their quarrel is true of him: "When anyone wants first to establish the kingship of God, he considers himself too readily the instrument of God, and he strives to rule so that He might reign" (*Bruderzwist im Hause Habsburg*, I). His methods repel; the expected prostration of his opponents does not follow. His ambition alienates his fellow-priests. Finally, he is ignored by everyone, obviously by his opponents, but also by his brothers. He is left alone. He is no longer taken seriously.

That doesn't confuse him; he keeps on going right ahead, thinking and doing things in the same way. Those not of the Faith take him to be a "papist," a champion of the priests' fixed craving for power. He meets hostility with more of the same, and as the proverb has it, thinks that the biter must be bitten; he does so with a will. He thinks his fellow-priests are slovenly and cowards.

He can no longer get himself out of this frame of mind, even when his bald spot starts spreading and all he has left are tufts of hair over his ears. He will not admit to himself and much less to others that he is in a rut and helpless, and so he doesn't get out of it.

He is still thundering against sinners in his pulpit—but they aren't coming to church—and against sins that his hearers don't commit, so they only learn to beat a penitential breast—for others, "O God, I thank thee that I am not like the rest of men, robbers, dishonest, adulterers . . ." (Luke 18: 11). He finds fault with everything else that is done in the Church or in the ministry. He wants to get away from old methods and considers all but his own as ridiculous, but it is precisely this of his method that is not recognized. He had zeal; he had a strong consciousness of his rank and dignity. He thinks that he might have expected that all this would have been seen by his ecclesiastical superiors and given some external recognition. Nothing happens.

So he is surrounded by loneliness. He becomes bitter, and helpless, for the reason that no one can help him. Superficially he resembles the fanatic. But strictly speaking, this type is overcharged with religious energies, and he is not lacking in the charity which is the heart of the Christian and the priest.

The case of the embittered man is rare. The things that bring on his bitterness are not always the ones we have listed, but we have brought out only those rooted in priestly existence.

The Hysteric

The hysteric is even more unusual: he has a certain affinity with the type just described. There can even be experiences which are the same for both, but in the one man they result in the type above, and in another, they develop into the form we are about to describe.

How does he get this way?

Apparently the psychoneurotic condition of which we are speaking is determined psychogenetically, in a predisposition resulting in an ethically faulty orientation, and finally ending in a lasting reaction. And this determines the character of the man permanently, or until something else happens.

The priest has a lofty dignity. But it is not one of this world, and in this world can even mean derision and martyrdom. There is a genuine self-consciousness of his dignity in the priest. But there is also one that takes its measure from this world. This can become a complex. Then, his title of "Reverend" is referred, not to his ordination and state of life, but to himself. And then it is not entered in his books as a standing debit, but as a matter-of-course credit.

That is objectively a lie. Or, expressed in the terminology we have used up till now, the tension that necessarily exists between the sanctity of the vocation and the humanity of the priest is either overlooked or denied. Reverence and the concrete *Reverend* are identified, and in a profane sense at that. That doesn't make sense. Whenever anyone wants to consider what is objectively a lie as the truth, reality will take its revenge. (We are not speaking here of the reverence and respect that the faithful have for the priest. Even the people know how to distinguish in a particular case between the priestly dignity and the priest.)

While sanctity and every kind of Christian and priestly existence grow and mature by respecting their proper tensions, the ignoring of these tensions must lead to a human distortion. Man proves and matures himself in the call that comes from above and the response that comes from below. So too the priest. Grace is given him, but not sanctity, and not even his personal dignity. That is always a debit, and will be a debit all his life, because the goal is infinite. "Be perfect as your Father in heaven!" This demand of our Lord and Master is just as certain as is the duty of always trying to realize it.

The man who is obsessed with a craving for importance takes his dignity to be something that is naturally his own, and relies on it in the ordinary affairs of life. But he can only do so with a bad conscience, because his poor humanity cannot be overlooked by anyone. If the honor that is meant for the state in life is referred to the person, it is not only a misunderstanding, but a kind of theft. It is an attempt, which he would deny, to receive recognition for something that not only does not, but cannot exist.

But suppressed humanity, a reality that cannot be explained away, takes revenge on the one who suppresses it: it makes him a caricature and soon exposes him to ridicule. He was always out for distinctions, ecclesiastical and otherwise, honors and titles. Winning them, he saw admiration in the eyes of those who appreciated his dignity and importance. And now there is no more of this external sign. And his reaction is sour. He betrays himself by it and becomes an object of ridicule.

Or he has succeeded in winning a few ornaments, medals, or rings, or even a bit of violet piping, and now he is intent on showing himself off at every solemn and less solemn occasion in studied gestures and with gracious smirks in all directions. But with time, the effect of this becomes a little out of place, and even a cause of laughter. For serious Christians it can be a scandal; only for the very naive is it a source of admiration. And this state of affairs is only aggravated if he doesn't suspect it. (But then it would no longer be our case. He would have to be called something like "A Saturated Hysteric" or "An Extreme Hysteric." And that is a case in itself, or at any rate, a "case".)

Let us keep on with those who aren't cured. A comic situation now results, and the prospect of escaping it is dim. Many a one has also had a run-in with his superiors, perhaps even with the Bishop. The effect of this is like a wound that will not heal (the "trauma" of depth psychology) and this aggravates his condition. There are priests to whom injustice has been done, humanly speaking. Joseph Scheicher can tell of his "Poor Brothers" who were summarily condemned and suspended without an opportunity of justifying themselves. But he adds that this happens "every day." We can hardly accept that, at least today. The literature that deals with priestly existence today has Bishops who are humane and wise, like the one in

Power's *The Encounter*, or the one in Marshall's *Father Smith*, even men who are pious seers, like the old man in Coccioli's *Heaven and Earth*, or the Bishop on a grand scale, like the Stephen Cardinal Fermoyle in the novel by Henry Morton Robinson. Only Msgr. Cherubini in Stefan Andres' *Das Tier aus der Tiefe* is a certain exception. Even Msgr. Robert Gillespie, whose nickname is "Plus Robert" (from his signature: ✠ Robertus), is amusing, but fundamentally kind (Marshall, *Father Malachy's Miracle*). Henri Bordeaux relates of Bishop Helouard of Bellerive that he "was a strict old man, lacking all sense of humor, who transformed his reception room into an ice house just by opening the door and appearing on the threshold" (*Le Fil de la Vierge*, p. 15). On this point the times have changed. Or have they, everywhere?

Nevertheless, there are priests who are still going around today with the idea that there is something due them. They feel that they are overlooked, misunderstood—and they complain to everyone they meet who has the patience to hear the story of their reversals. By this they make themselves a carnival figure among those who are here described. It has a painful effect on their audience. They pity *him*. But he takes it for agreement.

There are varieties of this type: the ascetic who pities himself and looks for sympathy; the sensitive type, who is easily hurt and feels rebuffed and is always out of humor because he applies harmless remarks to himself; there is a third type that thinks that one should always put up with things humbly, of course, and think of our Savior, who was also misunderstood . . . When visiting Deforis, the old ex-communicate, Emile Baumann says of him: "He gave in to the need for reassuring confidences, which is proper to old and sick men who, in their concern about their sinking egos, only want those who come near them to be concerned about their own person" (p. 51).

Hysteria is etymologically, historically, and according to the percentage of those afflicted with it, a woman's disease. That is what makes it so ridiculous when it flattens a man, especially one whose profession is so manly as is the priest's. But here again—they are rare. And the fact that it is a disease, at least half and half, is some excuse.

The Misunderstood Idealist

These were men with highly conceived goals. As long as these goals tended to one's own perfection, and the reformer started with himself, there was scarcely a sign of resistance. But when he wanted to sweep others along with him, even though they be his fellow-religious, the weight of habits, the indifference of old age, which cannot, and therefore will not easily change, was felt.

The history of all the Orders knows the tragedy of their one-time necessary reformers, who really dared nothing more than a return to their original ideal. Ludwig von Blois had to learn that. But he was not broken by the experience. Because he was steadfast in the face of years of opposition (which he suffered in Liessies as a young abbot), he did indeed grow weary. But it made him a wiser and more knowing man.

But we are speaking here primarily of the secular priest. Opposition has not only made many idealists weary, but hardened them. They were disillusioned by supposing that their ideal and their verve would win a hearing and following. Then followed disenchantment, and they ate their hearts out over it. Their idealism became a danger even for themselves. That is the case especially when their high intent is not aimed at their own and their brothers' sanctification, but attempts to reform their whole condition, a thing they are not qualified to attempt. But when did the saints, idealists, and reformers ever doubt their competence? I knew a country pastor who published an anonymous work on the reform of the whole Church. It was only with difficulty that he could be brought to recall it. There were and are those in the clergy who are especially fearless champions of social justice. They often have programs that far surpass their view of affairs and their intellectual ability, but they are sure that they have found the place to apply the Archimedean lever that will save everything. They throw themselves into their self-appointed duty with incomparable intensity and try to sweep others along with them. And despite all their occasional naiveté and audacity, there is usually a real concern in their daring. Often enough, that is recognized too late.

Then he comes upon the opposition of the comfortable, the ones who need peace, the know-it-alls, the mockers; and they shake him off. Perhaps he is denounced. Finally he has a clash with his superiors. One runs off, as did Auke in *Das geschändete Antlitz;* another retreats, sorely wounded. Others give in, honorably. But their experience of the sense of mission that drove them on does not quite leave them in peace. It crowds in on their hours of quiet and their dreams. Their ideals and goals still affirm themselves victoriously; and it can happen that one goes through the daily duties and offices of his vocation absent-mindedly, while he is living in a dream, day and night, of how all the possibilities of his ideas are realized. That is his world.

Those who are really great become even greater through their difficulties. Others are later justified, as were John Henry Newman and Johann Michael Sailer. Others are not, like Martin Deutinger, not to speak of the many idealists in our country.

There are idealists of fact, who become defiant and would sooner be ruined than give in. In his book *Die beiden Hänse* Peter Rosegger sketches a young idealist who takes himself to be the pastor of a girl who has fallen, whom he has rescued from suicide, and who no longer knows what she will do in life. (He doesn't know that she is the bride of his former school-fellow, the other celebrated Jack, who had been seduced and betrayed.) He takes the young mother and child into his home, contrary to the understandable misgivings and finally the prohibition of his ecclesiastical superiors. He is not at all bothered in his idealism despite the fact that he is endangering his good name. It is enough for him that he remain pure and that he does his work as his conscience tells him. As a final extreme he is punished by being transferred to the mountains to a secluded place of pilgrimage. He takes the poor mother and her child there with him, and he cares for the many pilgrims with all the love of a pastor, amid incredible hardships, until he dies prematurely of overwork.

Let us ignore for the moment what Peter Rosegger had in mind in writing this story. No one will deny that there are such priests. It is not always the case, of course, that they themselves have to make a great decision. It is thrust upon them in an hour of greatness or in a testing encounter. These devout idealists are more common than one would suppose. Many later shake off the call of their hour. Compared to them, this man, who is still imprisoned by his idealism, is great, even when, restricted as he is, he becomes a sacrifice of his good heart. It will only be on the great day at the end of time that the priest-idealists among them, of whom no historian and no poet has written, will be revealed.

The Priest in a Rut

A General Description. In his memoirs, Joseph Weingartner has this to say about one of his teachers: "When I entered the seminary in Brixen in 1895, Father Ivo Sint (from the canons' foundation) was the oldest professor. He was teaching mathematics and physics and was goodness itself. Our best fun was to get him to tell little stories from his life again and again, since he always told them in exactly the same words. For example, there was his story of the total eclipse: 'Wh . . wh . . when' (Father Ivo stuttered a little)—'when I was a little boy we had just sat down to dinner in the dining room. Then my father said 'It's getting dark all of a sudden!' So my mother said, 'I'll go to the kitchen and get a light.' 'Well, well,' my father said, 'you'll find your mouth all right.' 'Y-y-you see,' he concluded, every time with a solemn gesture, 'It was a total eclipse' " (*Unterwegs,* 1951, p. 26). Two pages later Weingartner tells almost the same story about another teacher.

Who doesn't know "characters" like that in clerical dress? Nice, old gentlemen, too: you hear their stories for the first time and are delighted. But at the next opportunity, they repeat them again word for word, and you're surprised that they don't remember that we know all about the affair. But they come back a third and a fourth time, and you get bored. But not young people, and especially students! Especially is this true when it's a priest-teacher, no matter how beloved he is, who tells them. On the contrary: they prompt him to tell the ancient stories and pretend curiosity and astonishment, the rascals! And the better known the stories are, even down to the last gesture and wink, the funnier they find it.

When I was a curate in my first post, one priest came every summer for one or two weeks' vacation. He was the oldest living priest who had once worked in our parish, a reverend old chatterbox. He was then a pastor in Vienna and a prelate, of which he prided himself not a little, although in an attractive way. He had the beautiful name of Pax. Mischievously, the other priests cited the Book of Wisdom in referring to his curates: *"Illi autem sunt in pace"* (Wisd. 3: 3)—"They rest in peace." But they themselves described their situation in the words of the Prophet Ezechiel: *"Pax, ubi non est pax"*—"Pax, where there is no peace" (Ezech. 13: 10). But that was hard to believe. At least during the nice days of summer he had a winning manner, even to me, his successor and junior by fifty years. But—and here we finally get to the point—as often as he came, he would tell me at breakfast about the time when his predecessor was standing in the sacristy, just before going out to preach. He had his hands folded, when just at the last minute, the local farmer burst in: "Father, I've lost a yearling. Would you mention that after the sermon, so I'll get it back again?" "Sure, sure, glad to do it." And the farmer was gone. Only then did the priest, a city man, ask himself, "Well, just what is a 'yearling'? Oh, that makes no difference!" After the sermon he said, "The local farmer has asked me to tell you that he has lost a yearling. The finder will please hand it in at the sacristy." Delighted but suppressed laughter followed. It was only afterwards that he learned from the pastor that a "yearling" was a year-old steer.

Every year I heard this story. And many a year, several times! But these twice-told tales are just a part and a symbol of all these types. Even their sermons become more and more alike and finally say the same thing. Not everyone has the wit of that old pastor; when he was told that his sermons were all the same, he said that, when they had done what he told them, he would come up with a new one.

There are some, too, who not only serve up the same old stories and jokes, but whose lives have become like clockwork, and the stories and jokes are told even on the same date and hour. They are just as predictable as everything else in their lives, by watch and calendar. That happens less frequently to pastors, because life, in its unpredictability, is always making new demands upon them and it doesn't give the dust time to settle on their minds. It is more of a danger to those who are obliged to the same yearly and daily order, or have obliged themselves and others to it: that provides a good foundation for the deposit of rust.

His Process of Development. Is this a question of priestly or Christian existence at all? Or is it only biological or histological? If that were the case, we would find only one person to explain the very complex phenomenon.

This is doubtless something that comes with old age; and it is manifested not only by the repetition of the same old anecdotes: there is a definite narrowing of existence and engagement. But it is not at all to the detriment of existence. The hardening of the arteries, according to physical laws, not only endangers them, but likewise and primarily protects them. In the course of nature there is a gradual loss of agility and adaptability. The life processes have a narrower basis. But that, too, is a source of strength.

There are fewer possibilities of decision for the older man. It is no longer possible to speak of hazard in the same way that one does of the younger priest. And yet there is still a hazard that is essential to his existence; that hazard is based on the possibility of danger. The experience of the threat is not danger itself. That danger is considerably greater and more diverse in the younger years, but it is experienced less by the younger priests than it is by the old ones. That is attributable to the extreme situation in which the old priest finds himself. For the man of faith, every moment has something of an extreme situation about it, because every moment is under the judgment of God. But the young man doesn't experience it that way, even though he does live it in faith. He has a totally different experience of time than the old man. For the young man, time is future, incalculably long, and so far as his consciousness is concerned, infinite; for the old man time is past and his experience of time is that of time speeding past and running out. The young priest still has to reckon with many possibilities of decision; the old man knows that there are only a few essential ones and all others are not worth considering. And he could not avoid this last one, even if he wanted to.

That is why things that were once important are repeated, even if it is only a joke. In fact, it is all the same to the old man that he has already used it. For everything is completely indifferent to him except that one thing which alone is important. They speak more in jest than the young man can imagine. That is what constitutes the wisdom of old age. And these wise men among priests—how could it be otherwise?—are very numerous. What the young men smile at in them, and take for weariness, lack of interest, and narrowness, even what in their youth sounds to them like theological audacity, is in reality a strength for which the young can have no adequate concept: it is the really unconfused look at what is essential.

"Omnes pene virtutes corporis," says St. Jerome in his letter to Nepotianus, *"mutantur in senibus, et crescente sola*

sapientia, decrescunt cetera": almost all the powers of the body are changed in the old man; and while wisdom alone increases, all the others fail.

We know the beautiful story about St. John the Apostle and Evangelist in his extreme old age. All of those who had been called with him by the Lord had been dead for half a century. Already an era was on them which was entirely different from Apostolic times. They were whispering among themselves that he would not die until the Lord returned—and whenever he was brought to the Holy Sacrifice of the community and the bishop had spoken, they asked him if he would not say a few words to them, too. He got up and said, "Little children, love one another!" And when he had said that a second and a third time, and again and again and never said anything else, many may well have laid it to the weakness of his old age. And when they asked him, "Father, why do you always say the same thing?" he answered them, "Because that is the commandment of the Lord and because it is enough, if it is fulfilled."

Then repetition appears in a different light, especially when they hit off the essentials so well. The decisiveness of the old priest is a different thing from the audacity of the young priest, which takes all possibilities into account. His decision comes from his eschatological seriousness. It is no longer boldness and the broad-minded willingness to try anything. It is preparedness for one thing! There is nothing else besides this that is of any importance. At any hour the door can open and the Angel of the Lord can summon him to one accounting. Compared to this attitude, all the existentialism of this time becomes empty talk.

It may be because of this simplified outlook, joined to the decisive experience of his final years and his old age itself, which explains why, toward the end of his life, many a priest sets on one thing: on a miraculous medal, a third order, the liturgical movement, on Our Lady of Fatima, the parish principle, or on St. Thérèse of the Child Jesus.

Charity as an "Arrested Form." But it is not by chance that many set all on charity, as did St. John the Evangelist. For charity is proved to be the heart of mastering the Christian existence . . . as the fulfillment of the "new commandment that the Lord gave us" (John 13: 34 ff.), "For he who loves his neighbor has fulfilled the Law" (Rom. 13: 8; Gal. 5: 14). In this charity old priests see more than they could have understood in their youth, and therefore they are more vital.

Little Rose in Brighton by accident had learned of the murders committed by a band of gangsters. In order to "shut her up," the seventeen-year-old gang leader "married" her, and now he wants to kill her too, while all the while he is abusing her touchingly stupid loyalty to him. Now she is kneeling in the confessional, she herself knows not why, since she wants to be damned with her Pinkie if he is to be damned. The old priest behind the screen merely says to the child before him, quietly and calmly: "We must hope and pray!" He recognizes her love for her dead Pinkie and sees in it from the first nothing sinful, but rather the crack into which grace can force its feet. "I cannot give you absolution now—but come back—tomorrow." "Yes, Father . . . And if there's a baby . . ?" And the priest says: "With your simplicity and his force . . . Make him a saint—so that he can pray for his father" (Graham Greene, *Brighton Rock*).

Where did Father Mellowes get his smile, and how did it freeze on his face? (Francis Stuart, *Redemption*, 1952) It was with astonishment and some fright that he saw a kind of life, after his seminary years, to which he could build no bridge by means of his theological formulas. He sees how good the devout can be, but how dense, self-righteous, and remorseless, too. And how sinners, even criminals, are in many ways more perceptive and willing to help. That is when his "smile" started. Nothing surprises him any more. Ezra, the nihilist, has seduced the pastor's sister, Romilly, merely because he can't stand a girl being pure and imperceptive. Mellowes knows it and sits at lunch with Ezra the next day and can still enjoy his fish. His sister marries the sexual criminal Kavanaugh, so that he would be helped in that regard. The smile still lingers on the negroid lips of the pastor. Foolishness or wisdom? Just helplessness, or helplessness as a virtue? There is a peace that goes out from him. "It was the smile of a man on whom the answer to a difficult problem was beginning to dawn, the smile that one would give to the unfathomable simplicity of a long-sought solution unexpectedly stumbled upon."

Why is it that Don Ardito, at that time a celebrated lecturer and famous writer in the large city of M., is attracted to Don Carlo Andreini? "Don Carlo was the rector of San Damiano, in one of the poorest sections of the city, a little man about sixty years old, with something in his face that made him seem ageless or else extremely aged. He had a long, smooth face, a head of hair as thick as that of a young man, and faded, pale blue eyes which opened and shut spasmodically. His voice was feeble and at the slightest provocation he laughed. In fact, he laughed a great part of the time, making a gurgling sound like a parrot. He was the poorest and loneliest priest of the diocese, yet he was invariably in a cheerful frame of mind, and spent all his days thanking the Lord for what He had given him. An outsider would have said that the Lord had given him absolutely nothing" (Carlo Coccioli, *Heaven and Earth*, London, 1953).

He kept this parish for which no one contended. "Joy was the essence of Don Carlo Andreini's nature. He lived very much alone, and for this reason there were always people about him: ragged urchins, chronic drunks, prostitutes, petty criminals, an occasional deformed creature that is always to be found in such poor surroundings. Don Carlo gave a bit of cheer to each one of these, perhaps no more than a kind word, a gurgling laugh, a tolerant look of his clear eyes, but in any case, a parcel of his joy. He never voiced any complaint, but his poverty was so obvious that no one could help wondering how he lived. A dirty little lame woman came every now and then to clean his rooms and cook him a meal, and never failed to steal what she could of the money he gave her for the marketing, although she was devoted to him. But he praised her work and treated her like a queen. Don Carlo Andreini never wearied of saying how happy he was and praising God for His gifts."

To get his blessing and some advice, Don Ardito sought him out, even though it was close to midnight. His advice always had the same theme: charity. "I say to you that you should see to it that they suffer as little as possible. If they must suffer, you should try to lighten their pain . . . God is with those who suffer, but He is not their suffering." And then the gifted and famous Don Ardito asks what he himself should have known better, according to all presumptions; but the poor priest who was sitting before him in a nightshirt, with only a jacket thrown over it, was supposed to answer him. In reply to the question, "In what does the love of God consist?" he said succinctly, "It means to love him in our fellow men." And he blesses him.

The poor people's priests of Naples go even further. Their love of neighbor is only more human. Perhaps it got that way by their innumerable unsuccessful attempts to love their parishioners any other way.

Don Ardito, in his latest book, had correctly interpreted the concept of poverty as an inner freedom from all attachment to possessions and goods. In writing of "Blessed are the poor in spirit," his final definition of poverty was one word: "wishlessness." The priests of Naples' poor are moved by the candor of Don Ardito's language. They sense that in him they can see one of their own kind, and they invite him to join them, even though the invitation came in a letter in which one of them explained how they differed from him. He said:

"You say that poverty belongs to God. With the Gospel you maintain that 'whosoever he be of you that forsaketh not all he hath, he cannot be my disciple.' But since, according to you, poverty is the absence of acquisitiveness or desire, it is a spiritual state rather than a material one, and even an oil magnate can enter heaven.

"This may be the truth, but just listen to me and look at the world in which I live, this abode of poverty, Naples.

"My people live in *bassi* or basement rooms, or else in the attics of great palaces, accessible only by foul and rickety stairs. Some of them live in the street, because either they have been bombed out of their homes or else they never have had a home at all. In this case they take an empty gasoline tin, bore a hole in it, fill it with wood they have picked up among the debris, and use it for a stove. Right out in the street or square they lie down to sleep with the numerous children, that is, unless they take their beds into the bowels of the Underground. The men and women wear rags and the children go naked . . . and play with horse dung on the street. Pray, where is this? you may ask. And I answer that this is the greater part of Naples and many more of our cities—Palermo, Catania, perhaps even Milan besides. In order to understand, one must live in the heart of them; and in order to do that, one must love sin, as I do. Because these poor people are incredible sinners. That is a discovery we make every day, living among them; and every day we discover a new sin and a new love. All they do is sin, because they are in want. If they didn't desire and hope for something better in the future, they would have no more reason to go on living . . . This is the nearest thing they have to a soul. For generations they have kept themselves going with the desire and hope for better things to come.

"If Jesus meant to include poverty of this kind in His blessing, then He must also have meant to bless sin, which is its inevitable companion . . . This is not the kind of poverty Jesus meant, you say, and you may be right. My ideas are all mixed up because this is the only poverty I know and love. For years now I have lived with two fellow priests among these people. And if you say that poverty which is blessed lies in the absence of desire, then they are even greater sinners than I supposed. . . . For every time they think, they only wish for something.

"Of course, the oil magnate desires less than they do, and so his must be the kingdom of heaven. They want a gramophone on which to play their favorite songs while they lie on the ground, a woman to go to bed with, some Sunday clothes, a car, an iced drink for a summer day. Their only ambition is to possess some of these things, and they are ready to rob or cheat their neighbor in order to obtain them. Yes, their hope is a violent one! And so these people are not poor, by your definition. It is easier for a camel to go through the eye of a needle than for them to enter the kingdom of God . . . Is this the conclusion to which I must come, Don Ardito? And if so, what are we priests here for? One answer may be: just leave these people to their fate.

"Leave them to their fate? No, never.

"If you knew how calm I am as I write this negative answer! It seems to me that I am bearing witness to something extremely important and that there is (if you will forgive me) something solemn about what I have to say. No, we must not leave them—we must remain with them always, cover them up and merge ourselves in them, until we can say that we and they are one. I don't know why. But I do know my two companions and I love them, and that is why we live the way we do. They call us the little brothers of the poor, but we are in constant danger of incurring ecclesiastical disapproval, and with some reason. After all, in order to love these people we have to love sin."

And the priests of the poor, who were supposed to give Don Ardito's answer to these people's one religious question, join them in chorusing this question to Don Ardito: "Where is the justice of God?" For He has become one of them, surely, in whose name He cried out for justice.

The priest of the poor continues, "To tell the truth, I envy you. Your room may be neat and clean, while mine is a filthy hole that costs only a very few lire a month for rent. And I'm hungry, not just for bread, but for well-cooked food, for meat and fancy sweets and for good wine. I'd like to pray before an altar decked with flowers and sleep in a soft bed. For all these things I have an incurable and irresistible desire!

"Vanities, if you like, but let me have a taste of them! God, if You made me what I am, why do You treat me like this? And what right have You to reproach me for loving these people and their sins? You put love for them into my heart and then intimate that I shouldn't feel it . . . You make me into a hopeless sinner!

"Perhaps, Don Ardito, I am writing to you in order to receive the answer: No, my brother, you are no sinner. In spite of your love for sinners and their sin, in spite of your own sinful desires, you are not wholly guilty, and there will be a little place for you, beside the oil magnate, in heaven. That is what I should like you to say. Because I need to have you comfort me."

And on the other side of the letter was: "Come and join us! For we may have our justification in the fact that in these men and women it is Jesus Whom we love" (p. 205).

It would be an easy thing with or without a moral book in hand to show that the priests of the poor in Naples had come to an erroneous theological conclusion. But can we satisfy ourselves with that? I remember something that Karl Sonnenschein once said: I do not dare to raise the question of the Christian moral law in the Wedding [the poor section of Berlin]; there it cannot be kept.

There are social conditions in which the "contradictions of human existence" (J. Messner) are aggravated to such a degree that they are unbearable, so that at best every attempt at preaching is met with speechless amazement. In the usual case, however, it is met with a hatred that is sure of itself. There is an objective order of morality, and it is therefore all the more necessary because in the sight of conditions like these, every reasonable demand and every moral admonition is met with the words of sin, hatred; and every proclamation of religion is met with self-confident godlessness. As long as a society, as long as a Christianity looks on that situation in ignorance or indifference, every word is in vain.

But all of this is not the object of our investigation. Nor is the fact that the Communists have an easy job of winning recruits when such circumstances exist. And Carlo Coccioli, we may well be supposed, drew his picture from life.

It is the fact that the position taken by the priests of the poor is false that here concerns us. But it is one that has gradually developed out of long experience and many vain experiments. It is not one that has been chosen as a result of moral reflection, but one that has just grown. It is the result of many components. The least of them has had its own decisive influence on it. They, yes, they themselves, are like ropes that have been stretched between heaven and earth and they have been trying for years to withstand the pull from above and the terrible wrenching from below. Now they have let themselves sink. They know that they have their obligations to God above, but they no longer know of any other bond that binds them but a boundless trust that no moral theology any longer has any probability for them.

Exactly the same thing is to be said about Father Mellowes' "smile." It is simply immoral. (The whole novel sets up a problem but never solves it: the encounter of the traditional blind Christianity of a little Irish city and the nihilism of Ezra, who had taken part in the destruction and conquering of Berlin.) His smile is a numbness that can no longer be thawed, deriving from the unresolved contradictions of human existence.

These men are not sinners. Therefore they do not belong in the chapter on "Priest and Sinner." Probably they have allowed their lives to succumb, along with their flight from the tensions of their ministry. But not their moral life: for theirs is a heroism of spiritlessness and half-despair. A logical kind of nonsense? Life is determined by other laws than those of logic. They no longer have any strength. They no longer see any way out. They have restricted themselves to a degree of existence which corresponds to their strength.

Does no one know of other similar examples? They are, at first glance, far different from the cellar holes of Naples. "Blessed are the poor in spirit," says the Lord. Here are the poor who cannot grasp these words. But there are those, too, who sleep in luxurious beds and travel in luxurious limousines; and when they come to Naples, they spend enough in a single day at the Grand Hotel to support a whole tenement for a month. The same words are true of them, too: "Blessed are the poor in spirit." And they understand them just as little. And the priests who work for the care of their souls have come to much the same agreement with them as the priests of the poor with their poorest, in one of the most beautiful cities in the world: a city through which the rich man has traveled admiringly in his limousine, without so much as an inkling of the misery that is vegetating between the Via Partenope and the Museo Nazionale.

And these arrested forms are far more frequent than those of the poor priests of Naples. "Let him who is without sin among you be the first to cast a stone" (John 8: 7).

PROGNOSIS

We have tried to give a typology of Priestly existence: beginning with the experience of the vocation, through the foundation, the first attempts at its realization, up until those decisive hours and years in which the final forms develop and assert themselves.

The task could have been done differently, no doubt, and in the introduction a number of different possibilities were indicated. The types could be multiplied. The Christian world is spacious, and varied according to continents and countries. Our viewpoint is central Europe, and therefore it is strongly determined throughout by Europe. The New World was included, insofar as it was attainable through witnesses. The types that we have described would be found among different peoples in varying proportions. Life is always much richer; it defies every attempt to describe it in general, and many of the individual characters could only be described because we have put them under not one, but several of the types herein described. There have been many examples that cost the author much thought before deciding under which type he could most reasonably put them.

These individual types all have had their day in the history of the Church, when they were the characteristic group. We have tried to relate the historical role of these types to an understanding of their origin, to their relative right to exist, and to the fact that they have outlived their usefulness.

And along with this, we have dared not only a genesis, but even a certain prognosis.

Here we had to be careful. All predictions of the future depend on the superstition that history's law is that of evolution. That is at best only partially true, or it may even be wholly false. The law of history is revolution. Oswald Spengler saw the truth of that.

And that is why the question, "What types will determine the future?" cannot really be answered. One can predict more easily which types are likely to die out. But even here every prediction is contingent and hazardous. At any rate, it is conditioned according to the history and future of each place. Of course this component of place has less and less effect, since man is becoming, in all his national variety, a citizen of the world. The priest of the World Church becomes a secular priest in a new sense, a priest-type of the Christian communion.

There are many novels about the future in recent times that attempt to project tendencies which are existing and effective today. One should not overlook the fact that they primarily intend to be a warning to the present, or a judgment on contemporaries. And each wants to say no more than he himself can say. George Orwell's novel has the forms of organization and the techniques of the employment of men in a dictatorship which has developed into the year 1984. We should have in about thirty years, he thinks, a world which mercilessly sifts out all that is personal and abolishes all freedom, if, indeed, the law of history is evolution and not revolution. Orwell says nothing of the role of religion in this world of his. Apparently it is uninteresting for him.

Hermann Gohde (*Der achte Tag, Roman einer Weltstunde*, Innsbruck, 1950) portrays life in the year 2074. Christianity has been supplanted by the World State (the "self-governing society of humanity") and its "office," as one supposes, has been rooted out, because it disturbs the world-immanent computations (p. 190). Rome is destroyed. Everyone who shows himself to be a Christian is liquidated. But there are also priests in this era. They are workers like the others, street cleaners, engineers, tractor drivers; they administer the sacraments secretly. They are set off by nothing except the invisible but ineradicable seal of their ordination (p. 310). Even Gohde scarcely mentions them. They are bedded down in a universal Christianity of love, whose "consolers," banded together in teams, work everywhere and are the secret hope of the "suppressed, tortured, and oppressed of this earth," of the "expelled and deported, the forced slaves of the Office-Apparatus" (p. 312).

Franz Werfel's *Stern der Ungeborenen* (Vienna, 1948) extends the course of time a hundred thousand years ahead, to an "astro-mental" man of an artistic, unfruitful, completely rationalized life under the earth. This life happens to be threatened by the revolution of the men in the jungle on the earth. But even after a hundred thousand years, according to Werfel, there will be religion, Christianity, priests, and Bishops.

Much more seriously to be considered are Romano Guardini's bold predictions (*The End of the Modern World*, New York, 1956): out of the culture and freedom of yesterday there arises "a risk of life and death" with the demon of an inner-worldly omnipotence, whose bearer is the World State. The State exercises determination over the whole planet, even into the realm of the person. The individual will be tremendously lonely and defenseless. This future will also bring about the unmasking of the last deceptions of modern man, and therefore a seriousness that has never before existed, one of transformation and decision. The last loan of Christian values by this world will fall due. "When future times oppose Christianity, it will become serious for the first time. This era will show up secularized Christianity as sentimentality and the air will be cleared: full of hostility and danger, but clean and open" (p. 129).

"The cultural heritage of the Church will not be able to extricate itself from the general collapse of all tradition; and wherever it continues to endure, it will be wracked with many problems" (p. 130).

The real and true, the absolute and unconditioned values in Christianity will remain. In fact, in this air, which will act like *aqua fortis*, Christianity will be recognized in its original contradiction to this world.

Christian existence will be characterized by a strangeness and loneliness that it has never before experienced, and because of that, priestly existence will be strengthened: "It is strange, what a consciousness of holy possibilities will well up in the midst of this spreading World of Coercion! The relation of absolute and personality, of the unconditioned and freedom, will enable the Faith to endure its homelessness and defenselessness and know its way . . . The loneliness in the Faith will be fearful. Charity will vanish from the attitude of the world (Mt. 24: 12). It will no longer be understood or possible. That will make it all the more precious when it is between one lonely person and another" (p. 132).

In this world all "misfits and forms of compromise" will not only disappear, but in this atmosphere everyone will hold his head in his hands, to think that they were ever possible, and because of the fact that they once were, do penance for them. "The priest as man of the world" hasn't an inch to stand on in this knife-sharp either-or decision. The "official of God with fixed salary" will give way to the steel worker and the electrical technician who visits the sick secretly after his work and administers the sacraments.

Not only does he get no salary for that, but he even gives his week's wages to those who are even poorer than he. Monsignors and prelates are advised to leave the purple at home. The old "pastor idyl" will become a fairy tale: "once upon a time . . ." But it will no longer be regarded sentimentally. The parish buildings have long since been turned into children's homes and centers of the "Enlightenment." All the "forms of escape" collapse of themselves, for there is only *one:* to be hidden in work, and in loneliness, and this means not only danger but strength. All the other misfits will be recognized, somewhat late, as the consequence of the confusion between what is Christian and secular.

How will priestly existence look in individual details in this world? Will there still be roads, roads that are still trod today, that lead in the direction of this existence? . . . The saints and saintly men on the model of the Curé of Ars; the priests of the *Mission de France;* the "Rucksack Priests" in the pitiful misery of those Germans expelled from the East? All paths that follow in the footsteps of "St. Sebastian of Wedding" . . .

August Zechmeister (*Das Herz und das Kommende,* Vienna, 1945) finds that the last refuge of Christianity which is unassailable even in the most difficult time of persecution will be the family. The priest would only be able to celebrate the holy liturgy as a father in his own family circle. This priest, too, "will have to belong to the total Work World of the future, whose foundations are beginning to be laid everywhere. When he comes home at night, he will have to get ready to care for his congregation. In his free time and at night he will give instructions. He will baptize and bless the marriages. He will warn the sinners to do penance; he will console the sick, and his wife and grown sons and daughters will naturally help him in the ministry" (p. 94). The Christians will live unknown in a hostile world. And if they are known, then it will be only "as they were in the beginning, by their love for one another" (p. 92).

All of these predictions are fraught with a depressing gloom. In their favor they have both the logic with which they are deduced from the present, and the predictions of our Lord about the end of the world. But who can say that the end of the world is at hand? Even Guardini refrains from a "cheap apocalypse" in that regard (p. 133).

The logic of the events that seem so certain in all of these predictions again presupposes that the law of world history is evolution. These authors do not see that the slavery and oppression of human nature cannot be long endured, in spite of all use of force. It does not reckon with an ineradicable longing of men for God. This gift can be lost or concealed for a time, but it is just in the distress of soul which then ensues that it will break out anew. Above all, those predictions do not take grace into account, nor the breathing of the Spirit, which does not blow according to the will of dictatorships, but where it wills. The boundless blindness of the Apostles, who had had three years of association with our Lord, gave reason for the gravest fears about the founding of the kingdom of God, even immediately before our Lord's ascension to the Father (Acts 1: 6). But the revolution that came with the descent of the Holy Ghost upon the apostles made those same petty fishermen saints and fearless heralds of the Gospel. Or: had one made a prediction for the Church based on a cross-section of the clergy in the year 1500, that prediction would have been hopelessly gloomy. And yet there followed the century of the great saints, the renewal of the Church on which we are still living.

The final words of our Lord before His ascension to the Father: "And behold, I am with you all days, even unto the consummation of the world" (Mt. 28: 20) and those others of St. Paul, "I can do all things in Him Who strengthens me" (Phil. 4: 13), can permit no crippling pessimism to thrive, even if the predictions mentioned above should come true. The Christian, the priest, must prove himself in the world of today. Tomorrow others will do it. Anticipation of the possibilities of the future can only mean a consideration of his hour. And the priest is not faced with the "rush of centuries"; he is always, in every hour of the world, under the power of grace and in the superabundance of the Redemption.

That is his foundation. The times can never be so dark that this foundation will not bear him up.

Index

INDEX

A study of personality and character types is always interesting, but when the category under consideration is the priesthood it takes on an unusual fascination.

"This book does not intend," notes the author, "to provide a typology on the grounds of any characterological predisposition, nor one based on a predetermination dating from the time before a man has chosen the priesthood. We want to try to explain the modes of priestly existence from the data of the priestly experience itself, from the experience of the tension, the necessary and unavoidable tension between the vocation to be a priest and the fact that such a vocation is given to a man who lives in this world."

Mature and realistic in his analysis, Father Pfliegler examines a wide spectrum of characteristics found among priests. The extremes (both the good and the bad), as well as the more familiar ground of mediocrity, are dealt with in detail, and the temptations, trials, and tensions of the priest in the contemporary world are discussed with candid awareness of practical problems.

A work of unusual merit, this study will be of particular usefulness not only to priests and seminarians, but to all those who wish to deepen their appreciation of the profound significance of the sacerdotal vocation.